Lionel Tertis

The First Great Virtuoso of the Viola

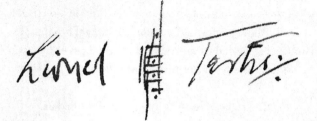

The First Great Virtuoso of the Viola

JOHN WHITE

THE BOYDELL PRESS

First published 2006
The Boydell Press, Woodbridge

ISBN 1 84383 278 X

The Boydell Press is an imprint of Boydell & Brewer Ltd
PO Box 9, Woodbridge, Suffolk IP12 3DF, UK
and of Boydell & Brewer Inc.
668 Mt Hope Avenue, Rochester, NY 14620, USA
website: www.boydellandbrewer.com

A catalogue record of this publication is available
from the British Library

This publication is printed on acid-free paper

Typeset in Adobe Warnock Pro
by David Roberts, Pershore, Worcestershire
Printed in Great Britain by
Athenaeum Press, Gateshead, Tyne & Wear

To Lillian – Mrs Lionel Tertis

To speak of the viola is to speak of that great musician Lionel Tertis, who has done more than any man living to rescue his instrument from its former position as the Cinderella of stringed instruments and has inspired almost all the leading English composers of our time to write a work especially for him.

— Robert Elkin, 1944

✂ Contents ✂

❦ List of illustrations ❦

Frontispiece: Tertis in the early years of the twentieth century

Plates 1–52 appear between pages 208 and 209

The author and publishers are grateful to all the institutions and persons listed for permission to reproduce the materials in which they hold copyright. Every effort has been made to trace the copyright holders; apologies are offered for any omission, and the publishers will be pleased to add any necessary acknowledgement in subsequent editions.

❧ Foreword ❧

A s a b o y growing up in South Africa, I had relatively few chances to hear string playing of quality; and it was through recordings by William Primrose and Rudolf Barshai (especially the latter's interpretation of Mozart's *Sinfonia concertante* with Menuhin) that I came to love the sound of the viola. Not long after I returned to Britain in 1966, an LP of Lionel Tertis was issued. I had never come across his name and might not have bothered to buy the record, had I not – as so often happens – heard him mentioned in a totally different connection. Whoever this Tertis was, he was clearly someone of consequence, so I invested in the LP and discovered his performance of the *Sinfonia concertante* with Sammons, as well as some short pieces and transcriptions.

What I heard on those old recordings from the 1920s and early 1930s was an amazing tone, which I now know was unlike anything before or since. It had the sort of warmth and opulence that only the very greatest artists can draw from a violin, viola or cello; and it was deployed with an instinctive command of legato and portamento. In the intervening years I have heard virtually all Tertis's records, and the best of them still have the capacity to astonish me. I envy those for whom this great artist's playing is a pleasure still to come. All Tertis's recordings have now been issued in two boxes of compact discs, so he may no longer be a cult figure confined to violists and string music enthusiasts.

His achievement was exceptional. Beginning at an age which nowadays would be thought too old to learn a stringed instrument, Tertis took the hitherto unsung viola and raised it, by his endeavours alone, to solo status. He still reigns as one of only three British string players to have made a worldwide reputation, the others being Primrose and Jacqueline du Pré. We ought to be proud of him and now, thanks to the researches of John White, we can base that pride on a solid body of fact. Tertis's memoirs were written when he had reached an advanced age and could no longer recall his own exploits accurately. John White, who as a member of the Alberni Quartet had a coaching session with Tertis, has uncovered an extraordinary mass of material.

This book will stand for a long time as a memorial to Lionel Tertis, a single-minded man who triumphed over tremendous odds to bring us the authentic voice of a uniquely beautiful instrument.

Tully Potter
Editor, *Classic Record Collector*

❦ Preface ❧

Lionel Tertis was a legend in his own lifetime – in his prime he stood shoulder to shoulder with Ysaÿe, Kreisler, Thibaud, Casals, Cortot, Rubinstein and a whole galaxy of stars in the first four decades of the twentieth century. He was the first great virtuoso of the viola. His former students often described him as one of the century's most forceful and intense musicians: a powerful personality, small in stature but upright and vigorous. Bernard Shore told me that 'magnetism seemed to flow out of his immensely strong figure, rooted to the platform like an oak tree ... and one became inevitably drawn into the very heart of the music he was performing'.

In the first decade of the twenty-first century it is well to remember that one hundred years ago Lionel Tertis had begun to change the history of the viola and viola playing for all time. Tertis did not start playing the violin until he was well into his teens, and on the viola he was virtually self-taught – there simply was no one capable of teaching the instrument when he took it up in 1896. Even the great conservatoires of France and Belgium would not have viola classes for several more years, and the Berlin Hochschule would not have one until the 1920s. The viola sections of most orchestras were the least regarded of all the strings. By the time Tertis died, on 22 February 1975, in his ninety-ninth year, the situation had completely changed, and he had been largely responsible for that change. This book is an attempt to put that long life into perspective and to bring the Father of the Viola back into the limelight, where he belongs.

Lionel Tertis's name was known to me from my childhood, when I collected information about musicians mainly from *The Strad* magazine and the *Radio Times*. Photographs and written information were cut out and pasted in a scrapbook with a different page for conductors, pianists, violinists etc. – the page devoted to viola players consisted mainly of pictures of Tertis.

Coronation year, 1953, was memorable for so many reasons. In the sporting world, for example, another hero of mine, the Yorkshire cricketer Leonard Hutton, led England to a thrilling Ashes victory against Australia at the Oval. In my own small world things were also beginning to change. I heard the records of Albert Sammons and Lionel Tertis playing the *Sinfonia concertante* by Mozart, and from that moment I was hooked on the viola, and gave up the violin for ever. Later I borrowed a copy of Tertis's book *Cinderella No More* and his story captivated me.

Tertis was one of the external examiners for my final examination at the Royal Academy of Music, and later with my colleagues in the Alberni String Quartet I had coaching from him at his home in Wimbledon.

After Lionel Tertis's death I founded the British Chapter of the International Viola Society. To coincide with the great violist's centenary in December 1976 a concert was arranged at Hockerill College, Bishop's Stortford, at which we remembered Tertis. The distinguished British viola player Harry Danks, a former pupil of Tertis, gave a very moving talk about his teacher, and led a performance of Tertis's arrangement of Beethoven's Trio in C, op. 87, for three violas. Our viola society's first newsletter was published to coincide with the centenary and included personal memories of Tertis by former students, colleagues and friends; a number of these are included in this book.

Two years later I hosted the first International Viola Congress to be held in the British Isles; the programme included tributes to Tertis: a lecture by Bernard Shore and a concert of duos for viola and cello originally written or arranged for Lionel and Lillian Tertis; on this occasion, Lillian was joined by the American viola player Paul Doktor. At the conclusion of the congress Mrs Tertis invited me to join the committee that had been set up to organize the Lionel Tertis International Viola Competition and Workshop. This was launched in 1980, and attracts violists from all corners of the world.

JOHN WHITE

∽ Acknowledgements ∞

During the last twenty-five years or more Lillian Tertis has become a dear friend of our family. She encouraged and helped me to build my Tertis archive, and I am very grateful to her and the Tertis Foundation for all their generous help and support during the many years it has taken to bring this book to fruition.

I am also grateful to Anthony Shaw, Lionel Tertis's great-nephew, for allowing me to see the family tree and some memories of past generations of the family which were written down by Tertis's nephew Harold Milner during his lifetime.

I would like to thank the Royal Academy of Music Research Committee for their grant towards my initial research, my colleagues at the Academy, members of the RAM Club and all associated with the RAM library for their help.

A few individuals need a very special word of thanks: Michael Dennison (Comus Edition), who transferred all the original text to the computer and much more besides; David Hermann for preparing the most comprehensive Tertis discography ever issued; Mary Worthington for her professional editorial skills and practical advice; and a huge thank you to my old friend Tully Potter, who has been helpful in so many ways; besides contributing the Foreword, his vast editorial experience and encyclopedic knowledge has been a source I have tapped on many occasions. I would also like to acknowledge his invaluable assistance and encouragement at all stages in the book's preparation; and finally my wife, Carol, for endless hours spent at her word processor typing out all the information that I have collected, for reading and correcting the text at different stages, and above all for her support and encouragement. Unfortunately I am unable to elaborate on the contributions that so many other people have given me; all have been so generous and helpful and nothing has been too much trouble for any of them.

I must apologize if I have inadvertently omitted any individual or organization from the list. I am grateful to the following libraries, librarians, publishers and organizations: Christine Abbott (Newcastle City Library), Kathryn Adamson (Royal Academy of Music Library), Nicolas Bell (British Library), Chris Bennett (The Elgar Birthplace Museum), Paula Best (Wigmore Hall), Robert J. Bruce (Principal Library Assistant, Bodleian Library), Rosalind Caird (Hereford Cathedral Library), Hugh Cobbe (British Library), James Codd (BBC Written Archives Centre), Paul Collen (Curatorial and Administrative Assistant, Centre for Performance History, Royal College of Music), Sophie Currie (Oxford University Press), David Day (Primrose International Viola Archive, Brigham Young University, USA), Ian Gammie (Corda Music), R. J. H. Hill (Hereford Library), Peter Horton (Royal College of Music Library),

Rosemary Johnson (Royal Philharmonic Society), Kevin La Vine (Music Reference Librarian, Library of Congress, Washington, DC), C. J. Lloyd (Tower Hamlets Local History Librarian), Jim McGrath (Athenaeum Archive, Strathclyde University, Glasgow), Morag Mackie (Glasgow University Library), Nicholas R. Mays (News International plc), Bridget Palmer (Royal Academy of Music Library), Christine Penney (Head of Special Collections, University of Birmingham), Stuart Robinson (Hallé Orchestra), Allison Rubia (W. H. Bell Music Library, University of Cape Town, South Africa), Patricia Sheldon (Newcastle City Library), Mrs C. Slade (Bideford and District Community Archive), Floortje Smehuijzen (Concertgebouw Orchestra), Janet Snowman (Collections Registrar, Royal Academy of Music), Jeremy Upton (Music Librarian, Reid Music Library, Edinburgh University), John Wells (Cambridge University Library), David Weston (Keeper of special collections, University of Glasgow), Gerard Whelan (Royal Dublin Society Library, Dublin); The British Council, The British Library Music Collections, The British Library National Sound Archive, Alan Bush Music Trust, University of Cape Town, The Clarke Estate, University of London Library, Mitchell Library (Glasgow), National Archives, Royal Dublin Society Library, *The Strad*, Trinity College of Music Library, Westminster Music Library, Worcestershire Record Office.

The following individuals have helped me in countless ways: John Amis, Marion Aston, Marjorie Baker, Andrew Bellis, William Benham, Patricia Berry, Roger Best, John Bethell, Luigi Alberto Bianchi, Claudine Bigelow, Tor Johan Bøen, Sheena Booth, Sue Branch, Carmel Byrne, Fiona Cameron, Roger Chase, Harold Coletta, Noel Cox, Gill Cracknell, Bryan Crimp, Paul Cropper, Liane Curtis, David Dalton, Harry Danks, Oliver Davies, Howard Davis, John Denison, Michael C. Doughty, Padraig ó Dubhlaoidh, David Dunhill, Leslie East, Phyllis Ebsworth, Lionel Elton, Csaba Erdélyi, Barbara Errington, William A. Everett, György Fazekas, Christopher Fifield, Carl F. Flesch, Christopher Foreman, Lewis Foreman, Michael Freyhan, Peter Fribbens, Christopher Gaches, Andrew Gillett, Bernard Glicksman, Livia Gollancz, Amy Griffiths, Graham Griffiths, Arnold Griller, Rusen Günes, Edith Harding, Thomas B. Heimberg, Penny Howard, Margaret Hubicki, David Hume, Veronica Leigh Jacobs, Cambray Jones, Michael Jones, Guy Jonson, Dédre Kelleher, Michael Kennedy, Norman Kent, David Kershaw, Stephanie Kershaw, Liz Kilpatrick, Geoffrey Kimpton, Bernard Knight, Valerie Langfield, Louise Lansdown, Ysobel Latham, Hazel Leslie, Robert Lewin, Martin Lincé, William Llewellyn, Dennis Lockyer, Margaret Lyons, Robert Lyons, Simon Marlow, Fiona Marney, Andrew Marsden, Michael Messenger, John Milnes, Mary Miskin, Gordon Mutter, Jane Nicholas, Christopher N. Nozawa, John Offord, Martin Outram, T. J. S. Patterson, John Paynter, A. T. Pickard, Dennis Plowright, Michael Ponder, Timothy Quinn,

Martin Roberts, Ronald Roberts, Roger Rowe, Jon Samuels, Wilfred Saunders, Colin Scott-Sutherland, Catherine Scudamore, Geoffrey Self, Bernard Shore, Yvonne Slater, Carlos Maria Solare, Diana Sparkes, Michael Stubbs, David Squibb, Frank Stiles, David Stone, Thomas J. Tatton, Philip Towell, Nancy Uscher, Yvonne van der Pol, Michael Vidulich, Peter Voigt, Sarah Walton, Elizabeth Watson, Christopher Wellington, Robin Wells, Eric Wenn, Ivo-Jan van der Werff, Eric Wetherell, Adam Whone, J. P. Williams, G. K. Woodgate and Betty Wyatt.

The Tertis Family

Humble beginnings – début – student days – the viola

T HE DATE of 29 December 1876 presents musical history with a remarkable coincidence. For on that day Pau Casals was born in the small Catalonian town of Vendrell, while Lionel Tertis came into the world in the industrial town of West Hartlepool in the north of England. Each of these two remarkable men was the son of a musician, and was destined to bring his chosen instrument to new heights of virtuosity and popularity. Many books have been written about the legendary cellist Casals, but the equally charismatic Tertis has been comparatively neglected, perhaps because he played the more self-effacing viola.

Like so many great string players, Lionel Tertis was of Jewish origin: he was descended on both sides from cantors who sang the synagogue services of the Ashkenazi tradition. His maternal grandfather, whose surname was Hermann, was a Polish cantor with a brood of children. All of these emigrated in their early youth in order to escape the growing anti-Semitism in Poland, which culminated in the pogroms of the 1880s. One son, David, went to Germany, took the name Loewenstein; he became a prominent physician, and was honoured by the Kaiser for his paediatric work. One of his four daughters, Antonie, was a professional pianist and a member of Anton Rubinstein's circle. She came to England in 1898, taught at the Matthay School, and died in 1947.

Cantor Hermann's daughter Phoebe came to England around 1860; according to Tertis's own account, she came with her father, who himself became a British subject. Eventually Phoebe Hermann met her first husband, Harriss Cohen, a jeweller who was also from Poland. Harriss and Phoebe Cohen had three children: Solomon, Joseph – who became a doctor and a rabbi – and Rebecca (who became Mrs Reeve). Harriss died of tuberculosis on the last day of May 1868, and Phoebe looked after the children on her own for a number of years. She then met and married Alexander Tertis, born in Koudanov in the Russian province of Minsk, the son of Benjamin and Sarah Tertis, who emigrated to England when Alexander was thirteen. Phoebe and Alexander's children were Lionel, Annie and Samuel. Lionel's birthplace, West Hartlepool, County Durham, where the family lived at 14 Regents Place, was not to play a large part in his life. In March 1877, when Lionel was three months old, the Tertises moved to a Victorian slum in the borough of Stepney in the East End of London, where Alexander became cantor at the Princes Street Synagogue.[1]

Lionel was always proud that he was born in Britain; and he grew up with the tastes, attitudes and outlook of someone who had come to maturity in the late Victorian and Edwardian eras.

The Tertis family lived at 8 Princelet Street, Spitalfields. In adjacent Brick Lane the 'poor man's market' on a Sunday presented a scene Lionel remembered, 'with piles of cast-off clothing and boots and shoes spread on the ground for sale ... Petticoat Lane nearby was also a place of such intensity and squalor. At that time the one bright spot in Spitalfields was Christ Church, so tall and so calm with its lovely pale-grey stone.' The 1881 Census gives the following information about the family:

> Alexander Tertis, head of family, age last birthday 30, occupation Minister, Jewish, born Russia.
>
> Phoebe Tertis, wife of Alexander, age last birthday 36, born Poland.
>
> Rebecca Tertis (Cohen), daughter, age last birthday 12, occupation scholar, born Sheffield.
>
> Lionel Tertis, son, age last birthday 4, born West Hartlepool.
>
> Annie Tertis, daughter, age last birthday 2, born London, Spitalfields.
>
> Samuel Tertis, son, age last birthday 2 months, born London, Spitalfields.

The Census of ten years later added the following to the Tertis household:

> Joseph Cohen, stepson, 24, student of medicine, born Hoyland, Yorkshire.
>
> Frances R. Cohen (Rebecca), stepdaughter, 22, born Barnsley, Sheffield.
>
> Harris [*sic*] Cohen, boarder, 24, cabinet maker, born Russia.
>
> Ellen Hennessy, servant, married age 34, general servant, born County Cork, Ireland.

Alexander Tertis became a British citizen in 1895; at that time he was fifty-one and had three children living with him: Lionel, aged eighteen, Annie, aged sixteen and Samuel, aged fourteen.

Lionel's earliest musical impressions were gained from hearing Alexander practising at home. 'My father had a fine tenor voice, and later on I began to realize how beautiful his phrasing was – he was naturally musical, good music absorbed him, and to him principally I owe my passion for it.' Lionel started playing the piano at the age of three. He always said he loathed the piano, and found it so extraordinarily mechanical that he could not therefore express his feelings on the instrument. He was fortunate that 1880 was the year the Education Act was passed, making schooling compulsory for children aged five to ten. He was taught at the local London County Council school in a street off Petticoat Lane; for his piano lessons he went to a German teacher called Professor Wasser.

Aged six years old, Tertis made his public *début* as a pianist at a concert in Highbury, North London. Wearing a black velvet coat and deep white-lace collar, he played a Tarantella by Stephen Heller. In later life he recalled that he had no nerves at all during the concert, and played at an excessive pace to show off. The piano soon lost whatever attraction it had for him, and at the age of seven he had to be locked in a room to practise, something he resented. All the same, both of his parents were keen that he should take up music as a profession; as Tertis said, 'I took to it ... Like a duck to water.' With his parents' blessing, he left home to earn his living as a musician when he was thirteen – the family expenses were becoming onerous and his decision helped to lighten his parents' load. His aim was to earn enough money to learn the violin. He consulted two periodicals, *The Era* and *The Stage*, both of which carried advertisements offering employment to musicians. His first engagement at Scarborough was as a member of a 'Hungarian band', distinctly fashionable at the time. He then accompanied a blind violinist who played many of the concertos as well as salon pieces; their performances took place on Brighton promenade. The violinist gave Tertis accommodation and also paid him well. In the summer of 1892 he obtained an eleven-week contract with a small ensemble who performed daily on the pier at Southend-on-Sea.

He now had sufficient funds to enrol at Trinity College of Music in the autumn of 1892, studying piano with R. W. Lewis, harmony with Dr Saunders, and violin – as a second study – with Bernhard Carrodus.[2] Of Dr Saunders, Tertis later said that he had 'not the smallest recollection of him, having no particular interest in the rudiments of that subject at that time. But the college, in its archives, has me down as having been in his class.' Tertis played piano concertos with the college orchestra, but above all enjoyed his violin lessons. His money ran out after two terms, so once again he had to look for work and took a job as music attendant at a lunatic asylum in Preston, Lancashire. Bradbury Turner, Principal of Trinity College of Music, wrote to congratulate Tertis on his appointment and gave him the maxims: 'The laws of morality are also those of art' and 'Remember, study is unending.' His duties besides making music included helping the patients dress themselves. He could not endure this situation for long, and finally accepted a position as pianist at Clacton-on-Sea before returning to Trinity College for one term. Meanwhile he continued his violin studies on his own.

He was led to believe that he would receive better tuition on the Continent, and, with financial support from his mother, who, according to Tertis 'pawned her few trinkets', he enrolled at the Leipzig Conservatory. 'When I arrived I found my professor, he was called Bolland; I came into an immensely long room, and he would be at one end of it, examining his stamp collection and bawling what I oughtn't to do ... to me at the other end of the room. And that's as far as my lessons went. It was a farce.' This disappointing episode only served to convince him that he could receive much better teaching at home and he returned after six months.

At the Michaelmas half-term of 1895 Tertis entered the Royal Academy of Music, where he was to remain until the end of the Michaelmas term of 1897. From 1822 to 1911 the Royal Academy was housed in a building in Tenterden Street (off Hanover Square) which was eventually demolished to become the back premises of an Oxford Street store. In the early days of Tertis's time at the Academy the building was described by a contemporary student, Vivian Langrish:

> One entered by going up three or four steps into the entrance hall ... From the front hall, passing a passage on the left leading to the Principal's room, one went through an archway into the main hall which, in a way, was the focal point of the Academy. It was a large open space lit by a large skylight. Stone stairs round three sides led to the concert room. This was a fairly spacious auditorium with a gallery round three sides. ... The annual prize giving and all orchestral and chamber concerts took place in the Queen's Hall and attendance was compulsory for all students.

Tertis was helped financially by a small bursary from Lionel de Rothschild. He studied violin with Hans Wessely, 'who was a very good violinist but kept all his secrets to himself and did not tell us all the tricks of the trade', piano with Mr Kiver and harmony with Frederick Corder. Wessely, born in Vienna in 1862 and a pupil of Heissler, Hellmesberger and Grün, had been a professor at the Academy since 1889. He often appeared as soloist at the Crystal Palace concerts under August Manns, and composed numerous technical works for the violin, including a scale manual. He had the reputation of getting his pupils to progress quickly, but was also a bully, with the ability to break the more sensitive students. He shouted and even screamed at his pupils, and newcomers to his chamber-music class were often humiliated in front of their colleagues. Wessely was not initially impressed with Tertis's playing; according to Tertis, 'Wessely ... informed my father that I was better fitted for the grocery trade.' However, in the next two years progress was made. During his time at the Academy Tertis made friends with another of Wessely's violin students,

Spencer Dyke, who came from Plymouth, and the two shared a flat in Green-croft Gardens, Hampstead. They were both full of youthful ambition, and every day each would try to outdo the other in the amount of practice they did. Dyke and Tertis spent a number of holidays together, staying in quiet, out-of-the-way places where they could work without disturbance. Tertis remembered an occasion at Coston in Norfolk when Dyke was working hard at the Bach *Chaconne*; when any difficulty occurred he stood in the corner of the room, facing the wall, repeating the awkward passage for a considerable amount of time without using any excess movement. Dyke felt he could concentrate best in this position.

It was another fellow student, Percy Hilder Miles,[3] who made the casual request that would change the course of Tertis's life. Tertis recalls how Miles suggested he should take up the viola so that they could form a string quartet. 'And I did, with an old cut-down instrument … very nondescript, but I loved the timbre, I loved the quality from the first moment I studied it, and from that time I worked at it myself, for the simple reason that there were no pedagogues for the viola – it was either a drummer or a pianist that taught it.'

During the academic year 1896–7 Tertis played both the Mendelssohn and the second Wieniawski violin concertos on the viola in Royal Academy concerts. Alfred Gibson, one of the violin teachers at the Academy, who on occasion played the viola in the Joachim Quartet, was horrified: 'The viola is not meant to be played high up. That is the pig department! I suppose you will in due course be playing behind the bridge.'

There were no viola students at the Academy; one old man was engaged to play viola for orchestral rehearsals and was described by the Principal, Sir Alexander Mackenzie, as a 'necessary evil'. In an interview near the end of his life, Tertis described the state of viola-playing in the 1890s:

> The condition was extraordinarily bad, with the exception of two or three viola players. Most of them were looked upon as Ugly Ducklings of the orchestra. They were absolutely despised by the other string players. Anybody could get into the viola section, simply because they were down-and-out violinists, they could get nobody else to do it. They produced a perfectly appalling sound – which made your hair stand on end, there was no vibrato, as cold as ice, and very bad, and they played on instruments that had been cut down and had no semblance of C-string sonority.

Tertis often referred to C-string sonority, meaning the resonant tone he produced on his lowest string with a technique unique to himself.

Tertis practised the instrument for a week, and the quartet rehearsed for two weeks. They then played Beethoven's Quartet in F, op. 18 no. 1, to Mackenzie, who told Tertis that he would never regret his decision to take up the viola. As there was no one to teach him he resolved to study it independently.

Tertis's account in his own memoir of how he progressed within a few months from the back desk of the second violins to principal viola in Henry Wood's Queen's Hall Orchestra has never been questioned; but the concert programmes of the orchestra tell a different story. The first mention of Tertis occurs on 20 November 1897, where he is listed as a member of the second violin section. In that year Émile Férir was appointed principal viola, a position he held until 1903. Interestingly, Tertis's name does not appear again until 12 December 1903 (after Férir's departure to the USA), when he is listed as principal viola. He continued to be listed as principal viola until 10 May 1904, a month before the inaugural concert of the London Symphony Orchestra.

It was as a member of Percy Hilder Miles's quartet that Tertis began his association with the popular South Place Sunday Concerts.[4] For their concert during the society's 1898–9 season Miles and Tertis were joined by Stephen Shea and cellist Herbert 'Bertie' Withers in a performance of Brahms's Quartet in A minor, op. 51 no. 2, and Schumann's Piano Quintet with the composer Joseph Holbrooke[5] at the piano. Typically for the period, the remainder of the programme comprised violin and cello solos, three groups of songs, and a performance by Holbrooke of the first movement of Brahms's Sonata in F sharp minor, op. 2.

When Tertis's first solo recital at the Queen's Small Hall received a short mention in the *Musical Times* of 1 January 1900 it was the harbinger of many such events to come. Bernard Shore commented: 'The incredible speed in which Tertis mastered the viola ... with no guidance whatever, was typical of the man himself. Once he decided on anything, he would concentrate every minute he could find on the job. There were no half-measures in anything that he did in his life.'

Early Career

*A career in music – early days as soloist, orchestral principal,
chamber musician, teacher – Kreisler's influence – new works*

A S A N E W century dawned, Lionel Tertis was probably one of the finest
violists in the world, although he still had some way to go before he
made the public aware of his quality. At home his only rival was Alfred Hobday,
who was almost seven years older and a member of an outstanding musical
family – his wife Ethel, née Sharpe, was a splendid pianist who had been part
of Brahms's circle in Vienna, while his younger brother Claude was a superb
exponent of the double bass. It is difficult to judge Alfred Hobday's playing,
because his only recordings were made as second violist in ensembles, but it
would seem that he played essentially in the nineteenth-century fashion, making very little use of vibrato. Behind his back his colleagues referred to him as
'Cold Mutton' – perhaps his style contributed to the canard which was common currency among the orchestral musicians of those days that the three
coldest things one could encounter were a gravestone, a woman's feet in bed
and a viola solo.

Abroad, Tertis's major rival was the Bohemian player Oskar Nedbal, almost
three years his senior and another player schooled in the nineteenth-century
tradition. A founder member of the celebrated Bohemian Quartet in 1892,
Nedbal caused a sensation all over Europe with his playing of the viola solo at
the start of Smetana's E minor Quartet, 'From My Life'. One of those who was
smitten was Arnold Bax, who first heard the Bohemians on their *début* tour of
Britain in 1897. But Nedbal, a gigantic man, earned his sobriquet 'King Viola'
by more than quartet playing: in his repertoire he had such staples as Mozart's
Sinfonia concertante, Berlioz's *Harold in Italy* and the Rubinstein Sonata. And
the viola was only one facet of his busy musical life. A pupil of Dvořák, he
was a superb composer of light music. He was also a great conductor, and as
conductor of the Czech Philharmonic was largely responsible for the popularity of the 'New World' Symphony. As with Hobday, it is difficult to make any
definitive judgement about Nedbal's playing, because he left only two recordings and never had the opportunity to become thoroughly accustomed to the
tricky business of making acoustic discs. Nevertheless it is clear that he did not
employ much vibrato.

And Tertis? At the turn of the century he, too, was probably a virtually vibrato-less player, relying on his excellent tone projection and intonation to make his impact. The major epiphany that was to turn him into the Tertis of legend was still to come.

During 1899 Tertis had become a sub-professor at the Academy. One of his duties was to play in the weekly string ensemble class directed by Émile Sauret (1852–1920), then professor of violin. 'Sauret possessed the most amazing left-hand technique, and his bow arm was wonderful – in fact he was a virtuoso in the true sense of the word', Tertis recalled. 'He turned out a galaxy of brilliant fiddlers during his professorship.' Today Sauret is remembered solely for the virtuoso cadenza he wrote for Paganini's D major Concerto. In his day he was the intimate friend of Brahms, Liszt and Tchaikovsky, and the favourite violinist of Emperor Napoleon III.

At the meeting on 28 March 1900 of the Awards Committee of the Academy Tertis was elected an Associate of the Royal Academy of Music (ARAM). Others so honoured were the cellists Herbert Withers and May Mukle. At the RAM Appointments Committee held on 10 October 1900 the Principal, Alexander Mackenzie, suggested making Tertis professor of viola; it was agreed 'that Mr Lionel Tertis be appointed at a fee of five shillings per hour'. Tertis, the first viola professor in the Academy, took up his duties during that term.

In the same year he joined the Wessely String Quartet, considered one of the best groups in the early years of the twentieth century. 'My first engagement with [Wessely] was at the Holloway Polytechnic, for which he paid me the fee of five shillings', Tertis recalled. The quartet had well over 100 rehearsals before giving that first concert. They soon established a reputation for their beautiful tone and perfect ensemble, and they premièred many British works. Both Tertis and Spencer Dyke, the second violinist – later a distinguished quartet leader – were Wessely's pupils; one assumes the group's playing style was unified.

Tertis returned to the South Place Sunday Concerts on 11 March 1900 in two guises – as a member of the Wessely Quartet (Wessely, Dyke, Tertis and R. V. Tabb) and as a pianist. They substituted Mozart's Quartet in C, K465 ('Dissonance'), for the D minor originally announced, and were joined by Josephine Troup in Dvořák's Piano Quintet in A, op. 81. In between were groups of songs and piano solos, and a performance of Max Bruch's *Romance* in A minor, with Wessely accompanied at the piano by Tertis.

A year later, in a Special Vocal Concert at South Place on Sunday 24 March 1901, Spencer Dyke was the instrumental soloist with Tertis as his accompanist in Wieniawski's Second Violin Concerto in D minor, op. 22; later in the programme they played Alexander Mackenzie's *Benedictus* and Sarasate's *Zigeunerweisen*, with Pierné's Serenade as an encore.

At an Academy students' chamber concert at St James's Hall on 24 July 1900 the Intermezzo and Finale from a Quartet in F by W. H. Reed (1876–1942) were given their first performance by the composer and Stephen Champ (violins), Tertis (viola) and R. V. Tabb (cello). Twenty-seven years later Reed would write his *Rhapsody* for viola and orchestra for Tertis.

On 24 May 1901 Tertis premièred the Viola Concerto by John Blackwood McEwen at the Royal Academy of Music, with the composer conducting; this was the first twentieth-century concerto for the instrument. He gave a further performance on 11 December 1901 with the Bournemouth Municipal Orchestra, conducted by Dan Godfrey. McEwen, a fellow student and later colleague at the Academy, also wrote a Nocturne in D flat for viola and piano for Tertis, and his poetic Sonata in F minor, originally for piano and violin, was included in many of Tertis's programmes at this period. One of Tertis's early recordings with the pianist Frank St Leger was another short work, *Breath o' June*, which McEwen dedicated to him.

The Wessely Quartet often appeared at the Bechstein Hall (renamed the Wigmore Hall in 1917). Two of their earliest concerts were given on 30 October and 25 November 1901, shortly after the hall was opened, when their programmes included quartets by Brahms, Dvořák, Haydn, Mozart and Beethoven. The cellist was now B. Patterson Parker.

On 1 December 1901 the quartet opened a South Place Concert with Beethoven's first 'Razumovsky' Quartet, op. 59 no. 1, and the ensemble returned on 9 February 1902 to participate in an Austrian Concert. The publicity stated:

> The object of this concert is not to bring forward compositions of the famous Austrian classical masters (Mozart, Beethoven, Schubert etc.), but to give an idea of the music played and sung by the people of the various nationalities which form the Austrian Empire. Examples will be given of the Volkslied of the Viennese; the sentimental Carinthian folk-songs; the charming songs of the people of Upper Austria and Styria; and the characteristic Jodlers of the Tyrolese. The Hungarians and Bohemians will be represented by specimens of their instrumental music, the Bohemian work being Smetana's String Quartet in E minor (Aus meinem Leben).

The quartet played two Austrian Airs and ended the concert with Dvořák's Quartet in F, op. 96 ('The American').

It was a red-letter day in Tertis's life when he first heard the violinist Fritz Kreisler (1875–1962), who made his London *début* at a Richter concert on 12 May 1902, playing the Beethoven Concerto. During Tertis's time as principal viola Kreisler appeared as soloist with the orchestra on 23 February 1904; the programme included three violin concertos by Brahms, Vieuxtemps and d'Erlanger, and he played Bach's E major Prelude as an encore. Tertis was inspired by this Viennese musician, whose style, tone, phrasing and vibrato all influenced his future development.

> For me the experience of hearing him play was like falling in love. His glowing tone, his vibrato, unique and inexpressibly beautiful, his phrasing, which in everything he played was so peculiarly his own, the manly grace of his bow arm, his attitude, at once highly strung and assured, the passionate sincerity of his interpretations ... the most heavenly tone-quality and expression I've ever heard from any violinist living ever since.

Kreisler was among the first violinists to use vibrato continuously throughout a piece, and its unusual intensity gave his tone great warmth and vitality. Giving advice some years later, Tertis commented: ' [Vibrato] should be continuous; there must be no break in it whatsoever ... there is nothing so dead or ruinous to an expressive phrase as the sound of a cantabile slow passage in which one or two notes are partly or wholly devoid of vibrato.' It was by adapting Kreisler's technique to his own playing that Tertis was able to produce the rich, sonorous tone which was his hallmark.

In the early 1900s the published repertoire of music for viola solo was very limited, so Tertis was delighted when he discovered two captivating short pieces, *Romanza* and *Allegretto*, written for the viola by the blind composer and organist William Wolstenholme.[1] Although he may have been considered a provincial musician, Wolstenholme was, by all accounts, an exceptional organist, who gave regular recitals both at home and abroad, and was noted for his improvisations on themes provided by the audience. Tertis wrote enthusiastically to the composer in praise of the *Romanza* and *Allegretto*, suggesting that he would travel to Blackburn with the composer and pianist Stanley Hawley and play the pieces to him. They could then talk over an idea that was beginning to excite him; that the *Romanza* might form the second movement of a new viola concerto. The flying visit took place, and was even considered worthy of a report in the local press, although its outcome is unclear. Wolstenholme may have agreed to write a new work, but if he did so, it is strange that there is no record of Tertis's having received it. Rather tantalizingly, the Society of British Composers yearbook for 1907–8 lists Wolstenholme as the composer of a 'Legende' for viola and orchestra, op. 45. Could this have been intended for Tertis? We shall probably never know, as the Wolstenholme archive does not have the manuscript, and the work must be presumed lost.

The *Romanza* and *Allegretto* featured in a programme at the South Place Concerts on 12 October 1902, when Tertis's talents were amply demonstrated. On this occasion the Wessely Quartet opened the proceedings with Beethoven's monumental E flat Quartet, op. 127; between two groups of songs Tertis was the soloist in the Wolstenholme pieces; he then accompanied Hans Wessely in the Violin Concerto by Mendelssohn (before Tosti's song 'Les Filles de Cadix'); the quartet ended the concert with Haydn's 'Sunrise' Quartet, op. 76 no. 4.

The relationship between Wessely and Tertis seems eventually to have become somewhat strained. We learn from Eric Coates that when he joined Hans Wessely's ensemble class in 1906 he had his playing ridiculed. His technique was likened to a poor amateur, and Wessely laughed at the fingerings Tertis had given him. Apparently the two men had been carrying on a feud and had not spoken to each other for months. Coates gained the impression that Tertis had managed to have the last word, and the arrival of Tertis's student in his ensemble class gave Wessely an opportunity to get his own back.

Their differences do not seem to have prevented their occasional collaboration in future years, but on 18 January 1903 Tertis made his final appearance with the Wessely Quartet. This was again at South Place, where they played Dvořák's 'Slavonic' Quartet in E flat, op. 51, and, with John Ansell as second viola, Brahms's String Quintet in G, op. 111. Both Wessely and Tertis played solos: Wessely the *Airs russes* by Wieniawski, and Tertis the *Canzonetta* by D'Ambrosio, and his own arrangement of the *Romance* from Wieniawski's Second Violin Concerto. A couple of months later (29 March 1903) he returned to South Place to accompany Wessely in Bruch's well-loved Violin Concerto in G minor and the *Rêverie* and *Aubade* by D'Ambrosio.

The original Wessely Quartet reassembled on 20 June 1925, when they performed J. B. McEwen's First String Quartet, which they had premièred in 1900 at an RAM Club Social meeting. Nearly 500 people attended this event, which also included a performance of Dvořák's Terzetto, op. 74, played by Wessely, Dyke and Tertis.

Wessely and Tertis shared a platform as soloists on other occasions. In 1902 they had performed the Mozart *Sinfonia concertante* with the Bournemouth Municipal Orchestra and subsequently would do so again, with the Queen's Hall Orchestra. The *Sinfonia concertante*, one of the glories of the violist's solo repertoire, was reasonably well known on the Continent – although relatively little Mozart was performed anywhere in those days – and it seems astonishing, from today's perspective, that British audiences were almost ignorant of it. One London critic described it as 'A practically unknown work'; another referred to the manuscript as 'a five-finger exercise'. In *My Life of Music*, Henry Wood stated that Arthur Payne, who led the Queen's Hall Orchestra from 1897, and Émile Férir gave fine performances of the work. He also wrote:

It is always pleasing to secure really beautiful renderings of Mozart. Two stand out in my memory, both occurring during the same season. The first was when Mathilde Verne and her sister Adela played the Concerto in E flat for two pianos, and the other was when Lionel Tertis – that superb artist with the golden tone – took part in the performance of the Sinfonia Concertante in the same key for violin, viola and orchestra. The violin part was played by Hans Wessely, who had been a Professor at the RAM since 1889, some of our most distinguished violinists being his pupils.

Tertis had by now become principal viola in Wood's orchestra, and continued to play in quartet ensembles which were often associated with his colleagues at the Academy. Among these were the London Quartet led by Philip Cathie (later to become the Zimmermann Quartet),[2] the Kruse Quartet and eventually the Walenn Quartet. The *Musical Times* reported of a recital by the Kruse Quartet at the Bechstein Hall *c.*1906: 'The volume of tone was remarkable in richness and resonance, and the precision of attack, shades of tonal force and delicacy in pianissimo passages were enthralling. No finer quartet playing has been heard in London.' For a brief period Tertis played in a quartet led by Willy Hess. Before becoming a professor of violin at the RAM (1904), this illustrious German player led the Hallé Orchestra in Manchester and the Gürzenich Orchestra and Quartet in Cologne; in 1904 he left to become concertmaster of the Boston Symphony Orchestra; in 1908 he invited Tertis to join the Hess–Schröder Quartet he was forming in the USA. Tertis initially went along with the plan but, on arriving in the USA, found he was being offered far less favourable financial terms than originally agreed, and so immediately returned to London. Férir took his place in the quartet. Hess ended his professional career in Berlin as professor of violin at the Hochschule.

The crisis in the Queen's Hall Orchestra in 1904, which led to the formation of the London Symphony Orchestra, resulted in Tertis's being invited to be the LSO's principal viola; but he declined, as he wished to devote most of his time to establishing himself as a soloist. Alfred Hobday took the post instead, and remained in it for more than thirty years. Not that Tertis gave up orchestral playing altogether; in the following year, at a concert of the Ipswich Orchestral Society, he not only played solos but also led the viola section: 'I had greatly benefited by my experience as a member of Wood's orchestra. I learnt from him what good phrasing was, the accurate value of notes and of rests, and many other details of help to musicianship, not to speak of discipline and punctuality.'

During 1905–6 Tertis gave four major recitals to promote his beloved viola. After the first recital the following report appeared on 1 June 1905 in the *Musical Times*:

As a solo instrument the viola is certainly the Cinderella of the string family, and there exists so little music written for it that exceptional interest was attached to the viola recital given by Mr Lionel Tertis, on the 19th May at the Aeolian Hall, for he gave first performances of no fewer than six new compositions for viola and pianoforte. The most important of these was a Sonata in C minor by York Bowen, who played the pianoforte part. This work is another testimony to the great talent of Mr. Bowen. ... A Cantilena and an Arab Love Song by Mr. W. H. Bell, also proved pleasure-giving music, and a Nocturne in D flat, composed by Mr. J. B. McEwen, showed originality. The list of novelties was completed by two bright little pieces, severally entitled Andante Espressivo and Allegro Scherzando by Mr. Harry Farjeon. In all these Mr. Tertis showed not only great executive skill, but produced a variety of tone-colour which dissipated that sense of monotony not uncommonly felt when the viola is listened to for any extended period.

Other works premièred in this series of recitals included a Sonata in E minor[3] by W. H. Bell, and two more works by York Bowen,[4] his second Sonata in F and 'a beautiful Fantasy' for viola and organ. The *Daily Telegraph* reported: 'Mr Tertis and Mr Bowen ... are beyond question musicians of the highest order. Mr Tertis' viola playing is marked by a great richness of tone, while Mr Bowen's soft and delicate touch as a pianist is especially noteworthy in view of the fact that he also plays the organ.'

Three days before this recital, there was a report in *The Times* of a concert at the Aeolian Hall:

There was naturally a great deal of disappointment at the announcement that, owing to the sudden illness of Herr Oskar Nedbal, the famous violist of the Bohemian Quartet, the new Serenade by Herr von Dohnányi promised for last night at the Broadwood concert would not be given, and that the viola part would be played by an artist who had not played with the others before. No doubt many of the capable viola players in London would have given much for a chance of acting as Herr Nedbal's substitute, but the choice of Mr Lionel Tertis for the signal honour was amply justified by the masterly way in which he threw himself into the task. If one had never heard the Bohemian Quartet before, one would have noticed the excellent ensemble, and philosophical reflections would doubtless have been made on the impossibility of obtaining such results without constant association among the players. Mr Tertis has, in fact, never done anything better than this, and the performance of Dvorak's string quartet in E flat, and of Schubert's delicious work in A minor, had all, or nearly all, the spontaneity for which the Bohemian players have been famous for years.

What Tertis did not know until afterwards was that Nedbal's 'sudden illness' was of a romantic nature. A widower since 1903, he had run off with the wife of Karel Hoffman, the quartet's leader. There can be no greater testimony to the status Tertis enjoyed than that he should be asked to substitute for his famous rival. Apart from Hoffman, his colleagues in this concert were the composer Josef Suk, Dvořák's son-in-law, and Hanuš Wihan, the cellist for whom Dvořák had written his concerto. Wihan was rather older than the others – he was originally the quartet's coach and joined only when his protégé Otto Berger became fatally ill. Tertis filled in for the rest of the Bohemians' British tour, and enjoyed the experience.

Tertis was also establishing himself as a viola teacher at the RAM, where in January 1906 his hourly rate was increased from 5s. to 6s. for principal-study students. One of his most talented students was Eric Coates, who studied with him from 1906 to 1909, and was later to distinguish himself as one of the finest composers of light music. Tertis wrote of their first meeting:

> From the moment I heard him at his first lesson, I spotted that here was the nucleus of a good viola player even though his efforts were rather crude, and I took an interest in him at once. His demeanour was of a charming, meek nature, but I was soon to learn that his pecuniary circumstances were of slender proportions, and I recollect that whenever I was able, I invited him to take lunch with me and saw to it that he had a good nourishing meal, for he always looked so fragile. He did indeed turn out to be one of my best pupils and eventually became principal viola in the Henry J. Wood Queen's Hall Orchestra.

Coates in his turn remembered entering Tertis's room for his first viola lesson at the Academy:

> I was at last in the presence of the Great Master and, mercifully for me, he was alone. What hands! What fingers! And what an enormous viola! I could not describe my first impressions of Lionel Tertis – I was in far too excited a state to notice anything except his hands and his instrument, though I remember his smile was irresistible. My little Testori [*sic*] was taken out of its case and closely examined. Much too small, was the verdict. We must try and find a larger one when we can. Then my treasured Tourte bow was the next thing to come under scrutiny. Yes, that was good – well balanced.

My master then seated himself at the piano and ... I stumbled through some Tartini. (I don't mind admitting that he played the piano a great deal better than I played the viola!). Not at all bad. An excellent bow arm but not a very good left hand. I should have to work hard at tone production first, though, and then technique later on. Could I put up with practising nothing but slow bowings for the next month or so? (sometimes 3 or 4 hours a day). I should have plenty of playing otherwise in the weekly orchestral practices. Of course I could. To please the master I would do anything. And with an encouraging smile and 'That's the spirit!' I settled down to my first lesson. His tone was glorious – if only I could make my viola sound one-tenth as lovely I would practise slow bowing for the rest of my life. I could feel he was a fine teacher, but what his playing was like I could not imagine.

At last the monotonous slow-bowings came to an end, and although it had been an exacting ordeal for me, I was glad I had stuck to it for all these weeks. Tertis had said to me, on that first memorable day in his room at the top of the old wooden staircase overlooking the chimney-pots at the back of the Academy 'If you will put up with it for a little time, Eric, you will not know yourself' – and I certainly did not. The difference in my tone was remarkable and I think Tertis was satisfied with the improvement, and I am quite sure he was pleased to find his new pupil had a streak of determination in him.

I sometimes wonder whether he had given me this test to see the kind of stuff I was made of. And then began the gruelling business of technique and, as facility had never been one of my strong points, I started on a period which taxed my strength and my patience to the utmost.

Coates, in his autobiography, goes on to say:

My master's command of the viola was incredible. I had thought that no one could have possessed such a technique as, or a more beautiful tone than, Oskar Nedbal ... but the sound which Tertis produced out of his huge instrument was something the like of which I had never heard before, and as for his technique, the more intricate the passage, the more did it seem as naught to this great virtuoso. ... The glorious tone ... seemed to permeate the entire room. It went from a tremendously vital, white-hot fortissimo down to a trembling, limpid pianissimo so distant that it was difficult to sense whence the mysterious sound could be coming. (Later on, I heard Tertis many times in large concert halls, and on each occasion I marvelled at the way in which he could make the softest sound carry to the farthest corner of the building. It was almost ethereal.) Scales, double-stoppings, arpeggi, fantastically-awkward passages, up and down staccato bowings, and all taken at such a breathless pace that it was bewildering.

Despite his success as a teacher it was not long before Tertis decided that he should devote more time to performing. In 1909 he was appointed principal viola in Thomas Beecham's new orchestra, and on 8 December his resignation was formally accepted by the Academy. Beecham had written to Frederick Delius earlier in the year:

> Last Monday my new orchestra made its first appearance[5] – they played very well and got a few brilliant notices … I do not however have the full contingent until February 22nd when I fire off my heavy gun. I can honestly declare that I shall by then have an orchestra which will simply wipe the floor with all others combined … The violas are led by Lionel Tertis who is the best viola I have heard anywhere.

However, some time later Beecham was to add: 'Tertis remained with us for about eighteen months, after which, unable to endure longer the strenuous routine, the long hours, and the close atmosphere of the Opera House, he resigned his position, and I do not think has ever been seen in an orchestra again.' Eric Coates, sub-principal in the Beecham Symphony Orchestra which at that time was led by Albert Sammons, said:

> I doubt if there has ever been heard in this country or elsewhere a more electrical-sounding body of players than that which went to make up the personnel of the orchestra … In the viola section alone there were eight at-one-time-or-another principals, and as the leader was Lionel Tertis himself it goes without saying that the eleven players behind him were on their mettle. Never before or since have I heard an orchestra play with greater brilliance than the Beecham Symphony Orchestra.
>
> … [Beecham] calling rehearsals at ten o'clock in the morning and keeping the orchestra waiting until eleven thirty, and then running straight on without a break till three and four in the afternoon, is enough to try the temper of an angel. That is what happened frequently during the rehearsals for the first performance of Elektra at Covent Garden, and it brought the orchestra nearly to the point of breakdown. Lionel Tertis gave in after the first night.

During the years Tertis had taught at the Academy he had taken every opportunity to encourage his friends and colleagues to write for the viola. The general recognition of his extraordinary ability as a performer and the driving force of his personality led to a response which would change the way in which the viola was perceived by fellow musicians and the concert-going public. Many new works were written and what had previously been considered a limited repertoire for the instrument was enriched with new and original music of worth. Some of the most significant new works were written by Arnold Bax, York Bowen and B. J. Dale.

When Tertis asked Benjamin Dale[6] to write a work for him, the commission resulted in the composer's most extrovert work, the Suite, op. 2, for viola and piano. The first two movements received their première by Tertis and York Bowen in a recital at the Aeolian Hall on 30 October 1906. The second movement, *Romance*, became a great favourite of Tertis. Tobias Matthay, a distinguished pianist and teacher, described it as 'The best slow movement since Beethoven'. The Suite attracted considerable praise,[7] and it has remained a popular item in the repertoire. At Tertis's request the composer orchestrated the *Romance and Finale*, and in this form the two movements were first played at a Philharmonic Society concert on 18 May 1911. The original set of orchestral parts was lost in the *Titanic* disaster in 1912.

In 1910, now professor of harmony and composition at the Academy, Dale accepted a commission from W. W. Cobbett to write a *Phantasy* for viola and piano. Cobbett's stipulation was that the composer should write a one-movement work consisting of several sections. They were to be of moderate length and to maintain a continuous flow in all moods. This form was said to come from the Elizabethan Fancy, which flourished until about 1670. Dale's *Phantasy*, op. 4, lasting about nineteen minutes, was completed on 26 May 1910 and premièred by Tertis at a RAM Club concert on 14 December of that year.

Tertis specifically asked Dale to write a work for six violas for a lecture recital he was giving at the Aeolian Hall on 9 June 1911. Playing with Tertis on this occasion were Eric Coates, Raymond Jeremy, Dorothy Jones, James Lockyer and Phyllis Mitchell; Dale wrote for them the *Introduction and Andante*, op. 5, a richly romantic and original score, a worthy English counterpart to Schoenberg's *Verklärte Nacht*. Dale's old teacher Corder wrote in the *Musical Times*: 'The Introduction and Andante is a work of remarkable beauty, power and originality', and went on: 'The effect of the whole is almost Beethovenian in majesty and grandeur and has a melodic sweep such as none other of the present generation of string-writers seems able to approach'. Dale revised the work in 1913, and it received at least a dozen performances before 1917, but it was not published, largely because of the First World War.[8]

Dale's *English Dance*, op. 10, formed part of the incidental music to *The Knight of the Burning Pestle*. Dale was in Germany at the outbreak of war, and was interned. The *English Dance* was scored for a small string orchestra when he was in Ruhleben civilian prisoner of war camp, and later arranged for violin and piano. He finally returned to England in October 1918. Dale's great friend York Bowen made a transcription of the *English Dance* for viola and piano, which he and Tertis performed in a concert of British music at the Steinway Hall on December 1918.

Bowen partnered Tertis at the piano on many occasions,[9] and in 1907 they had a tremendous reception and excellent reviews in Berlin. Their programme at the Mozart Saal in October included Brahms's E flat Sonata, Dale's op. 2 Suite, and a viola sonata (probably the C minor) by Bowen. The *Berliner Tageblatt* reported on 18 October 1907:

> Lionel Tertis and York Bowen gave us ... an exemplary performance of Brahms's Sonata in E flat, op. 120 no. 2, for viola and piano. Besides the viola player, whose magnificent tone and musical power entirely conquered the audience, there came forward a significant interpreter of the pianoforte part, and so we had the pleasure of welcoming an artistic conception, unfortunately only too rare in this place. The Suite by B. J. Dale contains much talent and dexterity. The performance was full of temperament and won for the work a triumph.

On their return from Germany Bowen completed a *Fantasie* for four violas for Tertis;[10] its first performance was given at a musical evening arranged by the Society of British Composers[11] at the music publisher Novello & Co. on 3 March 1908. The performers, Tertis, Eric Coates, James Lockyer[12] and Phyllis Mitchell, repeated the work at a RAM chamber concert on 25 May 1908.

This was also the year of York Bowen's major contribution to the viola repertoire. The Viola Concerto in C minor, op. 25,[13] was written for Tertis, who gave the first performance at the Philharmonic Society concert in Queen's Hall on 26 March 1908; Landon Ronald conducted and W. H. Reed led the orchestra. Both Tertis and Ronald were making their *début* appearance at a Philharmonic Society concert. A member of the audience that evening was the young Adrian Boult, who noted in his diary: 'An interesting but long viola concerto well played by Lionel Tertis.' The work was enthusiastically received by audience and press alike. Tertis would play the concerto a number of times during his career, including a performance at the Wigmore Hall in July 1923, and the first American performance in Chicago, where it was again well received. *The Times* review after the first performance said:

> Unlike some modern composers Mr Bowen has not aimed merely at orchestral colouring, but has packed all his movements with melodies, the second subject of the first movement and the theme of the Andante being very attractive and also lending themselves easily to development.

In these development sections Mr Bowen has written with a great deal of fluency and the writing, as might have been expected from his previous works, has a decided character of its own. The orchestral colouring and the harmonic progressions are often reminiscent of Debussy, but it is a case of influence rather than imitation ... Mr Lionel Tertis played the concerto with remarkable vigour and fine tone, and both he and the composer were several times recalled.

The *Morning Post* wrote:

He appears to have a predeliction [*sic*] for the viola, having completed two sonatas for the instrument, also a duet for organ and viola and a quartet for four violas. Very modern in spirit, it is admirably scored, with effects here and there which remind one of Debussy. The solo instrument is throughout treated with great effect and thorough knowledge, and if the first movement seems a little unduly spun out, the Andante is very expressive and the Finale very quaint and animated. The solo part was superbly played by Lionel Tertis.

After Bowen's sudden death in 1961, Tertis wrote in the Royal Academy of Music magazine:

York Bowen is indeed a great loss to our Alma Mater – the Royal Academy of Music – I have known him for over sixty years. He was a brilliant pianist and prolific composer. He was an example of how one should plan out one's daily life systematically, and conscientiously use every minute of it to good purpose. ... He and the late Benjamin Dale were the closest friends. They were both crazy about Wagner and went to every Covent Garden performance. I shall always feel indebted to both of them for their generosity in writing compositions for the viola. ... Bowen was always full of exuberance and this characteristic permeated his works. He could play most of the instruments of the orchestra, and added to all these talents he was a very fine pedagogue.

Arnold Bax arrived at the Academy as a student in 1899 and enrolled on the same day as B. J. Dale. Already alerted to the qualities of the viola by Nedbal's playing, he found his ideal violist in Tertis, and was to write a number of works for him over the next three decades. The earliest, *Concert Piece* for viola and piano, is full of youthful, romantic high spirits, and was composed when Bax was twenty and in his fourth year of study at the Academy. Although instructions such as 'con molto passione', 'molto cantabile' and 'con passione più e più' appear in the score, the Celtic influence so predominant in all Bax's music is already evident.[14] It was considered revolutionary in Academy circles when first performed by Tertis and the composer on 6 December 1904 at a Patron's Fund[15] concert at the Aeolian Hall. The *Musical Standard* critic wrote: 'one of the most advanced works in the programme … Consisting of one movement only in the usual sonata form, somewhat modified, it breathes a spirit almost of rebellion and riot throughout its fervid pages.'

Two years later Bax completed his first published chamber work, the Trio for piano, violin and viola in E major. This one-movement work was written under Tertis's influence; the viola part is often high in the treble clef, rising to the high D above the stave. *Musical Opinion* described it in January 1911 as

> a work of great brilliancy; a virile energy that carries one along with it; a rhythmic vitality and a splendour of harmonic colour that reminds one of Strauss's *Heldenleben*, an occasional harshness caused by the clashing together of elements which refuse to mingle harmoniously; these, together with passages of delicate and intricate beauty combine to make a quite remarkable work. The theme in A flat (page 8 of the score) is perfectly delicious, it makes one 'nudge oneself to listen', although it has a decidedly Straussian flavour. The trio as a whole opens up quite new vistas in chamber music.

In those days there were many music clubs, mainly in the London area, which supported the love and development of all aspects of chamber-music playing, both amateur and professional. One of the most influential was the Oxford and Cambridge Musical Club, founded in 1899 by Alfred Gibson; its object was 'to promote and extend knowledge of chamber music among its members, to hold fortnightly meetings for the playing of chamber music, and to provide a central resort in London, combining the advantage of a social club with the cultivation of that particular form of art'. It consisted mainly of members of the two universities, who arranged opportunities for its members to play, often with a visiting professional, in a private situation and also to promote professional chamber-music concerts. Sir Henry Wood was president for many years. The club organized regular concerts at the Broadwood Rooms.

Two other organizations, the Music Makers' Guild and the Hampstead Music Club, arranged chamber-music parties in private houses. Owing to the lack of violists, Tertis was often invited, and paid a fee, to join some of these amateur ensembles under the auspices of the Oxford and Cambridge Musical Club and a similar organization arranged by Sir William Evans Gordon at 4 Chelsea Embankment.

Many of Tertis's recitals had an educational bias, and through lecture recitals and demonstrations he attracted a good deal of interest from the press and the public alike. One event that he had hoped would stimulate interest in the viola was the annual conference of the Incorporated Society of Musicians[16] in Folkestone on 4 January 1910, which featured an important lecture on 'The Viola': its history, famous makers, treatment in the orchestra and chamber music, and its neglect as a solo instrument. The lecture was written by the Revd Henry Carte de Lafontaine, and delivered by Stanley Hawley. Tertis then played the Bach *Chaconne*, the Dale *Romance* and Bowen's *Fantasie* for four violas, in which he was joined by Eric Coates, Raymond Jeremy and James Lockyer.[17] This significant historical event for the viola shows the pioneer spirit of the Society. Tertis's performance of the Bach *Chaconne* also marked a personal achievement of which he was proud. 'I took my courage in both hands in 1910 and gave the first performance of the Chaconne on the viola. I had practised it for years, and in the simplicity of my heart imagined that the audacious enterprise would make the viola talked about all over town.' (Tertis was here forgetting that he had first performed the *Chaconne* in 1906, during his recitals with York Bowen at the Aeolian Hall. A review appeared in *The Strad* magazine in December 1906: 'Mr. Lionel Tertis has again shewn his talent for the viola at a concert given in conjunction with Mr. York Bowen, who is equally at home in composition and as a pianist. Mr. Tertis made the experiment of playing Bach's "Chaconne" on the viola – as someone said it is better so than as a pianoforte piece, to which arrangement Signor Busoni treated us ...')

What happened next was something for which Tertis was unprepared – the Folkestone performance was altogether ignored by the press, except for Edwin Evans reviewing in the magazine *Outlook*. Tertis wrote to Frederick Corder, who was then curator at the RAM, angrily suggesting that being British was the reason why the newspapers neglected to review his performance. He even threatened to go abroad. Corder replied:

> Is it any consolation to know that others are suffering even more than yourself? I have had five such disappointments during the last fortnight, and if I were twenty years younger should certainly feel like chucking the whole thing up. As it is, I endeavour to console myself with the belief that no really good effort is in vain. Such a performance as you gave the other night will long live in the memories of those who were present, and some good must come of it eventually.

Despite Tertis's disappointment at the reception of his Folkestone recital, other concert programmes provide ample evidence of the growing interest in the viola. Performances of music by Dale and Bowen featured in a concert at the Aeolian Hall on 9 June 1911 alongside new pieces from Joseph Holbrooke and Cyril Scott. All these works were performed for the first time, and Bowen,

Holbrooke and Scott all participated in the premières of their respective works. The other artists were Sylvia Dalton (Mrs York Bowen, soprano), Miriam Timothy (harp), Henri de Busscher (oboe d'amore) and York Bowen (organ).

Short Piece, op. 5 for six violas	B. J. Dale

[This was the *Introduction and Andante*, played by Tertis, Eric Coates, Raymond Jeremy, Dorothy Jones,[18] James Lockyer and Phyllis Mitchell[19]]

Fairyland, op. 57	Joseph Holbrooke[20]

[Nocturne for viola, oboe d'amore and piano]

Romantic Poem for viola, harp and organ	York Bowen
Fantasia for viola and piano	Cyril Scott
At the Midhour of the Night	York Bowen

[Song with viola obbligato]

Holbrooke was a prominent figure in London musical life at the time and a prolific composer and pianist. His chamber music, and that of Cyril Scott, another popular composer and pianist, often featured in pre-1914 concert programmes, as did that of Dr Ernest Walker,[21] Thomas Dunhill,[22] and Percy Grainger, whose *Arrival Platform Humlet for middle fiddle* was composed in 1912. Tertis remembers his impression of the work in his autobiography:

> Grainger invited me to come to a railway station to meet his fiancée. While walking up and down the platform he sang a tune, bouche fermée, a strange sort of noise to my ears to say the least of it, and when I asked him what it was he replied that it had just come to him, that he would write it out and dedicate it to me for unaccompanied solo viola and would give it the title A Platform Humlet. However, when I received the manuscript and played it through it sounded so devastatingly ugly that I never performed it either in private or in public – neither do I remember to what infernal end I consigned it!

Tertis did, however, edit the work for publication, and often played arrangements of Grainger's 'more melodic and traditional style' pieces. He recorded the composer's *Molly on the Shore* for Vocalion Records in a version for viola and piano.

A composer whose work and influence upon British music has proved to be of lasting importance was Frank Bridge. It is perhaps surprising that, as a fine violist who performed in a number of well-known ensembles, he did not write any major work for the viola. Two early pieces, *Pensiero* and *Allegro Appassionato*, were published by Stainer & Bell in 1908 as the first two instalments in the Lionel Tertis Viola Library, but after that the two men seem to have drifted apart. It has been suggested that there may have been some disagreement. However, as Bridge's style matured, it probably became less congenial to Tertis. If one compares the melodic style and uncomplicated harmonies of the two early pieces with the more unusual harmonies and extended melodic ideas of Bridge's viola duet from 1911, it is apparent that the later music must have seemed very distant to Tertis, whose taste was catholic but conservative. He performed the *Lament* and *Caprice* for two violas by Frank Bridge in a concert organized by the Society of British Composers on 18 March 1912, probably with the composer; the programme announced that they would be published shortly. In fact *Lament* was published only recently, and the manuscript of *Caprice* has disappeared.

Tertis began spreading his wings internationally. He appeared in Holland as soloist with the Concertgebouw Orchestra, directed by Willem Mengelberg, on two occasions, in 1911 and 1912. In the first concert he played Dale's *Romance and Finale* for viola and orchestra. Shortly before the 1914–18 War he paid his second visit to the USA as a member of the Harold Bauer Piano Quartet. This was a high-powered ensemble of soloists: Bauer was an exceptional pianist with a beautiful *cantabile* touch, who had been a professional violinist and therefore knew how to combine with string players; Bronisław Huberman was the most distinctive fiddler of his age, almost self-taught and not entirely in command of the subtleties of vibrato – one wonders how he combined with Tertis – but imaginative and creative in his phrasing; and the London-born Felix Salmond vied at that time with W. H. Squire as Britain's leading cellist (after settling in the USA in 1922, he occupied two of that country's most important teaching positions, at the Curtis Institute and the Juilliard School). The four men travelled about by rail; Tertis remembered:

The ordinary Pullman of an American train has a good-sized wash house at either end, one for men and the other for women. Huberman was an insatiable man for practising, and on our journeys he would be found in the men's wash-house playing his violin from morning to night, meal times excepted. He never stopped, no matter how many passengers were performing their ablutions, and how it came about that he was not forcibly restrained from turning the wash-house into a practice room I shall never understand.

A few months before Europe was plunged into war, thirty-six-year-old Tertis married Ada Gawthrop, aged fifty-three, a vicar's daughter who also played the viola. He had first met her in 1902 at Stafford House (later the London Museum), where she had come to hear him play, and they met again some time later at a concert where she was playing in the London Diocesan Orchestra, an amateur group of about forty women players. Lessons with Tertis followed, and over the years their friendship developed. On 2 December 1913 they were married at the register office in Epsom, Surrey. Following their marriage they went to live in a small house in Belmont. Harold Milner, Lionel's nephew, often visited them when he was a schoolboy at Epsom College during the early years of their marriage, when they had a pet monkey called Chippy who lived in a cage in a super-heated room. Milner, who liked to take the monkey for walks in the garden, remembers Ada as a kindly, gentle lady who was intensely musical. She was certainly good for Tertis. Domesticity introduced an element of fulfilment and calm into the life of this restless and turbulent man who had so single-handedly battled to sustain his vision since leaving home as a twelve-year-old boy. It also allowed him to explore, to a point, other enthusiasms outside his musical existence.

He had always been fascinated by the new motorcycles which were becoming popular, and eventually bought a second-hand machine. It had no gear changes, but that was of no consequence to him, because he was very ignorant of all things mechanical, and knew nothing of such matters as carburettors, plug points and correct vaporization of petrol. After some helpful advice from a knowledgeable motorcyclist and an instruction book, Tertis used this form of transport to travel to and from his professional engagements. Later he progressed to a 'Model T' Ford, which he found a much more comfortable way of getting about. But when he noticed that he was spending too many hours with his car, and his practice was being affected, he gave up motoring.

Likewise, he was an enthusiastic golfer who achieved the proud handicap of nine at the Banstead Club until his viola practice began to suffer, and he put his clubs away for ever. Gerald Moore remembers his golfing prowess: 'he reduced his handicap to a single figure in the space of a few years, much to the envy of Solomon the pianist and me, we played frequently together but remained rabbits. I once asked Lionel the secret of his low handicap and he confessed it was his putting, "I always putt with one hand." I asked "Does it work?" His answer was conclusive, "I never take three putts." '

Throughout his life, whenever Tertis took up a new interest it very soon became an obsession, but the one obsession he would not relinquish was his determination to see the viola achieve the recognition and respect he believed it to be due in order to be considered equal to the violin and cello as a solo instrument.

In his treatise on chamber music written in 1913, Thomas Dunhill was able to say about Tertis:

In this country the advocacy of Mr Lionel Tertis, a great artist, the eloquence of whose playing gives the viola a unique position as a solo instrument, has found a ready and most gratifying response. It is not too much to say that he has directly inspired some of the most notable British compositions of recent years, and that his performance of these works have convincingly shown that there are still greater heights and depths waiting to be explored.

❦ 3 ❦

The First World War

The Great War – Belgian connections –
lifelong friendships – Queen Elisabeth of the Belgians

TERTIS was thirty-seven at the start of the Great War, and too old for any meaningful military service. When he was eventually called up, he turned out to be unfit. Like others in the same situation – the great bass Robert Radford, for example – he threw himself into helping the war effort by entertaining those on the home front. He was to look back on the war as a ghastly watershed in history: 'Whatever our apprehensions, we little realised that it would spell the end of the sanguine, prosperous, hopefully forward-looking Europe most of us regarded as becoming solidly established.'

The German occupation of Belgium and the accompanying atrocities horrified the British nation. One of the best-selling publications of the 1914 Christmas season was *King Albert's Book*, produced by the *Daily Telegraph* in association with other leading newspapers under the editorship of Hall Caine. Among the musicians who contributed were Elgar, Lange-Müller, Liza Lehmann, Mackenzie, Mascagni, Paderewski and Saint-Saëns. The Belgian refugees who flooded across the Channel into Britain included many musicians, some of whom were to play a large role in Tertis's wartime career. Eugène Goossens, himself of Belgian stock, described the musical scene in Britain:

> At the outbreak of war all German professional musicians in Britain – and their number was legion – were sent back to the Fatherland, to the great delight of many British artists, who found themselves with increased work and considerably improved chances of livelihood. The public were soon to realise that in Albert Sammons, Felix Salmond, Lionel Tertis, William Murdoch, Myra Hess and many other instrumentalists (and singers) England possessed the equal of the fine German artists who had, up to that time, almost completely monopolised the British musical scene.

Tertis consolidated lifelong friendships during the war with others among Europe's finest musicians in addition to the Belgians. They met at the private chamber music parties held in 'Mrs Draper's cellar' in Edith Grove, which Eugène Ysaÿe called 'La Cave'. This is where, in 1913, Artur Rubinstein[1] had met Tertis for the first time. In his memoirs, Rubinstein described him as 'an unassuming little man in his middle thirties with the kindest eyes in the world behind his glasses, and a ready smile. A thick, tobacco-blonde, oppressive moustache belied the rest of his friendly face.' On that occasion Rubinstein heard Tertis play in the Debussy Quartet with Jacques Thibaud, Sammons and the Spanish cellist Augustín Rubio.

From the first bars on, I became aware of a new element in their ensemble, a sonority I had never heard before. The sound came to light by the powerful, singing, soulful tone of the viola as played by Lionel Tertis. Here was one of the greatest artists it was my good fortune to know and to hear. Our close, lifelong friendship dates from that night on. After the Debussy I played with him, Thibaud and Rubio in the C minor Piano Quartet by Brahms. The sound of his solo in the first movement still rings in my ears. It was a glorious night of music.

Tertis met Thibaud again at a farewell party for Paul Draper before the First World War. In an unusual play-through of the Brahms B flat sextet, at Casals's suggestion Paul Kochanski played first violin while Casals, taking Thibaud's violin and holding it low between his knees in place of his cherished cello, played the second violin part, Tertis and Pierre Monteux took the viola parts, and Rubio and Felix Salmond were the cellists.

Tertis wrote of these informal chamber music meetings: 'No public performance could ever have reached such a pitch of carefree, rapturous inspiration. There were no rehearsals; the music came fresh and the executants were no duffers – they included Ysaÿe, Casals, Thibaud, Cortot, Harold Bauer, Kochanski, Szymanowski, Arbos, Rubinstein and Sammons.' Artur Rubinstein said of Tertis:

He is the greatest glory in England in the way of instrument or players ... I remember him playing with Kreisler, the famous concerto for violin and viola by Mozart. I can tell you he had much better success than Kreisler. He knocked Kreisler out on that occasion, his tone was bigger, more human and more musical.

Tertis remembered another occasion when he played a Brahms Piano Quartet with Ysaÿe, Casals and Rubinstein.

Prodigious, the lusciousness and wealth of sound! Ysaÿe with his great volume of tone and glorious phrasing. Casals playing in the slow movement with divinely pure expression, Rubinstein with his demoniacal command of the keyboard (his ferocity in the Scherzo was frightening) – what an experience for me to be associated with such giants.

Brahms featured again at Edith Grove a few days later, when Thibaud, Kochanski, Tertis, Monteux, Salmond and May Mukle played the two string sextets. Tertis always cherished the unconscious compliment Casals gave him when the cellist arrived late for a chamber music evening and, hearing a Mozart quartet being played, asked his hostess at the front door: 'Who plays the viola?' Muriel Draper said that the greatest performance in her life of the 'Trout' Quintet was given in her house by Rubinstein, Thibaud, Tertis, Casals and Salmond (who presumably substituted for a specialist double bassist). She described Tertis as

> unique among viola players. He made of that ungrateful but necessary instrument a solo instrument of manifold beauties and possibilities. Its heavily grained tone texture, which in less gifted hands presents an obstacle to be overcome or a limitation to be regretted, became for him the chief asset of his art. Every note was a full convinced statement that between the brilliant clarities and penetrating flexibilities of the violin and the rich serenities and shapely flow of the cello, was a province of sound where the qualities of both were accessible to one instrument, and that was the viola. Phrases given to the viola emerged with startling value when played by Tertis, instead of sinking anonymously into the general musical whole. Too fine an artist ever to intrude his virtuosity in ensemble playing, or over-emphasize by the tiniest fraction of a phrase the emotional power he could extract from it, he made a definite contribution to the structure of a work by the just importance he was able to give to the viola part. Sonatas and one concerto for viola have been written for him to play, and more of his kind might encourage a real literature for the viola which at present it so conspicuously lacks.

One evening in 1915 Ysaÿe and his wife Louise came to listen to the music at Edith Grove, having crossed the Channel that day. Jacques Thibaud played a Mozart Sonata, and later, with Warwick Evans, Albert Sammons, Waldo Warner and Tertis, ran through Brahms's piano quintet and string quartet in C minor. Ysaÿe wept with pleasure at these performances. On another occasion Sammons, Sylvia Sparrow, Tertis and Rubio played in Ysaÿe's honour the Debussy Quartet, which had been dedicated to the Ysaÿe quartet. He was delighted with their playing, kissed Tertis on both cheeks and then said, to the amazement of all present, that he could not understand the music; it was too modern for him.

Sixty years later Tertis remembered the musical parties held at Mrs Draper's home: 'I never forget one work we did which was the César Franck Piano Quintet with Ysaÿe leading, Jacques Thibaud as second violin, Arthur Rubinstein piano, Casals cello and my humble self as violist. He took the finale at a terrific pace ... inspiring, exhilarating, wonderful!'

In 1914 Joseph Holbrooke arranged four concerts featuring some of his own compositions and other works at the Arts Centre, London. The first concert, on 27 February, included his works for clarinet and strings and the Piano Quintet; the second concert, a month later, included his Nocturne for violin, viola and piano and Sextet, op. 46, for strings and piano. The artists in the two concerts were John Saunders and Charles Woodhouse (violins), Tertis (viola), Herbert Withers (cello), Claude Hobday (double bass), Charles Draper (clarinet) and Holbrooke (piano). In the third concert, on 24 April, Holbrooke was joined by Albert Sammons, Thomas Petre, Tertis and Withers in the Franck Piano Quintet and Bax's new Trio for violin, viola and piano. The same artists participated in the last concert of the series on 29 May, when string quartets by Richard Cleveland and Ethel Smyth (E minor) were played alongside Holbrooke's Four Dances for piano and string quartet.

During 1915 Holbrooke's chamber concerts took place on 24 April and 7 May, this time at the Aeolian Hall. The first concert introduced his new work *Impressions* for string quartet, together with his Sextet, op. 43, and Piano Quintet, op. 40; the string personnel were the same as the previous year, with the addition of Raymond Jeremy and E. de Vlieger. The second concert in the series included Holbrooke's dramatic Piano Quartet 'Byron', and Tertis and Walthew played the latter's *Mosaics* for viola and piano. The following review appeared in *Musical Opinion*, June 1915 (Concert Notices by 'Capriccio'):

> The first performance was given at one of Mr. Joseph Holbrooke's chamber concerts on 7 May 1915 of Richard Walthew's Five Diversions for String Trio. A series of perfectly finished little numbers, abundantly melodious and full of deft turns of phrase and rhythm, they fulfil the highest demands of the form in which they are written. They are quite innocent of ethical or psychological complications, and prove that even now the case for absolute music is by no means obsolete. The balance of parts has been very skilfully preserved, and the faculty for clean and finished workmanship that forms so admirable a part of Mr. Walthew's equipment as a composer is displayed throughout. The last number in the suite, by the way, takes the form of a set of variations on the old ecclesiastical tune, 'Christus Natus Hodie'. A remarkable diversity of tone colour is obtained even from so limited a medium as the trio of strings. The Diversions should become popular. The soloists were Messrs. John Saunders, Lionel Tertis and Cedric Sharpe, and it would be difficult to imagine a better ensemble. Mr. Tertis further added to the joy of the occasion by playing Walthew's

'Mosaics' for viola and piano. These delicious little pieces are deservedly beloved of all who know and appreciate the value of spontaneous melodic writing and a cameo-like clarity of instrumental diction.

Among the distinguished Belgian musicians with whom Tertis became involved during these years were Désiré Défauw and Émile Doehaerd, the leader and cellist of the Allied Quartet. Défauw was a fine violinist who played the 1729 Stradivarius previously owned by Arbos and René Ortmans; he would later make a considerable reputation as a conductor. Doehaerd had been the cellist of the Quatuor Zimmer, the finest Belgian quartet after the Ysaÿe. The original players of the inner parts in the Allied Quartet were La Prade and Alfred Hobday. Tertis joined instead of Hobday in the latter part of the war, when the second violinist was the American-born conductor-violinist Richard C. Kay (later replaced by Charles Woodhouse). Défauw, Tertis and Doehaerd were also members of the Belgian Piano Quartet, brought together in London by the pianist-composer Joseph Jongen.[2] They gave their inaugural concert on 8 June 1915 at the Steinway Hall, playing quartets by Jongen and Frank Bridge.

The South Place Popular Concerts on 18 April 1915 included viola solos by Wolstenholme and Joseph Jongen's Trio for piano, violin and viola with the composer, Désiré Défauw and Tertis. The Trio was repeated in a concert for the Société des Concerts Françaises at the Aeolian Hall in June 1915. In the same hall, on 20 October, the Belgian Piano Quartet included Beethoven's Serenade for string trio, op. 8, and Chausson's Piano Quartet in the second of a series of concerts under the auspices of the Classical Concert Society.

Tertis was featured in a special article in the *Musical Standard* on 31 July 1915:

> He finds the public quite ignorant of the charm of the viola and is doing all he can to break down the prejudice against what is often regarded as the 'Cinderella' of the string family. ... 'You asked me for a few words to viola players', he said to us recently. 'What I should like said is as follows. Why do viola players show such little interest in their much neglected instrument? Why do they not help the cause of the viola as a solo instrument by playing solos? We get public recognition for our instrument with only two exponents! It is such a beautiful solo instrument. There are so many fine viola players, and it is extremely disappointing that they do not sacrifice a little for arts sake.'

On 22 January 1916 Tertis gave an afternoon concert at the Steinway Hall[3] in aid of Queen Mary's Convalescent Auxiliary Hospitals. With York Bowen and the violinist Daniel Melsa they premièred Bowen's new Trio (probably the

Phantasie Trio, op. 24, with viola instead of cello). Melsa was a fine violinist who made a career as a soloist as well as a session player. Max Jaffa remembered him around 1946–7: 'He used to sit way behind me – in the third or fourth desk – but he could play absolutely anything. "Go on, Danny, play something," we used to say when we were bored, and he would rattle off something like Paganini's *Moto Perpetuo* – which is non-stop virtuosity and high-speed violin technique from beginning to end. He would just play it without a mistake in sight.'

Artur Rubinstein and Tertis had often played together at Edith Grove, but their first public performance took place early in 1916, when they played two British works written for Tertis. The *Musical Times* on 1 March 1916 wrote:

> This performer is generally acknowledged to be one of the finest viola players we have heard in this country. He played with Mr Arthur Rubinstein Dale's Phantasy and York Bowen's Sonata no. 1 in C minor. Such fine artists presented these British works in the most favourable light ... Mr Tertis amazed his audience by his virtuoso playing on the viola of the famous Chaconne written by Bach for violin, and transposed on this occasion.

Ysaÿe, who was in the audience, went on to the platform and publicly embraced Tertis. The two of them were invited to play Mozart's *Sinfonia concertante* for the first time at a Royal Philharmonic Society concert, on 28 February 1916 at Queen's Hall, with Beecham conducting. At their first runthrough Ysaÿe suggested certain phrasings to Tertis and they adhered to these at the rehearsal with orchestra. At the performance, however, Ysaÿe changed everything, and Tertis had to imitate him on the spur of the moment. Ysaÿe promised to write a cadenza for the performance but did not finish it in time. In 1950 Tertis received the manuscript of the cadenza from the violinist's son, Antoine; it was inscribed 'À mon ami Lionel Tertis'. As it was interminably long and frightfully difficult technically, Tertis returned it to the Ysaÿe archive. During the time the cadenza was in Tertis's hands his former student Harry Danks made a copy, which is now in the author's possession.

When conscription was introduced in February 1916 Tertis was finally called up for military service, but was saved by old injuries to his nose and antrum which had been inflicted when he was eight. He had been knocked down by a thief, his face had hit the pavement and the mishap had led to a number of nasal operations over a period of years. With hindsight, all this discomfort was a blessing in disguise, as he was not accepted by the recruiting board for the army. Instead he was appointed a special constable. His duties included guarding the Ventor Road reservoir, by the side of which there was a hut where he used to practise surreptitiously, using a heavy brass mute to subdue the sound.

Through his friendship with Ysaÿe, Tertis met the King and Queen of the Belgians and developed a lifelong friendship with the violin-playing Queen Elisabeth, a pupil of Ysaÿe. In the summer of 1916 the king and queen asked Ysaÿe to come to their part of free Belgium to play for them and the troops. Ysaÿe invited Tertis to join him, and the violist went for an eight-day stay that included making music for soldiers on the front line and a tour of the trenches facing the German forces. Germaine Prévost (1891–1987), founder member and elder statesman of the Quatuor Pro Arte, spent several years in the trenches on the Dixmude sector. When Ysaÿe visited the front line in the summer of 1916, Prévost was summoned to take part in a Mozart quintet at the royal villa, La Panne, with Tertis playing first viola.

The sightseeing engendered paroxysms of nervousness on the part of those charged with the visitors' safety; Tertis was a small man, but hiding or camouflaging Ysaÿe was nearly impossible. Tertis kept a diary of the visit in three small notebooks, extracts of which are reproduced below for the first time in their original form:

1916 Friday 15 June

Left Belmont at 6.15 a.m. with darling Addle [Ada Tertis] and travelled by 6.40 to Victoria. …

We had a very good journey to Folkestone arriving there at about 10.45. The train was of course full of military officers some going to India and Egypt etc. Civilians had to go in a private room to have their passports re-examined before being allowed to go on board. Hundreds of soldiers came on with us. In the harbour we saw a submarine partly submerged. …

We started our sea journey at about 11.30, and all had to put on life belts (very cumbersome things) … We were escorted by a torpedo boat, and I saw at least ½ dozen troop ships all going to France (simply crammed with troops). When we arrived close to Boulogne Harbour, I saw the masts of a munition ship sticking out of the water which had been sunk 8 months ago. It has not been removed[,] it being considered too dangerous at the present moment. It was torpedoed by a German submarine immediately outside the harbour. I must admit was quite glad to get off the boat. Major Gordon passed us of course through all officials and we had no trouble. At Boulogne we had our lunch and then started off for La Panne in a Royal motorcar, through myriads of English soldiers five inside and two outside a pretty good pack. … Our first stop was at Calais where we met the youngest of Ysaye's sons. He went away rejoicing from papa with a 100 franc note in his pocket. Our next stop was Dunkirk where we saw a good many ruined houses and also a church the result of bombs. From there on to La Panne. All this accomplished in a Royal Autocar so that we passed all barriers with the greatest ease. We arrived at La Panne about 4.45 and had our tea, the sea shore patrolled by Belgian soldiers with their Kaki [*sic*] steel helmets. At about 6 the Royal car came for Ysaye and Rousseau to go to the Queen. We, Doehaerd, Theo Ysaye [Eugène's brother] and myself went for another stroll and saw a company of Belgian soldiers form up ready to march to the trenches to Nieuport about six miles away. It seems this happens every day for they work in the trenches at night and return in the morning. When we returned we had a note commanding us to join Ysaye at the Royal Villa and bring the music and instruments at 8.30.

At 8.25 the car came and we were met by two high officers who took us into a sort of Hall-sitting room where we all waited, officers as well for about ¼ hour. The moment then arrived. We were ushered in. Ysaye introduced me to the Queen and then to the King and said so many complimentary things about me that I simply burnt with uncomfortableness (though fortunately I did not understand). The great impression I had during the evening was their most delightful simpleness. Their kindness and graciousness was too touching added to which their simple surroundings left an impression never to be forgotten.

We began by playing a Quartet of Fauré and then Ysaye asked me to play a solo. I played Wolstenholme's pieces, which were liked. Then Ysaye played most wonderfully. After which we finished music with Brahms (piano) quartet in G minor. (*during conversation with King Albert I remember him saying to me 'I have often seen the Zeppelins in broad daylight going over to pay you a visit.' The Royal Villa looks out to the sea.*) During the evening I had quite a long and animated conversation with the King. Both the King and Queen thanked me for the pleasure I had given them and were very complimentary. Refreshments afterwards and then they left us. We soon after departed, and so ended a most memorable day.

1916 *Saturday 17th June – 2nd day*

Got up about 8.30. No bell in room – utmost difficulty to procure de l'eau chaud. Had breakfast very quickly, and then Major Gordon called to take us for a motor drive which was to include the Belgian headquarters. En route we saw plenty of captive balloons including two German ones which seemed to be quite close. No end of houses smashed to pieces, eventually arrived at Furnes. The market place (like a town of the dead) many houses in it practically demolished. It gave one an extraordinary feeling. One could hear the guns at Ypres going on all the time. In this square the great review of troops took place last year before King Albert and King George of England. I stood at the same lamp post as they did and saluted. ...

Just before lunch we heard a pretty good bang from a cannon and Ysaye said there goes the dinner gong! After lunch Major Gordon took us out again (Ysaye stayed at home this time). We went to Nieuport ... by mistake of the chauffeur (took the wrong road) and got properly into the danger zone. The road and district where we were now travelling was in charge of the French in their blue-grey uniforms and we were right in the thick of the trenches all along the dunes barbed wire everywhere. It looked almost like a scene in central Africa with all the camps on the dunes. We were within two miles of Nieuport at one place and saw a shell bursting – a huge column of smoke. ...

1916 21st June – 6th day

This has been the day of days for [?]me. A walk in the morning on the promenade, on sea front (where De Page hospital is) and talked to a patient, a French Priest who (had) *both* his legs amputated – terrible!!! (felt frightfully depressed after). ... At 2.15 we left for Hoogestate, a Belgian field Hospital – not very far from Ypres. General de Koeninke (commander of this sector) met us at the door. We arrived 10 minutes before the Queen. There was no programme so everybody had to announce what they would perform (myself included!!!) The programme was as follows:

> Trio for strings Beethoven: Ysaye, Tertis, Doehaerd
> Solo Ysaye
> Solo cello Doehaerd
> Piano solo Theo Ysaye
> Viola solo Tertis
> Violin solos Ysaye

The best concert we have had. We were all so 'bein [*sic*] disposé' when my turn came, I announced in French 'Deux petite pieces anglais'!!!! I wonder now where I got the courage from (before the Queen and all those high officers). After the concert we had tea with the Queen and many many generals etc. After the Queen left General de Koeninke said he would show us something in his section. We all got in his car, and travelled in the direction of Ypres!! His car had a misterious [*sic*] flag on the bonnet and all sentries and soldiers stood at attention as we passed – as we proceeded he pointed out to us huge shell holes. These became more frequent as we travelled. We were getting nearer and nearer to the Germans.

We also passed many little wooden crosses the graves of soldiers. We passed through Loos, every single house absolutely smashed to pieces, and then on to Niewe Cappelle. The church here was simply a mass of broken bricks and iron. It was too awful a sight – half the roof gone and the other half hanging as by a thread. Home after home blown to bits and still some of the peasants (real Flemish ones) living on in their cellars.

1916 22nd June – 7th day

Went for a walk and saw them shooting shrapnel at a Hun aeroplane, could not see the aeroplane it was so high up but very interesting to see the puffs or balls of smoke in the sky following the aeroplane. ... At 7.30 p.m. Doehaerd arrived from some excursion with Ysaye to say I was to come at once to camp (really they were the reserves to the first trench) at Eggeraertscapelle via Steenstrate to play for the soldiers. The camp was commanded by a most charming man Major [?]Reding, who heard me play yesterday at the hospital and said I had made him weep! I arrived and found the officers dining in a wooden shanty with wooden benches and curtains made of sandbag canvas. Two long flowing curtains in the middle of the room draped back with string. Outside the shanty (which was in the middle of a field) there were I should say about 500 soldiers waiting for the music. The programme was quite extraordinary. In the first place, we played in the open air in a field and secondly there was no piano to be had. We began with a Mozart Quartet – Ysaÿe, his son, Doehaerd and myself to which the soldiers listened most attentively and applauded enthusiastically. After Ysaye and his son played solos, Doehaerd and myself accompanying as best we could. The next item was all the national airs which Ysaye played, we filling the harmonies (the soldiers standing at attention all the time) and I finished up by playing Tipperary. The soldiers simply went wild. They all sang it so splendidly and with such vim that it was impossible to imagine other than British Tommies. It was an experience I shall never forget. It would have done any Englishman good to have seen and heard these Belgian Tommies absolutely yelling it out for all they were worth.

1916 23rd June – 8th day

... Packed my bag and went for a stroll on the sea shore. ... the Queen came along in her car on the way to the hospital and saw us and stopped to wish us goodbye. She thanked me and said my playing had given her so much pleasure and she was sorry I was going. ...

1.30 arrived and there was tremendous farewells and embracing. Ysaye kissed me on both cheeks – Oh! la la, – la la.

The Royal Car arrived with a gendarme sitting on the box seat. He accompanied us all the way, and we passed along like Kings. All the sentinels saluted us, also every soldier we passed. Davreux accompanied us as far as Dunkirk and then presented us with a report of the doings of the Armée Belge during the first year of hostilities. ... All went well and we got to Folkestone where the Kings courier again got us most expeditiously through all difficulties. I am sitting in the train now at 8.20 p.m. whirling along to London ready to give my own darling Addle ... a surprise. Voila!

Queen Elisabeth of the Belgians had sent her children to stay with Lord Curzon, former viceroy of India, for the duration of the war, and had asked Ysaÿe to visit them on occasion. In 1916 Lord Curzon invited Ysaÿe, Sammons, Tertis, Doehaerd and Rubinstein to spend the weekend playing chamber music at his country house near Basingstoke. On the Saturday morning after breakfast Tertis and Rubinstein played a sonata together, and after tea the group ran through Dvořák's Piano Quartet in E flat. At the end of the first movement the ensemble noticed that his Lordship was fast asleep – when they finished their performance he woke up suddenly and said: 'This was quite, quite delightful, gentlemen.' They were all so engrossed in their music-making that they missed the last train back to London. Lord Curzon produced one unused toothbrush and lent Tertis a pair of pyjamas, which were twice his usual size.

Tertis described Ysaÿe as a huge man who smoked a correspondingly huge pipe. 'Even his matchboxes were outsize. Only his violin was of standard dimensions, and in his hands it looked a toy. He was a glorious artist, with a tone of prodigious volume and inordinate technical powers.' In Liège there is a piece of paper on which Ysaÿe has written down a list of his colleagues for whom he intended to write a sonata. He planned to write two viola sonatas, one for his quartet violist Léon van Hout, the other for Tertis.

After Ysaÿe's death in 1931 André Mangeot, first violin of the International String Quartet, wrote an article about the great man which was published in *Gramophone*. One of his personal recollections concerned the time when he and Tertis joined Ysaÿe in the second performance of his Trio for two violins and viola, at a reception for Ysaÿe at the Grafton Galleries, London, on 1 December 1916.

We had worked on this very hard, as it was fairly difficult with double stoppings almost all the time, and the very afternoon before the concert we rehearsed till the last minute, and he corrected a note here and there on the manuscript, until Tertis and I thought we'd better stop in case he would correct the whole work. So we parted from the 'master', but when I arrived in the evening I was greeted by the great tall figure handing me a little piece of note paper on which he had traced staves with corrections of two more passages, saying, 'Tiens, mon petit. Voilà deux petites corrections que j'ai faites depuis notre répétition de cet après-midi. Ça n'est rien du tout à changer et tu venais que ça sonne beaucoup mieux.' I was flabbergasted as I had fixed all the notes in my mind definitely to do honour to the great man, but when I met Tertis I found he had a little bit of paper too, so it comforted me, and I thought if I went wrong we should all go wrong! But it passed off smoothly enough and the Trio was quite a success.

Early pencil sketches of Ysaÿe's trio are dated December 1914, but it was not finally completed until 1925–6.

Sammons and Tertis played the *Sinfonia concertante* with the Hallé Orchestra conducted by Sir Thomas Beecham on 30 November 1916 in Manchester. Their performance was reviewed in the *Musical Opinion* of January 1917: 'Mr. Sammons and Mr. Tertis were the soloists and each in their contrasting and matured styles provoked by their easy mastery a continual challenge for the orchestral players.'

In 1916–17 Tertis organized a series of six London concerts at the Steinway Hall, in aid of Queen Mary's Convalescent Auxiliary Hospitals for sailors and soldiers who had lost their limbs in the war, and who learnt new trades in the workshops at Roehampton and Brighton. An impressive list of fellow artists joined him in these concerts, all donating their services for the cause, and a letter from Tertis appeared in the programme. One of the works played was B. J. Dale's 'Short Piece' (*Introduction and Andante*, op. 5) for six violas. On 7 November 1916 his guests were the soprano Blanche Marchesi, accompanied on the harpsichord by Violet Gordon Woodhouse, and Défauw, Rubio, Tertis and Woodhouse gave a performance of Henry Purcell's 'Golden' Sonata – 'The chief feature of a programme of rare interest was a beautiful performance of Purcell's Golden Sonata' (*The Lady*, 16 November 1916). The programme ended with Mozart's 'Kegelstatt' Trio for the unusual instrumentation of violin, viola and harpsichord, which Tertis had also played that year with Ysaÿe and Vladimir De Pachmann. Tertis and his pianist friend Mark Hambourg contributed the Dale *Romance* and Bowen's Second Sonata in F to the penultimate concert of the series on 19 December 1916. The *Musical Times* in December 1916 wrote:

Mr Lionel Tertis, with more consideration for the musical saturation point of audiences than is shown by some concert promoters, is giving 'One Hour' chamber concerts on Tuesdays at Steinway Hall. He gathers round him some of the finest artists now in London, including Madame D'Alvarez and M. Ysaÿe. One of the items played recently was B. J. Dale's 'Short Piece for Six Violas'. At the concert given on November 7th, Mrs Gordon Woodhouse at the harpsichord provided a wonderful satisfaction. Why does this instrument played in this exquisite fashion induce a mood of content and delight?

In December 1916 Tertis included York Bowen's *Poem* for viola, harp and organ in a concert he shared with the singer Muriel Foster. In the same month he joined his Belgian colleagues at the Steinway Hall in a performance of Florent Schmitt's mammoth Piano Quintet with the composer at the piano. The performances were repeated a few days later, described by the *Musical Times*:

> as a masterly reading by Messrs Défauw, La Prade, Lionel Tertis and Doehaerd ... The interest in the Quintet was so great that another performance was given by the same artists on 11th December 1916 in Mr Heinemann's studio for the benefit of some fifty or sixty leading professionals and amateurs, Belgian, French and British. The prince of viola players Lionel Tertis played also on this occasion two movements from Benjamin Dale's Suite for viola, thus contributing further to cement the musical entente.

One of Tertis's, and the viola's, many friends was Frederick Corder, who felt obligated to defend Dale's *Introduction and Andante*, op. 5, for six violas. The following letter to the editor of *Musical Times* on 1 October 1917 outlines the position of the viola and Tertis's efforts around this period.

> Sir, My attention has been drawn to the following sentence in the brief notice of a Royal Academy Students' Concert in your August number: 'B. J. Dale's Fantasia for Six Violas was an item. It is difficult to see why a composer should write for such a combination'.
>
> The matter seems to demand explanation, and as the composer is a prisoner of war and the other person responsible for the work too modest to tell his share, elucidation seems to fall on me. The proper title of the work is 'A Short Piece (Introduction and Andante) for Six Violas', and it was written at the special request of Mr. Lionel Tertis and produced by him at his lecture-recital on June 19th, 1911, to testify to the interesting fact that in the short time that he had honoured his Alma Mater by teaching there this great artist had produced five first-class players of his beloved instrument. Through his efforts also were half a dozen other additions made to the meagre repertory of the viola, all of great interest and mostly

now published. The Sextet, however, is a work of such remarkable beauty, power and originality that it has received first and last about a dozen public performances, one last year at a de Lara Concert being by a wonderful team of executants. It is difficult, indeed, to see why a composer should ever enter the realms of concerted chamber music, considering the limited public interest even in quartets; but it is the nature of the true artist to love to grapple with difficulties, and where would you find a more striking instance than the present? The six instruments have all highly independent parts, they imitate the sounds of other instruments, they do things that one would have thought impossible for any viola-player, and ... I should not omit to mention that Mr. Tertis gave the whole proceeds of the first concert towards the publication of the Sextet by the S.B.C., and if this has been so long delayed the causes are firstly the well-known fastidiousness and love of revision of the composer, and then – the War'. A remarkably fine gramophone record of a special performance of the Sextet has been made, and the people who are empowered to lay hands on a composer's works without leave are trying to make a pianola roll out of it. This is an even more fatuous undertaking than murdering the 'Siegfried Idyll.' It is also interesting to note that the performance so kindly noticed in the *Musical Times* was repetition, by desire, of one given a month before, which was thought a veritable *tour de force* on the part of six young girls.

Some time later Tertis said: 'I would like to say how much I am indebted to my harmony professor (at the RAM) Mr. Frederick Corder. I shall never forget his unfailing kindness, sympathy, and help in all my struggles, and there are many students who would say the same. We all owe him much gratitude, and the Academy is indeed fortunate to have him.'

At the Aeolian Hall on Saturday 17 March 1917 a 'Mark Hambourg Afternoon of Music' was reviewed in the April number of *Musical Opinion*:

A Chamber Concert in which Mr. Mark Hambourg co-operates is but a rare event. It might be thought that a player of such strongly marked individuality would be unhappy in the discipline demanded by chamber music, but it must be admitted that at the concert on March 17th, at which he appeared in company with Messrs. Défauw, Tertis and Doehaerd, he kept himself well in hand. The works played were sufficiently interesting. Joseph Jongen's Trio for pianoforte, violin and viola is a cleverly written piece of work for a combination requiring much deftness in manipulation. It is not of vast emotional significance, but at the same time it is characterised by a distinct feeling for beauty. Mr. Hambourg and Mr. Lionel Tertis gave a performance of Cesar Franck's Violin Sonata in A, arranged for viola by Mr. York Bowen. It is quite possible to question the wisdom of such an arrangement, and it is not easy to determine what object the composer had in view beyond adapting the sonata to Mr. Tertis's violin like viola playing. The effect of the transcription is to increase the gravity of the more sombre passages and to impart a certain plaintiveness to the cantabile portions. No overpowering improvement upon the composer's original version is to be noted.

On Saturday 7 July 1917 an Allies Concert was organized by Madame Maria Levinskaya in aid of the Allied Prisoners of War (Educational) Book Fund. Tertis and York Bowen gave the first performance of the latter's Melody for G String in G flat and the finale from his Viola Sonata in C minor. Chausson's *Chanson perpétuelle*, op. 37, was also in the programme, played by Isabeau Catalan (soprano), Défauw and Sylvia Sparrow (violins), Tertis (viola), Doehaerd (cello) and Madame Levinskaya (piano).

Tertis was a member of the jury for the Cobbett Competition in 1917. The other jury members were composers Frank Bridge, John Ireland, York Bowen, Thomas Dunhill, Algernon Ashton, Baron Frédéric d'Erlanger and the chamber music players John Saunders, Alfred and Ethel Hobday, Hans Wessely and Ernest Tomlinson. The prizewinner in the Folk Song Phantasy for string quartet was H. Waldo Warner (tune 'Dance to your Daddy'), and the second prize went to Herbert Howells.

On 5 October Tertis gave a recital at the Aeolian Hall organized by Edwin Evans, and on 24 October he gave a joint recital with Albert Sammons at the Wigmore Hall (Bechstein Hall), when they played Mozart's *Sinfonia concertante* (with piano) and Handel–Halvorsen's Passacaglia; Tertis's contributions were the Bach *Chaconne*, the première of J. B. McEwen's *Chaleur d'été* and Sammons's Theme and Variations. Tertis later wrote of Sammons: 'What a natural born violinist. If only our country had done its duty by him and given him in his early life the facilities he deserved he would, I feel, have been the greatest of all.'

Stanley Hawley, who had been a good friend to Tertis in his campaign to promote the viola, died on 13 June 1916. The following year a memorial concert was arranged on 24 October at the Wigmore Hall; Tertis, with Sir Henry J. Wood at the piano, played Dale's *Romance* in a version in which the notations and time signatures of this movement were revised by Stanley Hawley. Lena Ashwell, with Wood as her accompanist, gave a number of recitations with Tertis playing viola obbligato – *Young Colin* (traditional), John Lyly's *Cupid and Campaspe, Fie, Shepherd, fie!* (traditional) and Sir John Suckling's *My Heart and Thine*. Myra Hess also played a group of piano solos by Stanley Hawley.

The venue for the first of six recital-lectures on 26 October 1917 was the Aeolian Hall in New Bond Street. Edwin Evans spoke about the viola, and Tertis, William Murdoch and five other violists played three works by B. J. Dale. The programme stated that

Benjamin J. Dale, who has been interned at Ruhleben since the beginning of the war, is known chiefly by his fine pianoforte sonata, the suite played today, a piece for six violas, written to commemorate the effect of Mr. Tertis's teaching of the viola, and a piano piece, entitled 'Night Fancies', dedicated to Mr. Edwin Evans. A well-known musician said of him the other day that 'He has written fewer and better works than anybody in his generation. The viola suite took just seven years passing through the press solely on account of his ultra-fastidiousness.'

Five days later Tertis and Murdoch were heard once again in Dale's Suite; the Wigmore Hall programme also included two sonatas originally written for violin by McEwen and John Ireland, both being played for the first time in the version for viola and piano.

The second concert of the Royal Philharmonic Society's 106th season was given at Queen's Hall in early December, conducted by Sir Thomas Beecham. The centrepiece of the programme was Mozart's *Sinfonia concertante* for violin, viola and orchestra There were several reviews of the concert the next day, including the following, from the *Daily Telegraph*:

As often happens when he is in command, the chief feature of the whole scheme was a Mozart work – the 'Concertante-Symphony' for violin and viola. With two such artists as Mr Albert Sammons and Mr Lionel Tertis as the soloists, a striking performance was a foregone conclusion, and certainly neither the protagonists nor the orchestra who supported them gave any grounds for disappointment. The playing of the solo parts could hardly have been bettered for perfection of balance, clarity and sheer beauty of tone; and the whole interpretation was listened to with the rapt attention which belongs only to the worthy presentation of such music as Sir Thomas Beecham takes the keenest delight in conducting.

When Tertis gave a recital at the Wigmore Hall in December 1917 it was not merely a rare opportunity for the instrument but another significant extension of repertoire, with what was described as 'a Mozart Concertante for violin and viola – with piano accompaniment'.

An interesting concert took place at Queen's Hall on 4 February 1918: Adrian Boult made his London *début* conducting the London Symphony Orchestra, with Tertis as soloist. He played the Dale *Romance*, the Bach *Chaconne* and gave the first performance of Kreisler's *Tambourin chinois* arranged for viola and orchestra by York Bowen. An article in the *Musical Times* on 1 March reported: 'Interest centred on pieces by native composers and the very remarkable skill of Mr Tertis. The performance of the Chaconne was one of those executive feats that stagger ... One of the most significant points of the concert was the warmth of the reception accorded to Dale's *Romance*, which is so full of charm and which was so delightfully played by Mr Tertis.' Proceeds went to The Wounded Soldiers' Concert Fund; Boult recollected: 'Owing to an air raid, the audience on February 18th hardly outnumbered the Orchestra.' Tertis remembered: 'What was indelibly impressed upon me was how, on this first occasion and the very many others when thereafter I made music with Adrian Boult, I always felt comfortable in any variations of tempi, dynamics and so on knowing that Boult's control of the orchestra would be coordinated with every whim of my personal reflection in the work I was playing.'

Like Tertis and other artists, Clara Butt gave concerts for wounded servicemen. Tertis joined her at one of these concerts at the Assembly Rooms, York, during the 1918 season. He also gave a recital at the Wigmore Hall on 25 May 1918 in aid of the Minesweepers Fund. He played the viola version of John Ireland's Violin Sonata no. 2 in A minor, with the composer at the piano. Tertis followed with some short solos; finally, with York Bowen, he played Bowen's Sonata no. 1 in C minor.

At the Wigmore Hall on 6 December Tertis premièred York Bowen's *Phantasy*. The composer was advertised as playing the piano, but owing to his indisposition he was replaced at short notice by Samuel Liddle. The *Phantasy* received the W. W. Cobbett Composition Prize in 1918.

Isidore de Lara arranged over a thousand concerts under the scheme of War Emergency Entertainments. In his series of concerts of British music at the Steinway Hall, Tertis was featured in the fourth concert, on 12 December, with Victor Borlee (flute) and Gwendolen Mason (harp) in Bax's *Elegiac Trio*; Tertis also played Richard H. Walthew's *Mosaic in Ten Pieces* and Dale's *Phantasy*, op. 4; together with York Bowen he also gave the first performance of Bowen's arrangement for viola of Dale's *English Dance*.[4]

The Chamber Music Players

William Murdoch and The Chamber Music Players

D URING the latter part of the First World War Tertis's recitals brought
him into close contact with the Australian pianist William Murdoch, who
was to be the linchpin of one of the great British chamber music groups. From
the point of view of posterity, it was the most important ensemble that Tertis
played in, because – although the group as a whole did not leave recordings
– he made records with some of its members. As he wrote:

> My next venture in ensemble playing was of a more or less permanent
> nature, and took the shape of another piano quartet: Albert Sammons
> the leader, William Murdoch pianist, Felix Salmond cellist and myself.
> My wife christened us with the splendid title of 'The Chamber Music
> Players.'[1] We made music together for the best part of 22 years with only
> three changes (all cellists – Arnold Trowell and Cedric Sharpe followed
> by Lauri Kennedy in place of Felix Salmond who had gone to America).
> Some of the happiest hours of my life were spent with these good friends
> and excellent musicians.

Born in Bendigo, Victoria, in 1888, William Murdoch came to the Royal
College of Music on a scholarship before the war, and may well have encountered Tertis there. In 1911 he went on tour to South Africa as Clara Butt's
accompanist; he then spent three years touring the world as a recitalist. He
quickly became well known as a Beethoven player. Early in 1916 he was introduced to Albert Sammons by a mutual friend, Viscount Coke, then a captain in
the Scots Guards. In May that year Murdoch and Sammons were conscripted
into the army; both joined the Grenadier Guards as bandsmen. In their spare
time they began giving recitals together, and eventually Murdoch and Tertis
began appearing together as well.

The Chamber Music Players – consisting of Murdoch, Sammons, Tertis and
Felix Salmond – grew out of these contacts. It was this group, though with
Raymond Jeremy instead of Tertis, that gave the first private performance of
Elgar's Piano Quintet and String Quartet, with the composer's close friend
W. H. 'Billy' Reed as second violinist, at Frank Schuster's house on 26 April
1919. The same musicians gave the public premières at the Wigmore Hall on 21
May, with Sammons and Murdoch adding the Violin Sonata.

During the 76th year of CUMS chamber concerts, a programme of twentieth-century Spanish music was presented on Tuesday 4 March 1919 in the large room of the Guildhall, Cambridge. Pedro G. Morales, the Spanish composer-violinist, participated in the concert and also wrote a programme note about the new group of Spanish composers whose works were being played. Tertis, Salmond and Murdoch were joined by Marjorie Hayward (violin), Herbert Kinsey (violin) and Morales (violin/viola) in the English premières of two important works by Turina – his Piano Quintet and his *Scène andalouse*, with Tertis playing the solo viola part.

After a fair amount of rehearsal, the first known concert by The Chamber Music Players was given on 6 January 1921. On this initial outing the group played Beethoven, Handel, the Bridge *Phantasy Quartet* and Fauré's G minor Piano Quartet. A review appeared in *The Strad* (February 1921):

> I was much interested to hear a new organisation 'The Chamber Music Players' at their first concert the other day at the Wigmore Hall. As it consists of such experienced artists as Mr. Albert Sammons, Mr. Lionel Tertis, Mr. Felix Salmond and Mr. William Murdoch, the playing was of a very high quality. It will be seen they constitute the piano quartet, but evidently do not intend to only practise that particular class of work. On this occasion we had an early Beethoven String Trio, while, in addition to two quartets Messrs. Sammons and Tertis gave a delightful performance of the Handel-Halvorsen Duo for violin and viola.

Their next concert was given as the inaugural event of the British Music Society, Hampstead Centre, at the Town Hall, Haverstock Hill, on 13 January. The *Musical Times* commented: 'An interesting event is the formation of the new combination which elects to be known as "The Chamber Music Players" ... Individual excellence is not always a guarantee of fine ensemble, but this is one of the exceptions which proves the rule. Their success has been instantaneous, and they will no doubt be an important factor in the making of chamber music in the near future.'

Their next assignment was to give six weekly concerts at the Earl of Lathom's home in Mayfair. Works by Dale and Bowen were played, and there was a rare performance of William Hurlstone's Piano Quartet in the fifth concert in the series, on 13 February 1921.[2]

Two further concerts followed in February. On the evening of 21 February Tertis participated in performances of Mozart's Trio in E flat, K498, and Fauré's Piano Quartet in C minor; the concert on 28 February included the E flat piano quartets by Schumann and Dvořák.

In April The Chamber Music Players gave two Wigmore Hall recitals: the first, on Monday 11th, included Mozart's Divertimento for string trio and Brahms's G minor Piano Quartet. Five days later, on the 16th, their afternoon concert featured two A major piano quartets, by Brahms and Chausson.

The Chausson was repeated at the Wigmore Hall on the afternoon of Monday 4 July, alongside the quartets by Jongen, op. 23 in E flat, and Josef Holbrooke, op. 21 in G minor. On 13 June at Seaford House The Chamber Music Players were once again promoting music by British composers in a mixed programme of instrumental works and songs by Ireland, Goossens, Holbrooke, Bridge, Bantock, Bax and Scott.

The viability of an ensemble of four top soloists depended on the vast infrastructure of music clubs which flourished throughout the British Isles in those days. A group might not earn large fees – especially when the money had to be split four ways – and would never match what a quartet of similar status in Germany would attract, but could make a decent living through carefully planned tours. On the other hand, personalities could clash when such major artists were working on their joint interpretations. William Murdoch's daughter, the oboist Mary Murdoch, remembers The Chamber Music Players rehearsing at their house in the 1930s:

> Lionel and Albert found it hard to be of one mind and my father was invariably the peacemaker. I think it was due to Lionel's love of 'portamento'. His old wife was an invalid and Lionel used to ring her up in the hall while I sat on the stairs. On one occasion a tour of Scotland was cancelled at the last minute due to a disagreement between Albert and Lionel – so they played trios instead. The last time I saw Lionel was in 1961 when I was giving a recital at the German Institute. Lionel was then with his much younger wife. After the concert he said to me in amazement, 'But you play so well!' My reply was, 'Well it must be because I am Bill's daughter!'

Despite the occasional disagreement, the variety of the group's programmes – made possible by Murdoch's ability to play anything put in front of him – kept boredom at bay; and there was a good deal of camaraderie among the musicians, which helped if things went wrong when they were 'on the road'. Sammons was adept at all things mechanical – he even made the violin he used when Beecham heard him at the Waldorf Hotel in 1909. On one occasion The Chamber Music Players were about to give a concert in Bradford; while they were making their way on to the platform, Tertis jarred the scroll of his viola against the door jamb and the soundpost collapsed. Sammons called for a fork and a teaspoon and manoeuvred the soundpost back into position. Tertis swore that his instrument sounded even better than before.

The autumn of 1921 was a busy period for The Chamber Music Players, with

numerous concerts throughout the British Isles. On 3 October 1921 they gave
the opening concert organized by the Derby Municipal Concerts Committee, following their afternoon recital with another in the evening. The Cardiff
Chamber Music Concerts Society, founded in 1903, pioneered the cause of
chamber music in Wales; The Chamber Music Players gave the first concert
in the society's 1921–2 season at the High School Hall on 21 October, playing
piano quartets by Schumann (E flat, op. 47), Fauré (C minor) and Dvořák (E flat,
op. 87). Four days later the group was in Lancashire, playing in Rochdale; the
Brahms C minor Piano Quartet concluded their programme.

Three further concerts followed at the Wigmore Hall in November 1921. On
the evening of the 8th, under the auspices of Daniel Mayer & Co. Ltd, they played
piano quartets by Dvořák and Chausson in the opening concert of the London
Chamber Concert Society, and on the following afternoon they repeated the
Dvořák and added Bridge's *Phantasy Quartet* in F sharp and Beethoven's String
Trio no. 3. The *Musical Opinion* of December 1921 reported:

> ... it is surely not possible to say much of a programme which included
> E. Chausson's Piano Quartet in A major, Brahms' Sonata in D minor and
> Dvořák's Pianoforte Quartet in E flat in view of the fact the performers
> were Albert Sammons, Lionel Tertis, Felix Salmond and William Mur-
> doch. It might be possible to get a finer quartet together for these works,
> but we take leave to doubt it. The concert, for all lovers of what is finest in
> chamber music, was consequently a veritable feast.

At the end of the year they made the first of a number of visits to Newcastle.
The concert was reviewed in the February 1922 issue of *Musical Opinion*:

> The visit of The Chamber Music Players here created great interest, and
> the audience at the Chamber Music Society's December (1921) concert
> was very large in consequence. One was vastly impressed by the way in
> which such brilliant solo executive artists ... combined together to form an
> equally brilliant quartet. The late hour at which these concerts commence,
> together with the necessity of having to catch a train, prevented me hear-
> ing the Fauré Quartet in C minor (op. 15). The other quartet played (Schu-
> mann's op. 47, in E flat) was splendidly performed and well deserved the
> great applause it evoked. Messrs. Albert Sammons and Lionel Tertis were
> brilliant in their duet – the Handel–Halvorsen 'Passacaglia' – and were
> obliged to give an encore. In a similar collaboration Felix Salmond and
> William Murdoch played the first movement of Ropartz's Cello Sonata in
> G minor, the rendering of this also rousing the audience to enthusiasm.
> This concert was one that had quite a numbing effect on one's provincial

critical faculties, in fact – one wishes for many more similar experiences, however.

The Chamber Music Players gave only one Wigmore Hall concert in 1922, on 2 May, with Arnold Trowell playing the cello. The programme included a number of solos. Tertis played his transcription of the Bach *Chaconne*; the programme also included Beethoven's String Trio, op. 9 no. 1, and Brahms's Piano Quartet in G minor, op. 25. Trowell, a New Zealander who was also a noted composer, played with the group during 1922 and the first months of 1923. His arrival was announced in *The Strad*, June 1922: 'One hears that Mr. Felix Salmond has had great success in America and will no doubt remain there for the time being; good for him and bad for us. His place among The Chamber Music Players has been taken by Mr. Arnold Trowell.'

The reorganized Chamber Music Players entertained the Newcastle-on-Tyne Chamber Music Society on 14 December 1922, at the Great Assembly Rooms, Barras Bridge. The first half of the concert comprised Brahms's Piano Quartet in C minor and Mozart's 'Kegelstatt' Trio in the version with violin replacing the clarinet. After the interval Cedric Sharpe and William Murdoch joined forces in Eugène Goossens's *Rhapsody*, op. 13, for cello and piano, and the recital ended with Schumann's Piano Quintet, op. 44, with Herman McLeod as second violin. This review appeared in the February 1923 issue of *Musical Opinion*:

> There is something singularly satisfying about a really good chamber concert, one in which all the items are undeniably worthy. Of course, their very fewness makes it easier to go astray, as even one item can spoil a programme. At the 184th concert of the Chamber Music Society, we had Brahms, Mozart, Goossens and Schumann as the composers, and the Chamber Music Players as the performers. It would be difficult to find four artists such as Messrs. Sammons, Tertis, Sharpe and Murdoch who sink their individuality as successfully as they do. Considering the comparatively short time they have played together, their unanimity of purpose and execution is little short of wonderful. One could do little more than admire the playing, whether it happened to be the Brahms C minor Quartet, the Mozart Trio in E flat, or the Schumann Quintet in E flat, op. 44. Even Goossens' Rhapsody for cello and piano, op. 13, sounded more beautiful than strange – and one can hardly pay the players a greater compliment. In the quintet, Mr. Herman McLeod, a local violinist, played creditably the second violin part.

Cedric Sharpe, who replaced Trowell in The Chamber Music Players early in 1923, was professor at the Royal Academy of Music for nearly fifty years. Born in Maida Vale on 13 April 1891, he came from a Yorkshire family. His father, Henry, was professor of piano at the Royal College of Music, where Cedric studied with W. H. Squire. Cedric was to record a considerable amount of chamber music in collaboration with Albert Sammons, William Murdoch and Marjorie Hayward. He was principal cello in the London Philharmonic, London Symphony and Covent Garden orchestras. He published a cello tutor and *The Principal Cello Book*, with a foreword by John Barbirolli.

The programme for the concert at the Chelsea Music Club in 1923 was Beethoven's String Trio in C minor, op. 9 no. 3, Ireland's Piano Trio no. 2 in E minor, the Handel–Halvorsen Passacaglia and Fauré's Piano Quartet in G minor, op. 45.

With Ethel Hobday replacing Murdoch, The Chamber Music Players gave recitals in Newcastle and Liverpool in late 1924, written up in the January and February issues of *Musical Opinion*:

Music in Liverpool – Rodewald Society

The other outstanding event was the recital by The Chamber Music Play-ers ... who have not previously been heard together in Liverpool. We were rather disappointed in them; individually brilliant, there was not the mutual consideration and intimacy of style that one expects in cham-ber music. But the hall was against real intimacy, and the atmospheric conditions were bad. The works included the Dvořák Piano Quartet, op. 87, the Fauré Quartet and a Beethoven String Trio; not a very exciting programme.

In 1924, before a Chamber Music Players concert in Newcastle, Tertis visited the home of Edgar L. Bainton to try out his newly completed Viola Sonata. Helen Bainton, in her book *Remembered on Waking*, wrote: 'I remember a day when a chamber music concert was to be given by The Chamber Music Players ... Our excitement was increased when we heard Lionel Tertis was coming to our home in the afternoon to try over father's newly completed Viola Sonata. I was not allowed in the room, but I can remember sitting on the stairs outside listening, and though I had no great musical knowledge at that age, I know how entranced and how proud I felt.' Sadly Tertis never played this sonata publicly.

The Chamber Music Players played the two Piano Quartets by Fauré in a concert in memory of the composer at the Wigmore Hall on 9 June 1925. Tertis also performed the composer's *Élégie*, with Sir Henry Wood at the piano; other artists who took part were Kirkby Lunn, Olga Lynn, Anne Thursfield, Mark Raphael, Sir Landon Ronald, Eugène Goossens, Roger Quilter and Daisy Bucktrout.

On 9 March 1926 The Chamber Music Players gave a Wigmore Hall recital of piano quartets: Brahms, op. 60, Schumann, op. 47, and Dvořák, op. 87. The *Times* critic took them to task for including a work as tedious as the Schumann: 'and even ... the admirable performance given could not arouse any interest nor conceal the positively bad writing of parts of the work'.

The Chamber Music Players appeared in Derby on 10 December. In that month favourable reviews appeared of their recording of the Mendelssohn Trio in C minor (with viola instead of cello). For their annual visit to the Newcastle Chamber Music Society, on 16 December, they prepared a rare and interesting programme:

Piano Quartet in G minor	Mozart
Concerto in D minor (originally for 2 violins)	Bach
Albert Sammons (violin), Lionel Tertis (viola),	
Edgar L Bainton (piano)	
Sonata in A minor (1st movement)	Boëllmann
Cedric Sharpe (cello) William Murdoch (piano)	
Sonata op. 21	Dohnányi
Albert Sammons (violin), William Murdoch (piano)	
Piano Quartet in A major op. 30	Chausson

The *Musical Opinion* of February 1927 reported in its 'Newcastle Notes':

> The Chamber Music Players (16th December 1926) were a great attraction at the Chamber Music Society's two hundred and fourth concert. Mozart's Piano Quartet in G minor opened the programme, and put us all in good humour. Then Albert Sammons, Lionel Tertis and Edgar L. Bainton gave an attention-compelling performance of Bach's Double Concerto, the marvellous way in which Tertis made the viola part sound as fine as the violin being one of the features of the evening ...

The Chamber Music Players appeared once again at the Newcastle Chamber Music Society on Thursday 15 December 1927, when their programme was Schubert's Piano Trio in B flat, op. 99, Brahms's Sonata in F minor, op. 120 no. 1, for viola and piano, Delius's Sonata no. 2 in C major for violin and piano, and Brahms's Piano Quartet in G minor, op. 25.

In February 1928 The Chamber Music Players shared a recital with the singer Megan Foster at a subscription concert in Bradford, given on the same evening that the British National Opera Company performed *Götterdämmerung* at the Alhambra Theatre. The concert was reviewed in *Musical Opinion*:

Chamber music in which the piano takes part in the ensemble being so often given in a more or less casual manner, it was extremely enjoyable to hear The Chamber Music Players. Messrs. Murdoch, Sammons, Tertis and Sharpe being in constant association, have achieved an exactness of ensemble on a level with the finest of string quartets, and this was felt in their entirely sympathetic performance of piano quartets by Brahms (G minor) and Chausson (A major).

On 21 January 1931 The Chamber Music Players embarked on a ten-concert tour of piano quartets, starting in Birmingham, where they played Brahms's op. 60, Mozart's K478 and Dvořák's op. 87. On the next three days they had concerts in Cheltenham, Gloucester and Liverpool, and ended their tour in Inverness on 2 February. A review appeared in the March 1931 edition of *The Strad*:

> There is a goodly amount of musical activity to report in Liverpool. For chamber music lovers the outstanding event has been the visit of The Chamber Music Players in the Max Mossel subscription series of concerts. They played pianoforte quartets by Dvorak, Mozart and Brahms. Little need be said about the playing as here is one of the finest combinations in existence. Those who were present heard playing which they are not likely to hear bettered perhaps in a lifetime.

Tertis contracted influenza after the fourth concert, and the tour continued without him; the others changing their repertoire to piano trios. Perhaps it was 'diplomatic flu', and this was one of the times when Sammons and Tertis did not agree on musical matters, as Murdoch's daughter remembered. A newspaper, however, clearly stated that the violist had influenza.

With the addition of a second violinist, The Chamber Music Players played a programme of great piano quintets by Elgar, Dvořák and Brahms on 18 October 1934 for their Newcastle audience. *Musical Opinion* of December 1934 reported:

Music in Newcastle-on-Tyne

To open the fiftieth season of the Chamber Music Society came, very fittingly, the Chamber Music Players towards the end of October. The playing was superbly worthy of this jubilee occasion in a programme which consisted of Elgar's Quintet in A minor (op. 84) for piano and strings, Dvorak's Quintet in A major (op. 81) and after the interval the Brahms Quintet in F minor (op. 34). Perhaps some of us found the meal rather too liberal and unvaried for natural appetite, – a matter so entirely personal to the individual, of course, as to leave little room for argument. But whatever might be said about the quantity, nothing but praise was evoked by the quality of the works, as of the playing of them.

In 1935 Cedric Sharpe had to withdraw from the ensemble, but an ideal replacement was found in Lauri Kennedy (grandfather of the violinist Nigel Kennedy), a fine Australian cellist with a beautiful, cultivated tone, who is best remembered as principal of the BBC Symphony Orchestra. Marion M. Scott reviewed the first concert of the new line-up in the *Musical Times*:

> Lionel Tertis was concerned in another chamber concert – this time at the Grotrian Hall and given by the organisation known for many years as The Chamber Music Players. Messrs. Albert Sammons, Lionel Tertis and William Murdoch, are of the original team, but they have a new cellist in Lauri Kennedy. He has become one with them in refinement, discretion and tone quality. For Fauré's Piano Quartet in G minor, the elegance and faultless discrimination of the playing almost persuaded one the Quartet was a distinguished composition. But in Brahms' tremendous work in the same key, one felt the polish a little repressive. Murdoch was almost too self-sacrificing in his concessions of tone to the strings. Delightful as the performance was (and the same thing applied to the performance of Frank Bridge's Phantasy Quartet) the authentic fire radiated only from the viola.

The Chamber Music Players took part in the Queen Mary Hall Concert Series in Great Russell Street; these concerts were arranged in conjunction with the Incorporated Society of Musicians. The group gave ten concerts at the Grotrian Hall during the 1935–6 season. Works performed included Fauré's Piano Quartet no. 2 in G minor, op. 45, Bridge's *Phantasy Quartet*, all Brahms's piano quartets, Dvořák's Piano Quartet in E flat major, op. 87, and Mozart's Piano Quartet no. 1 in G minor, K478. *The Times* commented after one of the concerts:

> Perhaps the greatest praise should go to Mr Murdoch, who had it in his power, had he wished to do so, to overwhelm his colleagues with the powerful tones of the piano. But the warmth of the expression and the timely gentleness of Mr Sammons, Mr Tertis and Mr Kennedy were also factors of supreme importance in securing the inspiring interpretations.

In Newcastle on 19 March 1936 the four men played a programme of piano quartets by Dvořák (op. 87) and Brahms (op. 25 and op. 60); and a week later, on 26 March, they appeared at the Bath Spring Festival in the Pump Room. Later that year they made a short tour, starting with a programme of the three

Brahms Piano Quartets at Queen's Hall on 17 October and continuing in Scotland, with concerts in Dundee, Glasgow and Edinburgh; their programmes north of the border included one Brahms quartet and the Walton Piano Quartet. The December issue of *Musical Opinion* reported:

> The surprise in the programme was the Walton, written when the composer was about seventeen years of age, and not only worthy of comparison with, but showing greater individuality and technical skill than most examples by the great composers. Even in this early work, Walton's indebtedness to others is slight. The Brahms and Dvorak were, with the Walton, thoroughly enjoyable. There is a danger at the moment in Glasgow of over-indulgence in the classics, and we hope the Chamber Music Society will continue the policy of introducing new works, a policy which has greatly helped to create interest in its concerts in past years.

When The Chamber Music Players performed piano quartets by Fauré (op. 15), Walton and Chausson for the Newcastle-upon-Tyne Chamber Music Society on Thursday 17 December 1936, it was not only Tertis's farewell to his Tyneside audience for the time being, but his swansong with the group. On his retirement, which at the time seemed permanent, and the departure of Kennedy for America (and then Australia), the ensemble was suspended.

However, on Tertis's return to the concert platform at the outbreak of the war in 1939, The Chamber Music Players reformed, Cedric Sharpe resuming his role as cellist. On 9 December 1939 the *Star* newspaper reported on the foursome's first appearance at a National Gallery concert:

> After a lapse of some years The Chamber Music Players have once again appeared in London. This organisation, one of the best in this country or any other, consists of four musicians, each famous in his own particular metier. William Murdoch (pianist), Albert Sammons (violin), Lionel Tertis (viola) and Cedric Sharpe ('cellist) are a perfect combination for the exploitation of chamber music.

In 1940 they made at least two further appearances at these concerts, but Tertis did not play in July, when the fare consisted of two piano trios, Mozart's K542 and Schubert's B flat. Tertis joined the group again in December, when once again the programme included Brahms's C minor Piano Quartet.

On 12 February 1940 The Chamber Music Players opened a fortnightly series of concerts called 'Monday Seven O'Clocks' at the Colston Hall, Bristol. The *Bristol Evening World* reported: 'Chamber music is not a super-attraction in Bristol, so the audience, by its size, was no indication of the value of the concert as a musical entity ... Dvorak's quartet in E flat ... was given an individual interpretation that left nothing to be desired ... and it was noticed with pleasure that Mr. Tertis had lost none of his old fascination of tone.' The other works in the programme were Bridge's *Phantasy Quartet* and Brahms's Quartet in G minor.

This formation of The Chamber Music Players remained unchanged until William Murdoch's untimely death in 1942, when the group was disbanded. It had always been an alliance of like-minded friends; and although it had survived easily enough the changes of cellist and the occasional spats between Sammons and Tertis, such a key member as the pianist could not be replaced without completely altering its make-up. Murdoch had played in virtually every piece at virtually every concert, and was irreplaceable.

Bernard Shore remembered: 'Hearing Tertis play with The Chamber Music Players there was no question of the viola being lost in the background – and what a group that was. ... They played for the joy of playing and no holds barred.'

American Tours

Allied Quartet – new works by Bax – Mrs Coolidge

M USICAL LIFE in Britain was strangely reduced immediately after the
Great War, the most remarkable aspect being the almost total absence
of foreign artists. However, musicians from the newly created state of Czechoslovakia, such as Ema Destinnová, Jan Heřman and the Bohemian Quartet,
were quick to reappear, as were French stars such as Emma Calvé and Alfred
Cortot, Russians such as Benno Moiseiwitsch and Joseph Coleman, and the
occasional Italian such as Tetrazzini or Busoni. (Even though Italy had been
on the same side as Britain in the war, the majority of her musicians were slow
to return.) Hungarians were in short supply: the Hungarian Quartet would be
back by the early 1920s, but Joseph Szigeti and the new Budapest and Léner
Quartets would take a little longer to arrive. Anti-German sentiment had run
so high during the war that it would be years before the heavy Austro-German
presence in British concerts would be restored; and it would never regain the
level it had reached before 1914. German-speaking musicians who had just
been establishing themselves on the London scene when war came did not feel
welcome for a number of years. The Klingler Quartet did not play in London
again until 1928. Adolf Busch, who would end up giving more concerts in London than anywhere else, did not make his rentrée until 1925, and did not bring
his quartet until 1930. Even Kreisler, beloved of English audiences, left it until
4 May 1921 to play in London again – he need not have worried, as after his
'Vivaldi' and Viotti concertos at Queen's Hall Dame Nellie Melba and Albert
Sammons presented him with laurel wreaths.

The net result of the chauvinistic attitude of British audiences was that for
several seasons musical programmes had a somewhat porridgy, insular air. Of
course, this situation meant that there was more work for native musicians, but
it was not a happy state for true artistry to flourish in. One saving grace was
that some of the musicians who had come to Britain as refugees had made such
strong ties that it was a while before they returned home. The Allied String
Quartet, for instance, with its strong Belgian contingent, kept going longer
than one might have expected, which was good for Tertis.

From 1919 Tertis occasionally borrowed a viola (once attributed to Mariani,
1645, but more recently ascribed to Maggini, 1600), from the barrister Chetham
Strode. As a student at Trinity College, Cambridge, Strode showed great

enthusiasm for music, and in 1899 he and a group of fellow students founded the Oxford and Cambridge Music Society. He heard many of the greatest artists throughout his long life, developed an exceptionally wide knowledge of music, and had the reputation of being one of the best amateur viola players of his time. He often gave lectures about string instruments and possessed a number of fine ones himself. On 20 August 1919 Tertis wrote to him:

Do you think you could spare me your viola soon? I have practically decided to give a recital in October and I am asked to make some gramophone records at the beginning of September. I should simply love to do them on your viola, and meanwhile I should get to know the instrument for the recital. I would also like to give a good comparison with mine. If you think you could do this I should be awfully grateful to you. I could let you have the Amati now, and my own a little later (after I have given it a good trial with yours).

On 8 January 1920 Tertis again wrote to Strode.

I am at the end of my tether – I mean my viola is driving me crazy. I have spent days and hours with Beare but with little success. You were good enough to say I might come to you, and indeed I should be most grateful if you would let me have your viola again for a time. Meanwhile I am trying hard to find another. I am on the track of one which is in Scotland and Beare is enquiring about a Gagliano abroad. I have some important concertos coming on, including a longer programme at Belfast. I could not possibly play at these affairs on my wretched beast. If I did, my propaganda work would be finished, hence this appeal to you to be self-sacrificing once more and I hope you will forgive me.

The making of the 'gramophone records' Tertis mentioned in his first letter to Strode was remembered ten years later by the Vocalion Company's official accompanist (later Music Director), Stanley Chapple:

I had the unique experience of playing the Bach double concerto with Sammons and Tertis, the latter of course having arranged the second violin part for viola. His consummate playing really seemed to make his transposition improve the original score, except in the second movement, in which one missed the wonderful effect of Bach's pattern-weaving for two violins ...

One of the finest pieces of recording ever achieved was the result of a lucky seizing of a chance opportunity. During the waits in the studio, whilst the double concerto was being recorded,[1] Sammons and Tertis started to play the great Handel Passacaglia. They played from memory, and I am sure in a spirit of fun and bravado, to see how far they could continue. Whilst they were playing a test was made unbeknown to them. It was so good that they were persuaded to record it properly, and the record was made almost before they realised what had happened! That disc still remains as a memento of one of the finest displays of string playing I have ever heard.

On 11 January 1919 B. J. Dale's song with viola obbligato, 'Come away, Death', was premièred in a concert to welcome the composer home from internment in Germany; it was sung by its dedicatee Frederick Keel, with Tertis and Dale playing the other parts. The programme also included a performance of Dale's *Introduction and Andante* for six violas, op. 5, with Tertis as usual on the top line and Eric Coates taking the third part. The *RAM Magazine* reported:

RECEPTION TO MR B. J. DALE AND MR F. KEEL

A crowded audience of professors, students and members of the RAM Club and the Society of British Composers and their friends, assembled in the Duke's Hall of the Royal Academy of Music on Saturday evening, January 11, to welcome Mr. B. J. Dale and Mr. F. Keel after their long internment in Germany. The programme was made up entirely from works by these two musicians, and included Mr Dale's Phantasy for viola and pianoforte (admirably played by Mr Lionel Tertis and Miss Myra Hess), and his Viola Sextet for six violas, which received a beautiful interpretation under the leadership of Mr Tertis ... After the interval Miss Myra Hess played Mr Dale's Pianoforte Sonata in its entirety. The remarkable performance which Miss Hess gave of this fine and difficult work will long remain in the memories of those present. It formed a notable conclusion to a unique occasion ... Mr Keel sang six songs, four by himself and two by Mr Dale, all of which had been written at Ruhleben ...

The schedule of the Allied Quartet (Désiré Défauw, Richard C. Kay, Lionel Tertis and Émile Doehaerd) increased, with regular concert series at the Wigmore Hall and others throughout the UK. In the first three months of 1919 they appeared at the Wigmore Hall on four occasions, beginning with a concert in aid of the King's Fund for Disabled Soldiers and Sailors. The two major works in the programme were Mozart's Quartet in F, κ590, and Debussy's Quartet; there were also individual movements by Brahms, Bridge and Grainger, and the first performance of Joseph Jongen's *Serenade tendre*. Florent Schmitt was the pianist at the Wigmore Hall concert in March in another performance of his Piano Quintet in B minor, op. 51. Raymond Jeremy played second viola with the quartet in their third recital in Brahms's String Quintet in G, op. 111. The final concert of the series on 9 April consisted of Frank Bridge's Piano Quintet in D minor with Harold Samuel, and Schubert's String Quintet in C, op. 163, in which the second cello part was played by Thelma Bentwich.[2]

Tertis's Wigmore Hall appearances included concerts on 4 and 5 March; in the first programme the tenor John Coates made his reappearance after war service, and sang songs by Amy Hare. Then Tertis, Miss Portman, the Canadian violinist Kathleen Parlow and the Welsh cellist Arthur Williams (who, like Benjamin Dale, had been interned at Ruhleben)[3] played a number of chamber works. The next day the Allied Quartet shared a programme with the pianist Moiseiwitsch and other instrumentalists – a highlight was a performance of the Ravel Introduction and Allegro for harp, strings, flute and clarinet.

On 14 March Tertis played the Brahms Sonata in E flat with Gertrude Hopkins. The violinist Marjorie Hayward joined them for the Mozart Trio, K498, and the concert ended with Franck's F minor Piano Quintet in which the cellist was Cedric Sharpe.

Just over two weeks later Tertis performed with the Harrison sisters and pianist Leonard Borwick in Dvořák's Piano Quintet, but illness prevented him from appearing at the Wigmore Hall a few days later, when he was booked to play Beethoven's first 'Razumovsky' Quartet with Emanuel Compinsky, Richard Brinkman and Felix Salmond. His place was taken by Alfred Hobday. The quartet's first appearance in Manchester was reviewed in *Musical Opinion*, 26 February 1919:

> At an afternoon concert the Allied String Quartet made a first appearance in Manchester at the Gentleman's Concert: Beethoven's B flat Quartet (op. 18), and Ravel's, with pieces and single movements by Franck, Jongen and Brahms, made up the programme, and the playing won especial admiration for its mastery of delicate effects of detail. Miss Elsie Cochrane was the vocalist.

A short article, 'The Viola', by Towry Piper in *The Strad* of March 1919 gives us a picture of Tertis at the age of forty-two:

> On the executive side the instrument has in Mr. Lionel Tertis a protagonist whose commanding technique and sound musicianship have compelled the attention and admiration of all who have been privileged to hear him, and has perhaps done more than any other living artist to promote the cause of the instrument of his choice, and to foreshadow the future which lies before it in the domain of solo and chamber music.

In April 1919 a new series of municipal concerts was started in Derby; Tertis was one of the artists booked to give two recitals on the same Friday, one at 3 p.m. of a more serious nature and a more popular programme in the evening.

The autumn of 1919 included a further series of four recitals by the Allied Quartet. In the opening concert the quartet played the first of Mozart's six quartets dedicated to Haydn, K387 in G major, and Beethoven's 'Serioso' Quartet, op. 95. These two works were separated by a group of viola solos in which Tertis was accompanied by Ellen Tuckfield. Besides popular favourites, such as the *Londonderry Air* and *Tambourin chinois*, they played the Ireland Sonata.

A week later the second concert of the series included Ravel's String Quartet as part of a special concert devoted entirely to the composer's music. On 5 November they performed Mozart's String Quintet in D and Bridge's String Sextet with violist Frank Bridge and cellist Ivor James. Richard Kay was absent from the fourth and final concert in the series; his place as second violin was taken by Thomas Peatfield. There were performances of Brahms's String Quartet in C minor, op. 51, and Fauré's Piano Quartet in G minor, in which the guest artist was Alfred Cortot, who would participate with them on other occasions, and in the autumn of 1921 they gave a performance of Fauré's less well-known Piano Quintet in C minor.

Quartets by Vincent d'Indy and Ravel were the main works in a programme of French music which the Allied Quartet contributed to the London Chamber Concert Society Wigmore Hall series (1921–2 season). They repeated the Ravel in a recital for the Newcastle Chamber Music Society in February 1922 and also performed Beethoven's op. 18 no. 1 and short movements by Bridge and Brahms.

When Artur Rubinstein first returned to London after the end of the war he stayed for only a short while, but found time for chamber music sessions which he would remember for years to come: 'The hours of music with my friend Tertis and the others, Sammons, Warwick Evans and Salmond at Sylvia Sparrow's house were a great inspiration.' Rubinstein's former landlady arranged a big party, invited all the artistic and titled people she could and employed Thibaud, Sammons, Tertis, Salmond and Rubinstein to play quartets and quintets.

From 1919 onwards Tertis was very active travelling throughout the British Isles to further his cause. A recital for the Newcastle Bach Choir with Ellen Tuckfield in November included sonatas by Brahms and Grieg's op. 45. The *Musical Times* commented: 'The viola has been undeservedly neglected as a solo instrument, and the superb playing of Mr Tertis should do much to induce a greater number of instrumentalists, especially amateurs, to take it up.'

It was the fashion in the 1920s for singers to make their Wigmore Hall *débuts* assisted by famous instrumentalists, as the following review from *Musical Opinion*, March 1920, aptly describes:

At her recital at the Wigmore Hall on February 2nd, Miss Annabel McDonald had the assistance of Messrs. Lionel Tertis and Albert Fransella, and there is nothing fresh to be said of the playing of these artists. The former was specially fine in the Tartini Fugue. He was also heard in works by Saint-Saëns, Rebikoff and Fauré. Miss McDonald was heard in traditional and modern English and modern French songs, but it is not possible to say much that is encouraging because of her many lapses from perfect intonation and her faulty production.

During his busy professional schedule Tertis on occasions found time to attend social functions such as the dinner party given by the Foster family at Brockhampton in March 1920. The guests included Lady St Leonard, the Petres of Ingatestone Hall, Sir Gilbert Parker and Elgar's wife, Alice. Lady Elgar died shortly after, on 7 April 1920. She had expressed a wish to be buried in the cemetery of St Wulstan's Church on the side of the Malvern Hills. The funeral took place on 10 April 1920. W. H. Reed wrote:

Frank Schuster and Carice (the composer's daughter) begged me to bring my colleagues to play the slow movement from the string quartet. Lady Elgar loved it; and they thought it would comfort Sir Edward a little. I hurriedly arranged this: Sammons, Tertis, Salmond and I went to Malvern and played it in the little gallery at the west end of the church. It was very sad to see Sir Edward there with bowed head, leaning on Carice's arm.

At the third concert of the Belfast Philharmonic Society's 1919–20 season, Tertis and William Murdoch contributed instrumental items to the programme, including a transcription of Franck's Violin Sonata and a number of shorter items. A review of the concert stated that 'The quality of the performance of these celebrated artists is beyond criticism.'

In a return visit to the Grosvenor Room, Birmingham, for one of Madame Minadieu's Matinées Musicales, Tertis and Murdoch were soloists in Turina's evocative *Scène andalouse* for solo viola and piano with a string quartet led by Arthur Beckwith.[4] This performance was part of a programme of modern Spanish music arranged in conjunction with Pedro Morales.

On 28 May 1920 Rebecca Clarke played her new Viola Sonata to Tertis, her former teacher. In her diary she wrote: 'Tertis … was really thrilled and will play it on June 29th.' Five days before the concert Clarke went to hear Tertis rehearse the work with pianist Helen Bidder, who, however, was not up to the task; the composer managed at short notice to get Arthur Alexander to replace her. The sonata was included in an afternoon concert at the Wigmore Hall, advertised as a song recital by Norah Scott Turner assisted by Tertis, Arthur Alexander and William Wolstenholme, with H. Gruenbaum at the piano. Tertis's other contributions included the *Romanza* and *Allegretto* by Wolstenholme, with the composer at the piano, *Tambourin chinois* and the viola obbligato to a *Provençal Carol* (1672) arranged by C. Kennedy Scott.

During the summer of 1920 Tertis arranged Szymanowski's lovely 'Chant de Roxane' from the opera *King Roger* – taking his cue from the composer's friend Paul Kochanski, who had done it for violin. He performed it often in his future concerts.

Around the same time he recorded the Brahms Sonata, op. 120 no. 1, for the Vocalion label with the pianist Ethel Hobday, who had known the composer well. This slightly abridged historic recording was marketed in an awkward fashion, on two 12-inch discs and one 10-inch; but the performance exuded a frisson which Tertis did not quite recapture in his electrical remake with Harriet Cohen. In view of the importance of Tertis's recordings – they are, after all, what remains to us of his actual playing – it is necessary to say a little about the difficulties of making 78 rpm records. In the early 1920s the sound waves were still collected entirely by a large horn, which conveyed them directly to a needle cutting a groove in a wax disc. From this fragile 'positive' the factory produced a metal 'master'; and from that master came 'negative' stampers which were used to press the finished shellac discs. Although the acoustic process had been perfected by this time, it was still primitive, with volume partly controlled by the proximity of the player to the horn. The pianist had his stool and piano jacked up several feet off the floor, to bring the sounding board closer to the horn; and the violist had to stand in one place, not indulging in the body movement so necessary to a string player, in case he moved the viola too far from the horn and affected the sound quality. Tertis became quite adept at the technique, but inevitably some of his earlier discs betrayed his inexperience in the studio.

During the concert season 1920–1 Tertis and a few other musicians joined Dame Nellie Melba on an extensive concert tour throughout the UK. It was reported that 'A large audience flocked to hear Dame Nellie Melba at the Town Hall, Portsmouth on 2 November.' They also gave the first concert held in the Brighton Dome since its occupation as a military hospital. The tour included a visit to West Hartlepool, the town where Tertis was born. Later in life he remembered that they arrived at night in dense fog and left the following morning in pouring rain and the concert room was overheated.

In the early years of the decade Tertis shared a concert with the singer Adelina Delines with the composer Roger Quilter at the piano. Recently Tertis's signature has been found in the composer's visitors' book.

At the Newcastle-on-Tyne chamber music society concert on Thursday 10 February 1921 the Allied Quartet played quartets by Debussy and Schumann (op. 41 no. 3) and the *Novellettes* by Glazunov; they shared the programme with the singer Mme Gardner Bartlett, who was accompanied by Edgar L. Bainton.

Also in 1921 the Belgian Embassy in London informed Tertis that, in recognition of his services to the Belgian cause during the war, HM the King of the Belgians had bestowed upon him the decoration of Knight of the Order of the Crown. He later learned from Ysaÿe that the decoration also concerned Tertis's efforts in raising the status of the viola.

After the end of the war Tertis re-established contact with Arnold Bax, who was once again inspired by his friend's wonderful virtuosity; this led to a number of new works, starting with a Concerto (later renamed *Phantasy*) for viola and orchestra. Tertis premièred it at a Royal Philharmonic Society concert at the Queen's Hall on 17 November 1921; Albert Coates conducted a programme that included Holbrooke's symphony 'Les Hommages'. The concert was reviewed in *Musical Opinion*:

> Mr. Bax's Concerto for viola and orchestra was given its first performance. The work follows classical tradition in consisting of three distinct movements, though these are linked together without a break in the flow of the music. The viola, like the cello, does not make an ideal instrument for concerto purposes; and Mr. Bax's fondness for ornament and arabesque has led him to write passages not altogether suited to the genius of the instrument. The Concerto, however, contains some very pleasing music, and the solo part was finely played by Mr. Lionel Tertis.

In the winter of 1921–2 Bax wrote his Sonata for viola and piano, and dedicated it to Tertis. The first movement was completed on 9 December 1921 and the rest followed within a month. Harold Truscott was one of many musicians who felt that this, one of Bax's most outstanding works, is perhaps the greatest duo sonata for viola and piano. Tertis and the composer gave the première at the Aeolian Hall in 1922.

In the spring of the following year he joined Bax in another performance of the viola sonata at one of the 'Concerts Intimes' organized by Lady Dean Paul at the Hyde Park Hotel. A few weeks later he assisted the young violinist Miss Murray Lambert in her Wigmore Hall recital, in which they played Tertis's arrangement of Bach's Double Concerto for violin and viola.

On 15 August 1962 Tertis wrote to Colin Scott-Sutherland.

> I owe a deep debt of gratitude to Sir Arnold Bax, for he wrote many works
> for the viola which was of immense benefit for the viola as a solo instru-
> ment. I consider one of the best of his works was the viola and piano
> Sonata. I am proud that he should have written so many works for me and
> for my campaign for the instrument.

Tertis's admiration for Bax was reciprocated. The future Master of the King's
Music wrote the following glowing appreciation in the *Musical News and
Herald* of 27 May 1922:

> Were any keen student of the musical life of the past twenty years to be
> asked the name of the personality who (apart from composers them-
> selves) has been responsible for the greatest amount of creative activity
> in music during that period, the answer would certainly be Lionel Tertis.
> The reason is as simple as it is striking. Many years ago Mr Tertis discov-
> ered the soul of an instrument, and in the light of this revelation com-
> posers have been inspired to create an extensive repertoire for this new
> medium of expression. It was a fortunate chance that turned Mr Tertis's
> attention to the Ishmaelite of the orchestra, for he is one of the few
> authentic geniuses in the executive and interpretative world, and there
> is no reason to doubt that had he persevered with either the piano or
> the violin, the instruments to which he first applied his wonderful gifts,
> the outcome would have been equally remarkable, if less important. But,
> luckily, a peculiar physical aptitude decided otherwise, with the result
> that the technique and emotional capabilities of the viola have been
> developed in Mr Tertis's hands to a point undreamed of, as I believe,
> before his time. There have been other great viola players, both among
> Mr Tertis's forerunners and contemporaries (notably in Czechoslovakia),
> but whilst these have, on the whole, been content to concentrate upon
> the characteristic sombre and sardonic moods of their instrument, Mr
> Tertis has extended its possibilities until it has been proved capable of
> almost all the nuances of the other strings besides (among other quali-
> ties) that peculiar acrid poignancy which this great artist derives from
> the higher register of the A string, and which no other medium known
> to me can produce.
>
> It must have been in my student days that a prominent British composer
> remarked to me, 'Surely Tertis's viola playing is the best performance on
> any instrument to be heard in this country.' Time has only justified and
> solidified this judgement.

Mr Tertis must owe a great measure of his success to the fact that he has ultra Continental ideas of adequate practice and rehearsal. The seductions of the typically English 'All right on the night' theory have for him no appeal. Hard work added to a unique genius have made him what he is. It only remains to add that Mr Tertis is the most modest of great artists. Apparently never satisfied with his own work, he must sometimes feel a kind of wonder that his achievements win the enthusiasm and veneration of every musician – creative or executant – fortunate enough to enjoy them, nor can he fully realise, I think, that he has permanently ennobled an outcast to a position among the princes of musical expression.

On Christmas Eve 1921 Tertis played a concerto and a group of solos at St Andrew's Hall, Glasgow, with the Scottish Orchestra conducted by Landon Ronald, who called Tertis 'The Kreisler of the Viola' in pre-concert publicity. Tertis returned a year later, on 19 December 1922, and performed Dale's *Romance* with the orchestra and the recently knighted Sir Landon. He also included the unaccompanied Fugue of Tartini, plus a group of solos with Mr Wilfrid Senior at the piano. They played Fauré's *Élégie*, Tertis's arrangement of Rebikov's *Dance of Satan's Daughter*, J. B. McEwen's *Breath o' June* and Kreisler's *Praeludium and Allegro* (then thought to be by Pugnani, just as *La Chasse* was alleged by Kreisler to be Cartier's work). It is interesting that at the next concert in this series, on 23 December, the violin soloist was the 'Promising Young Glasgow Violinist' Mr William Primrose, who played Max Bruch's Concerto in G minor, *Scherzo-Tarantelle* by Wieniawski and Achron's arrangement of Mendelssohn's famous *On Wings of Song*.

On 16 February 1922 the Allied Quartet returned to Newcastle, this time sharing a programme with the bass Norman Allin. The quartet's contribution was Beethoven's op. 18 no. 1, Bridge's *Sally in our Alley*, the Intermezzo from Brahms's Third Quartet and the Ravel Quartet. With Sammons that year he played Mozart's *Sinfonia concertante* at a Robert Mayer children's concert.

In 1922 he undertook a three-month tour to the USA, including recitals and a number of concerts with the New Zealand-born soprano Frances Alda.

During the Royal Academy of Music's centenary celebrations, in which Tertis played in two concerts, he was elected a Fellow (FRAM) of the institution. The first concert, at the Aeolian Hall on 10 July 1922, was a programme of chamber works by John B. McEwen, when Tertis and the pianist Dorothy Howell played the composer's Sonata in F. The second concert, on 18 July, which all who attended remembered as a triumph of his quiet compelling personality, was given in the presence of King George V and Queen Mary. In a packed Queen's Hall, Tertis, by the sheer beauty of his playing in the Dale *Romance* with orchestra, forced the attention of the audience away from the Royal Box, on which it had previously been riveted, and focused it on the music. *The Times* commented:

> To a few of us at least the anticipation of hearing Mr. Lionel Tertis play B. J. Dale's 'Romance' for viola and orchestra created a climax in the construction of the programme. In spite of the anticipation we were not disappointed. It is difficult to say which is the greater tribute – that of the composer to fine viola playing, or that of Tertis to the composer. In any case last night both were united in purpose, and we and they and music itself were richer for their outpouring.

The orchestral viola section on this occasion included three of his former students: James Lockyer, Eric Coates and Raymond Jeremy.

A concert of some of Bax's newer works was mounted at the Queen's Hall by his publisher on 13 November 1922. Included was his *Phantasy* for viola and orchestra. Bernard Shore was a member of the orchestra, and recalls the occasion in his book *Sixteen Symphonies*:

> One of the most exciting concerts that come to mind is that of his [Bax's] works given under Eugène Goossens at Queen's Hall on November 13, 1922. There was a picked orchestra, and Goossens was in wonderful form, brimming with vitality and feeling. The programme included 'The Garden of Fand', some choral pieces and the then new Phantasy for viola and orchestra, with Tertis as soloist. The music was not typical of the 1920s, and for that very reason has lasted all the better. The Phantasy is still a grand work to play, though the scoring may be a shade too brilliant. The solo tends to be obscured unless the orchestra is tactfully handled; but the music is spiritedly lively and youthful and the slow movement melting in its deep romanticism.

At the Wigmore Hall on 22 November Tertis took part in a concert with Harold Bauer, Myra Hess, Irene Scharrer, Sir Landon Ronald, Albert Sammons, Cedric Sharpe, the Ladies' String Quartet and the Philharmonic String Quartet; the programme was Brahms's Piano Quartet in G minor, Bloch's Suite for piano and viola and Bach's Concerto for three pianos and strings. As the programme stated:

> This concert is given by Mr. Harold Bauer and the Eminent Artists, who are so whole-heartedly co-operating with him, for the pleasure of making music together as comrades, and it has no object beyond that. It is not intended to provide a musical sensation, nor is it given for financial profit,

for none of the participants receive any remuneration. The proceeds will be devoted to an object of general musical interest subsequently to be decided upon.

There were many reviews of the concert:

> And, as may be imagined, the public responded nobly to the appeal of an 'all star' programme in the carrying out of which there was never a touch or trace of self glorification, all concerned being united for the common good. To an audience packed to the doors Mr Bauer addressed at the outset a few words, in the course of which he extended to those so minded an invitation to smoke. But really a concert of this very rare order required no such additional stimulus to enjoyment, however grateful some of those present may have felt for the unaccustomed privilege ... Brahms led the way with his Piano Quartet in G minor, and truly memorable was the performance of that happily-inspired work at the hands of Messrs. Bauer, Sammons, Tertis and Sharpe. A reading so virile and delicate in turn, so rich in its feeling for the romantic element in the music, so aglow with warmth and colour, and of such irresistible rhythmic impulse – as, notably, in the Rondo alla Zingarese, of which the performance was a miracle of unanimity and brilliance – would surely be difficult to match ... For reasons that are perfectly obvious, the appeal of an entirely unfamiliar work, particularly one of which the phraseology is often so uncompromisingly modern as that in which Mr Bloch expresses himself, could not possibly have proved so powerful, however flawless the performance of it – and superb was the playing of Mr Tertis and Mr Bauer in the new suite.

In *My Viola and I* Tertis states: 'Bloch originally composed his Suite for viola and piano. I gave the first performance of it with Harold Bauer at the Library of Congress in Washington. Bloch was present in the audience and some years later he arranged it for viola and orchestra.' However, this was later discovered to be incorrect. As reported in volume 1 of Maurice Riley's *History of the Viola*: 'The Suite for viola and piano won first prize in the 1919 Elizabeth Sprague Coolidge Chamber Music Competition, held at the Berkshire Music Festival. Louis Bailly, violist, and Harold Bauer, pianist, gave the premier performance at the Festival.' Tertis and Harold Bauer gave the first London performance of the Suite on 22 November 1922 at the Wigmore Hall.

Tertis was invited by Sir Walford Davies to give a recital at Aberystwyth University in the 1920s. Just before he was to perform the Bach *Chaconne*, Sir Walford suddenly said to him: 'I would like to say a few words to the audience about this great masterpiece – I will only be one or two minutes.' But to Tertis's horror, this one or two minutes developed into a lecture of over twenty minutes. Tertis always felt nervous throughout his career before any performance:

> In fact I always felt as if I was being prepared for the operating table! I paced up and down in the artists' room like the 'little lion' of my name but, as the minutes passed, becoming more like an infuriated bull. When at long last Sir Walford returned to the artists' room, I somehow or other pulled myself together and proceeded onto the platform literally shaking from top to toe, but when I played my first notes, nervousness as usual disappeared. I have often heard artists say they are never nervous. Those that are worth their salt who say this are telling a great big fib.

On 10 February 1923 the *Daily Telegraph*, in a column entitled 'Music of the Day', included an article by Tertis: 'The Viola – Its use as a solo instrument'. The following is a short extract:

> When I began playing the viola I had to keep going on arrangements of violin pieces I made. There was nothing to play on the viola in the way of solos. Fortunately for me, I attracted the attention of some composer friends of mine – Arnold Bax, York Bowen, B. J. Dale, J. B. McEwen, W. H. Bell, and others – with the result that the British Library of Viola Solos … is stronger and more important than that of any other country. There is a field with regard to the viola so far very little exploited by composers. I refer to the viola as an obbligato to the voice – its middle register being much more suitable for that purpose than either the violin or cello. The viola has a peculiarly sympathetic human character, which blends most readily with the voice.

In a concert conducted by Eugène Goossens at the Wigmore Hall in June 1923 Tertis played three major works with orchestra: the Bloch Suite, Bowen's Concerto and the Dale *Romance and Finale*. The following review appeared in the *Musical Times*:

> Mr Lionel Tertis is our 'one and only' violist. He cannot add to his fame, for it stands at the highest point; he can only insist on the claims of the beautiful and neglected instrument he has chosen – which he did very convincingly … York Bowen's Concerto, B. J. Dale's Romance and Finale and Bloch's Suite … in different ways these works fulfilled a common purpose – to show in the best light the adaptability of the viola; tender and gentle in the Bowen, austere and poignant in the Dale, while the Bloch was performed with feats of acrobaticism. (1 August 1923)

The Tertises became acquainted with Mrs Elizabeth Sprague Coolidge, and on 20 June 1922 Tertis sent her a copy of the programme he was to give at the Wigmore Hall on the 29th, in the hope that she would be able to attend. Mrs Coolidge was described by W. W. Cobbett as 'the Lady Bountiful of chamber music. Her benefactions are on a scale so generous as to transcend the bounds of what any lover of the arts could in his most sanguine moments have expected from a single individual ... and I must be satisfied with offering her the homage of every musician the world over, whose interest is centred in the branch of chamber music.'

The Berkshire Festival was founded in 1918 and the concerts were given in Pittsfield, Massachusetts, in a hall with a capacity for 500. Generally the audience consisted of invited guests, who also received hospitality in a pleasant 'British' type hotel. From 1918 to 1924 an annual festival was held for three days each time, with two concerts each afternoon plus three evening concerts. Mrs Coolidge gave warm, generous hospitality to her European friends and also arranged many concerts in Europe where her favourite artists took part. In 1926 she was awarded the Cobbett Medal 'for services to chamber music' by the Worshipful Company of Musicians, London.

During her visit to England Mrs Coolidge invited Tertis to participate in her 1923 festival. He wrote to her on 10 August 1922:

> Ever since you were good enough to say you would like me to play for you in America, I have been thinking it over, and have felt that the minimum sum which I would like guaranteed to me, to be able to come would be £500 ... firstly, because I cannot go without my wife, and secondly because I would like, if you could allow me, to put your engagement through a New York manager, to whom of course I would pay the necessary commission on the engagement as naturally I want to give him as much inducement as I can to work for me.
>
> I hope I am not asking too much of you, and if you could see your way to this I shall be most happy to come and play for you in September 1923, and play the programme I would like.
>
> Since I last had the pleasure of seeing you, I have met, through my friend Mary Anderson at Broadway, Mr Chas. L. Wagner the New York manager who heard me play there. I gather he is enthusiastic about my going to America. He would like me to give a recital in New York after your festival. I have sent him at his request press notices of all my European Engagements ...

Mrs Coolidge visited the Tertises at their home in Belmont during the summer of 1922, and in early August confirmed with Tertis that she would like him

to play at the Pittsfield Festival in September 1923 plus three other engagements at a fee of $500 per concert. Tertis accepted this offer direct with Mrs
Coolidge, and therefore did not need to use his New York manager. In a letter dated 23 November 1922 Tertis suggested to Mrs Coolidge that she might
consider programming Dale's *Introduction and Andante* for six violas in her
forthcoming festival. Tertis was in communication with Mr Wagner about the
possibility of his arranging further concerts during his American visit. Wagner
promised Tertis at least twenty concerts and a New York recital.

A letter from Tertis dated Boxing Day 1922 asks if it would be possible
for Harold Bauer to play for him, and encloses a list of viola works that Mrs
Coolidge might consider to be included in the festival: Bax, Sonata; Brahms,
Sonatas op. 120 nos. 1 and 2, Songs with viola and piano, op. 91, String Quartet
in B flat, op. 67, String Quintet in G, op. 111; York Bowen, Sonatas nos. 1 and
2, Poem in G flat for viola, harp and organ, *Fantasie* for four violas; B. J. Dale,
Phantasy, *Introduction and Andante*, op. 5, for six violas; Dunhill, *Phantasy
Trio* for violin, viola and piano; Fauré, two Piano Quartets; Grazioli, Sonata;
Handel–Halvorsen, Passacaglia for violin and viola; Ireland, Sonata in A minor;
Loeffler,[5] *Four Songs* with viola and piano, op. 5; Meyer-Olbersleben, Sonata;
McEwen, Sonata no. 2; Mozart, Trio in E flat for clarinet (violin), viola and
piano.

Mrs Coolidge wrote to Tertis in January 1923, inviting him to play in concerts
she was arranging in Rome, one of which was for the American Academy; the
plan was that he would give a recital including the Bloch Suite, and participate
in a chamber music concert with Casals, Thibaud and Cortot. Tertis suggested
a fee of £50 per concert plus travelling expenses.

Mrs Coolidge wrote a long letter to Tertis on 12 February 1923 outlining the
changes of artists and arrangements for the forthcoming concert in Rome in
May. The Italian composer Alfredo Casella (1883–1947), who was in New York
in the early part of 1923, was very interested in the proposed concerts. Unfortunately May was not suitable for Casals and Thibaud, and Casella suggested he
would be happy to arrange for a fine quartet (the Pro Arte) from Brussels plus
some other players, and that he would be the pianist. Casella would join Tertis
in the Bloch Suite on 2 May. Mrs Coolidge asked Tertis to play the viola part
in Leo Sowerby's Trio for flute, viola and piano on the 5th, with the composer
at the piano and the Frenchman Louis Fleury playing the flute – this work was
written for one of Mrs Coolidge's festivals. In the event, a number of famous
musicians attended, including the Spanish composer Manuel de Falla. Mrs
Coolidge also suggested to Tertis that they might consider repeating the 'Rome'
concerts in London in June with the assistance of Albert Sammons, Myra Hess
and other colleagues.

The letter ends with reference to Tertis's recital at Pittsfield in September; Mrs Coolidge decided that she would like Tertis to play the Brahms Sonata in F minor and the Bax Sonata, both with Myra Hess. In between, her choice was Mozart's 'Kegelstatt' Trio with Gustav Langenus (clarinet) and Katherine Goodson (piano).[6] Other British musicians who participated in the 1923 festival included the London String Quartet, Frank Bridge, Rebecca Clarke, B. J. Dale and Eugène Goossens. Both the Bax and Dale were receiving their first performances in America.

Ada and Lionel saw Mrs Coolidge on a number of occasions during her visit to England in 1923.Tertis was one of her guests at a soirée in St John's Wood on 18 June. He hired a Rolls-Royce for one of their outings at the cost of about 10 guineas. Many of the letters between them are intimate, and show a strong bond between the Tertises and their American friend.

In July 1923 Mrs Coolidge asked Tertis to keep nagging the composer Eugène Goossens to complete his string sextet which she had commissioned the previous year – a fantasy for three violins, viola and two cellos. Mrs Coolidge had been upset by Goossens's prevarications and wrote to Tertis from her home in the USA on 3 August 1923:

> As might be expected, I received no wireless message or any other kind from Mr Goossens, but I wrote to him from the ship saying positively that if the manuscript was not here in time for weeks of rehearsals that I should cancel it and play it some other time. I mean this and I have said the same to my musicians so if Mrs Bridge arrives without it I have already chosen the composition with which I will fill its place, one by Arthur Bliss. I am sorry to be peremptory or unkind about this, but after all, my first duty is to the artistic performance of the Festival programs and I cannot allow even Mr Goossens to upset it.

Mrs Frank Bridge did in fact bring the Goossens manuscript with her when she sailed from England at the end of August. By all accounts the sextet was played superbly by a group that included Tertis on viola and May Mukle as one of the cellists.

Other British works featured at the Berkshire Festival were Frank Bridge's String Sextet on 27 September, and Dale's *Introduction and Andante* for six violas, op. 5, on the following day – Tertis, Rebecca Clarke and Waldo Warner (violist of the London String Quartet) were joined by three eminent American immigrants, Austrian-born Hugo Kortschak, Polish-born Edward Kreiner[7] and Russian-born Nicolas Moldavan. None of the local players seemed to have a good word to say about the Dale, and Mrs Coolidge was upset by the 'quarrelsome rehearsal' which gave vent to such jealousy and bickering that Waldo

Warner 'put his instrument back into its case, refusing any longer to take part'. Frank Bridge, who had declined Mrs Coolidge's invitation to participate in the Dale Sextet, overheard the rehearsal of the work from his bungalow.

> One viola in hot weather is too much. Consequently six! are as you can imagine. The most glorious out-of-tuneness. Pheugh. How damned glad I am that I refused to play. The solo viola is gliding about … The slides are the prima donna stunt. An apportamento or portamento in front of the note every time. Like a sick sea gull. Gives me the creeps.

Rebecca Clarke many years later recounted to Veronica Leigh Jacobs her memories of the occasion: 'an uncomfortable situation arose when one of the American players made a possibly high-handed remark about how the music [Dale's *Introduction and Andante*] should be played and Tertis was sufficiently annoyed that he threatened to return to England immediately.' Extracts from Rebecca Clarke's diary entries concerning rehearsals for the first American performance of Dale's piece document the events:

> *22 September 1923* rehearsal of Dale 6tet. Stormy rehearsal. Kreiner very rude to him (Tertis) and the whole thing nearly gave up.

> *24 September 1923* The atmosphere is beginning to feel thick with musicians and rehearsals! Went through the Dale again, and it passed off without mishap this time, though Kreiner was still unduly argumentative. Tertis came back with us and stayed for dinner, for which Harold Bauer also came. Bauer played and told stories in great style.

> *26 September 1923* Tertis and Myra Hess rehearsed the Brahms F minor Sonata with an audience of Mrs Coolidge, Rebecca Clarke and May Mukle.

> *27 September 1923* Further rehearsal of the Dale Sextet.

> *28 September 1923* [comment on the Brahms F minor Sonata in 11 a.m. concert] Myra and Tertis at the morning concert; they played marvellously. [Re the Dale] I played in the Dale 6tet. Only woman and much the tallest!

Part of Mrs Coolidge's idea of inviting foreign artists to appear at her festival was to help launch them afterwards in other parts of the USA. Tertis, on his first major solo tour, stayed until February 1924. *The Strad* announced Tertis's visit to the USA in its October 1923 edition: 'Everybody seems to be paying a visit to the States. Mr. Lionel Tertis is one of the latest to have gone. He is to play in about thirty concerts before his return in the new year.'

Tertis had asked Mrs Coolidge if she could pay him his Washington fee in advance. On 31 January 1924 he wrote to her:

This is what I have done with the $775 which you so generously have loaned to me. Last week's Musical America had a full page of notices, the cost of which was $300 – a page is going in next week's Musical Digest at $135 and I am going to divide the Musical Courier page at $400 with two insertions of the Kreisler appearances at New York and Boston ... The Musical America has interviewed me. I believe solely as a result of my putting in the advertisements and it will be in next Saturday's issue.

In Chicago Tertis played the Dale *Romance and Finale* and the Bach *Chaconne* in a programme conducted by Frederick Stock that included the first American performance of York Bowen's Concerto, which was generally well received. Tertis was, however, disappointed by the reception given to the work by some of the critics, and wrote to Mrs Coolidge: 'I don't think it is at all bad and it shows off the viola. I have never played it better. I haven't got a Brahms or Beethoven Concerto to play and they don't seem to realize that.' He then doubted if it was a good idea to repeat the concerto in Boston, and even considered giving a recital instead.

The high points of his five-month tour were the performances with Fritz Kreisler of Mozart's *Sinfonia concertante* in New York and Boston. They met three days before the New York concert (29 January 1924); Kreisler sat down and wrote two difficult cadenzas which they had to commit to memory in two days. Jacques Thibaud attended the second of two rehearsals of the *Sinfonia concertante*, and it was after this that he invited Tertis to play it with him in Paris. Kreisler then suggested he and Tertis should perform it in London at the Royal Albert Hall. Tertis's comment was 'a dream come true'. In a letter to Mrs Coolidge, Tertis wrote: 'I have never worked so hard in my life as this last week. Kreisler at the last moment sprang on me that we should play the work plus the new cadenzas from memory! No light task and I hope I shall get through.' On another occasion Tertis complained to Mrs Coolidge that he had been unable to master some difficult passage in a work he had been slaving at for weeks. Her reply was: 'Go on practising the difficulties and forget about all the work you have put into them, and remember these two words ... DON'T WEAKEN!'

There were numerous reviews of Tertis's concert tour of America from October 1923 to January 1924. A selection is given below:

This is a musician who insures for himself a hearty welcome. He plays with very beautiful tone, with exquisite finish of style, with clarity of insight and sharply defined artistic purpose.

Finally, those who may have feared that the viola would prove to be a comparatively monotonous voice were agreeably disappointed. In the hands of such a master as Mr Tertis it becomes a singer of varied moods, not indeed readily lending itself to the expression of gayety but capable of dramatic vigor, classic dignity and genuine feeling.

(*New York Herald* 6 October 1923)

We know that all the praise which has been spoken of Mr Tertis is more than justified. He is a consummate player upon his instrument. A superb musician, he draws from it a tone of such rich, umbrageous loveliness that you are tempted to divorce from your affections that frivolous, chattering soprano, the violin, and cleave only to her gravely passionate contralto sister, the once despised viola. But it is despised no more; for Mr Tertis has made its cultivation seem extraordinarily worth while. He is a great and rare artist. Bach, who was himself a viola player from choice, and usually played the viola part in chamber music, must surely have tuned in on yesterday's concert with his paradisiacal radio.

(*New York Tribune* 24 December 1923)

We recognized in Lionel Tertis an artist of the first rank, one of the type of Joachim, and in our days of Cortot, sensitive yet virile, tender yet masculine. In the hands of Tertis the viola rivals the fiddle. When he played the 'Tambourin Chinois' it seemed as if Kreisler's violin had discovered an elder brother as marvellous as itself. (*San Francisco Examiner*)

⚮ 6 ⚭

Return to the RAM

His greatest moment – Montagnana viola –
Flos campi – teaching – Griller Quartet

LIONEL AND ADA Tertis returned to England on 16 February 1924 on the
Cunard liner RMS *Berengaria*. No sooner were they back in circulation
than the pianist Katherine Goodson invited them to a party in honour of
Ernő Dohnányi. The Hungarian composer, then forty-six, was at the height
of his fame, and his country's foremost musical ambassador as creator and
performer; Bartók and Kodály – both much better appreciated today – were
hardly known to the wider world. In conversation that evening Tertis mentioned that he played Dohnányi's C sharp minor Violin Sonata exactly as written for the violin. The Hungarian was amazed that he could get up so high; the
music was produced, a viola borrowed from their host, and they proceeded to
play the sonata. Tertis remembered: 'It was a most exciting performance for
me, as Dohnányi, besides being a world-famous composer, was a magnificent
pianist.'

Tertis's first recital on his return to England was at the Wigmore Hall on
4 March, when he played the Bax Sonata with the composer at the piano, a
sonata by Martini, and his transcription of the Bach *Chaconne*. The following
review from *The Times* was one of many:

> After a performance at Wigmore Hall on Tuesday ... the player addressed
> his audience. He said that he was sorry to see so many empty seats; he had
> been told by his agent that he could fill the hall by giving away free tickets,
> but he preferred to play to those who thought the artist worthy of his
> hire. He proposes, therefore, to follow the example of the American con-
> cert managers who are refusing to 'paper' their halls. This was Mr. Tertis's
> reappearance in his own country after a prolonged tour in America, and
> it was interesting to discover that there were about 60 people in London
> who thought it worth while to pay to hear the finest living exponent of his
> instrument. So much for the taste of the London public! ... Mr. Tertis's
> distinctive gift is to show that the viola can be as gracious as the violin.

Tertis's solo career continued unabated, and included a concert in Cardiff on
1 May. He visited Milan later in the month to take part in a Coolidge-sponsored
concert of contemporary music, staying in Paris for one night; Mrs Coolidge

– who since 1922 had been becoming increasingly enthusiastic about Italian composers such as Casella and Malipiero – paid all his expenses. At home he was awarded the Gold Medal of the Worshipful Company of Musicians.

In June 1924 Tertis and Myra Hess gave three recitals together at the Wigmore Hall. The main duo items were the Beethoven Variations on a theme of Mozart, op. 66, Mozart's Sonata in A, K305, and sonatas by Bax, Dohnányi, Franck, Ireland and Brahms. *The Strad* printed the following review:

> I heard the last of the three recitals given by Miss Myra Hess and Mr. Lionel Tertis and delighted in their playing of sonatas of Martini, Ireland and Cesar Franck. Mr. Tertis has a remarkable faculty for suggesting somehow that he is really playing on a violin all the time, by which I mean he has such flexibility and lightness. It is only now and again that the real violin tone is missed, while in not a few places, especially, I thought in Ireland's music, the viola tone seemed to be more suitable.

During the 1924–5 season the Tertis–Hess duo played recitals for the Clef Clubs of Nelson, Burnley and Colne in Lancashire – branches of the British Music Society. At the Nelson Clef Club, each concert was accompanied by short explanations and analyses.

The violist Bernard Shore[1] was a student of Tertis from the 1920s and subsequently became a friend. This is how he remembered Tertis as a player:

> Tertis, like all great soloists, had personality and magnetism; he gripped you when he played, you felt under a spell. On the platform he stood as firm as a rugged oak tree, no unnecessary movement, but just that illimitable bow, from the use of every blessed inch of it, to the minutest movement at the tip. There was no particular elegance about it, it just worked! When Tertis really began to look at the instrument, he realised that he would have to develop a new technique, not only overcoming the particular problem of tone production – far more tricky than violin or cello – but enabling him to shift all over the large instrument with complete ease. This helped him to use the strongest fingers where most needed and add nearly an octave to the then accepted compass. His thumb was so strong that it acted like an anchor and his fingers could scrabble about at the top of his huge viola, like a violinist. If one could point to any particular quality of his playing, it was his genius for expressing his inmost thoughts and feelings, whether in a major work or in the slightest of pieces. He could bring out every nuance and latent subtlety of colour that existed in the viola, hitherto almost unknown. He could make a marvellous sound in pianissimo – even with 2 inches of bow he got a certain colour he wanted.

He had a passion for perfect intonation, as all of us students knew to our cost – if we dropped even a tiny brick, out would come a pencil and a cross was put over the offending note. 'NO – NO – NO, could you hear that A flat was sharp, you must listen.' He had such perfect confidence (rightly so) in his sense of intonation that he once had an argument with Sir Henry Wood and his first oboe during a rehearsal. Sir Henry complained that Tertis wasn't playing an A flat in tune with the oboe. Tertis fairly snorted. 'What? – it's not me that's out of tune, it's the oboe playing flat. Listen to my note.' 'Hoity Toity', said Sir Henry.

Tertis was right! That short but sturdy figure was always utterly absorbed in the music he was playing, and every detail studied until everything was perfect; and he could not stand anything dull. Unless the playing came from the heart it was rubbish. Yet despite the fantastic range of expression he always had at his command (like Beecham, who was his favourite conductor) – his stance was always rock-like, and no mannerisms or unnecessary movement ever came between him and the audience. However he demanded 100 per cent from whoever he was playing with, and I remember one dreadful time when a friend of his wanted to conduct the Romance of Dale, in the orchestral version – now Tertis had to be absolutely free to express himself and expected every subtlety to be immediately followed and even anticipated. Unfortunately this poor conductor hadn't a clue, so Tertis walked out of the rehearsal and refused to come back until the composer himself finally took charge. This upset Tertis as much as all of us, but he simply could not tolerate anything amateurish. Eventually we enjoyed a fine performance. In the same way, God help an accompanist who played too loud for him! (or not sensitive enough).

I was lucky enough to play with him in public occasionally, and though it meant an awful lot of rehearsing, they were unforgettable experiences as one couldn't help borrowing some of his terrific confidence and inspiration.

Tertis always strung up his viola a semitone as directed by Mozart in the *Sinfonia concertante* – 'It's too growly in E flat', he grumbled. Tertis always said the most thrilling moment in his life was playing this work with Kreisler, who he adored above all string players. Indeed their playing had much in common; both had the priceless gift of touching their audiences' heart. Many artists may fill us with admiration by their playing but only those rare ones veritably get inside our tenderest feelings. Kreisler and Tertis both had this magic. It is not surprising, therefore, that Tertis arranged many of Kreisler's pieces for the viola.

His playing was unique. No one before or after produced such a marvellous tone, fantastic range of tone colour – a technique unsurpassed by any violinist. His playing had a magic of its own; he was able to express his deepest feelings and communicate them to his audience ... For those of us who heard Kreisler, he was Tertis's most adored God and inspiration.

Without doubt the greatest moment in Tertis's career was when he played the *Sinfonia concertante* with Fritz Kreisler at the Albert Hall on the afternoon of 22 June 1924 in front of a capacity audience of 8,000. The review in the *Daily Mail* by Richard Capell described the effect of the expressive, dark-toned viola:

> It was a different beauty, but a well nigh equal one, and it was enchanting to hear the two singing, as it were, in affectionate mutual emulation. The violin would seem to be playfully challenging the viola to imitate its gay upward flight. The viola was not loth, and if it could not reproduce the other's brilliant accent its own turn would come after a time when the violin was demurely invited to match the viola's peculiar gravity of expression ... The viola has in the past been the Cinderella of the string family, always overshadowed by violin and cello. It was very graceful of Mr Kreisler yesterday to help it to a new place. It was, perhaps, a turning point for the viola and Mr Tertis, so long a splendidly gifted devotee.

The critic of the *Daily Chronicle* was equally complimentary: 'The performance yesterday was one the flawless beauty of which will be remembered; each artist in perfect sympathy with the other, each of wonderful beauty of tone and perfect finish of phrase.'

Soon after this concert Tertis played the *Sinfonia concertante* with Jacques Thibaud in Paris. The trip, on which he was accompanied by Ada, had added resonance because he bought his beloved Montagnana from a Paris dealer, Maucotel & Deschamps. He described it as 'an eighteenth century Montagnana viola which eventually proved to possess a truly wonderful tone'. (Behind the word 'eventually' one senses a great deal of trouble in setting up the instrument.) 'I took a chance on buying it', wrote Tertis, 'for it was shown to me in an unplayable condition, without bridge, strings or fingerboard. I was informed that ... it would be some months before they would be able to put the Montagnana in order. In other words, I could take it or leave it. I was tremendously attracted by the fine craftmanship, lovely wood and varnish.' He agonized for three hours until Ada persuaded him to take the plunge. 'No case was available – it was such a large instrument, 17⅛" – so my wife came to the rescue by wrapping it in her waterproof coat, and that is how it was taken across the channel.' Tertis had often been frustrated with his instruments and he was looking forward to the Montagnana, which he would use for all his recordings for Columbia and until his retirement in 1937, before selling his 'beloved and most trusty servant' to Bernard Shore.

On 28 May 1924 Tertis wrote to the violin repairer-restorer William Voller[2] at 57 Drewstead Road, Streatham, London SW16.

Many thanks for your note, I have now given my viola a good trial with the piano – and I am delighted with the result. There is no doubt about it you have saved the viola again and your new bass-bar has brought out all that there is in the instrument ... I am now waiting patiently for your summons to come and try the Montagnana. I wonder if it will have that rich tone which I have always longed for (but have never yet found in any viola that I have tried) – combined with quick responsiveness.

Tertis was still attracting intense interest in the musical press. The following extracts are from an article by J. Wharton Sharp in *The Strad* of June 1924:

Amongst our present day musicians who have made a reputation both at home and abroad, the viola-player, Mr. Lionel Tertis, holds very high rank. In addition to this however, greater praise and acknowledgement are due to him since he has entirely devoted his exceptional gifts, as a musician and executant, to furthering the cause of the viola, which, as a solo instrument, has been neglected for years. ...

Prejudice, Mr. Tertis mentioned, is one of the hardest things to fight and overcome, and chiefly through it the viola has always been relegated to the background by musicians generally, who have only regarded it as a necessary and useful adjunct in orchestral and chamber music works. The possibilities of the viola as a solo instrument have not been realised, which is all the more peculiar, as its tonal qualities possess a beauty and charm entirely distinct from other string instruments. Amongst amateurs especially this fact has been absolutely overlooked. Then the general idea concerning the viola, its different clef, its greater finger manipulation and somewhat heavier weight, as compared with the violin, biased many from taking it up. However, it may truthfully be said that any capable violinist, turning to the viola and studying it for some little time conscientiously, would soon find that these imaginary 'defects' disappear.

Also, the general belief that the viola tone is nasal in quality would shortly vanish. This idea concerning the tone of the instrument is more than probably due to the unfortunate fact that there are in existence what are known as 'small violas'. Strictly speaking, there are no such instruments, as a violin, slightly larger than the ordinary, can be strung up as a viola and played upon as such, but the tone emitted is neither that of a violin or viola. Instead, the tonal quality will be gritty, harsh, and probably nasal in character, thus creating a bad impression as regards true viola tone. ...

In a few years' time musicians of all classes will be deeply indebted to Mr. Tertis, who not only through his great ability and power as a soloist, but also by sheer hard work, determination and enthusiasm, is assuredly bringing the viola into that important position in the musical world which for so long past has been its due.

In August Tertis and Harriet Cohen performed in Salzburg after several performances at home. Harriet Cohen described the tour:

I began to rehearse with Lionel Tertis for the Festival of Contemporary Music that was to take place at Salzburg that summer ... We *were* to play the Arnold Bax Sonata for viola and pianoforte. Some of the most delight-ful, and I must say, alarming chamber music rehearsals (for he could get into sudden rages – soon over) were those with Lionel. He charmed and scolded me into becoming a real chamber music player. He taught me the true meaning of rubato and with him I learned to 'manage' my tone so that every note of a string instrument could be heard through it. I remained his partner in sonata recitals for many years.

They went to Paris with a group of British artists to play for the Semaine Anglaise at the Colonial Exhibition. Harriet Cohen reported that 'Tertis's playing of Handel, Delius and Bax was the marvel of the town.'

During 1924 J. B. McEwen, having succeeded Alexander Mackenzie as Principal of the RAM, invited Tertis to direct the ensemble class as well as teach the viola. Tertis was paid one guinea per hour, considerably more than most other professors, according to the minutes of a meeting on 1 October 1924. (He would resign from this appointment in 1929, once again to devote all his energies to solo work.)

Tertis already had a lofty reputation in the profession as a private teacher and an ensemble and orchestral section coach. Bernard Shore had this to say about the master's pedagogy:

Though he never founded anything like a 'Tertis School', the influence he had was immense. ...

Faulty intonation was anathema to him, and having an incredibly acute ear, every lesson was a strain to try and satisfy that terrible ear of his. Coming away from a fierce lesson, with music annotated by little crosses on the top of the offending notes, made one scared of fixing up another lesson until a long spell of concentrated practice brought enough courage to try again. Tertis always regarded faulty intonation as sheer careless-ness, and his own confidence was superb. Then his other particular foible – expressive playing, which of course covered every aspect; tone produc-tion, phrasing, rhythm, technique – the lot. He could not bear dullness, and his continual cry for 'Keep your fingers alive – you play so many of them dead', and 'Why do you make that shift so slovenly?' He would ham-mer and hammer at a phrase, until every subtlety was expressed. One was literally forced to pour oneself into the music until the last drop was emptied.

On 28 August 1924 Tertis wrote to Mrs Coolidge about the forthcoming Pittsfield Festival, which he looked forward to reading about in the musical press. He went on to say: 'I have only just got my new viola back after having been in the hands of various experts – but it has led me into enormous expense – however I think it may prove a success but I cannot tell until it has a good six months playing on. It is the most beautiful thing to look at I have ever seen. Certain notes are as big in tone as a cello.'

Tertis wrote a further letter to 'Dearest Elizabeth' on 19 October, congratu-lating her on the success of her recent festival and confirming that he and Ada would arrive in New York a few days after Christmas. He continued:

I have come to the conclusion that I shall have to part with the 'Montag-nana' viola. It is just a trifle too big in size for the acrobatic things I have to do on it. It has a tone like a cello, indeed I have never come across a better viola, so perfect for chamber music and sonatas etc. I wonder whether Sprague would be interested? It would be a never ending source of joy to him I know. I very much doubt if there is a finer viola in America! It has cost me something over 1600 dollars, which is not over much, considering how unique it is and in such a wonderful state of preservation. If he would like to see it when I come I will let him have first refusal of it. In any case I had decided to sell it in America …

Sprague Coolidge declined the offer. Another letter from Tertis to Mrs Coolidge dated 18 November 1924 says:

I am very disappointed with my forthcoming season in America, not only is it financially bad but musically also – most of my engagements are Quartet ones. The only really important engagement I have is with the Chicago Orchestra. The other four I have are unimportant and includes [*sic*] playing with Dushkin in the Mozart Double Concerto [*Sinfonia concertante*]. He is not only a bad musician but plays out of tune. I did not know what he was like until I played with him the other day. I was not even consulted about playing with him in America and I am afraid if I had been I could not have refused because of the financial aspect. What is more trying than anything to me is the fact that the object of coming to America as a Viola Soloist will be very largely defeated this time.

He then goes on to say he has booked a berth on the *Caronia*, sailing from Liverpool on 20 December, and that his wife Ada will not be coming this time.

On 25 November Tertis began recording for the Columbia Graphophone Company at its studios in Petty France, London. After making test discs, including the Hornpipe from Korngold's *Much Ado about Nothing* Suite (which fortunately has survived, as it is his only record of the piece), his first assignment was the Bach *Chaconne*, which he had been playing in public so often that year, and for which he was allotted four sides. He turned in a magnificent performance, although in later years he always regretted having indulged in so many portamenti. This recording was still made under the old acoustic process, as were two short pieces, Bach's 'Come, sweet death', for which he had the services of the young Malcolm Sargent as pianist, and Porpora's Aria.

Owing to ill health Tertis had to cancel his proposed tour to America. He wrote to Mrs Coolidge on 5 December 1924:

This is to let you know that Sir St Clair Thomson has absolutely vetoed my going to America this season – my nose has been giving me trouble lately, and Sir St Clair considered it dangerous for me to travel in its present condition. I am to have an operation on 20th December (the day I was booked to sail!) Unfortunately it will not cure me as my trouble is chronic but I shall be much better after it. It has been a great upheaval as you can imagine after all my arrangements had been made but I am trying to take it philosophically ...

A letter dated 4 January 1925 from Mrs Coolidge to Ada Tertis confirms that Tertis did after all go to America – Mrs Coolidge probably persuaded him to continue with his tour: 'I hope that Lionel's health and spirits will be adequate to his American duties. I know that they will be hard for him but I think it was the only thing to do to come and discharge them ...' On his American tour Tertis played in Northampton with a quartet on 7 January, which was followed by three weeks touring with them from 13 January – they appeared in Buffalo on 16 January, Minneapolis on the 26th and New Orleans on the 28th. He played in Washington on 17 March and returned to England on 21 March on the *Leviathan*.

On 21 December 1924 the *Daily Express* wireless concert from the BBC's

Chelmsford station was heard throughout the UK. Hundreds of telephone calls and telegrams were received at the BBC and the *Daily Express* office congratulating the organizer on the epoch-making night. The artists taking part were Miss Maggie Teyte (soprano), Mme Edna Thornton (contralto), Mr Ben Davies (tenor), Mr Frederick Ranalow ('a star of light opera'), Mr Lionel Tertis ('a master player of the viola'), Mr John Goss ('the finest ballad singer in the world') and Mr George Reeves ('a pianist of marvellous touch').

Writing to Elizabeth Coolidge on 12 March 1925 Tertis said: 'I fear I shall not be coming again to America. I am too much a loser financially. Had I been a younger man, I would of course have persevered with my mission to America. I am delighted that there are two Viola Recitals in New York this month, given by Bailly and Krainerl [*recte* Kreiner].'

On 6 April 1925 Tertis appeared as soloist at Queen's Hall with the London Symphony Orchestra under the Finnish conductor Georg Schnéevoigt. It had been hoped that this concert would include the belated British première of the Sibelius Violin Concerto, played by Achille Rivarde; when this plan fell through, Tertis was given the chance to present a rare performance of York Bowen's Viola Concerto, although his name was inadvertently omitted from the programme. *The Times* reported:

> Mr. Bowen's concerto goes near to being a fine work. It is not dull anywhere, and, though the themes are not specially attractive in themselves, a good deal of interest attaches to their development, especially in the slow movement, and in the last moment it is well sustained all through. Mr. Tertis's standard is always high, and he raised it last night. He knew the concerto absolutely, and there is little he does not know about the viola. His tone stood out equally distinctly against brass, wind and strings.

Tertis received a handsome apology from the directors of the LSO for the omission of his name, and was so mollified that he reciprocated with a donation to the orchestra's endowment fund.

Tertis's centrality to British musical life was demonstrated on 9 June, when the London Symphony Orchestra celebrated its twenty-first birthday with a replica of its first concert – except that Elgar and Koussevitzky conducted, Hans Richter being long dead. Sir Thomas Beecham presided at the dinner afterwards in the Hotel Cecil, and Tertis was one of only two string players at the top table, the other being W. H. Squire. The other guests of honour who were not conductors or composers were the publisher William Boosey and Robert Radford.

In the May 1925 issue of *Musical Opinion*, under the heading 'Music in Wales', it was announced that four celebrity concerts were to take place at which Carrie

Tubb, Maggie Teyte, Leila Megane, Morgan Kingston, Tertis, Lamond and Solomon would appear at the resort of Llandudno during the coming season.

At the Wigmore Hall on Wednesday 10 June Tertis joined violinist Marian Jay in a performance of Mozart's *Sinfonia concertante* with the Aeolian Chamber Orchestra led by W. H. Reed and conducted by Maurice Besly.

Mrs Coolidge visited the Wembley Exhibition with Ada and Lionel, and stayed the night at Belmont on 12 June 1925. They also arranged a Welsh tour, for which Lionel hired a car and acted as chauffeur. He invited Mrs Coolidge to attend a chamber concert at the Royal Academy of Music in which his ensemble class were participating. A letter from him outlines the Welsh holiday:

> I have been carefully going through the mileage of our little tour, and to do it comfortably we must get to a place called Llangollen the first day – this is impossible by car (nearly 200 miles). This is my suggestion. You and Ada go by train to Shrewsbury on July 1st leaving Paddington at 11am and arriving at 2pm (and I will take the car down the day before). I will meet you at the station – we will spend two hours in Shrewsbury and then motor to Llangollen, in time for dinner. Let me know if this meets with your approval. I am writing for reservations at the hotels today … I will write to Lord Coke at once about Holkham and will keep 10th, 11th, 12th free and let you know as soon as I hear. [Tertis was planning to take Mrs Coolidge to meet his old friend at Holkham Hall, Norfolk.]

At the Royal Academy of Music graduation ceremony on 24 June 1925 there were performances of Grainger's *Molly on the Shore*, Glazunov's 'Interludium in modo antico' (from *Five Novelettes*), and arrangements by John B. McEwen of two Scottish dances – Reel 'Johnny Lad' and Strathspey 'Tullochgoram' – played by Jean Pougnet, Hugo Rignold, Tertis and Douglas Cameron. One can only assume that Tertis's star pupil, Harry Berly,[3] was undertaking paid work elsewhere, and that his teacher deputized for him in his absence. On 18 November the RAM minutes book stated that: 'Mr. Lionel Tertis asked to be relieved from giving lessons to Harold Berly owing to the inability of the student to give sufficient time to his studies', and 'The Principal mentioned several other cases where students had accepted engagements which prevented them giving the necessary attention to their Academy studies, and proposed that in such cases the alternative should be placed before them of either remaining as students, with the Academy having first choice on their time, or of leaving the Academy and taking up their professional work.'

The first performance of Vaughan Williams's *Flos campi* took place in the Queen's Hall in October, with Tertis as soloist and Sir Henry Wood conducting. Arthur Jacobs writes in his book about Wood:

A symphony concert conducted by Wood on 10th October 1925 unveiled Vaughan Williams's newest work, Flos Campi, rather obliquely based on the biblical Song of Solomon. It had the distinction of Lionel Tertis's solo viola-playing, still regarded as one of the wonders of instrumental performance. Tertis also contributed to a Wigmore Hall concert marking the recent death of the composer Gabriel Fauré, with Wood as his piano accompanist – a role he had rarely assumed since Olga's death. [Olga was Wood's first wife.]

Tertis played Fauré's *Élégie* in his memorial concert on 9 June 1925. On the October performance of *Flos campi*, Rebecca Clarke noted in her diary: 'Went to the symphony concert to hear Vaughan Williams new thing for viola, orchestra and choir. Very fine. Tertis played.' The following review appeared in the November issue of *Musical Opinion*:

Perhaps the most noteworthy event at the Symphony Concert on October 10th was the production of Vaughan Williams Flos Campi Suite for solo viola, orchestra and choir, the solo part being taken by Lionel Tertis. The work is intended to illustrate certain portions of 'The Song of Solomon', but, in our opinion, is far from beautiful. The opening portion, headed 'As a lily among thorns', seems to portray the thorns very vividly and to leave out the lily. In polyphony, 'the old-fashioned mind', as we suppose it would be called, likes the parts to bear some sort of relation to one another; but the writers of the day seem to be especially proud of themselves when no such relation can be traced (though we confess we had not expected Vaughan Williams to go as far as this). He, Wood, and Tertis received a great ovation, though it is difficult to think that either he or the audience really enjoyed the sounds we heard: it strikes one as having been rather a succes d'estime.

On 19 November at the Newcastle Chamber Music Society's concert Tertis performed with Walter Gieseking for the first and only time. The concert[4] was reviewed in the January number of *Musical Opinion*:

... the visiting artists, Gieseking, Lionel Tertis ... collaborated to give a fine performance of the Dohnányi Piano and Viola Sonata (op. 21), a work of much interest and one which we were pleased to be able to hear given by such fine musicians. Tertis, as usual, made the viola sound just like the large violin ... A transposed version of the well-known Pugnani–Kreisler Prelude and Allegro did not convince one that it was preferable to the original violin, despite Tertis's very skilful handling. He also played his own 'Sunset' and a couple of pieces by Marais and Wolstenholme.

On 25 November 1925, virtually a year to the day after making his initial Columbia records, Tertis essayed his first electrical recording, his own arrangement of Dohnányi's C sharp minor Sonata, with William Murdoch at the piano.[5]

With his friend and colleague, Tertis gave a recital for the Royal Dublin Society on 30 November 1925, in which Murdoch contributed piano solos by Chopin and Liszt and, with Tertis, such favourites as the Dale *Romance*, the Grieg Sonata, op. 45, and Kreisler's *Tambourin chinois* and *La Chasse*.

At the Aeolian Hall on 3 March 1926 Jean Robley gave a violin recital assisted by Tertis and pianist Ethel Hobday, who joined Miss Robley in a performance of Mozart's *Sinfonia concertante*. Also in that month Tertis gave a concert with the singer Adelina Delines in Bideford, a seaside town on the north coast of Devon, about thirty miles from Crediton, where the violin-maker Arthur Richardson lived. This was a difficult journey in those days. However, Richardson had always had a special interest in the viola from his early studies of Stradivari. He went backstage after the concert and was allowed to look at, and even take measurements of, the famous Montagnana, whose fine tone had intrigued him. On returning home he soon realized there would be little point in making such a large instrument because there would be no market for it. This was the first encounter between Tertis and Richardson; they were not to meet again for a decade or so.

Tertis's letter to Mrs Coolidge on 1 April outlines his programmes and plans for a forthcoming Italian trip: 'I have at last found for viola players – a classical work of first importance (for viola and orchestra) – the D major Cello Concerto of Haydn! and I am giving the first performance of it on the viola in Turin with the orchestra there, on April 18th!! (I have written two cadenzas for it).' Tertis was unaware that someone had arranged it already: a transcription made by A. Spitzner had been published by Breitkopf & Härtel in 1907.

Tertis toured Italy in the spring of 1926 with Alfredo Casella. Their programme included violin sonatas by Dohnányi and John Ireland transcribed for viola by Tertis, together with Bloch's Suite and the Bax Sonata. At their recital in Turin Tertis produced the transcription of Haydn's D major Cello Concerto. During his tour he gave a recital with Lamond as pianist at the American Academy on 9 April, which included the Brahms Sonata, op. 120 no. 1, and the Franck Sonata. On the following day he and Casella played sonatas by Martini and Bax and the Bloch Suite. He gave further recitals with Casella in Modena on 12 April, Turin on the 13th, Florence on the 16th, with orchestra in Turin on the 18th and in Palermo with Casella on the 22nd.

In 1926 Dame Nellie Melba undertook a farewell tour of about twenty concerts in the provinces,[6] at which she invited Tertis to play solos. When he accepted she wrote to him from Venice:

> My dear Lionel, I am delighted that you honour my farewell tour in England by playing for me. We must do the Mozart Aria. I wonder if you have a copy of my cadenza. I can't find mine (so like me). I return to England (for a few days) about 17th September, so do ring me up, 5581 Mayfair, and we might have a little rehearsal and then you could give me the song.
>   Bless you, Nellie Melba

The Mozart aria in question was 'L'amerò, sarò costante' from Mozart's *Il re pastore*, originally for soprano and violin. Tertis adapted the violin obbligato for viola. The aria included an elaborate cadenza with florid decorations and a chromatic scale rising an octave to the B flat above the treble stave, with the viola accompanying chromatically a third below. Tertis described her singing of this scale as 'always a miracle of exactitude'. He remembered,

> Her singing was very nearly unique. She seems to have received as a natural gift what others strive for with toil and tears and never quite attain. She sang with a perfectly lovely and perfectly even scale, and the effect was of simplicity and ease. I believe it is true, as a matter of fact, that she did not have to work much in her training time. Her intonation was always faultless, her phrasing was ideal. No singer I ever heard could trill as she did. The two notes of her trill were dead in tune, and the utmost brilliancy was maintained for its duration.

The following review appeared in the February number of *Musical Opinion*:

> Dame Nellie Melba is at present in Scotland on her farewell tour. In Glasgow a crowded audience gave her a splendid reception. Every available seat was occupied. The prima donna was in brilliant form and gave generously of her best in a programme which included Il Re Pastore (obbligato played on the viola by Lionel Tertis). Tertis as solo viola added a genuine instrumental distinction to the programme, his solos including Prelude and Allegro (Pugnani-Kreisler), Bach's 'Komm Süsser Tod' and short excerpts by Wolstenholme, Marais, Kreisler, and his own composition Sunset. Harold Craxton as accompanist and solo pianist was the hardest worked member of the party; his accompaniments were models as such. In Edinburgh, the famous prima donna's farewell concert was not only marked by a crowded audience, but she was further honoured at a complimentary luncheon given by the Lord Provost and members of the

City Council. Dundee, Aberdeen, Perth and other Scottish centres were included in her farewell tour.

Melba took farewell of Manchester at two concerts in the Free Trade Hall on January 30th and February 6th (1926) and naturally the hall was filled on each occasion. Mr. Lionel Tertis played viola solos, Mr. Hackett-Glanville sang and Mr. Harold Craxton accompanied and played piano solos. At the close of the second concert, Melba made a short farewell speech from the platform, and the audience responded with Auld Lang Syne.

It is noted in a minutes book at the Royal Academy of Music that 'the fee of Mr Lionel Tertis be increased from 21 shillings to 25 shillings per hour as from 1 January 1927.' Later in the year Tertis wrote to the Academy offering to present a prize (anonymously) of 10 guineas for the best viola playing, to be competed for annually in the Lent Term. The offer was accepted with gratitude. The annual prizewinners were Adolf Borsdorf, Philip Burton, Winifred Copper-wheat.

Winifred Copperwheat (1905–76) was encouraged in the mid-1920s by J. B. McEwen to concentrate on the viola and study with its champion Tertis. She so impressed Tertis when she first played for him that he undertook to give her lessons, knowing also that she had the strong will and determination to overcome any obstacles that came in her path. Later on, after one of her recitals, he was heard to say: 'She played like an angel.' He always spoke of Winnie with warmth and affection, constantly paying tribute to her musicianship and the wonderful work she did for the viola through her solo playing and teaching. She was professor at the RAM from 1940 to 1976.

During the 1928–9 academic year Tertis offered a termly prize of £5 5s. at the Royal Academy of Music for a competition for students who had not played the viola before September 1928. The set piece for the first competition was the third movement (Tempo di Minuetto) from the Sonata in F by Grazioli. The first three prizewinners were Esme Haynes, Marjory North and Eileen Grainger, adjudicated by Tertis, Rebecca Clarke and Mary Stewart,[7] respectively.

On 25 June 1927 Sir Edward Elgar's seventieth birthday was celebrated by a distinguished body of people from the social, musical and literary worlds at Frederick Schuster's house in Bray. The composer's three chamber works, the Violin Sonata, First String Quartet and Piano Quintet, were played in the music room that stood in the middle of Schuster's garden. The artists were the original members of The Chamber Music Players – Sammons, Tertis, Salmond and Murdoch, joined by W. H. Reed as second violin.

W. H. Reed (1876–1942) was leader of the London Symphony Orchestra for a long period. He composed a great deal of music, little of which was published. He was a close friend of Elgar and his book *Elgar as I Knew Him* is a must for lovers of Elgar's music. In 1927 he composed and dedicated to Tertis his *Rhapsody* for viola and piano, which was published by Augener in the same year. Its première was reviewed in *The Strad* in July 1927: 'A good solo written with a knowledge of the viola, and with good thematic material well worked out. The Andantino which follows a broad Allegro is very musical, and there is a striking technical development in the Finale.' In a letter to Mrs Coolidge on 29 April 1927, Tertis reported: 'I played a new work last Monday by W. H. Reed, with the London Symphony Orchestra at the Queen's Hall, and everyone raved about my viola – it certainly has improved out of all recognition and I would like you to hear it. Its tone is mellow and enormous.'

W. W. Cobbett, author of *Cyclopedic Survey of Chamber Music* and instigator of the Cobbett 'Phantasies' Prize, celebrated his eightieth birthday on 11 July 1927. Many well-known musicians attended a dinner in his honour at the Princes Restaurant, London and Ethel Hobday, Albert Sammons, Tertis and Ivor James gave a performance of Frank Bridge's *Phantasy Quartet* during the evening.

Tertis visited Germany in September. He confirmed his arrangements with Mrs Coolidge on the 7th, saying that he would leave London on the 25th and rehearse that evening with Madame Emma Lübbecke-Job (a friend and colleague of Hindemith who premièred a number of his piano works). Ada Tertis received a letter from Mrs Coolidge on 8 September saying how delighted she was that Lionel would play again for her in Berlin. Other people she had invited were Bliss, Respighi, Schoenberg and their wives, and possibly Ernest Bloch. Mrs Coolidge paid Ada Tertis's expenses for her visit to Berlin with Lionel, and she stayed with the Tertises at Belmont later that month. The German press called Tertis 'a brilliant virtuoso on the viola' (*Deutsche Zeitung*) and 'the greatest viola player in the world' (*Berliner Zeitung*).

On 3 November 1927, at the first concert of the Royal Philharmonic Society's 116th season, Tertis played Vaughan Williams's *Flos campi*, conducted by Sir Henry Wood. The reviews were glowing; the *Manchester Guardian* reported:

To-night London was given a second hearing of the Flos Campi Suite by Vaughan Williams, first heard two years ago, with Mr. Lionel Tertis as the solo violist, and a small chorus from the Royal College of Music. The performance under Sir Henry Wood was exquisite, and Mr. Tertis played so beautifully that one almost wished he would make his viola part more conspicuous, but he is too sensitive an artist even to think of himself before the work he serves.

Teaching at the RAM was an important part of Tertis's life. Many years later he described his time as director of the ensemble classes:

During my five years of chamber-music coaching at the RAM I used to pick out the best string players with the purpose of constituting permanent teams. I chose for association players I thought would match in as many ways as possible and might in time make acceptable string-quartet combinations. One of these teams, to which I gave much time and care, cohered and in due course made a name for itself: everyone knows the Griller Quartet.

Tertis was a big influence on the Griller Quartet (Sidney Griller, Jack O'Brien, Philip Burton and Colin Hampton), both individually and as an ensemble; he founded and coached the young quartet and instilled a passion for the great classical masters. His obsession for practice, detail and the attainment of perfect intonation had a profound effect on his young protégés. Sidney Griller's own coaching had much of the rigour and vigour of his former mentor; he often said he learnt his technique from Tertis:

I adored him – and he was very strict. But he was good-hearted with money and generous with his time. If he took it into his head to teach all morning and afternoon, he would give me lunch money. He made me take an interest in painting and reading – he was making me go to galleries when I was fourteen.

Griller remembered how Tertis built the quartet:

He was absolutely ruthless. Adolf Borsdorf was the viola, Philip Burton was the second violin and the cellist was a boy called Blyth, then Tizard. I won a scholarship, the only one at the Academy where you got money – £14 a term. Jack O'Brien came second to me, so Tertis said we'd better get him into the quartet as second violin, Philip Burton was moved to viola, then Tertis himself chose Colin Hampton.

Under Tertis's benevolent tyranny they learned to like and respect the great masterpieces of the quartet repertoire.

Tertis spent a whole session on the Schubert A minor, concentrating on the two-bar introduction. In two hours I never came in once. He went on and on at the intonation, and at the ensemble between viola and cello.

Another group of which Tertis had high hopes consisted of Jean Pougnet, Hugo Rignold, Harry Berly and Douglas Cameron. The Pougnet Quartet appeared at the Wigmore Hall on 19 March 1926 and played Beethoven op. 18

no. 3, the Vaughan Williams Quartet in G minor and the Ravel Quartet. Berly was a violin pupil of Ethel Martin at the Tower House School of Music in East Sheen before entering the Royal Academy of Music where he changed to viola; he was perhaps the finest of all Tertis's students, and gave his first major London recital at the Grotrian Hall on 9 February 1926. With Harry Isaacs he performed the complete Dale Suite, op. 2, and sonatas by Bax and Rebecca Clarke.

Four students from Tertis's ensemble class at the Royal Academy of Music – Phyllis McDonald (an Australian), Hilda Parry, Winifred Copperwheat and Joan Mulholland (all Londoners) – were suddenly asked on Monday 14 March 1927 to deputize for the famous Léner Quartet, who were unable to give a private concert at the Academy when their leader fell and broke a bone in his right arm. The Academy authorities were informed after midday that the concert would have to be cancelled. Although the Léner Quartet was one of the finest in the world, it was decided that Phyllis McDonald and her three colleagues should be asked to appear in their stead. 'It was such a shock to us that we hardly knew what to think', Phyllis McDonald told an *Evening Standard* reporter:

> Mr Lionel Tertis, the viola player, who is teacher of the ensemble class, came to us and asked if we would do it. We did not realise what a big task it was or no doubt we should have been terribly nervous. We were a little nervous as it was, but we simply had no time to think about it. We realised it was a great chance for us, and determined to do our best. Fortunately, we have been playing together for about four years. We played two Beethoven quartets – the whole of op. 59 no. 1 and two movements from op. 135. We practised from twelve o'clock right up to four, when the concert was due to begin, and everyone seemed pleased with the result. Mr Tertis told us afterwards that he thought the fact that we were suddenly called upon to take the place of such a quartet as the Lener had inspired us, and he had never known us play so well before.

After the concert Mr Tertis was beaming with satisfaction over their prowess and told the *Evening Standard*:

> Not many of the professional quartets could have done so well and the girls made excellent deputies for the quartet we were expecting. Opus 59 no. 1 is a huge task for any musician to tackle, and the fact that they did it so well at such short notice was a great achievement. Many able quartets would be shy of undertaking it except after mature consideration and adequate rehearsal.

In the academic year 1927/8 the McDonald Quartet, with a different second violinist (Adna Ryerson replacing Hilda Parry), undertook the performance in the Duke's Hall of the complete cycle of Haydn's quartets. Tertis informed the critic Ernest Newman about the forthcoming Haydn Festival:

> Dear Sir, I hope you will pardon my troubling you, but I venture to send the enclosed. I am hoping that the performances (which will take until about June to complete) will arouse some interest with the outside public, as being of educational value.
>
> We should feel tremendously encouraged if we could hope for your presence on the first Thursday or any other.

The following review was written by W. W. Cobbett:

> They were given weekly, in chronological order, on Thursday afternoons beginning on 3rd November 1927, no charge for admission being made by the Academy. Fresher or more refined performances than those given by these young people can hardly be conceived, nor can too much stress be laid upon the splendid coaching they received from Lionel Tertis, whose influence was felt in every bar. They illustrated the part that youth can play in making manifest the beauty and variety of this wonderful music, which is the world's inheritance from the father of the string quartet. Their performance, in particular, of the early quartets was a revelation to me.

After the end of the series Tertis was presented with a silver inkwell, inscribed: 'Lionel Tertis, Souvenir of the Haydn String Quartets, Phyllis McDonald, Adna Ryerson, Winifred Copperwheat, Joan Mulholland'.

Tertis's ensemble class was held in public, and took place in the Duke's Hall, so that any students or colleagues could attend if they wished. He did not confine his coaching entirely to questions of ensemble, but also laid down the law on tone production. His viola was out of its case during these sessions and he was forever demonstrating. He could be very demanding and even tyrannical, and simply would not tolerate any faulty intonation.

Max Gilbert, who studied with Tertis at that period, remembered two things – his insistence on perfect intonation and the importance of a rich C-string sonority.

Tertis also had a great influence on the Welsh-born violist Gwynne Edwards. In 1928 he encouraged Gwynne to switch from violin to viola at the RAM, where he taught him both viola and chamber music. Edwards said:

> The essence of Tertis's teaching was also characteristic of his coaching in general – really detailed in excellence, and dedicated in such an impressive

way. His main, determined demand was for impeccable intonation at all times – this was powerfully brought to our notice. The clarity of musical intent – special reference to, and assistance with, observing every detail of colour and quality of tone. Ensemble playing had to be precise and recognition of important voices, in proper dimensions, made his predictions outstanding in all necessary characteristics. If these ingredients were not observed I think it is right to say that his attitude could be described as almost explosive!

As a performer Edwards found Tertis was absolutely confident and controlled, and he felt his reading of the Walton Viola Concerto was most convincing, though he thought that he perhaps over-bowed the opening. It is well known that Tertis rejected the Walton Concerto initially, but Gwynne remembered that when Tertis took to it he used it as a centrepiece with all his students.

Gordon Mutter was awarded a scholarship to the Royal Academy of Music in 1928; he was inspired by Tertis's playing to take up the viola, which he studied for a time with Tertis's former student Raymond Jeremy. On being demobilized after the Second World War, Mutter had some quartet coaching from Tertis (c.1946) before forming the quartet at the University of Cardiff. In August 2001 Mutter said: 'My recollections of Mr Tertis are his kindness and enthusiasm. He was a great inspiration to me as a soloist, and members of our newly formed quartet. The brothers Voigt made me a Tertis Model before I ventured for lessons and our quartet's success at Wigmore Hall recitals was due in no small measure to his coaching.'

Tertis's students travelled far and wide to make their careers; one of those was a young man from Shoreham-by-Sea called Edgar Cyril Glyde, who studied at the Royal Academy of Music in the 1920s with Spencer Dyke and Tertis. Glyde moved to Canada where, after gaining valuable orchestral experience, he became the violist in the Hart House Quartet in Toronto. Later he became violin and viola professor at Auburn University, Alabama, until his retirement in 1974.

Tertis (at the age of fifty-two) played the Mozart *Sinfonia concertante* with the young Scottish-born violinist William Primrose (aged twenty-four) at the Grande Salle Pleyel in Paris with the Lamoureux Orchestra conducted by Sir Thomas Beecham on 30 May 1928 in a Mozart Festival. Tertis said: 'Primrose, then, was a most brilliant violinist ... At the end of the concert in the artists' room Primrose suddenly said to me: "I am a disciple of yours from henceforth", and he immediately gave up the violin to become the world famous viola soloist.' Tertis and his young colleague made music together again in 1929 when they joined Alexandre Barjansky (cello) and Mathilde Verne (piano) in the

Schumann Piano Quartet in a lunchtime concert at the Aeolian Hall. Primrose commented:

> During the early part of his career Tertis was reviled – not looked upon as an upstart but a 'downstart'. Although a small man he was a feisty warrior and wouldn't take no for an answer at any time from anybody. He had the deepest faith in what he was doing and an unquenchable love for the viola – for what he felt and realized he was capable of ... When I first started to perform on the viola, Tertis was very generous in his praise. He encouraged me, and as the years went on we became close friends, though I didn't see him as often as I could have wished.

A letter from Tertis to Mrs Coolidge on 24 April 1928 included some very interesting news:

> The following I know will make you smile. I have got another viola! a Gasparo da Salo about 1590, an enormous thing. I am thinking of being put on a frame to be stretched out (like they do rabbit skins) so as to be able to play it – it beats my Montagnana for tone and that is saying something. I hope to play it to you one of these fine days. I have only had it a few days and am playing on it at the British Music Society's Congress at Bournemouth on May 3rd.

Tertis bought the instrument from the well-known collection of Silvestre in Paris. It was in wonderful condition. Tertis accounted for this by its large size, the body length 17¾", which prevented most violists from playing it. At the time Tertis also possessed the original pegs and small fingerboard, and considered it to be the finest viola in existence. It was known to both European and American connoisseurs and many tried to acquire it.

On 1 August 1928, in another letter to Mrs Coolidge, Tertis wrote that he was to play the Dale Suite (not Bloch) and the *Sinfonia concertante* with the Berlin Philharmonic on 6 December. Alas, the concert never took place, as Ada described in a letter to Mrs Coolidge:

> My poor Lionel had a nervous breakdown early in November. The doctor forbade him to touch his viola for a couple of months, so all his lovely foreign engagements had to be cancelled just at the very last. Our tickets had been paid for and even seats on trains engaged! There was great disappointment in Brussels, where he was to have played with the Conservatoire Orchestra ... Berlin of course was a disappointment, where he was to have played with the Philharmonic Orchestra. Of course he could not practise to prepare for the tour of Italy in January, so that also had to be

given up. As if all that wasn't enough – on one of the first days of the New Year he slipped on ice and severely sprained his right thumb – To end the whole story – he is only now able to again start serious work – and is at last beginning to accept engagements for the coming season.

The Elgar and Walton Concertos

Correspondence between Tertis and Elgar – genesis of Walton Concerto
– performances by Tertis in Liège and Edinburgh

THE LATE 1920s were momentous for the viola, with two concertos written by Paul Hindemith, and others by Tibor Serly, Darius Milhaud and William Walton. It was typical of Tertis's rather equivocal position in the musical world – on the one hand always searching for repertoire, on the other hand ignoring important new works or simply being oblivious of their existence – that in the midst of this glut of important music he busied himself with adapting a concerto written for another instrument. He could hardly have known about the Serly work, as the composer was at that time simply a member of the Philadelphia Orchestra viola section. But the other new concertos were either premièred virtually under his nose, in important European centres, or – in the case of the Walton – actually offered to him. He also ignored two fine works by Belgians, the Suite by his friend Joseph Jongen, which was published in 1928, and the Concerto by Jan Rogister, which had been available since 1914. Nor was Tertis aware of the three solo Suites by Max Reger, which had been in the Peters catalogue since 1916 and were given a new edition in 1928. When Tertis was an old man, Paul Doktor played him one of the Suites and he was mortified to think that this music had passed him by.[1]

He had perhaps left it too late to ask Sir Edward Elgar for a viola work, although the idea had been put to the composer already. On 5 February 1917, the day before his death, Dr George Robertson Sinclair, organist at Hereford Cathedral (the 'G.R.S.' of the eleventh of the Enigma Variations) wrote to Elgar: 'My dear Edward, I want to tell you about a wonderful viola player who played at my recital last Thursday. I never heard anyone to approach him … His name is Lionel Tertis. It would be splendid if you wrote something for him to play.' Elgar did not respond, but meanwhile Tertis found a suitable case for transcription. 'The first time I heard Elgar's Cello Concerto I had been struck by its suitability for the viola,' he wrote. 'How often I murmured to myself over the years – if only I could have a work from this great man's pen. Anyhow there was the next best thing. In 1928 I undertook the transcription and then wrote to Sir Edward in fear and trepidation to tell him what I had done.' When the transcription was finished, with Elgar's blessing, the following correspondence between soloist and composer took place:

Tertis to Elgar, 10 May 1929:

> Dear Sir Edward,
> When could you hear the Concerto? – I should be so grateful. Howard-Jones says he will play the piano part. We will come anywhere you like.
> Kindest regards,
> Yours sincerely,
> Lionel Tertis

Tertis to Elgar, 1 June 1929:

> I was very delighted to get your letter, and am sorry to be such a bore and worry to you. Howard-Jones happened to be here – hence my suggestion to come over to you. I shall be only too glad to come to Stratford at any time to play the Concerto. Would either of the following days suit you? June 18, 19, 20, 21, 22.
> The address at Bath will find me until June 8th.

Tertis to Elgar, 4 June 1929:

> I hasten to say that I am returning home to-morrow, and that Tuesday June 18th is awkward for me. All the other dates hold good, or any other day you appoint. Mr Howard-Jones cannot come, but I will bring Mr Eric Gritton to play the piano part. Forgive me for the trouble I am giving you.

Tertis later commented in his autobiography: 'To my request that he should hear me play his Concerto, I received, to my delight, a favourable reply, and it was arranged that George Reeves and I should go down to Stratford-on-Avon, where Elgar was then living, to give him a performance of it with piano.'

Elgar to his publishers, Novello, 20 June 1929:

> Mr Lionel Tertis has today played through to me a suggested arrangement of the Cello Concerto for viola; it is admirably done and is fully effective on his instrument. I hope you will see your way to print the solo part – the piano accompaniment and the full score will require no alteration. Mr Tertis would propose to play the Concerto in Rome etc. next winter: I think he will write to you on the matter: this is only to say I fully approve of the arrangement.

Sir Ivor Atkins, a great friend of Elgar and organist of Worcester Cathedral from 1897 to 1950, remembered that in June 1929 Tertis visited Elgar at Tiddington House; Elgar agreed to hear a play-through of Tertis's arrangement of the Cello Concerto before making a firm decision. Tertis and George Reeves played the work without a break. After this performance Elgar told Ivor Atkins that it had been a most impressive demonstration of the capabilities of Tertis's large viola, and that he had gladly agreed to the arrangement being published.

There followed a number of letters from June to August that year regarding the Concerto.

Tertis to Elgar, 21 June 1929:

> Yesterday was a most momentous day for viola players, and on their behalf and my own, may I be allowed to express intense gratitude to you. I shall at once see about getting the part properly copied and will send it to you as soon as it is finished. It was so good of you, yesterday, to take such infinite trouble, and go over the Concerto a second time, and make an arrangement of my derangement! Please remember me very kindly to your daughter. I shall often think of June 20th 1929 – your lovely garden – not forgetting the darling doggies, especially the divine spaniel.

Novello & Co. Ltd to Elgar, 26 June 1929:

> We thank you for your letter of the 20th inst. regarding the arrangement of your Cello Concerto for Viola, which we shall be happy to engrave if you will kindly ask Mr Lionel Tertis to forward the arrangement to us. ...

Tertis to Elgar, 28 June 1929:

> Here is the part. I hope it is not too full of mistakes and somewhere near what you wanted, but I should be grateful if you could possibly find time to look it through in case there are any further alterations you may desire. I have proposed it to Brussels and Rome where I play with orchestra next season, and also to our own Philharmonic Society. I don't know whether I am too late for the latter – if I am, I shall try and find the pennies! and give an orchestral concert myself for it.
>
> With kindest regards,

Tertis to Elgar, 28 June 1929:

> It is no use my trying to tell you the joy I feel – words fail me. I want more than anything to go over it again with you, and would come down to Stratford any day you are kind enough to appoint (after next week). Would you in this case play the piano part so that I need not bring anybody.

Tertis to Elgar, 2 July 1929:

> I have virtually done nothing to the Concerto. I would so much rather it could be 'arranged by the composer'. It would be such a valuable power

in breaking down the prejudice of the so called sacrilege of re-arrangement. Much as I yearn for this, if you do not wish it – would you allow to be printed on the part: 'The 'cello part arranged by L.T. (with the sanction of the composer)'. I have noted carefully all your marks, which will be attended to at once. With regard to the slow movement, – you are of course right about there being an alternative part – in fact if you agree – may I propose cutting out the tuning down of the C string altogether – it makes for difficulties and it is only for one note. As soon as I hear from you, I will take the part to Novellos. With many apologies for giving you all this trouble,

I am much honoured with the message from beloved Marco.

Tertis to Elgar, 5 July 1929:

I have taken the part to Mr. Harold Brooke of Novellos and explained everything to him. There will be two parts of the slow movement – one with the C string tuned to B♭ and the other with the normal tuning.

I am going away now to work at it and memorise it.

Tertis to Elgar, 29 July 1929:

I have been through the 2nd proof of your concerto today and now it only awaits your final approval. When may I come and see you? I want to play it to you again, and must consult you about one or two points.

Could I come one morning as I want to visit Mrs. Gordon Woodhouse in Gloucestershire to try over a piece for harpsichord and viola! the same day, and get back home in the evening (all in the little Austin '7').

Best love to Marco

P.S. I leave here to-morrow and Belmont will find me from Thursday.

Tertis to Elgar, undated:

I have just heard that the B.B.C. are trying to fix up March 21 or April 4. I do hope and pray that one of these dates will be suitable to you. I am very excited about it – no doubt they have written to you. I also heard this morning from Brussels that I am to play it with their orchestra there on March 2nd and 3rd. M. Désiré Défauw conducting and I am hoping to hear shortly that I am to play it in Rome in January. With my kindest regards and much love to Marco.

P.S. If this is allright please don't trouble to answer.

Tertis's transcription was reviewed in the December 1929 issue of *Musical Times*.

> We owe much to Mr. Lionel Tertis, whose playing has been an inspiration
> to others, whose arrangements have enlarged the limited repertory of the
> viola. And now Mr. Tertis has done violists the greatest service by arrang-
> ing Elgar's Cello Concerto for their instrument. It is, of course, impossible
> to form a final opinion of the arrangement from the score. Only an orches-
> tral performance can show how delicate problems of tone relations have
> been solved. But apart from this, everything points to a successful issue.
>
> On the one hand the tender melancholy which prevails in the compo-
> sition appears eminently suited to an instrument the timbre of which is
> most appealing when the music is of a reflective, introspective character.
>
> On the other hand Mr. Tertis's work has been exceptionally thorough
> – as witness the lowering of the C string from C to B flat to obtain cer-
> tain desirable effects in the Adagio. It is the work of one who has a per-
> fect understanding not only of the technique of the instrument but of its
> genius for tone colour and effects. Incidentally Mr. Tertis, aware of the
> objections some people may raise against the special tuning, provides an
> alternative arrangement which does away with the necessity of altering
> the pitch of the string.
>
> There is then every reason to hope that the new garb will reveal the
> nobility of Elgar's Concerto not less excellently than the old, in which case
> it will be the first great viola concerto in existence, as even 'Harold in Italy'
> is more a symphony with viola solo than a concerto. May it prove the
> founder of a prolific and valiant line! F.B.

Tertis to Elgar, 2 February 1930:

> Thank you for your letter. I have taken note of the rehearsals, and I am
> looking forward to it more than anything that has ever happened to me. I
> am playing it at Brussels on March 2nd and I shall be back about the 5th. Is
> there any chance of going through it with you again after this date (except
> March 11th when I am playing at Wellington, Som.). I am most anxious
> to eradicate anything you may not like as regards my fingering, nuance,
> portamenti, phrasing, tempi, etc. etc. etc. I do so want to try and play it as
> you would wish it.
>
> Best love to Marco, bless him.
>
> P.S. I have had the viola part inserted in my own score which I will let you
> have when I get back from Belgium.

The unofficial première of the Elgar 'Viola' Concerto took place on 2 March 1930 in Brussels, with Désiré Défauw conducting. It was repeated the next day.

On 11 March Tertis gave a recital in Wellington, Somerset. He wrote to Elgar three times later that month.

Tertis to Elgar, 13 March 1930

> Shall I send you my score? (It has the viola part written in over the cello.) If so where shall I send it?
>
> I am giving a little batchelor [*sic*] supper party after the concert (to let off steam!) and I should feel so very honoured and delighted if you will come. Sir Thomas Horder, Dr. Irwin Moore and Dr. Charles Corben are coming – (so anyway you will have three medical men in case you feel ill after it!)
>
> *Do say yes* – and is there anyone you would like to ask – I should be delighted. I will let you know details later. It will be adjacent to Queen's Hall either at the Sesame Club, Grosvenor St. or an interesting Italian restaurant I have heard of. I hope you will come.

Tertis to Elgar, 16 March 1930

> My dear Sir Edward,
>
> I am most delighted that you will come to my little supper party. I shall try and arrange it at the 'Berkeley' so that you won't have far to go to your club. I also wish you could have your dear doggies with you. Let's have them on the platform! on their chairs!! I will take the score to Brooks's club to-morrow (Monday) and ask them to hold it until your arrival, and meanwhile, I will do my best to find out about the definite hour of the rehearsals.
>
> Looking forward very much to seeing you.

Tertis to Elgar, 25 March 1930

> I have been longing to send you a little line, and this is the first opportunity I have had. It is just to tell you once again what an enormous thing you have done for the viola player. It is the first time in musical history that he is in a position to go into the music shop and find a *Master* work for his instrument. It is quite impossible for me to express the gratitude I feel.
>
> God bless you,

The January 1930 issue of *Musical Opinion* paid tribute to Tertis, as well as heralding the forthcoming first performance of his transcription:

The growing popularity of the viola is manifest in the number of viola concertos which are to be played during the present season, and the series of viola recitals which Mr. Lionel Tertis has undertaken. No other player in this country has striven so much as he to make the instrument popular. Tertis is a phenomenon on the viola, which is something more than a player of genius. It is he who has urged and encouraged the younger members of the British school to give their attention to the possibilities of the viola, with the result that some of the finest works by Bax, McEwen, Dale, and Vaughan Williams have been written for the viola. Recently, Hindemith, the viola player in the Amar String Quartet, and also famous as a composer, played a new Viola Concerto by William Walton. At a recent recital, Tertis played a Viola Sonata by Delius, originally written for violin, and during the coming season he will play the Elgar Cello Concerto which he has arranged as a Viola Concerto – such re-arrangements are an eloquent tribute to the virtuosity of Tertis.

Tertis was more than delighted when Elgar agreed to conduct the first public performance of his arrangement on 21 March 1930 at Queen's Hall. Unfortunately, in the last movement, Tertis's string broke. On the whole the press were complimentary about the new 'Viola' Concerto.

Sir Edward Elgar and Sir Thomas Beecham shared the task of conducting the BBC Symphony Concert last night at Queen's Hall. It was an extraordinarily interesting concert alike in respect of the music played and the way in which it was played. Four of the five items in the programme were by living British composers, and the fine orchestral playing made one realise what an incomparable single instrument an orchestra at its most unanimous can be. Interest in the programme naturally centred in the first performance of Mr. Lionel Tertis's arrangement for Viola and Orchestra of Elgar's mellow and philosophically wise Cello Concerto. For most of us it is of course difficult if not impossible to dissociate the concerto from the cello but Mr. Tertis has admirably succeeded in accommodating the orchestral mass to the viola's tone. Sir Edward Elgar, of course, conducted last night and Mr. Tertis himself played the solo viola, and the beautiful ensemble may have been due to their efforts but the expressive inflection of every phrase showed that Mr. Tertis deeply felt the poetry in the work. The viola did not give us all the ineffable beauty that the cello does in the Adagio, but Mr. Tertis and his instrument made the dainty little Scherzo appear to be merrier and more capricious than the cello does. Mr. Tertis broke a string in the last movement which caused a halt in the performance for a few moments, but he replaced a new string with incredible rapidity and the performance ended triumphantly. (Edwin Evans)

Bernard Shore, principal viola in the BBC Symphony Orchestra, remembered the first performance:

It was a truly memorable occasion and I was glad to be in the orchestra. Though one missed the magnificent sonority of the cello in the grand opening chords and the occasional upward jump of an octave in the main theme, the first movement sounded wonderfully impressive and 'right' somehow.

In the second movement, Tertis had made some changes, as the cello's sonorities in pizzicato could not be matched on the viola, but in the main part of the movement the feathery sound of his pizzicato seemed quite lovely and even more apt than the cello.

When it came to the slow movement, he surreptitiously tuned his C string down to B flat, quite unnoticed by the audience. One could plainly see by his face that Elgar was moved by his playing of this movement.

Unfortunately at the start of the Allegro in the Finale, he (Tertis) broke his A string ... But whatever Tertis's disappointment, he gave a magnificent performance and I have seldom known Elgar accompany this work with so much pleasure and sensitivity.

Incidentally, we noticed many cellists dotted about in the hall, all looking extremely sinister, as if their pockets were bulging with guns! They must have been driven to near frenzy at the theft of their beloved concerto.

Tertis performed his transcription of the cello concerto twice, on 14 March 1931 at St Andrew's Hall, Norwich, with the Norwich Municipal Orchestra conducted by R. J. Madden Williams, and on 14 May at the Queen's Hall, London, with the Strolling Players' Amateur Orchestral Society conducted by Joseph Ivimey.

Tertis to Elgar, 11 January 1932

I hadn't the courage, last week, to write and tell you, that I was broadcasting from London, yesterday evening – your Concerto, in case you could listen in – because, it has always been on my mind, the unfortunate, and very poor rendering I gave of it at the 'first performance' at the Queen's Hall.

This is to tell you, that it went very well last night, and that I feel I have retrieved the situation. It is a most divine work. The only drawback is, that no mere human interpreter will ever be able to express all the tremendous deep feeling contained in it. I feel I want the power of at least six violas, and then I should not be able to get to the bottom of it. Give Marco my very best love & please don't bother to answer this.

Elgar did write back to Tertis, and it was a letter of which he was very proud.

> Marl Bank, Rainbow Hill, Worcester
> January 12th 1932

My dear Tertis,
Thank you many times for your letter which arrived just as I was addressing this envelope to you. I listened with the greatest happiness: your playing was wonderful and we were thrilled. I admired your low C/Bb which came thro' marvellously. The whole thing was a picture and sounded to the miserable author (who has a vile cold) divine. Marco, who is still wearing his collar, listened also and sends his love with mine.
  Yours very sincerely and gratefully,
  Edward Elgar

Tertis to Elgar, 15 January 1932

> The Midland Hotel Manchester

I don't think I have any right for such a beautiful letter from such a great man as you are – all the same it has made me feel supremely happy and I would not take £1000 for it. Glad you liked the Bb. You may have noticed that I hung on to it as lovingly as the prima donna to her top note. I am very sorry about your cold and hope you are much better. Do take care. I am proud that Marco is still wearing the collar. Bless him and his dear Master.
  Played here last night with Sir Hamilton & Hallé Orch. marvellous conductor & orchestra. [At this Hallé concert Tertis introduced the Walton Concerto to Manchester, and also played *Harold in Italy*.]

Tertis to Elgar's daughter Mrs Carice Elgar Blake, 16 January 1932:

Dear Mrs Blake,
It was kind of you to write about the performance of your father's wonderful music. It is indeed a privilige [*sic*] to try and interpret it, and I was overjoyed to know that your father had listened. It is a most divine and soul stirring work, and the depth of feeling contained in it, is inexpressible.

On Tuesday 23 August 1932 the BBC Symphony Orchestra, conducted by Sir Henry Wood, presented a concert of British music at a Promenade Concert which included three movements from Holst's *Planets* and Rutland Boughton's Overture *The Queen of Cornwall*, both conducted by their respective composers. Tertis was the soloist in the Elgar Concerto. The October edition of the *Musical Times* reviewed the concert:

> Mr Tertis tried again to persuade us – and nobody could try more eloquently – that Elgar's Cello Concert is fit and proper music for the viola. And so it is, very nearly; but there are pages of it that would never have come into existence had there been no violoncellos, and they lose something without the instrument that created them. All the same, to hear Elgar and Tertis and a viola is a moving experience.

Reviews were not always favourable, as the following by Alex Cohen from the August 1934 issue of *Musical Opinion* demonstrates:

> But if the Violin Concerto enshrines a 'feminine soul', the Cello Concerto just as patently enshrines a masculine one. I know, too, that Elgar was very fond of the viola. Had he written a viola concerto, one scarcely dare speculate as to the soul he would have enshrined in that! In any case, it's more seemly to leave these considerations to the medical profession. But, shades of Hermes and Aphrodite! I was forgetting. What sort of unholy operation did Lionel Tertis perform when he arranged the Cello Concerto for viola? It only remains for him to transcribe the Violin Concerto for viola, and the transmutation of either musical sex to no sex at all will be an accomplished fact.

Ernest Newman, in his column 'The Week's Music by Wireless' wrote: 'Some of the things heard by wireless during the week came over extraordinarily well. Mr. Lionel Tertis, in his arrangement of Elgar's Cello Concerto for viola, gave us a noble performance of a noble work.' Basil Maine also reviewed it:

> the transcription of the work for solo viola which Lionel Tertis has so skillfully carried out, must be regarded as a half loaf, better than none, but, for all that, a rationed allowance. It is in the slow movement, especially, that the loss of the violoncello's peculiar poignancy and depth is felt, whenever the transcription is performed. The writer well remembers a performance which Lionel Tertis gave at the London Museum in the spring of 1932. It was an outstanding experience by reason of the soloist's easy and modest wearing of a superb virtuosity. In spite of this, however, it was impossible to avoid the impression that the music was on a lower plane of intensity throughout (compared to the original).

Tertis to Elgar, 22 January 1933:

> Dear Sir Edward,
> Harriet Cohen at the concert of your works she is doing with the Pro Arte
> Quartet – I believe in May, is most anxious to include something of yours
> with me. You once told me, years ago, that you had some sketches for viola
> hidden away somewhere. Dare we hope that you could piece one or two of
> them to-gether for this concert – even if it lasted only 5 minutes it would
> be wonderful for us and future viola players.
>   Ever yours sincerely,
>   Lionel Tertis
> Forgive me for worrying you.

Three days later Tertis wrote to Elgar's dog!

> Dear Marco,
> 'Bubbles' and I send our love to you. We are very excited about the pos-
> sibility – however slight – of a tune from your Master. *Please* help him to
> find it.
>   Yours affectionately,
>   Bubbles, and Lionel Tertis

Sir Edward Elgar once again agreed to conduct a performance of the viola
arrangement of his cello concerto with Tertis as soloist. It took place on
Wednesday 7 September 1933 in Hereford Cathedral as part of the Three Choirs
Festival; the London Symphony Orchestra was led by Elgar's friend W. H. Reed.
Two other composers conducted their own works for contralto and orchestra
in the programme; Julius Harrison (*Rhapsody*) and C. Armstrong Gibbs (Scena:
The Love-Talker) – the latter was especially composed for the occasion; Muriel
Brunskill was the soloist in both works. The remainder of the programme was
Arthur Bliss's Prelude to *Morning Heroes*, Edward German's Theme and Six
Variations, and César Franck's Symphonic Variations, with Myra Hess as solo-
ist. The concerto performance went well, and as they walked off the platform
together Elgar whispered to Tertis 'Good boy' – words like these from Sir
Edward were high praise indeed. Elgar was not well at Hereford, and this was
the last time he would conduct: he died a few months later in February 1934.
     After the performance Elgar wrote to Tertis:

                                        Marl Bank, Worcester
                                        13th September 1933

> My dear Tertis
> I have had no opportunity to write since the Hereford Festival or should

have sent you long ago heartiest thanks for your superb playing of your Concerto.

It was a wonderful reading, and thank you ... I wish we met oftener, but I am seldom away from home now.

Kindest regards to Mrs. Tertis and, with sincere thanks, to you.

Yours sincerely,

Edward Elgar

Tertis replied on 17 September:

How good of you to write to me concerning Hereford. The thanks are due from me to you, not from you to me, that viola players should have the privilige [sic] of playing such a Master Work. That I should have pleased you is unbounded recompense to me. I see that Piatigorsky is playing it in November. I understand – though I have not heard him – that he is wonderful. I am looking forward immensely to hearing him do it.

It was in 1928 that the young William Walton conceived the idea of writing a concerto for Tertis. On 5 December he started work on the piece; he finished the second movement on 1 February 1929 and began the Finale on the 12th of that month. But Tertis, on seeing the music and being invited to première the work, rejected the offer, sending the score back by the next post. 'With shame and contrition I admit that when the composer offered me the first performance I declined it. I was unwell at the time; but what is also true is that I had not learnt to appreciate Walton's style.' Edward Clark, who was in charge of new music at the BBC and a strong voice in the International Society for Contemporary Music, invited Paul Hindemith to be the soloist in the world première, which took place at a Prom in Queen's Hall on 3 October 1929, with Wood conducting. Tertis, who was in the audience, was quite converted by the music, although it is unlikely that he enjoyed the solo playing, for, as he used to say, 'Hindemith was so dry.' In his later years he recalled:

Well the Walton Concerto's rather a disgraceful part of my history. When I received the concerto from the composer I wasn't accustomed to play F natural when the octave above was F sharp. I remember I was rather unwell and I said to the composer 'I'm awfully sorry, I'm not very well, and I don't think I could undertake this'.

The suggestion that Walton should write a concerto for Tertis has often been attributed to Sir Thomas Beecham; but Bernard Shore, in a talk at the inaugural Lionel Tertis International Viola Competition and Workshop in the Isle of Man in 1980, expressed a less well-known view of the work's genesis:

in 1929 came our greatest concerto unsurpassed by perhaps many of the well-known violin and cello concertos; I was lucky enough to be involved at the outset. Walton, then a brilliant young man, was sitting next to me at a typical Tertis recital in which he was playing Bach's Chaconne. I felt the young man getting tense and excited, and during the ovation Tertis was receiving after this performance Walton got out of his seat and exclaimed – 'My God, I have never heard a sound like this before – and what an artist – I must write a concerto for him!' Not many weeks after this he came down to my house with some sketches and we played them through with Angus Morrison at the piano, and Hubert Foss from Oxford University Press turning pages for him. Eventually Walton sent the score to Tertis with his dedication. Unfortunately, Tertis could not come to terms with the new idiom and there was no piano score to help, so he returned the full score to Walton with much regret. However, when he heard the work, he at once realised its great power and beauty and finally gave superb performances – the most memorable in Zurich on the first European tour of the BBC Symphony Orchestra.

Bernard Shore gave the second performance at a Promenade Concert on 21 August 1930. Tertis first played it at the annual festival of the International Society for Contemporary Music in Liège on 4 September (1930). He also played the concerto in Germany, and afterwards Walton wrote to Harriet Cohen:

The orchestra was bloody, the rehearsal ditto – in fact everything seemed, with the exception of Mr. Tertis, who was a saint and angel throughout – to be all wrong, till at the performance, I found myself at the top of my form and behaved like Toscanini and it all went perfectly. If the orchestra had been good the performance could not have been better. It consisted of the professors and students of the Conservatoire, the average age of the former 90 and the latter about 15. However they did try and in fact rose a certain distance for the occasion, and the concert made the hit of the festival ... The applause – tears – and cheers, couldn't have been better and Tertis and I were more tired by walking on and off than by playing ... You have no conception what Tertis has made out of the work – if you liked it before, you will pass out when you hear him play it. I nearly did myself.

Rebecca Clarke, in an interview with Nancy Uscher in the spring of 1978, said of the concerto:

I remember going to the first performance ... Hindemith played it, and I was in Queen's Hall, in the circle side, and in the middle of the Hall was Tertis, listening. And Hindemith, obviously, was the kind of player who was a fine musician, but he didn't practise. And he was playing with practically no vibrato. And in a way that was quite different from the way Tertis would have wanted to. And I couldn't help now and then glancing at Tertis ... every now and then, his fingers would jump. They would do this, twitch. Because he felt Hindemith wasn't doing justice to the work. So I think that had something to do with making him change his mind.

Tertis even edited the solo part of the Concerto, which was published on 3 July 1930. Later Walton inscribed on Tertis's copy: 'For Lionel Tertis with gratitude for everything he has done for this work and for his magnificent playing of it – from William Walton, 3rd February 1931.'

In 1932 Walton heard Tertis play the work in Manchester with the Hallé Orchestra conducted by Sir Hamilton Harty, who then suggested to the composer that he should write a symphony. The concert was reviewed in the February 1932 issue of *The Strad*:

Mr. Walton is one of the most vigorous thinkers, among our contemporary composers, and he thinks to some purpose. This work is highly original and most attractive in style, and, of course, lost no whit of its point at the hands of Mr. Tertis, who is a consummate artist of his instrument. Mr. Tertis also played the solo part in Berlioz' 'Harold in Italy'. The beautiful viola playing – and Sir Hamilton Harty's well-known liking for Berlioz – produced in this case an interpretation of the first class.

Of Tertis's broadcast performance of the concerto from Birmingham that same year, Ernest Newman wrote:

The most interesting musical programmes of the week have all been accessible to radio users. They have had the opportunity of making the acquaintance ... of two fine concertos – that of Sibelius for the violin, and that of William Walton for the viola. ... Mr. Tertis, of course, brought out all the beauty and all the power of the Walton viola concerto at Birmingham on Thursday. But I am afraid the wireless engineers have still a good deal to learn before they can give us a thoroughly satisfactory transmission of a concerto. The same fault was noticeable at both Birmingham and Bournemouth: the solo instrument was so emphasised that when it combined with the orchestra it mostly reduced the tissue of the latter to a blur. We hear the orchestral mass moving about and supplying a changing harmonic background to the solo; but the chords and the colours are merely averaged, as it were; the musical ear is constantly irritated at being unable to get perfect definition of the individual notes of the harmony and of the instrumental timbres, the latter being merged into a sort of vague wash of tone.

At the Three Choirs Festival on 8 September 1932 Tertis was again the soloist in the Walton Concerto, with the composer conducting. In her book *William Walton: Behind the Façade*, Lady Walton writes: 'William met Elgar in the lavatory. He didn't much care for William's work, and was heard to mutter that William had murdered the poor unfortunate instrument.' There was a lukewarm review from Eric Blom in the October issue of *Musical Times*:

> Mr William Walton conducted his beautiful Viola Concerto, the prevalent tone of which is so limpid and lyrical in spite of the duckish pranks of the middle movement, which was odd enough in the cathedral, but no more so than gargoyles and satirical carvings made by masterly hands. The performance, in spite of the appearance of Mr Lionel Tertis, began extremely badly, but pulled itself together ...

Tertis was looking forward to playing the Walton Concerto at the Usher Hall, Edinburgh (1 December 1932) with the mainly amateur Reid Symphony Orchestra conducted by the redoubtable Donald Francis Tovey, who was appointed Professor of Music at Edinburgh University in 1914 and founded the Reid Symphony Orchestra the following year. Owing to Tovey's indisposition Dr Adrian Boult deputized at short notice for this broadcast concert. Apart from the Walton concerto, the programme included Haydn's Symphony no. 95, W. B. Moonie's *Springtime on Tweed*, conducted by the composer, and some short viola pieces (Szymanowski's 'Chant de Roxane', Tartini's Fugue) and four movements from Glazunov's *Scènes de ballet*, op. 52. After the rehearsal Tertis wrote to Tovey:

> Caledonian Hotel, Edinburgh
> 1st December 1932
>
> Dear Professor Tovey,
> I do so appreciate your kind telegram and good wishes. It has been a very great disappointment to me not to meet you and to be associated with you in tonight's performance.
> It came as a great shock to me to know that you had been so ill – I had no idea of it, and I send you my most warmest wishes for a very speedy and complete recovery. How they do miss you here.
> I have just tremendously enjoyed reading your intensely interesting notes on tonight's concert.
> I much hope my share of the programme will give you satisfaction when you listen in tonight.

With kindest remembrances and renewed best wishes,
Yours sincerely,
Lionel Tertis

P.S. The orchestra were splendid at rehearsal, of the tremendously difficult orchestral part of Walton's Concerto.

The soloist and conductor had contrasting memories of the occasion:

> At Edinburgh in December 1932 I played in the first Scottish performance of Walton's Concerto. Adrian Boult conducted ... the applause was long sustained, and Boult amused me between recalls by whimsically suggesting that we should play the Concerto all over again. We returned to bow yet another time and Boult flabbergasted me by addressing the audience and calmly announcing that in response to its appreciation Mr. Tertis had kindly consented to repeat the Concerto. Let me say at once that the audience listened attentively to the second performance and nothing was thrown at me. It was a gruelling experience but worth having, for I am certainly the only viola player who has played an entire concerto as an encore piece.

Michael Kennedy, in his book about Adrian Boult, gives a different version:

> The audience received the Concerto frigidly so Boult told them he would repeat it in place of the Glazunov. Tovey wrote to Boult two days later 'I should like to think that I might have had the gumption to do it if I had been there ... I hope the audience took it well the second time.'

In December 1932 Walton wrote to Tertis:

> Casa Giachetti, Ascona, Tessin Schweiz
>
> Dear Lionel,
> News about your success with my Concerto in Edinburgh (surely a phenomenon for the whole to be encored, or am I misinformed?) reminds me that a letter to you is long overdue – which remissness I hope you will, in your kind way, overlook.
> Owing to being in a state of complete dejection about my symphony, and there not being a possibility of it being ready for its proposed first performance on April 3rd, I wrote to Harty informing him (he has been extremely kind about it) and suggested that he should put the Viola Concerto in its place. I received a card from him yesterday and he seems to approve of the suggestion and is putting it before the LSO committee. As many members expressed a wish that they should include it in the

programmes when we mentioned it at Worcester, I imagine and hope that it will be put in the April 3rd programme, so there ought to be at last a really good performance, orchestrally speaking, in London. I hope you approve of the idea.

I'm considerably cheered up at hearing of the Edinburgh performance, having just received a stinking review of the concerto in some Italian paper. Also I've just had news that 'Belshazzar' has been accepted for the International Festival at Amsterdam next year. So perhaps with all that encouraging news and not feeling myself tied to dates I may be able to get a move on with my new work.

I hope sometime (not too distant) to write another Concerto for you as a present, for I'm really grateful to you for all you have done for this one. With all best wishes for Xmas and the New Year

Yours

William Walton

Tertis was booked to play the Walton Concerto with Boult and the BBC Symphony Orchestra in April 1934, but had to cancel. Ernest Newman wrote: 'Mr. Bernard Shore, who took over the solo viola part in consequence of Mr. Tertis's temporary disablement seemed occasionally to be in a slight technical difficulty, but on the whole the music received justice at his hands.'

In the July 1938 issue of *Musical Opinion* a review of new scores stated that the concerto 'is a work of great complexity, and with all its undoubted mastery over effect is not immediately appealing. And so it is not likely to be played in public at all frequently.' This remark prompted a letter to the editor from Alan Frank in the next issue:

Sir, In your kind review of the miniature score of Walton's Viola Concerto, you imply that the work is not likely to be frequently performed. May I point out that it has already been given with orchestra, at least forty-three times in eight countries, – Great Britain, Germany, Belgium, Switzerland, Sweden, Finland, South Africa and U.S.A. In addition it has recently been recorded (by Decca).

8

BBC Orchestra and
New British Works for Viola

The new BBC orchestra –
compositions by Delius, Bax, Bliss and RVW – Casals

I N THE SUMMER of 1929 Lionel Tertis and Albert Sammons were involved in a major undertaking. The BBC had decided to form its own symphony orchestra. The string principals were appointed individually, but auditions for rank and file players were held in London and the regions between May and the autumn. Sammons and Tertis heard more than 1,000 auditions to select the sixty-strong string section of the BBC Symphony Orchestra. To lick the players into shape, the orchestra's founding conductor, Adrian Boult, adopted Tertis's suggestion of separate sectional rehearsals.

Women had played for years in Sir Henry Wood's orchestra at Queen's Hall, and some were included on occasions in the orchestra at Royal Philharmonic Society concerts. During this period there was also the London-based British Women's Symphony Orchestra. Dame Ethel Smyth was very critical of the choice of players for the newly formed BBC Symphony Orchestra and wrote to the *Daily Mail* on at least two occasions about this matter. Tertis replied in a letter that appeared in the *Daily Mail* on 9 July 1929:

> Sir, – my name having appeared twice recently in The Daily Mail (in connection with the new BBC Orchestra) with what I might mildly call an unjust inference, I shall be greatly obliged if you will allow me space to refute the suggestions made.
>
> Now, if an official (as stated by Dame Ethel Smyth) told 'Musician' that 'Sammons and Tertis can at once recognise the sex of a concealed player', I, for one, did not know I possessed this peculiar X-ray faculty. Neither was I 'safely guided' by any question or answer.
>
> In adjudicating for the new BBC Orchestra I had no interest whatever as to whether the candidates were male or female. My sole and unbiassed purpose was to judge of their efficiency.
>
> As a matter of fact I was, with regret, unable to pass a single candidate I heard (and in most cases I did not know their sex). Their performances

were, unfortunately, all below the standard required for a first-rate orchestra.

The suggestion that the candidates were made fools of is childish. I undertook the auditions with a full sense of the responsibility laid upon me, and no indication was at any time given to me that only one sex would be acceptable.

I might add that – having been through the mill of a very wide experience of orchestral playing, and with all due deference to my friend Dame Ethel Smyth – I feel fully qualified to know what is wanted in an orchestral player; and if the qualification of teacher (as well as executant) is necessary, then, may I meekly say, I have also had experience.

Dame Ethel, writing in the *Daily Mail*, agreed with 'Musician' that it was a strange fact that 'so far not one single woman has been selected by audition for the BBC Orchestra'. She added: 'Of course, the enforced reply to "necessary questions" such as "Are you ready?" makes the screen business (designed to hide the sex of the applicant) a farce, and no wonder the women are angry. Moreover the suspicion that one is being made a fool of is enough to unnerve a sensitive spirit.' She suggested that artists like Mesdames Suggia and Fachiri, 'who are distinguished teachers as well as executants', should join the board of judges.

On 20 July 1929 the *Star* reported:

The National Orchestra which has been formed by the BBC in conjunction with Sir Thomas Beecham will soon begin rehearsals, and their first public appearance will be probably at the Queen's Hall on October 18. They may perform before then, though it is not likely, but it is definite that they will on that date start a series of 22 weekly symphony concerts, which will be broadcast.

Ten per cent. of the instrumentalists will be women. The orchestra will consist of nearly 100, all of whom have now received their contracts for signature.

The gallant 100 have been chosen from about 1,000 applicants, every one of whom was given an audition. The auditions took three months to complete. Marks were given for points in their playing, and far more than were wanted for the orchestra passed the audition. The percentage of women, I am assured, represents a fair proportion of those who passed the tests as compared with the men.

The autumn and winter concerts will be regarded as an experimental season, and the orchestra, it is hoped, will be placed on a permanent basis next year.

In 1929 Tertis played Bax's Viola Sonata and Delius's Violin Sonata no. 2 during a series of recitals to promote the viola, three at the Wigmore Hall and three at the Aeolian Hall. He began the series on 3 October at the Wigmore Hall, with George Reeves as his partner. They played Martini's Sonata in E, Dale's *Romance and Finale* and sonatas by Delius and Bax; Dale's *Introduction and Andante*, op. 5, for six violas, was played by Tertis, Rebecca Clarke, Dorothy Jones, Raymond Jeremy, Leonard Rubens and James Lockyer. They rehearsed at Rebecca Clarke's home on 30 September and had a further rehearsal at the Wigmore Hall on 1 October. Clarke noted: 'We feel like the advanced viola class.' As usual, the reviews the next day were glowing:

> Mr. Tertis is a highly skilled arranger as well as performer. The music, then, if it may sound different, will sound well. This was certainly the case with the Delius Sonata no. 2 yesterday, lately arranged with the sanction of the composer and played for the first time in this version. Mr. Tertis has a fine command over tonal variety, indeed in the upper register his instrument often sounds like a violin; he seems to be able to get rid of the somewhat 'pinched' quality of the viola, while it is seldom there is any passage in which he is unable to speed up its speaking power. With the composer at the pianoforte, the sonata of Bax also went extremely well, and the performance was warmly applauded.   (*The Times*)

> There can rarely have been so many British composers performed within a few hours as to-day. ... Arnold Bax's sonata with the composer at the piano, struck one as successful in a different way; it is music that seems to have grown to a definite shape and quality out of the viola's very peculiarities. A Romance and Finale by Benjamin Dale (with Mr. George Reeves at the piano) ... is pleasant and well made in a conventional manner. So is the same composer's Introduction and Andante for six violas, but this suffered from being written for a combination that is comparatively ineffective as well as impractical. To avoid too close a spacing of the harmony the treble parts have to be kept too long in the higher registers, the viola compares unfavourably with the violin, and the bass is not solid enough as a foundation for a longish work.   (*Manchester Guardian*)

The critic Ernest Newman suggested to the Columbia Graphophone Company that they should ask Arnold Bax to record his Viola Sonata with Tertis, the dedicatee. The sessions were held on 27 May 1929 and the two of them turned in a superbly dramatic performance. It seems likely, however, that the recording did not pass the factory 'wear test', as it was very vivid and therefore the 'highs' on any commercial pressings would have become worn very quickly on the clumsy playing equipment of the day. Had the project been a more commercial one, another session would have been scheduled, but Columbia merged with HMV the following year, the Great Depression put a stop to all but the most saleable recordings and so the Bax Sonata had to wait another decade before William Primrose and the composer's paramour Harriet Cohen made a rather less dramatic recording, sponsored by the English Music Society. Fortunately Tertis kept his set of test pressings and gave the precious discs to Harry Danks, who loaned them to Pavilion Records; the Bax–Tertis performance was released for the first time on a Pearl LP in 1981 and later on a CD.

The concert series continued at the Aeolian Hall on 7 December 1929, with Mozart's Sonata in A, K305, and Brahms's Sonata in F minor, op. 120 no. 1, Ireland's Sonata no. 2 in A minor (with the composer at the piano), the first performance of Bax's *Legend* (also with the composer), Bowen's *Fantasie* for four violas (Tertis, Rebecca Clarke, Dorothy Jones and Winifred Copperwheat), Ireland's *The Holy Boy* and the Tartini–Kreisler Fugue. The Bax piece had been written in July and dedicated to Mrs Coolidge. Clarke noted in her diary: 'Poor audience and he (Tertis) didn't seem very happy.' The concert was reviewed in the January issue of *Musical Times*:

> The new Legend for viola and pianoforte by Arnold Bax which Mr. Lionel Tertis introduced at his concert at Aeolian Hall on December 7 (1929), is in one continuous movement. A first, and single hearing impresses it on the memory as being in the rich style of shifting harmonic colour that Bax now most often uses. The viola part, played in this instance with Mr. Tertis' astonishing mastery and exquisite control of tone, is free and dramatic.

On 19 December 1929, for the second time in a few years, Tertis appeared as a soloist at the Newcastle Chamber Music Society, this time with Evlyn Howard-Jones as his pianist. The concert was reviewed in the February 1930 issue of *Musical Opinion*:

> A programme of varied music was heard at the Chamber Music Society's concert. Lionel Tertis and Howard-Jones played the Brahms Sonata in F minor, op. 120, no. 1, originally for clarinet and piano, but later usually played (with the composer's sanction) by viola and piano. As Tertis is probably as great on the viola as Herr Mühlfeld was on the clarinet, one had the feeling that nothing was lost by the substitution. At any rate, the performance was exhilarating. Grieg's Sonata in C minor, op. 45, and the Delius one-movement Sonata in C, no. 2, were also played in excellent fashion. The Delius work is a fine and characteristic example of the composer's mature style; it was completed in 1915. None of the beauty seemed

to evaporate in this arrangement, a tribute to the wonderful viola playing of Tertis. As solo items, Tertis played two short pieces, and Howard-Jones gave us some Chopin, his renderings being noteworthy for richness of tone and imagination, as well as scintillating technique. Leonard Gowings used a lyric tenor voice deftly in two groups of songs, the composers including Ford, Brahms and Rachmaninoff. Mr. Bainton accompanied artistically.

Returning to the Wigmore Hall on 30 January 1930 Tertis shared his programme with the harpsichordist Violet Gordon Woodhouse, Albert Sammons and the Russian-born harpist Maria Korchinska. The programme was Martini's Sonata in D, Porpora's Aria, Marais's *Le Basque*, Ethel Smyth's *Two Interlinked French Folk Melodies*, Vaughan Williams's *Folk Song Fantasia* (all with harpsichord), Bach's *Chaconne*, Bax's *Fantasy Sonata* for viola and harp, and the first performance of W. H. Reed's Sonata for violin and viola. The other concerts in the series were on 15 March at the Aeolian Hall, 1 May at the Wigmore Hall and 31 May at the Aeolian Hall.

In 1924 Delius composed his Second Sonata for violin and piano, the last work he was able to write down before his terrible illness; for the later compositions Eric Fenby acted as his amanuensis. The sonata is in one movement, divided into three sections. Tertis arranged it for the viola. He recorded it in 1929, and took a great deal of trouble over it, rejecting a first effort made with Evlyn Howard-Jones on 4 October 1929. Three days later he achieved exactly the balance and spontaneity he wanted, this time with George Reeves at the piano.[1] The result is a genuine period piece for the high noon of British Romanticism, and is accorded a uniquely authentic performance. The fill-up is an equally beautiful performance of the Serenade from *Hassan*. It won the approval of Delius's wife Jelka, who wrote to Philip Heseltine on 2 December 1929: 'Tertis has really played the Sonata II beautifully.' Delius wrote to Tertis from Grez-sur-Loing on 1 December 1929:

> I have only just heard my 2nd Violin Sonata played by you for the 'Columbia'. It is marvellously beautiful, and I am overjoyed. I cannot imagine it better played. You have got so inside the music, and I never thought the viola could sound so lovely. What a great artist you are! The Hassan Serenade is also quite beautiful. The few bars you repeat an octave lower only enhance the piece. Please thank Mr. Reeves for his excellent collaboration.

In 1933, after a concert in Berlin, Tertis returned via Paris with the sole aim of visiting the ailing Delius. Eric Fenby wrote to the author some years ago about the visit:

'Lionel Tertis is coming to tea, and he wants you to play the third sonata with him!' Thus Delius greeted me at lunch on 13 February 1933. I was taken aback by this announcement. I had never seen Tertis nor heard him play but, of course, he was legendary in my mind from all that I had read of him. He arrived late, a tiny, crumpled, dejected figure. He had taken a taxi from Paris – thinking Grez to be a village nearby – instead of coming by train to Bourron. His fingers, he said, were numb with cold after two hours drive in a blizzard. The driver had fleeced him shamefully, and he had left his wallet in his hotel. He was quite overcome on meeting Delius, and seemed thoroughly ill at ease. I dreaded the moment all through tea when Delius would ask me to take him upstairs to 'warm-up' in the music-room; not from anxiety about my playing so much as what he would say and do when he heard the low A of Delius's piano! I delayed this disclo-sure as long as I could, and then yielding, struck the note. Tertis stared at me aghast, put his instrument back in its case and flatly refused to play at all! I made no comment, but quietly and slowly strummed the open-ing arpeggios of my part, calmly explaining as I did that our blind old tuner from Fontainebleau stubbornly refused to raise the pitch! At this Tertis reopened the case and took out his viola again and made the nec-essary compromise. He continued protesting as we tried a few bars, but was silenced by the arrival of Delius being carried feet-first by his man through the door. As soon as he was settled down, Tertis motioned me to begin. Delius was rapturous in his praise and Tertis, with not a hint of dis-comforture, even suggested another piece! I little thought that four years later I would join his colleagues at the dinner at Pagani's in wishing him well in his retirement, or, indeed, that he would ever laugh in recalling his visit to Delius at Grez.

Fenby went on to say that one of his most treasured possessions was a beauti-ful letter Tertis wrote to him after his visit to Grez, complimenting him on his playing without rehearsal.

Tertis's European tour included concerts in Italy, Germany (Berlin) and Hol-land, where he played his transcription of the third Delius sonata. Later that month Tertis received a letter from Jelka Delius:

Dear Mr Tertis … The remembrance of your masterly and heavenly playing, so full of deep understanding, is with us all the time, and I hope you will come again when it is not so cold. Delius would love that. It was unfortunate that he had one of his bad days when you came, and he cannot bear such icy weather. Yet he loved and enjoyed your playing which, he says, is quite unique. Kindest regards from Fenby, who, of course, loved accompanying you.

In his *Sunday Times* column, 'The Week's Music', Ernest Newman wrote in October 1932:

On Monday evening, at Queen's Hall, Miss Harriet Cohen and Mr. Lionel Tertis delighted us with the fineness of their style and the sensitiveness of their understanding in Arnold Bax's viola sonata, and in the third violin sonata of Delius, which latter has been arranged for his own instrument by Mr. Tertis. As usual with these arrangements of his, it is all, so far as the listener is concerned, a matter of striking a balance between the losses on the swings and the profits on the roundabouts. Sometimes a passage that has always seemed to us to have been born in the violin, and is inseparably associated with it in our minds, will come to us, as Hamlet might have said, in such a questionable shape that we feel we must speak to Mr. Tertis about it; at other times we are surprised and delighted by the new meaning a phrase will acquire in its new and graver colouring.

Tertis's edition of Delius's Sonata was reviewed in the June 1937 issue of *The Strad*:

Sonata for Violin and Piano (1924) by Reid Stewart.

The edition for viola and piano (by Lionel Tertis) was published in 1932. It is interesting to compare the different styles of Mr. Sammons (who edits the original violin part) and Mr. Tertis. Their methods often vary. For example, at the very outset of the Sonata, Mr. Sammons takes the opening note, which is a crotchet immediately before the bar line, with an up bow. Tertis uses a down. Very often his bowing indications differ considerably from those of Sammons. Tertis is particularly fond of taking a note immediately before the bar line with a down bow, contrary to the accepted usage. I observe too that Tertis uses the mute for the second Lento passage (3/2 time signature, page 8 of piano score). This is a departure from the composer's original directions.

With Myra Hess, Isolde Menges, Orrea Pernel and Ivor James, Tertis played in a Wednesday evening concert at the Wigmore Hall on 9 October 1929; included were Mozart's Trio in E flat, к498, and Franck's Piano Quintet in F minor.

On 22 October he wrote to Elizabeth Coolidge from the Esplanade Hotel,

Prague, where he was staying with his wife. He was playing that night with the Bohemian Quartet in Martinů's Quintet (written for Mrs Coolidge and first performed at her Berkshire Festival in September 1928) and Roussel's Trio with the flautist Georges Barrère, whom he described as the greatest flautist who ever lived, and the cellist Hans Kindler. Tertis mentioned that the Quatuor Pro Arte had turned up at his hotel on the previous Sunday to greet both Mrs Coolidge and himself; he was rehearsing with them in Brussels on the afternoon of the 26th and also appeared with them in Paris on the 27th.

Back in England on 6 November Tertis was the soloist in W. H. Reed's *Rhapsody* with the newly constituted Municipal Orchestra of twenty-seven players in Brighton, conducted by Jan Hurst. The orchestra attracted large audiences at their special Wednesday symphony concerts. A notable series of great artists was engaged to perform on these occasions; besides Tertis, other eminent string players who appeared were Beatrice Harrison, Daniel Melsa, Isolde Menges and Segovia. Tertis would give another performance of the *Rhapsody* on 22 October 1930 in Bath, with the Pump Room Orchestra, conducted by Edward Dunn.

At the Wigmore Hall on 26 March 1930 Tertis joined Harriet Cohen, Maria Korchinska, Eugene Cruft, Léon Goossens, the Virtuoso Quartet and the Oriana Choir, conductor Kennedy Scott, in 'A Recital of Recent Works by Arnold Bax'. He began the programme with Harriet Cohen in a performance of the composer's Viola Sonata.

On 19 May 1930 Ada Tertis wrote to Mrs Coolidge:

> Lionel went through a very bad time in the early part of the year and many concerts had to be cancelled. The trouble began with a boil in his nose, which caused the side of his face to swell beyond recognition, with much pain – After that he subsided and was afflicted with a succession of boils on the back of his poor head – terribly trying and painful – However he managed to pull up in time to play the concerto which Elgar conducted at Queen's Hall.

Mrs Coolidge invited Tertis to play second viola in the Martinů Quintet with the Quatuor Pro Arte at the Huitième Festival da la Société Internationale de Musique Contemporaire in Brussels on 8 September 1930. At Tertis's instigation all the artists appearing at the festival signed a copy of the programme, which he sent to Mrs Coolidge.

The Robert Mayer Concerts for Children were resumed at the Central Hall, Westminster, under Dr Malcolm Sargent on 18 October 1930. Seven concerts were arranged. Among the soloists engaged were Tertis and Sammons, who played Mozart's *Sinfonia concertante*.

Four days later Tertis gave a concert which included the Brahms F minor Sonata with Nicolas Orloff (piano) and the Mozart Duo in G with Isolde Menges. The final work was the Dvořák Piano Quartet in E flat, op. 87, in which the cellist was Ivor James. The printed programme included a Columbia advertisement for Tertis's recordings: 'latest viola successes by this famous artist'.

At the Royal Philharmonic Society concert on 23 October Tertis and Isolde Menges gave a performance of Mozart's *Sinfonia concertante*, conducted by Sir Thomas Beecham. Reviews the next day included the following from the *Morning Post*:

> It was Richter, I think, some time in the first decade of the century, who said, after the unexpected success of some Mozart composition or other, that after all Mozart might have a future in England. Much has happened since then: Mozart from an unfashionable has become the fashionable composer – and we have in Sir Thomas Beecham a conductor who not only understands but makes an orchestra and soloists understand his music better, perhaps, than any other living man. The result of this happy combination of circumstances was evident at the first of the Philharmonic concerts at the Queen's Hall last night, when the whole programme was devoted to Mozart. The house was packed from floor to ceiling by serried rows of enthusiasts, and, more important still, we had a concert which for sheer perfection of interpretation can never have been surpassed and very rarely equalled.

Tertis and Sammons played the Mozart *Sinfonia concertante* at the Leeds Triennial Festival in October 1931. *The Strad* in November commented: 'This is a really delicious work, and it cannot have often been more beautifully performed. Well might it be so, too, for one might search the world over for two more talented players than these soloists, and then it would be by no means certain that you had found anything half so good.' On 25 November the critics were equally enthusiastic after a memorable rendering by the same artists of the *Sinfonia concertante* at Queen's Hall under Boult. This concert included the première of Holst's *Hammersmith* and the first performance of Walton's *Belshazzar's Feast*.

There were three more performances of the Mozart with Sammons in 1933, on 16, 17 and 19 January at Queen's Hall, conducted by Malcolm Sargent; in each programme Tertis was also the soloist in Berlioz's *Harold in Italy*. The first of these concerts was reviewed in the February edition of *Musical Times*:

> The performance of the symphony 'Harold in Italy', on January 16th, was a complete exposure, or revelation, of Berlioz's claims to be considered a

great composer. For musicians of either way of thinking it was an interesting study of the composer's musical system, and it was very largely a fresh
study, for the work is not too often performed. To those to whom it was
over-familiar the interpretation of the viola solos by Mr Lionel Tertis made
it welcome. There are some who will say that Mr Tertis could be given no
higher praise. After the Berlioz, Mr Tertis was joined by Mr Albert Sammons in Mozart's Double Concerto in E flat. The first and third movements contain too much of rhythmic and harmonic plain speaking to be
considered first-class Mozart, but the slow movement is Mozart mingled
with Bach, and that is something beyond classification.

Tertis and Sammons appeared again on 9 March at a Royal Philharmonic
Society concert with the London Philharmonic Orchestra conducted by Sir
Thomas Beecham, and once more on 29 April, this time on the south coast at
a Hastings Symphony Orchestra Society concert under the direction of Julius
Harrison. It was at this concert that Phyllis Ebsworth (later the violist in the
Macnaghten and Ebsworth Quartets) first heard the viola played as a solo
instrument; she was enthralled by the wonderful lyrical tone of the instrument
and decided that she was going to be a viola player.

In March 1934 Szymon Goldberg – who had just left the Berlin Philharmonic
– was the violin soloist in a performance reviewed in the April issue of *Musical
Times*:

> The London Philharmonic Orchestra conducted by Sidney Beer enter-
> tained us at the Queen's Hall with a Mozart programme, the salient fea-
> ture of which was the playing of the soloists, S. Goldberg, leader of the
> Berlin Philharmonic, and Lionel Tertis. Goldberg gave an admirable read-
> ing of Mozart's A major Concerto. He commands a fuller tone than most
> modern violinists with the neatness and finesse absolutely confident in
> spite of the conductor's nervousness, which might have told disastrously
> with a less experienced player. Tertis joined him in a brilliant performance
> of the Symphonie Concertante, a work one rejoices to see restored to a
> place in the soloist's repertoire.

During the 1931/2 concert season Tertis was one of the artists featured at
the monthly Tuesday afternoon meetings held during the winter months at
the Music Society, Tufton Street, Westminster. The programme for the twelfth
season such players as Harriet Cohen, Harold Bauer, the Trio Italiano (Alfredo
Casella, Alberto Poltronieri and Arturo Bonucci) and the Kolisch String Quartet.

In October 1931 Robert Mayer announced his ninth season of concerts for children at the Central Hall under Sargent. Tertis was among the artists engaged, and played the Walton Concerto.

Berlioz's *Harold in Italy* was championed by both Tertis and the conductor Sir Hamilton Harty. A review of a performance by the Hallé in Manchester on 14 January 1932 in the February issue of *Musical Times* demonstrates the general lack of appreciation for what is now a popular and recognized work:

> At the last Hallé concert, I heard the opinion expressed that there was not a true melody in the whole of 'Harold in Italy', which had just been performed with Lionel Tertis in the solo part, that Berlioz was totally incapable of doing anything with such scraps of theme as he managed to invent, and that the few moments of beauty, which incontinently emerged were absolutely obscured by the hideous noise of the rest. Well, it is a point of view; but just as amazing to me as my deep appreciation must have been to the musician who exploded in terms similar to those recorded above. One thing cannot be denied, however, and that is the excellence of the performance on both the part of the soloist and orchestra. Sir Hamilton Harty's championship of Berlioz, apparently still needed when opinions like those cited remain current, is well-known and can safely be authoritative. By performance like the one on this occasion he does real service to Berlioz, to his audience, and to himself.

Harty admired Tertis, as the following letters show:

> 1, Norfolk Road, St. John's Wood. London NW8
> Dec 6th 1933
>
> My dear Lionel Tertis,
> How good of you to write to me about the Berlioz, and how sincerely I appreciate the words of congratulation from a colleague such as you. I have never forgotten our 'Harold' in Manchester, and the players there often speak of it and of your beautiful playing of the solo. I wish we could do a Berlioz concert in Paris and include 'Harold'. Well, who knows, sometime it may come to pass.
> Best thanks – and warm good wishes,
> Yours ever,
> Hamilton Harty

In his memoirs Tertis recalled Harty's masterful conducting of *Harold in Italy*:

> I have often played this grand work, but Harty's interpretation excelled that of all conductors I have known. In two places in particular the effects

he made were incomparable. In the lovely Evening Prayer of the Pilgrims, with the answering intoning of the priests, Harty's expression was so vivid that one actually saw the picture. In the final Orgy those outstanding bars for trombones and tuba, with clarinets and bassoons, heralded by the violins' fortissimo shriek – Harty rendered the grandeur of these phrases of immense sound with an extraordinarily subtle rubato. What he produced out of these twenty-two bars was electrifying.

> 1, Norfolk Road, St. John's Wood. London NW8
> April 9th 1935

My dear Lionel Tertis,
Through shyness we often neglect to tell people just what we think. But I must tell you that among the very small group of artists I love and respect and admire – you are one of the very finest. Please accept from me my affectionate thanks for your great gifts. It is a joy to work with you, for we feel music in the same way. I wish we met oftener. Bless you, and good luck and happiness be with you. If so be you find anything in my Violin Concerto worth your attention I should be honoured and delighted. But be quite frank and simple about it, if either the music itself – or its adaptability, seems unsuitable. The 'Universal' people have it now, and will gladly send you a copy if you haven't got one.
    Yours ever,
    Hamilton Harty

Tertis's old friend Artur Rubinstein came into his life again in the summer of 1932. After many amorous adventures, Rubinstein decided to marry. He was forty-five; his bride, who was three days short of her twenty-fourth birthday, was Nela Młynarski, the younger daughter of the Director of the Warsaw Opera, Emil Młynarski. They were married in London on 27 July 1932 and Lady Cholmondeley gave the wedding reception. Their most unusual present was two nights of his favourite chamber music at Sylvia Sparrow's home before the wedding, when Miss Sparrow and Rubinstein were joined for this celebration by Tertis, Thibaud and Felix Salmond.

The Depression in the 1930s had a major impact on the music profession. Tertis wrote to Mrs Coolidge on 25 October 1932:

Dearest Elizabeth, I am writing to tell you I am contemplating coming to America next season (1933–1934) firstly, because for some little time I have had a growing urge and secondly, because I cannot get enough work to do here! ... I have got two good violas now, and don't know which I like best!'

In April 1931 the Tertises' old dog Triscie died; in the latter part of 1932 her place was taken by a little Pekinese puppy which they named Bubbles, who was a wonderful source of delight and amusement to Lionel. The housekeeper, Mrs Hatchett, left their employment in December 1931 and was replaced some months later by a young girl called Nancy. 'She is becoming a most invaluable member of the household', wrote Ada to Mrs Coolidge.

Despite the Depression, London was still attracting world-renowned soloists, as the following notice from *Musical Opinion* demonstrates:

The 'concert-club' arrangements of the Courtauld–Sargent concerts for the fourth season (1932–1933) have been altered to meet the increased demand for membership. Six concerts will be given in triplicate instead of duplicate. Each concert will be given on Mondays, repeated on the next day (Tuesday) and given again either on the following Thursday or Friday. All will be held at Queen's Hall, and Dr. Malcolm Sargent will conduct five of the six concerts. The soloists include Milstein, Suggia, Cortot, Sammons, Tertis, Kutcher, Leon Goossens and J. Alexander. New works to be performed for the first time are by Martinů, Bax and Kodály.

With Gerald Moore at the piano, Tertis played a popular programme, including the first Brahms sonata and a selection of shorter pieces at the Chelsea Music Club.

On 20 December 1932 Tertis wrote to Harriet Cohen from the Carfax Hotel in Bath about programmes for their forthcoming tour:

Dear Harriet,

I have tried to find out the date of your return, but have not succeeded. I hope you have had a really splendid time in the States. I am down here for probably three weeks taking the course, to try & get rid of some rheumatism and may possibly remain until about Jan. 8th. That will leave us time for rehearsal for Bowdon (Jan. 23rd) and the American Women's Club at 11AM! on Jan. 27th. I understand that they want some short viola solos – will you mind this? We could do the Chant de Roxane by Szymanowski and the Fugue of Tartini – both of which are really duets for piano and viola. I have put these down also for Milan and Rome.

The F minor Brahms is wanted at all three concerts, so suppose if we do Delius no. 3 and Arnold's Sonata, it will make a good programme. If you find this allright, would you be an angel and tell Ibbs & Tillett, and also let me know.

I am looking forward very much to seeing you and making music again. My wife and 'Bubbles' are here and join me in best love and all good wishes for Xmas and the New Year. I hope dear little 'Me too' is all right. Give him a hug for me.

Ever yours,
Lionel

In her memoirs Harriet Cohen remembered her European tour with Tertis in February 1933:

The concert in Rome for the august Società di Santa Cecilia was our highest achievement so far. Lionel was received with what amounted to reverence, which he deserved, and which he acknowledged with his usual modesty. We had been rather irritable with each other on the train coming from Holland (a reaction from the recitals, of course) and I had cried, vowing to return to London at once ... the warm appreciation of the Milan audience recharged our nervous systems and soon all was well. Our overwhelming reception in Rome heightened the feeling of accord between us.

In April 1933 the *Musical Times* reviewed their concert in Holland:

Harriet Cohen and Lionel Tertis have promoted the interests of British art by winning favour not only for their own playing (critics and public seemed pleasantly surprised at the possibilities of the viola as displayed by Tertis), but also for works by Delius, Bax and Orlando Gibbons. Vaughan Williams's 'Hymn-Tune Prelude' did not please the Dutch, but with all the prejudice there is against Bax, this composer's Sonata, written in 1923 and dedicated to Lionel Tertis, was accepted as one of considerable musical value. Nevertheless it was quite understandable that the most popular items were the Tartini/Kreisler Fugue and the Brahms Sonata op. 120 no. 1. (Herbert Antcliffe.)

The recital for the Società del Quartetto di Milano consisted of Delius's Third Sonata, Bax's Sonata, Szymanowski's 'Chant de Roxane', the Kreisler–Tartini Fugue and Brahms's First Sonata. While in Italy Tertis played a recital of works by York Bowen (Sonata no. 1) and John Ireland with Alfredo Casella.

About three weeks before Hitler came to power Tertis and Cohen gave a recital at the British Embassy in Berlin. Cohen remembered: 'The large hall was packed, for it was a musicians' programme and the audience was still the most rewarding to play to in the world. So great, I would say almost violent, was the applause that we had to repeat the last movement of the Brahms Sonata at the end of this long programme.' Mrs Kreisler attended this recital; she paid Tertis the glowing compliment 'I have never heard any string player whose tone quality was so like Fritz's.'

The following day, 30 April, Sammons and Tertis made their historic recording for Columbia of the *Sinfonia concertante*, with cadenzas (based on those by Hellmesberger) and amendments by Tertis. The orchestra was the new London Philharmonic, conducted not by its founder Beecham but by that other excellent Mozartian Sir Hamilton Harty. Tertis remembered that the recording 'was done so to speak, on the spur of the moment, in a very small room, and we had about a fifteen minute run through before the recording'.

Mrs Coolidge invited Lionel to play second viola in Bax's new String Quintet in London on 29 May 1933 for an inclusive fee of £25. In August Lionel wrote two letters to Mrs Coolidge: the first reported the death of his wife Ada's close friend Elizabeth Margaret-Haweis; the second bears printing in full, as it shows Tertis's state of mind at the time and his general feeling of dissatisfaction:

Dearest Elizabeth,

Following the hurried note I wrote to you on our calamity, if I am not troubling you too much, I should so like to have your opinion on an idea that is impressing itself very much upon me, and one that I have had subconsciously for some time.

I feel, if I could get a substantial, fixed appointment in America, at an institution, to teach the Viola, and possibly have charge of an Ensemble Class, I would leave England, and come.

Here are my reasons,

1) It would help Ada, to get her right away.

2) Until now, Ada's devotion to Miss Haweis, would not permit of our ever altering our anchorage, but now we can, we neither of us have any relations or friends we feel drawn to, or to whom we have any obligations.

3) I have not received in my own country, the support I should have had for my missionary work for the Viola.

Therefore before it is too late, I should like to go somewhere where I could spread the gospel of the Viola, by solo work, and where I could lay the foundation of a community of future Viola soloists, by teaching. I think that in America my efforts might bear fruit.

If you think there is anything in this, and you know of anyone in America, to whom you could moot this idea, where it might possibly take hold, I should be very grateful to you.

Ever affectionately, Lionel

Mrs Coolidge's reply on 30 August included the following advice:

I wish too, dear friends, that I had some suggestion of value to make in response to your appeal about coming to America but, dear Lionel, I wonder if you know that the musicians who are already living here are in a very sorry plight and that there would seem to be no probability of filling any position for which there are not already more applicants than can be supported. I am sorry to have to say this to you, as indeed I have to others. America just now is struggling to keep its head above water and the musicians have suffered keen distress by the closing down of schools, falling off of students, and the general inability to pay for even necessities. I believe that when we come out from the shadow other countries will do the same and that you will still find it wise to remain one of the most distinguished artists in Great Britain.

Tertis replied to this letter on 24 September, thanking her for her good advice, and continuing: 'I am hoping to make a good deal of propaganda for the viola this year – Five new works are being written! Bliss, Holst, Vaughan Williams, Bax, Goossens. I will send you accounts of them when they appear.'

A series of Six British Music Concerts was presented at the Queen's Hall in early January 1934. In the fourth of the series, on 8 January, Tertis was the soloist in Dale's *Romance* and Vaughan Williams's *Flos campi*, with the Wireless Chorus and the BBC Symphony Orchestra (leader Arthur Catterall) conducted by Adrian Boult. Also in the programme was Bax's Symphony no. 4 and songs by Rutland Boughton and Roland Bocquet sung by the tenor Parry Jones.

Tertis renewed acquaintance with Solomon Cutner, the great concert pianist known internationally as 'Solomon'. They had often made music together, and as a consequence of their meeting decided to establish themselves in a duo partnership. Solomon was a child prodigy who studied with Mathilde Verne, a British pianist of German descent. She had been a student of Clara Schumann and taught in London where she participated in many chamber music concerts. Verne opened a school of piano-playing a few years before the Great War, and Solomon became one of her pupils at a very early age. When he was barely ten years old he learnt the piano part of Dohnányi's Violin Sonata in C sharp minor and played it with Tertis in a concert for Woodford Music Society in Essex.

Tertis always had a great admiration for Solomon, and in their rehearsals they always strove to grasp the fullness of the composer's intentions and to achieve perfect tonal balance. Solomon was like no other artist Tertis had worked with before. The following story was recounted by Solomon's wife in an interview recorded in 1991, and is taken from *Solo: The Biography of Solomon* by Bryan Crimp:

Despite their hard work together – perhaps because of it – Tertis would, on occasions, explode. This was nothing new; the little man was famous for his gargantuan outbursts, as fiery as they were short-lived though, in the process, they did make him many enemies in the musical world. On this occasion, apparently prompted by some innocent remark from Solomon, Tertis flared like a rocket and launched into a tirade. Solomon's reaction was obviously not one that Tertis had previously encountered. Still seated at the piano, Solomon looked up at Tertis with a beatific smile on his face and during the first available opportunity to get a word in edgeways said 'It's no use Lionel, I'm not going to quarrel with you!' Tertis was so taken aback that he was reduced to a fit of the giggles.

Tertis and Solomon gave the première of Arthur Bliss's Viola Sonata, which is dedicated 'In admiration – to Lionel Tertis, the true creator of this work', at a private performance on 9 May 1933 at the composer's home before a distinguished group of musicians. William Walton turned pages. Bliss in his autobiography *As I Remember* describes the occasion:

> Musically speaking, 1933 was marked for me by my friendship with Lionel Tertis, and the completion of a large-scale Sonata for him. Tertis, like two former collaborators of mine, Leon Goossens and Frederick Thurston, was not only a master player, but the inspirer of a whole school of playing. It is no exaggeration to say that through his influence the viola, that Cinderella of instruments, was crowned a princess. I was determined to write something for him.
>
> As my Sonata grew, I realised that it was really becoming a concerto for the instrument and if today I had the energy and patience I would translate the piano accompaniment into an orchestral tissue, taking care that the mellow dark sombre tone of the solo instrument was not obscured by too thick a surround. But even if the length of this sonata was a deterrent it could not have had a more brilliant introduction to audiences. ... and of course I found it inspiring to work with him.

Bliss remembered the first time he heard Tertis play:

> it was in the late Twenties, and I went specially to hear his own arrangement of the Bach Chaconne, and of course his tone was absolutely personal, like Goossens' tone on the oboe is personal to him. It was a dark, sombre, rich sound on the lower strings; on the A string, when he got up high, you had this quality of a splendid mezzo-soprano singing voice, it was really a thrilling sound.

The official first performance was given by Tertis and Solomon on November 1933 at a BBC Chamber concert. Bliss continues:

> Shortly afterwards, in place of Solomon, Rubinstein accompanied Tertis.

I remember Rubinstein only had the score a day or so before the concert, but despite that he gave an electrifyingly assured performance. It is a wonderful moment for a composer when he hears his music given a deeper significance than he himself thought it could bear, and then, with two superlative players there is the certainty that for each and every section the right tempo will be found. I have come to the conclusion that I do not so much mind wrong notes or a disregard of dynamics provided the basic tempo is right. I have heard performances of this Sonata that have taken fully three minutes too long. Perhaps it is fatal to affix metronome marks to one's score, for the metronome may be inaccurate, and I feel mine must be. If my music is to make any impression it must move on, and not be static; that is the very essence of my own character. A right pulse is for me the first essential factor in pleasurable listening. I digress a little to emphasise my joy in the pulsing flow that great players like Tertis, Solomon and Rubinstein can give to any page of music. I think my Viola Sonata should have Tertis' name coupled with mine as joint composers, for many times in the course of its composition I would be called to the telephone by Tertis with his viola at the other end. I would hear his voice 'On page 17, line 3, do you like this' – I would then hear the tones of the viola – 'or this?' He would then repeat the passage. 'But, Lionel, I don't hear much difference'.

'But you must', he would answer; 'the first time I took two down bows, etc. etc.'

Well ... I had a master class in viola playing quite free, and I am grateful.

The BBC fortnightly Friday concerts were reviewed by Marion M. Scott in the *Musical Times* in December 1933:

The second concert (November 3rd) brought the premiere of a new Sonata for viola and pianoforte by Arthur Bliss, composed for and dedicated to Lionel Tertis, who played it with Mr Solomon [*sic*]. Seldom has a new work left one with a livelier desire to hear it again. In the first place, it is most beautifully adapted to the character of the viola. Arthur Bliss shows an ever-growing capacity to 'get inside' the genius of each instrument, so that his compositions strike one not so much as outward applications to the oboe, clarinet, viola (or whatever the instrument is) as expressions of their inward and spiritual grace. One result is that in this Viola Sonata the most striking tone colours, the deepest and highest notes, with their dark fullness or curlew plaintiveness, are sparingly used. The main progress of the music is maintained along the natural middle register, and the pianoforte writing is accommodated to give the viola enough support below and above without choking its middle breathing space. The gain in sustained interest is great; when the colour effects come, the ear has not been dulled by familiarity.

Secondly, whether he meant it or not, Arthur Bliss has mirrored something of Lionel Tertis's own character in the music – that exquisite artistic reticence which is yet compatible with such heartfelt expression. Thirdly, the Sonata attracts by its thematic material and the distinction of its design. This design challenged one on a first hearing, and even gave an impression of ending before it had expected it. Yet the longer one thinks of it afterwards, the more one comes to delight in its delicate symmetry. For what happens in the three movements – Moderato, Andante, Furiant – is this. The middle movement, which is very expressive, is prefaced and concluded by a short, strongly recognisable passage in which the viola plays pizzicato – these two pizzicato passages buttressing the cantilena of the movement proper. Now what Bliss has done in the span of the middle movement, he has done with the Sonata as a whole. The big, up-rushing theme which opens the first movement is introduced again as a Coda at the end of the last movement. Thus the Sonata itself stands between two noble buttresses, of which the form of the middle movement is a smaller replica. It would be a delight to analyse the work in detail. As to the performance, it was perfect.

The rest of the programme consisted of Mozart's Sonata in A (K305) and the Sonata no. 3 by Delius, both arranged by Lionel Tertis for viola and pianoforte; Chopin's B minor Sonata for pianoforte, played by Solomon too swiftly, yet attractively; and some viola solos, with Ernest Lush as accompanist. Of these, the Chant de Roxane by Szymanowski Kochanski–Tertis became pure enchantment when interpreted by Tertis. What a great artist!

Bliss's Viola Sonata was given the following review by Ernest Newman:

Arthur Bliss's new sonata for viola and piano received, at the hands of Mr. Tertis and Mr. Solomon, what even the composer would probably call a first-rate first performance at the B.B.C.'s chamber music concert on Friday. Detailed consideration of the work must be reserved until the score is available. On the basis of a mere first hearing all one can say is that the sonata shows Mr. Bliss emancipating himself still further from the influences that at one time threatened to do him and other young post-war composers so much harm. His musical constitution has been healthy enough to come unscathed through what will probably be known to historians as the Silly Epoch – the years from about 1919 to 1929; and, like so many of his young contemporaries who have steadied themselves he is finding that romanticism, in one form or another – and the form, of course, changes from age to age – is the diet that suits music best. (Even jazz pays its mewling and puking tribute to the romantic as it conceives it.) I am not sure whether the finale of Mr. Bliss's sonata hangs together quite as well as the first two movements, but this is a point upon which we shall know more later. What is certain is that the ideas of the work are distinguished, the fancy delightfully free, and the craftsmanship masterly.

It was also reviewed by Hubert J. Foss in the *Musical Times* of March 1934:

The collision of Arthur Bliss and Lionel Tertis is not one isolated episode in the new history of the viola as a solo instrument, nor in instrumental history as a whole. In other periods, a music-machine, or a school of players, or one virtuoso, has deflected the course of musical composition. Tertis's perfection has something legendary about it, like a Hans Andersen story – something that is parallel to the Bachs, Vivaldis, Paganinis, and Joachims to name only a few of the famous. Tertis's none-too-lovely heroine has coaxed many princes. But how this episode of ours will look viewed from the distance of fifty years is hard to guess but easy to doubt. Of the many works commanded by his wand, few seem to have the secret of youth, and one is tempted to wonder, as a speculation on the subject of idioms, whether the two concerti Paul Hindemith wrote for himself will not outlive some of the greater number written down by others for Tertis. Of the game shot down by Tertis's inimitable skill, I should be inclined to claim this Sonata as one of the first in importance. For it occupies a place of importance in the career of Bliss as a composer, and unless I am greatly mistaken, a rare one in the annals of modern English music.

In the last of three talks Bliss gave on 'Aspects of Contemporary Music' (22 March 1934 at 5.15 p.m.) at the Royal Institution, 21 Albemarle Street, the composer described the appeal the viola had for him: 'The viola is the most romantic of instruments; it is a veritable Byron in the orchestra. The dark, sombre quality – now harsh, now warm – of its lowest string, the passionate rhetoric of its highest string, and its whole rather restless and tragic personality, make it an ideal vehicle for romantic and oratorical expression.' Tertis and Solomon should have given another performance of the new sonata, but Tertis burnt his hand on the radiator of his car, so instead Frederick Thurston joined the Griller Quartet in the composer's Clarinet Quintet.

Tertis edited the Bliss Sonata, and it was published by Oxford University Press in 1934.

Musical Opinion in 1934 included an entry stating that Bax was writing a second Viola Sonata for Tertis; little more is known about this project except for two pages of manuscript which Harriet Cohen gave to Clifford Gillam, the founder of the Bax Society, after the composer's death in 1953. The pages are numbered 21 and 22; page 21 is the end of the second movement and page 22 is the beginning of the third. Many of the composer's solo and ensemble works have orchestral dimensions. His Piano Quartet was orchestrated and titled 'Saga Fragments', and the Third Piano Sonata became his Symphony no. 1. Page 21 of the proposed Viola Sonata became the end of his Sixth Symphony. It is hard to say what happened to the rest of the Sonata, but Harriet Cohen, Bax's mistress, had a habit of giving away pages of discarded manuscripts, and some have found their way into libraries and collections in Europe and the USA. Perhaps one day someone will discover the remaining pages of the Second Viola Sonata.

Tertis gave the first performance of Gustav Holst's *Lyric Movement* on 18 March 1934. After the performance Holst wrote to Tertis:

Dear Tertis,
I send you my warmest thanks for the great treat you gave me and thousands of others on Sunday night. Your playing was perfect. I'm sorry I can't say the same for the piece itself. There is one bad bit of overscoring which makes me ask myself when am I going to learn the elements of my job. This shall be put right before the next performance. If you have any critical suggestions I'd be glad to know them (the bad bit is, of course, the squiggles in four sharps.) Yours ever,
G.H.

Holst's daughter Imogen also remembered the première of the *Lyric Movement*:

But he (Holst) was too ill to go the BBC studio for the first broadcast performance in March 1934 of his Lyric Movement for viola and small orchestra, which was dedicated to Lionel Tertis. He had written a postcard to Adrian Boult saying 'You and Tertis are to have an absolutely free hand over my new thing. Just do what you like with it. And accept my thanks in advance, also my blessing. And the same to Lionel Tertis and the other players'. During the weeks before the broadcast Tertis had consulted Holst about many of the details and they had agreed on the bowing, so that

when the Oxford University Press published the score there was little editing to be done.

At a Promenade Concert on 14 August 1934 Tertis played the solo part in
the Bax *Phantasy* for viola and orchestra conducted by Sir Henry Wood. It
was reviewed in the October issue of *The Strad*: 'Lionel Tertis put in some
admirable work on Bax's lovely Phantasy for viola and orchestra. If Mr. Tertis
can persuade a few more composers like Bax to enrich the viola repertoire by
such brilliant works, he will be performing an incalculable service to music and
to posterity.' Ernest Newman wrote of the same concert: 'Mr. Tertis gave us a
noble reading of Bax's Phantasy for viola and orchestra – a fine work in spite
of the fact that the Irish type of melody that runs through some portions of it
does not quite cohere with the rest of the music.'

Tertis had played Vaughan Williams's *Flos campi* at its première on 12 October 1925, and the composer dedicated his Suite for viola and small orchestra to
him. Tertis gave the first performance on 12 November 1934 with the London
Philharmonic Orchestra conducted by Malcolm Sargent. The Suite consists
of eight short movements, each with its own particular character and atmosphere. *Musical Opinion*, December 1934, noted:

> The second Courtauld–Sargent concert was given on November 12th,
> when Malcolm Sargent returned to his duties, completely restored to
> health as a conductor. A new Suite for viola and orchestra by Vaughan
> Williams was played for the first time. It betokens no new departure for
> its composer: his work never lacks spontaneity when meditating on rural
> and pastoral subjects. The various short dance movements do not lack
> development, while the Suite is cast in that diatonic mould peculiar to
> Vaughan Williams which delights the ear. Lionel Tertis was the soloist.

The *Musical Times* (December 1934) reviewed the concert:

> Vaughan Williams has not exhausted his capacity to spring surprises. His
> Suite for viola and orchestra played by Mr Tertis at the concert on Novem-
> ber 12, could no more have been prefigured than the 'Pastoral' Symphony
> or Flos Campi. After the event one can perceive the composer's train
> of thought and agree with it. In the 'Concerto Accademico' for violin,
> Vaughan Williams' contrapuntal puzzles were the fashion. Still more so
> was the percussiveness of the Pianoforte Concerto. In the work for viola,
> however, he corrects fashion – rebukes it if you like – for treating the
> instrument in an unsuitable way. The recent elevation of the viola, he says,
> has been too respectful. The viola's dusky tone and gift of plaintiveness do
> not necessarily cast it for tragic parts: they are part of its homely nature

and are fit for homely thoughts. Its voice, unlike that of the aristocratic violin, is the voice of lowly humanity, with its simplicities and humours as well as its dumps. Its candle-light is that of the cottage. So Vaughan Williams does not write a three movement concerto with poignant subjects, burdensome developments and punctilious designs. He writes a set of short pieces, lively, peaceful, jocular, wistful – anything but portentous – with the voice of folk-song slipping in, as if by right, at every other breath. The lowering of the brow does not in the least lower the style. In fact, Vaughan Williams has written a work more crowded with points of musical interest, sudden gleams of beauty, inspired simplicities, and telling subtleties. Sometimes he is so quick-witted that his meaning loses itself in performance – Vaughan Williams is becoming too rapid for St. Cecilia, or her servants. The pieces are called Prelude, Carol, Christmas Dance, Ballad, Moto Perpetuo, Musette, Polka and Galop. It would be wrong to say which was the nicest: one does not listen so, and the next time the choice would be different. Judgement went by the board in the excited pursuit of things that flew past the ear, and it is only the leisured simple things that were remembered. One of them came in the Carol, where the viola had a sweet and simple tune and the flute followed it about, a bar or so behind, with fleeces as white as snow. Mr Tertis enthusiastically backed up the composer in this process of putting the viola in countenance. Debunking is too ugly a word.

In August 1937 the score was reviewed in *The Strad*:

Oxford University Press.
Suite for viola and orchestra by Vaughan Williams (6/-)

This Suite with an arrangement for the pianoforte of the orchestral score, should be an important addition to the viola repertoire. The Suite consists of three groups of pieces published separately at 2/6 or the complete work, as stated 6/- ... As usual the strong personality of the composer shows itself throughout the work. His sense of beauty runs through those of the numbers in which melody predominates, such as the Carol, Ballade [*sic*] and Musette. In some of the other numbers there is a certain harshness, and a lack of defined outlines, which make them difficult to understand on a first hearing. Much of it is music which one will either like or dislike – there will be no half-hearted feeling. The writing for viola shows a thoroughly sound knowledge of the instrument and the arrangement of the orchestral score for piano is a model of skill. The numbers vary in difficulty from moderate to virtuoso. The Moto Perpetuo is distinctly in the latter category – and brilliant.

A performance Tertis particularly cherished was one in which he joined Casals in Strauss's *Don Quixote* at the Queen's Hall on 14 November 1934, with Sir Henry Wood and the BBC Symphony Orchestra. There were several reviews the next day. In December the *Musical Times* reported:

On November 14 Casals played the Haydn Concerto (in D) and the cello part in Strauss's 'Don Quixote', and in so doing answered a question that has been at the back of a good many minds for some time. A solo artist who is nearing his sixtieth year is also nearing the period of technical decline, and if he is a string player the first weakenings will be inexorably conveyed to the least instructed listener. At this concert there were signs, no bigger than the first falling leaf of autumn, of this oncoming menace, from which there is no escape. More obvious, however, were the signs that it did not matter. Casals (said his playing) will go on being Casals, the great interpreter of music and personage on the platform, long after he has ceased to be the wizard of string and bow that he now is. His playing of the concerto was a model of style, and in the tone poem the parts that stood out were those in which the cellist was the principal performer. Mr Tertis was vivacious in the viola music; one felt that Casals needed such a partner.

Tertis later wrote about Casals:

One of the privileges of the generation was to hear him in his prime. A grand soul was housed in that small body – a body so small that it was always a wonder how easily his left hand climbed over the range of the huge cello he generally played upon. What supremely distinguished him was his consummate musical understanding, but his technique itself was fascinating, above all perhaps the cunning with which he would change position on the long fingerboard … Casal's portamento was miraculously discreet, no matter what the width of the interval.

Besides conducting the original BBC Symphony Orchestra, Adrian Boult was also the Corporation's Director of Music. This position involved programme planning and engaging the relevant soloists, a responsibility that sometimes caused problems with colleagues and friends within the orchestra. Tertis's former pupil Bernard Shore, a great friend of Boult's since 1921, was appointed principal viola when the BBC founded their orchestra in 1930. Through a remark by Mrs Shore to Boult's wife, he learned that Bernard Shore was very unhappy at not being asked to play Sancho Panza to Casals's Don Quixote in Strauss's tone poem at the concert in Queen's Hall. In a letter to Shore dated 29 December 1934, Boult outlined the reason for this decision:

Except for Tertis you are recognised as the leading viola player in the country. Your salary is probably double T.'s professional income ... The trouble therefore does not seem to be material – it must be artistic ... the Don Quixote business. I did not answer your letter to me about it – I thought it would be more friendly not to, though I disagreed with you on one point: the solo cello and solo viola are handled identically in the score; both are in and of the orchestra. As a matter of courtesy the names are printed in the programmes; but surely when the greatest living cellist is engaged for one part, it is up to us to put beside him the greatest living violist, particularly when he is an Englishman.

9

A Shock Retirement

Working with a harpsichordist – further tours – Tertis as teacher –
a shock retirement and farewell dinner – appreciations for a great artist

AMONG Violet Gordon Woodhouse's circle, who met regularly over the
years in London, Lypiatt and Armscote were the Sitwells, Ethel Smyth,
Arnold Dolmetsch, Augustín Rubio, Enrique Fernández Arbós, Arthur Waley
and Tertis. On 5 March 1935 Tertis gave a recital at the Wigmore Hall with
Violet playing the harpsichord; their programme took in pieces by Handel,
Martini, Mozart, Galuppi, Tartini, Scarlatti, Telemann, Porpora, Vaughan Williams, Kalnis, Poulenc and Marais. *The Times* reported that 'everything was
exceedingly well played, though one felt that the viola's tone was sometimes
too dry, especially on the top string. The viola tone seemed to take off some of
the sparkle of the harpsichord, which sounded better in the solo music'. The
review in *Musical Times* was of the same opinion:

> it must be confessed that the harpsichord does not partner the viola so
> well as the violin, owing to something inherent in the nature of the two
> tones. This together with the loss of the viola's low notes when playing
> violin music in its original key, just prevented Handel's Sonata in F from
> touching the superlative charm of the performances of two sonatas by
> Martini and various solos.

In the 1930s Tertis often played with Violet in the drawing room of her home
at Nether Lypiatt Manor. He must have achieved a gentle muted effect, for Eve
Simmonds thought his viola and Violet's clavichord 'very well balanced and
beautifully together'. A critic wrote: 'Segovia on the guitar, Lionel Tertis on the
viola, Casals on the cello and Violet Gordon Woodhouse on the harpsichord
may be classed together as the four who can distil from these instruments the
purest musical essence'.

Another of Tertis's concerto transcriptions had been taking shape, this time
of the double concerto for violin and cello by Frederick Delius. After Delius's
death in 1934 Jelka Delius wrote to Tertis:

> I have just come back to Grez, and I want to tell you that May Harrison,
> altho' she at first thought it would offend her sister (Beatrice) if she played
> the Double Concerto with you, has now found that her sister is not at

all against it. As you said you had no violinist yet, I venture to suggest that you take her. She studied it one whole winter, under Delius's own guidance, and he always thought her playing very beautiful and musical. It would also save you no end of trouble with a new violinist.

On 3 March 1935 Adrian Boult conducted the première of Tertis's transcription of Delius's Double Concerto with May Harrison and Tertis. Jelka wrote to Percy Grainger from Grez on 19 March about the performance:

Tertis was, of course, the soul of this performance and imparted to it such a wealth of true Delius tenderness and feeling, carrying May (Harrison) with him quite beyond herself; Boult at his best where discreet following a master mind is required. Of course I know that certain things could not help losing their effect thro' the deep 'cello-tone not there. But as the 'cello part is almost all thro' in the high ranges it had not to be changed and sang out so beautifully in Tertis's supreme playing.

Delius died on 10 June 1934 and was temporarily buried in Grez cemetery. At midnight on 25 May 1935 his body was brought back to England and laid to rest in the churchyard at Limpsfield, Surrey. The memorial service took place in Limpsfield church on the afternoon of 26 May. Amongst those who attended were Balfour Gardiner, Vaughan Williams, Sir Landon Ronald, Barbirolli, Albert Sammons and Tertis.

At a BBC recital in 1935, when Artur Rubinstein joined Tertis in the Bliss Sonata, the programme included a performance of the Bach *Chaconne* which so impressed the *Daily Mail* critic Edwin Evans that he wrote the following letter to Oxford University Press:

I heard Tertis play his arrangement of the Chaconne, and am in favour of it being published. Not many viola players will be equal to playing it as he does, but they will all want to have a stab at it. As it becomes known it ought to become the equivalent of the 'cordon bleu' among them. On the musical side it struck me, with listening, that in sonority it was a distinct improvement on the original, though I may be stoned for saying so! The chords and arpeggios spread across the strings gain much in dignity by starting from a deep foundation. Moreover with violinists I have always been conscious of a certain occasional scratchiness, which they complacently regard as inevitable but which, for my ears, mars the effect. With the mellower tone of the viola this becomes negligible. I was on the qui-vive for it on Friday and it never bothered me.

The concert was also reviewed in the March issue of *Musical Times*:

Many artists now blend chamber music with solos in their programmes. Lionel Tertis and Arthur Rubinstein did so at the BBC Chamber Concert on January 26. The fine Sonata by Arthur Bliss is true chamber music, carried out with the decorative richness of solo style. Further acquaintance sustains the admiration roused by the first hearing, and by Lionel Tertis's unapproached mastery when playing it. Yet somehow one felt that Solomon – the pianist of last year's performance – got nearer to the work than did Arthur Rubinstein notwithstanding his brilliance ... Lionel Tertis, for his solo, performed the amazing double feat of transferring Bach's Chaconne to the viola, note for note, and of restoring it, so far as possible, to bowing and phrasing Bach himself must have known when he wrote it for violin and out-curved bow of his day. The experiment was a noble success. The broader, slower style fitted well with the dark vistas of viola tone, and the unbroken continuity of thought and beauty in the great work were clear to a singular degree. Tertis always does seem to get close to the mind of any composer whose music he plays. He made close rapport with Beethoven in the set of Variations op. 66 originally written for cello and piano, but here played by viola and piano in his own arrangement.

In 1935 Dame Ethel Smyth invited the Tertises to her house in Woking with the purpose of asking Lionel if he would edit her *Two Interlinked French Folk Melodies* for viola. In *My Viola and I* Tertis describes the visit:

> In this connection my wife and I went to visit her ... In her sitting room we could not help being struck with the accumulation of incongruous objects. One such was a large and dilapidated kitchen-chair, with a huge rubber bed-ring upon it. Also present was an enormous, rough-haired, unkempt sheep-dog she introduced to us as her husband.

At Tertis's retirement dinner in 1937 Beecham recalled that when he, in the company of Ethel Smyth, met Tertis one day, Dame Ethel, having stared at Tertis for some time, plucked at Beecham's sleeve and said: 'That is the only man I have met in my life I should like to have married.' Beecham suggested that when the time came to erect a monument to Tertis, this remark should be inscribed on it as a tribute to his charming and popular personality.

Tertis wrote his Variations on the Passacaglia of Handel for two violas, based on the final movement of the Suite no. 7 for harpsichord. The dedication reads: 'Dedicated to Mrs Elizabeth Sprague Coolidge, a slight token of gratitude for all she has done for music and musicians. Lionel Tertis May 1935'. The manuscript is held in the Library of Congress in Washington. Tertis wrote to Mrs Coolidge on 9 May:

Dearest Elizabeth

I have just finished writing a set of variations for Two Violas on the Passa-caglia of Handel. You have probably heard the Halvorsen arrangement for violin and viola, and I am presumptuous enough to think that I have gone one better than Mr Halvorsen. I am going to play them with a pupil at his recital on 22nd June (he is a player whom I think will keep the flag flying for the viola. It has occured [*sic*] to me that if you thought them worthy (the variations) I would like to have the privilege of dedicating them to you, therefore if you will let me know directly you arrive in London and can spare ten minutes, I will get my pupil to come along, and we will play them to you for you to say yes or no.

Further if they really excite you and you think you would like it, we'll play them at your party as a sort of surprise but of course only on the con-dition that I do it for love.

Ever affectionately, Lionel

The new arrangement was aired in a Wigmore Hall recital on 22 June, given by Harry Berly with Tertis and Charles Lynch (piano). The concert was reviewed in the August issue of *Musical Times*:

From the music chosen by Harry Berly for his viola recital at the Wigmore Hall on June 22, it was clear he meant to 'swing himself up' (as Beethoven would have said) to a high plane. Three works were Sonatas for viola and piano, by three B's – Brahms, Bliss and Bax; the fourth a new set of Vari-ations for two violas by Lionel Tertis founded upon the Passacaglia from Handel's seventh suite and developed to the utmost heights of difficulty of which the viola is capable. Harry Berly thus first challenged criticism in chamber music, where the executive skill of the artist is so merged in that of the interpreter that his technique is usually unnoticed by the public save when it is absent; and secondly in virtuosity, where attainments, however dazzling must be supported by artistry if the difficulties are not to become dull. It can be said at once that Mr. Berly acquitted himself with honour on both counts: he is a genuine musician with a vocation for the viola. He has studied with a genius of the instrument, Lionel Tertis, and has absorbed a good deal of the master's method and style. However, at the moment Berly is more developed on the executive than the interpretative side. Thus while he and Charles Lynch gave an interpretation of Arthur Bliss's Sonata, that was clever and competent but not intuitive, Berly as first viola in the Handel–Tertis Variations, exhibited a virtuosity equal to every sort of brilliance and legerdemain. Such a façade of technique as he and Lionel Tertis put up here must have been astounding, even unsettling, to people accustomed to regard the viola as the melancholy Jacques of the orchestra.

Another impression gained from this performance was of the singular beauty to be obtained from the tone of two solo violas heard together – a sound more satisfying in pitch and mysterious in timbre than that of two violins. Yet even more than the violin, the viola demands consideration from other instruments. In the Sonatas a richly powerful grand piano joined issues with the viola, not altogether to the latter's advantage, despite the discretion of Mr. Lynch, and the admirable tone produced by Mr. Berly. The juxtaposition set one thinking how interesting it would be to hear a viola recital in which the piano employed was of the early clear-edged type, with more sostenuto than a harpsichord, yet without the enveloping sonority of a modern grand. After all, string players discriminate between the types of violins suitable for solo, orchestral or chamber music; might not analogous considerations attach to the work of pianists? Yet even in asking the question, one pauses. Lionel Tertis has something about his tone that makes his softest whisper come through not merely a grand piano, but a full orchestra – a tone whose quality is part of the magic of genius and personality which glowed in his playing of his own variations and (though he had modestly taken the second part) made it seem the origin and foundation of all.

The Handel–Tertis Variations received a second performance on 5 October 1935, at the opening concert in a series given by British artists, and organized by Mrs Augustus Ralli at the Hyde Park Hotel. It was reviewed in the November issue of *Musical Times*:

> Myra Hess and Lionel Tertis joined in an admirable performance of the Sonata for viola and piano by Arnold Bax. The work, written for Tertis, bears the impress of his unique personality. But it is unmistakably Bax, a composer who, by education, and friendship, Miss Hess and Mr Tertis are well qualified to understand. The result was a performance in which these factors reacted upon each other with the happiest results. An arrangement for two violas and piano of the Allegretto from Schubert's Quartet op. 161 and a set of variations for two violas on Handel's Passacaglia from the seventh Suite, both came from the pen of Mr Tertis. They were played by himself and William Primrose, and proved well contrasted, welcome additions to the viola repertory.

At a Courtauld–Sargent concert on 1 April 1935 at Queen's Hall, Tertis played Vaughan Williams's Suite for viola and small orchestra with the London

Philharmonic Orchestra conducted by Malcolm Sargent and again in a Prom concert on 5 September. On 18 December Tertis was again the soloist in the Suite in the winter series of symphony concerts in Bournemouth. The review of the concert in the February issue of *Musical Opinion* described the work:

> a sincere, sensitive and charming pastoral it is, with one or two quiet numbers, which, in their subtlety and suggestiveness of a delicate English landscape, are hardly to be matched in music old or new. Other numbers of more animated kind, one or two of which might be described as 'rustic' – afford ample contrast, if in themselves they do not carry the same conviction. Mr. Tertis played like the fine artist he is, but did not quite persuade one that the viola is an ideal solo instrument, the tone somehow tending to lose itself in the orchestral background, however delicately the latter might be woven and in spite of the large and powerful viola used on this occasion.

After another of his concerts that year Tertis met Alexander Glazunov, who promised to write a concerto for him but sadly died in the following March. The same year Tertis visited Maurice Ravel in Paris, and played for him the Dale *Romance and Finale*. Ravel was very complimentary, and promised to write a work for viola; the score was to include a small orchestra and concealed choir, and there was to be an alternative part for harmonium for occasions when a choir was not available. Tertis was thrilled, but it was never written, as Ravel died on 28 March 1937.

On 4 January 1936 Tertis performed the *Sinfonia concertante* with Sammons under Sargent at the Central Hall, and on 26 February he played the same work at Queen's Hall with Adolf Busch and the BBC Symphony Orchestra conducted by Sir Henry Wood. Busch, then forty-four, was at the height of his fame, and enormously popular in London, where a special society had been formed to promote his concerts. He had not played in his native Germany since 1 April 1933, in protest against the Hitler regime's treatment of the Jews; and although he himself was the typical blond Aryan so beloved of Hitler – who called him 'our German violinist' – he had resisted all the Nazis' blandishments when they had tried to lure him back. He had played the *Sinfonia concertante* many times, usually with the violist of his quartet, Karl Doktor. Although the tall, broad Busch and the stocky Tertis must have made an odd couple on the Queen's Hall stage, they merged their styles well enough, as reported in *The Strad*: 'The broadcast of Tertis and Busch playing the lovely "Sinfonia concertante" of Mozart was, as might be expected, a complete success.'

Between these two Mozart performances Tertis set off with Clifford Curzon to tour the capitals of Central Europe at the invitation of the British Council.

Their programmes included the Bliss Sonata, the Brahms Sonata in E flat, op. 120 no. 2, and the Bach *Chaconne*. The duo left on 5 January; their first recital was in Prague, followed by Budapest and Sofia. In 1960 Ivan Kaloferov wrote to Tertis from Sofia: 'a great number of my friends here are familiar with your name and activities and some of them still remember your recital in Sofia in 1936.' Tertis was to have played in Bucharest, Cracow and Warsaw, but was taken ill with influenza, and was unable to play in these cities. Artur Rubinstein, who was staying in the same hotel, did much to cheer him up.

On 1 March 1936 the first public performance in England was given at a chamber concert arranged by the Cambridge University Musical Society of a Septet for viola, harp, flute, oboe, clarinet, bassoon and horn by Cyril Bradley Rootham.[1] Elizabeth Sprague Coolidge was the dedicatee, and the work's première was given at her festival at Pittsfield, Massachusetts in 1934. Each instrument in the Septet has an interesting part to play, though the viola is given an even more soloistic role – at the time of its composition Rootham had Tertis especially in mind.

Tertis gave two performances in Zurich at the Tonhalle, the first with the local orchestra conducted by Volkmar Andreae, in which he played Mozart's *Sinfonia concertante* (with the orchestra's concertmaster Willem de Boer), Berlioz's *Harold in Italy* and Walton's Viola Concerto, and the second with the BBC Symphony Orchestra under its principal conductor Adrian Boult, who was also at that time Director of Music for the BBC. Each programme included a British work. At the opening concert in Paris on 20 April Clifford Curzon was the pianist in Constant Lambert's *Rio Grande*; the following day in Zurich Tertis was the featured soloist in the Walton Concerto; the orchestra concluded the tour with concerts in Vienna and Budapest. The orchestra at the time had a number of Tertis's former students in the viola section, including Bernard Shore (principal), Winifred Copperwheat and, at the back, Gwynne Edwards. Shore wrote an article for the Royal College of Music magazine about the orchestra's European tour in 1936:

> On Tuesday 21st April the orchestra took an early train from Paris to Zurich. During the journey a heavy suit-case fell on Dr. Adrian Boult's head and the conductor who was cut and bruised lost consciousness for a few minutes. On arrival he saw a local doctor who agreed he was fit enough to conduct the evening concert. A short rehearsal was taken by the concert-master Arthur Catterall and Dr. Boult appeared at the evening concert which began with an overture by Busoni. The soloist was Lionel Tertis who played Walton's Viola Concerto so splendidly that he and the work received the greatest reception it has probably yet had.

A new generation of viola players came under Tertis's influence in the 1930s. Three of them, Sydney Errington, Paul Cropper and Harry Danks, became long-serving, distinguished principal violists: Errington and Cropper in Manchester (the Hallé and the BBC Northern, later renamed the BBC Philharmonic), Danks in London (BBC Symphony). Errington remembered many years later his introductory lesson at Tertis's house in Belmont, near Sutton in Surrey:

My first meeting with Tertis was rather 'fraught' – I managed to acquire a king-sized nose bleed just as I left the train at Belmont. I felt more than ridiculous, but before I knew where I was I was flat on the floor with cotton wool being stuffed up my nose! Having dried me out we started the lesson and I suffered (willingly) for two hours whilst he proved to me that I had no idea of true intonation; at the end of that time I believed him without reserve. I then met his charming wife who served us with afternoon tea. After the short interval we carried on with the lesson – this time he got on to my tone. I well remember him saying, 'Well, you make quite a pleasant sound but it's all "flautando" – you must work for your sound, don't sound like a poor fiddler'. We did other things; I remember him saying 'I don't mind if you bow with your foot – all I want to hear is a pure and lovely sound suspended in the air – the listener must only be conscious of that. No bow, no string, no resin – only the perfectly pure and poised note'. I felt like a wet rag at the end of all this (about three and a half hours) but he was as fresh as a daisy and he had been playing with me a lot of the time on his great 'Montagnana'. That concluded a most inspiring lesson. He took me a brisk walk over the downs and then dinner, after which he packed me off back to Leeds. Fee (as I was a young professional) 25 shillings!

Here, taken from Errington's notebook, are some of the things Tertis told him during this lesson:

1. Feel every note you are performing all the time. Doesn't like my vibrato but every quaver must live.

2. Try to eliminate the bow, the hair, the resin and the strings and go directly to the music. In other words sound – beautiful and pure all the time. (Doesn't like Hindemith or Milhaud).

3. Watch intonation all the time; never let a slipshod note go by – tone three times as great with perfect intonation! (I [S.E.] have a tendency to play sharp.)

4. Change position smoothly – no jerk or bump. That is more naturally. Bound up with this – change string smoothly also – quietly and at the last moment.

5. Never attack with a jerk unless for a special musical reason (avoid actual 'nut' noises).

6. Chordal playing – take time over bottom notes of chords – give them a chance to ring. Do not come over too violently and hold bow back at beginning of down stroke.

7. At end of many up-bows let bow and string 'breathe'.

8. Sliding   a) Never slide down (2 3) with second finger in cases as this, it leads to this general rule:– Descending slide in new bow with new finger. b) Ascending slide (as a general rule) with old finger when both notes are slurred. When notes are separate slide (if slide is required) with new finger.

9. Never 'pull off' bow at end of down bow – keep same speed to the end.

10. Change bow quietly.

Paul Cropper, who on his retirement from the BBC Philharmonic was awarded the MBE for services to the viola, remembers Tertis as teacher and performer:

> As it is more than sixty years since I had lessons from Tertis, many of the details have become blurred or forgotten, but the salient points remain as clear as ever. His kindliness, utter sincerity, also his supreme confidence in his convictions and yet, as with most truly great artists, his great humility, are the things I remember most about him as a man.
>
> As a teacher these great attributes were evident all the time, along with infinite patience. Tertis was immensely thorough and would not let the slightest technical or musical fault pass, and any faulty intonation, no matter how slight, was anathema to him. When I was studying the Brahms F minor Sonata, I was guilty of some faulty intonation. He finished off the lesson saying: 'Cropper, for your next lesson you must play the first page of this sonata with every note in tune, and if you do not, I never want to see you again.' Harsh treatment but it worked wonders.
>
> During the time I studied with Tertis he did not use any etudes, but had evolved a system of using various difficult technical parts of sonatas, concertos, solos, etc., in extended form as studies, which I have found very useful ever since.
>
> One of the main things I learnt was the importance of concentrated contact between bow hair and strings, especially for a 'penetrating' pianissimo.
>
> Another point, he spent a considerable amount of time working out

fingering for an expressive passage, sometimes very awkward to do, but nevertheless the most effective. It made me realise that many string players often use the easiest fingering, but not necessarily the best.

Perhaps one of the most important functions of a teacher is to make pupils work very hard – but without wasting time – and to give their best; this Tertis did as well as imparting all his musical and technical skill. So what more can I say? He was a great teacher.

Harry Danks, perhaps the longest-serving principal viola in a London orchestra, did more than any other to keep Tertis's name alive to the present day. In 1934 he first heard Tertis in a recital at the Central Hall, Birmingham. The Wesleyan Central Halls in most large cities in this country promoted a series of Saturday evening concerts which provided an opportunity to hear fine artists for the minimum cost. Admission to the hall was sixpence, and for this one heard a top soloist of the day supported by other artists.

In 1934 a two shilling piece made it possible for me to travel into Birmingham by train for nine pence, pay sixpence admission for the concert and still have enough change left over for a cup of tea; finances in those days did not permit anything stronger.

In the first part of the programme Lionel played the E flat Sonata of Brahms and in the second a group of his own transcriptions. One in particular I remember vividly to this day – Tambourin Chinois by Kreisler. He had transposed the dance a fifth down and adjusted the piano score so that not everything lay in the lower part of the keyboard. It was a revelation. Here was this small man playing on a large viola and producing the most lovely sound that I had ever heard from a string instrument. He had everything; beautiful sound, consistent intonation, fine technique and a lovely way of phrasing a melody. He was the complete musician and artist. I think he gave three encores, I certainly remember the Serenade from Hassan by Delius played muted; it was exquisite and my mind was made up. I had fallen completely under his spell, as so many before me had done, and nothing short of studying with him would do. It has proved to be one of the best decisions I ever made. Five minutes in his company, while he demonstrated the colour and range of the viola, and one was captive to his cause.

At that time my prospects and finances were nil; nevertheless I wrote to Lionel and explained the position. His reply was typical – he invited me to travel to his home and play to him, which I did, though it was November 18th 1935 before this could be arranged.

Tertis's fee to a professional player was £1 10s. 0d. but, having read Harry's letter, he reduced it to a guinea. Danks's memories of Tertis in the 1930s are as vivid as those of Eric Coates nearly thirty years previously:

> In those days he lived at Belmont near Sutton in Surrey which was quite a journey for me from the Midlands, but I was determined. I remember quite clearly how he received me at the front door; quiet and reserved and with an introduction to Mrs Tertis who immediately offered tea, which he postponed until the conclusion of the lesson. I discovered at later lessons how impatient he was to begin, but if it was a cold day he would insist that I put my hands in hot water. He was very strict and firm in all he said and did with the viola.
>
> I had prepared his own arrangement of the Elgar Cello Concerto, but before I was half way down the first page he attacked my poor intonation; in fact throughout the years that followed he never ceased to do this, and on a number of occasions brought me to a point of despair. He was relentless on this question of intonation and would always ask if I could hear the faulty notes, insisting that I test the offending cause against other notes. He had a system of cross checking one note with another, how to listen intently until the sound came over a complete circle of sound. He maintained that every note in tune had a 'round' sound to it. At one point I touched the piano to check the note which I apparently could not determine correctly; he was furious, and today with hindsight I now understand the situation – I was doubting his judgment. 'Never trust the piano, it is the one instrument that is never in tune' he bellowed at me. The whole lesson ... was spent in this fashion without let up on intonation, and at the end he was just as adamant and relentless as at the beginning. His parting remark was: 'You must believe me Danks or we cannot work together'.
>
> Every word that Lionel said, of course, was noted and remembered and sometimes it was good. Mostly it was bad for me, because he was a tremendous idealist. My intonation never satisfied him, my vibrato was always too quick and I was always sent home, running for the train, almost in tears, many, many, many times, but I don't regret a minute of it. Some lessons would consist from start to finish with this type of situation. Many years later I told Lionel of this; he was shocked and simply refused to believe that he had been so strict or that my intonation problems were so troublesome.
>
> From the first lesson I received from Tertis the dominating drive was 'work', regularly and constantly, with a will to continue despite difficulties and disappointments that appeared to surface once or twice a week. He

insisted upon this attitude and was relentless even to the point of severe criticism at the end of a miserable lesson, pointing out that my standards of playing were not improving, therefore there was no point in continuing unless I worked harder. I travelled back to the West Midlands a number of times with a lump in my throat.

Things eventually improved one day when a copy of the Vaughan Williams Suite slipped out of Danks's music case. Tertis picked it up and suggested that Danks play the Prelude; at the end Tertis congratulated him on a musical and well-thought-out reading and suggested he play through the Carol and Christmas Dance (with Tertis at the piano). Their relationship improved from this point onwards, and lessons continued until the outbreak of war in 1939, resuming on Danks's release from the army in 1946.

Again I remember most clearly the effect on me when he took up the Montagnana and played the pieces back to me; what a sound, what quality and warmth. I know there are many recordings available today of his artistry, and I have them, but somehow they do not give me the impression I have in my own mind of his sound, for me something is lost in the transmission to disc or tape. He could be almost overpowering when demonstrating at a lesson, but I never left his presence without believing in him completely.

Throughout his life Tertis supported the work of such bodies as the Musicians' Benevolent Fund, and often championed his fellow professionals and criticized the unfavourable conditions and contracts under which they had to work. He was one of the first to write to the *Daily Telegraph* in protest at Malcolm Sargent's comments that orchestral musicians should not have long-term contracts and pension schemes. Charles Reid, in his biography of Malcolm Sargent, takes up the story:

In June 1936 the *Daily Telegraph* carried an admirably reasoned article by Ferruccio Bonavia about retirement pensions for orchestral musicians. Bonavia had played among the Hallé violins during Hans Richter's day, and it was under Richter that the Hallé's pension scheme started. It was this scheme that he commended to other orchestras and patrons. During the weekend a reporter sought Sargent's opinion on the matter. 'Orchestral pensions? By all means', Sargent replied. He was a humanitarian and loved his fellow man with the best. But, he went on, there is a snag. As soon as a man thinks he is in his orchestral job for life, with a pension waiting for him at the end of it, he tends to lose something of his supreme fire. He ought to give of his lifeblood with every bar he plays. Directly a man gets blasé or does not give of his very best he ought to go. It sounds cruel, but it is for the good of the orchestra.' His tone was that of one who briskly retails the economic facts of life to softies who shy away from them or are too dim to take them in. 'In a general way', he concluded, 'he was in agreement with the idea of a pension scheme'; but the pensions should be on the basis of one-year contracts, renewed only if the musician retained his finest form, and payable 'only at the end of the musician's life, when he has poured out ungrudgingly his whole strength'.

Tertis raised the point that the orchestral player 'has a far harder job to tackle than formerly – too much to do and too little time in which to accomplish it'.

From the Royal College of Music and the Royal Academy of Music Sir Hugh Allen and Sir John McEwen wrote to the editor in grave deprecation. Tertis agreed with Sargent that the player should give of his lifeblood, and added that he was only willing to do so. 'But', he added 'some conductors reduce him to stone, and from a stone nobody can get blood.'

On 13 February 1936 Tertis was playing in Sidmouth, Devon. During this period he invented, for the improvement of wire strings, a small cushion which was put on the bridge under each string; any profits of the sale of these 'cushions' went to the Musicians' Benevolent Fund. The February issue of *The Strad* reported:

> We understand that the sales of the 'Tertis' Bridge Protector, for use with wire strings on the violin and viola, have been very encouraging to its sponsors, and this device, which is the invention of Mr. Lionel Tertis, the eminent viola player, will, it seems, take a permanent place, alongside the wire E string and string adjuster, the only innovations for the violin which have stood the test of time. As wire strings appear to have come to stay, however much the purists may object to them, any appliance that eliminates their less attractive qualities is assured of a ready sale.

On 1 December 1936 Tertis and Solomon gave a sonata recital at the Royal Academy of Music as part of a series of concerts and lectures between 30 November and 5 December. A report of the concert appeared in the *RAM Club Magazine* (no. 107), signed B. J. Dale:

> The sonata recital by Lionel Tertis and Solomon was an artistic event of the highest quality; it is not often that an opportunity occurs of hearing in one programme the two sonatas of Brahms, op. 120. Whether these works be better suited to the clarinet or viola is a matter on which opinions may differ; when played by Lionel Tertis, however, there can but be one opinion, and that is that this noble artist is the ideal exponent of

these productions of Brahms' mellow genius. And when Tertis has as his collaborator a magnificent pianist like Solomon, the occasion is one of those rare ones to which the epithet 'perfect' must be applied. This was an hour of great music, worthily performed. The variations by Beethoven on a theme from 'The Magic Flute', played between the two sonatas, are the kind of thing which may, often enough, prove embarrassing to the Beethoven-lover. As played by Tertis and Solomon they sounded like a piece of inspired fooling and made an admirable foil to the glowing strains of Brahms' lovely works.

In the BBC archives there is a memo written on 27 January 1937 by Kenneth Wright to Julian Herbage concerning the BBC Symphony concert draft of 1936–7: 'Have we considered the alternative of inviting William Primrose to produce Walton's new version of his Viola Concerto instead of repeating Tertis in the old one?'

During the mid-1930s Tertis was afflicted by acute fibrositis in his right arm which had been affecting his bowing. He had discussed this problem in confidence with his colleague Albert Sammons, but he gradually had to reduce his repertoire. This major problem caused him much mental anguish, and he decided, without telling anyone, that his last public performance would be at a concert on 24 February 1937 for which he had been engaged by the BBC, in celebration of his sixtieth birthday (29 December 1936) to play both the Walton Concerto and *Harold in Italy*. After the Berlioz he collected his belongings, and without a word to anyone, even the conductor Ernest Ansermet, left the hall in a state of shock. The following review appeared next day in the *Daily Telegraph*:

Lionel Tertis on his 60th Birthday by F. Bonavia

… Mr. Tertis excels where most virtuosos fail; he is a master of the art which, when good reason is shown, can conceal itself. Music comes first with him. Whether it be instinct with high spirits, as in the second movement of William Walton's concerto, or imbued with the gentle melancholy of 'Harold', Mr. Tertis does not stand outside, but collaborates with the orchestra.

Some credit for the incomparable performance of 'Harold' must go to Mr. Ansermet, whose keen sense of orchestral colour was well employed in the two compositions with viola and whose just tempos did not allow us to feel that the Pilgrims' March is too long.

But one had the impression that the loveliness of the tone produced by the soloist was bound to have an effect on the orchestral players. There is so little power and so little brilliancy in the viola that the only way to persuade or subdue is the best and the infallible – sheer beauty of tone. The delicacy of the arpeggios which conclude the Pilgrims' March took one's breath away; it was matched by orchestral sounds which were just a distant shimmer.

The following personal reminiscence by Carl F. Flesch was shared with the author in 1999:

> In the 1930s, as a budding insurance broker, I had access to many musicians through my father, Carl Flesch, and Tertis was one of my clients for personal accident insurance. I found him a particularly nice and unassuming man considering his position, but the point I want to make is that he had to give up his playing career comparatively early due to, I forget whether it was rheumatism or arthritis. What struck me at the time was the philosophical uncomplaining attitude he adopted in the face of something which is obviously a calamity for any performing musician. Young though I was, I found it most impressive and it has stayed in my memory.

Tertis explained his retirement in a letter published in the *Daily Telegraph* on 27 February 1937:

> For some time I have been seriously handicapped with rheumatic trouble in my bowing arm. Lately it has deprived me of an essential part of my equipment – spiccato playing, without which no string player has a right to go on. My repertory has in consequence been curtailed. I do not wish to continue until the deterioration in my playing becomes apparent especially in view of my propaganda on behalf of the viola. It is futile at my age to think of a long rest from playing, with the eventual hope of attempting a 'come back'.
>
> I therefore deem it wiser to give up playing before it gives me up. And so tonight's BBC concert must be my final appearance. Needless to say that it is a wrench to sever myself from the music profession, in which I have been especially fortunate in my privilege of working for the viola as a solo instrument.
>
> This is my opportunity to express my gratitude to our English composers, who have so generously provided the world's best library for solo viola players; and at the same time my thanks to The Daily Telegraph for its never-failing readiness to give publicity to this hitherto neglected instrument.
>
> If you can see your way to publish this 'obituary notice' of mine, it will make my position so much easier in explaining the situation to my colleagues and the public.

No one who attended the concert had a suspicion of Tertis's decision. On Thursday morning the *Daily Telegraph* said:

> Viola playing of the kind we had heard from him last night has not been heard in this or any country before …
>
> It is understood that Mr Tertis's decision is irrevocable. He played the viola for the last time on Wednesday. He will not touch his instrument again.

On 27 February the *Evening News* reported Tertis as saying:

> I suppose I can claim that my campaign was a success, for plenty of fine modern composers have written for the viola, and there are now fine viola players to carry on.
>
> It is a great thing to feel there are artists like Bernard Shore and William Primrose to carry on after me. My one immediate regret is that I shall never play the Romantic Phantasy for violin and viola which I persuaded Arthur Benjamin to compose. He has finished it and I like it enormously. I was to have given it a first performance on April 4th. Somebody else will have to do that now, and the one thing that has been a great comfort and, frankly, an enormous surprise to me, has been the general interest that seems to have been aroused by my announcement today of my retirement. I had no idea that people cared so much.

Two reviews appeared in the *Musical Times* on 1 March; here is an extract from one of them:

> We did not know when we were listening with unbounded admiration to Lionel Tertis at the BBC concert that the event marked not only his sixtieth birthday but also his farewell to the public. It was evident that something had happened to give him greater determination. Wonderfully as he had played before, even Tertis has never played as he did then. Regrettable as his decision to retire must be, it is yet good to think that we shall always remember him as we last heard him – a performer whose genius surpassed that of any other violist of his time, whose playing could inspire a whole orchestra.
>
> For the BBC Orchestra, too, surpassed itself on this occasion – as happens when a soloist's conception of a piece of music is of such excellence that it rouses and stimulates his critical, sceptical colleagues of the orchestra. William Walton's Concerto and Berlioz's Harold in Italy were played then as they probably have never been played before. Certainly never before has the viola proved so conclusively its claim as a solo instrument.

Its tone matched or contrasted with orchestral tone in perfection; it was the tone composers must have dreamt of and, in all probability, despaired of hearing – soft yet penetrating, imbued with a natural nobility, exquisitely delicate and at the same time capable of 'standing up' against the orchestra. It is hard to think that we shall not hear him again in the Mozart Concertante or in the two great works which he chose to conclude his career. But it must be admitted that this parting was well made.

Tertis received the following letter from William Walton on 12 March:

My dear Lionel,

I have delayed writing to you until settled down in a quiet place, for I really want to tell you how very sad I was to read of your retirement.

I am glad that I did not know that we were hearing you play my concerto for the last time the other night. It was one of the most moving performances that has ever been given of it. I rushed round to try and see you afterwards; unfortunately but understandably you had already left.

You must know how very grateful I am to [you] for the care and trouble you have always taken with this work; – it is indeed entirely owing to you that it has become more or less well-known.

You will realise with us all what your retirement means to music, but I do not question that your judgement in this, is the best; and I cannot but admire the courage which must [have] been entailed in making this dreadful decision.

Your playing will always remain one of my most cherished and delightful memories. ...

I am Yours ever William Walton

William Primrose wrote to Tertis on 23 March from the Lotos Club, New York:

It is with the greatest consternation that I read of your retirement. This is indeed a decision that I sincerely trust you will reverse before long. There is really too great a dearth of fine musicians – and especially violists – for the public and your colleagues to lose you. Everyone over here is most surprised.

If it is your irrevocable decision then my very best and warmest good wishes go with you, and my heartfelt thanks and deepest gratitude too, for all you have done for me. Please believe that anything I may do in the future will be 'l'hommage au grand maître'. I am sure I voice the feelings of all your disciples and admirers.

Tertis later wrote:

> I was touched by receiving two letters, one from the viola section of the BBC Orchestra and the other from the principals of the sections. The first was signed by Bernard Shore, Philip P. Sainton, Eric Bray, Anne Wolfe, Mary Gladden, Norman Carrell, L. S. Southworth, Winifred Copperwheat, Hugh Wyand, Patience Lucas, G. H. Knowles, Gwynne Edwards and Muriel Hart.

The other letter ran:

> It was a great shock for us to read of your retirement after our concert together, which was for us, ignorant of the decision you already must have made, one of the finest concerts we have ever given with you. We feel proud that your last concert should have been shared with us, and we realise now that we have lost not only a great artist but a great friend. Paul Beard, Archie Camden, Ernest Hall, Ambrose Gauntlett, E. W. Hinchcliff, Sidonie Goossens.

From about 1913 until 1937 the Tertises lived at 'Smalldown', 63 The Crescent, Belmont. When they moved in, the house was third on the right after Belmont Rise as you approached The Crescent from the station. In fact, it was not until the 1930s that Belmont Rise was cut through as a bypass road avoiding the village. It would appear that several of their neighbours' houses must have gone in the development, leaving 'Smalldown' and one or two other houses isolated on the far side.

After Lionel's retirement the Tertises went to live in Broadstairs, from where he travelled to London two or three times a week to teach. *The Strad* in May 1937 wrote: 'After his retirement Lionel Tertis's celebrated viola, a Montagnana, dated 1717, and measuring 17⅛ inches, was acquired by Bernard Shore of the BBC Orchestra. This magnificent toned instrument is in a wonderful state of preservation and has a rich orange-red varnish.' On Shore's death the instrument passed to his former student Roger Chase.

Tertis taught for some time without an instrument, but felt frustrated not being able to demonstrate, and eventually, breaking his resolution, he borrowed a viola from Eric Coates, and his interest was rekindled. Coates had never lost touch with Tertis since his student days, and they became very good friends.

Tertis was moved to receive a letter from Albert Sammons, William Murdoch and Robert Mayer informing him that a dinner was to be given in his honour at Pagani's restaurant on 13 June 1937. Virtually every well-known musician of the time attended or sent their good wishes by letter or telegram. Robert Mayer received the following letter from Ernest Ansermet on 11 June:

> Hotel Kurhaus, Scheveningen
> I am extremely sorry not to be able to join you and the numerous friends and admirers of Lionel Tertis at the dinner given in his honour and I would be very much obliged if you would bring to your guest the expression of my fervent admiration and my sincerest respect. I had the honour and the good luck of accompanying him, last February, the day of his sixtieth anniversary, and it was the occasion for me, of an unforgettable perform-ance of Harold in Italy and a no less enjoyable performance of the Walton's Concerto [*sic*]. To those who heard Lionel Tertis that night, it is hard to believe to his retirement [*sic*] as he showed himself in the full mastery of his art, and I sincerely hope it was not the last time I could hear or accom-pany him.
>
> Anyhow, let me take the opportunity of your meeting for expressing the view which is surely that of many foreign friends of Lionel Tertis. The viola sections of the British orchestras are, to my mind, the best in the world and Lionel Tertis is the highest representative of this tradition of your instrumental school – which had, as an indirect result, the produc-tion of the part of the British composers, of the best works ever written for this particular instrument. I had the pleasure of introducing Lionel Tertis in my concerts in Switzerland and this experience made our audi-ence conscious of that double fact! The fame of the British school of violas and the personal significance of Lionel Tertis as a Casals of the viola. Let me believe that Tertis will enjoy still and for a long time the results of his admirable achievements and with my kindest regards, I remain
>
> Yours very sincerely,
>
> E. Ansermet

There were effusive tributes in the speeches after the dinner. The conduc-tor, composer and former violinist Eugène Goossens, who spoke first, said that he had come not to bury Tertis but to praise him. He recalled the early days when Benjamin Dale and York Bowen had composed works for Tertis, and how later practically all the greatest English composers had followed this lead. He mentioned one of his earliest associations with Tertis, when he conducted the concert that included the first performance of Bloch's Suite. On receiving the news of Tertis's retirement he said that all the troubles he had been expe-riencing of floods in Cincinnati, cancelled performances and so on paled into insignificance. He and Tertis had been friends for nearly thirty years, and had been loyal to each other except once when Tertis had asked him to write a work for him.[2] After four attempts he finally tore it up; but now all he asked was to be allowed to write another work and have the pleasure of hearing Tertis play it. He begged Tertis to resume his career.

Bernard Shore was proud to be a pupil and an intense admirer of Tertis, but valued above all their great friendship. He wished to acknowledge in public the great debt of gratitude he owed to Tertis, who, many years before, had promised that when he retired he would give Shore the first offer of his instrument. In spite of offers far greater, Tertis kept his word like a gentleman, and had passed the instrument on to him. In addition, he had included his unique library of music. Shore insisted that this was only being held in trust for Tertis, should he ever want to use it again. 'Please Heaven, may that day come soon!' He remarked on the inspiration which all Tertis's pupils had gained on their visits to Smalldown, and how Tertis gave everything he knew to his pupils, holding nothing back. He was still the world's supreme viola player, as his final performance at Queen's Hall had shown. Like all great artists, he was never satisfied with his playing, and in this respect a great deal was due to Mrs Tertis, who, at all hours of the day, might be called upon to give her opinion as to the most successful way of playing a certain passage. He paid a great tribute to her unswerving faith in her husband. His retirement was the brave step of a burning idealist. He hoped he would resume his teaching which he, from personal experience, knew to be even better now than ever. He wished Tertis 'good luck and happiness; and if you will, play to us again!'

Vaughan Williams told the story of how, having written a few small pieces for Tertis, he invited him down to play them over. Unable to find an accompanist, he had to play himself. As though this were not bad enough, they found that his miserable piano was half a tone flat. Tertis tuned down, set to work and after following the accompanist right through, apologized for his own shortcomings. The golden tones, passionate utterances and wonderful phrasing would always remain in the memory of those who had heard him, and even those who had not would live richer lives because Tertis had played, perhaps even before they were born. A beautiful thing, once created, remained with us for ever, in spite of the follies of all times.

Sir Thomas Beecham then spoke of the highly emotional and perfectly justifiable speeches that had been made on Tertis's retirement. He wished to paint another picture of his recollections of Lionel, and to touch on another which had received less attention. He spoke as a conductor. It was impossible to realize what the viola section of an orchestra was like when he started as a very young man. They were the despair of conductors, the diversion of the audience and the perpetual exasperation of the press, or at least of that section of the press which knew what a viola was. Then this worker of miracles appeared on the scene. How he did it, no one knows; but the fact that the whole balance of the modern orchestra was rectified was due from A to Z to Tertis. He had heard the long and justified praise bestowed on him as a virtuoso; but when the history of music here and abroad came to be written, this saving of the orchestra's 'distressed area' would be recognised as his greatest achievement. This was an imperishable contribution, by means of which he would be as well known as Queen Victoria, Gladstone, Casanova and any other historical figure. You cannot, he said, discern anything of Tertis's personal life from the tranquil façade of his face. He had wandered all over the world with this mysterious instrument, and knew every little town between London and Odessa. He had even played English music everywhere, but was still alive! He had been a rowdy, uproarious young bounder, unequalled in Chicago or Cincinnati. He recalled their early exploits on the football field, in hotels and railway stations and, in particular, one occasion when in company with Waldo Warner and Warwick Evans he had left the train and proceeded to uncouple the engine, to the subsequent amazement of the officials. The romantic side of his nature was a closed book to the present generation.

William Murdoch said that he wished to consider Tertis's career from another angle. The sudden and apparently irrevocable decision came as an even greater surprise to the members of The Chamber Music Players than to the public. Tertis had given them no inkling of his retirement. Their combination had worked together for the best part of twenty-two years. He described the personal blow on hearing from Tertis that their joy of music-making was so soon to cease. It was not easy to reconcile oneself to the loss of a companion; doubly difficult for a combination apparently as strong as the Rock of Gibraltar. They would probably not continue, as Lauri Kennedy was going abroad, and it required too much courage to make a fresh start at this stage. He would never forget the hundreds of hours spent with Lionel, working and fooling. For they did fool, although this facet of Tertis's make-up was not so well known. Serious musicians were not always serious, and many people would have been amazed, had they been present at one of their rehearsals, to see Tertis so hilarious that he couldn't play a note. Sammons was not only the leader but the ringleader, and sins at rehearsal were due to him. Once some musical point appealed to their sense of humour anything might happen. He was glad to see Felix Salmond present. He had been Albert's easiest victim, the ignition jet of his inspiration. He had often seen Felix twisted thrice round his instrument, sobbing with laughter, while Lionel rapidly caught the infection. But in spite of all this Tertis was always a serious artist, and was guilty of no deviation from sincerity and idealism. Art was his life and completely filled it. He had a splendid sense of concentration. He had confessed to the speaker that the happiest moments of his life were those filled with the laughter and work of The Chamber Music Players. 'This is true for us, as well as for him. If Lionel, in search of happiness, finds music once again a necessity, we and the public will welcome his return.' He then called upon his colleagues present – Felix Salmond, Lauri Kennedy and Albert Sammons – to rise and drink a toast to Tertis. Tertis then replied:

My advocacy of the viola was the result of accidental contact with the instrument about 44 years ago, when I at once realised its attractions and its undeserved neglect. It was as at that time the Ugly Duckling – barely tolerated – and however inadequate my efforts have been, I do take deep satisfaction in the fact that I was one of those who helped to rescue it from its invidious position. Of course this could not have been accomplished had it not been for our composers, who have provided the most extensive and the world's best library of solo viola music, for which viola players will ever feel the most intense gratitude.

Now I should like to make an explanation concerning the discontinuance of my work. I want to take this opportunity to try and remove a little scepticism which I know exists with regard to the cause of my retirement. I ask you all to believe me when I tell you that my resolution did not come about without good reason and mature thought.

For some two years I have had to resort to subterfuge to cover up the deficiencies in my playing. My colleague, Albert Sammons, will bear me out how some 18 months ago, in desperation, I sent him an SOS, and confessed to him the failing in my bowing technique which had come upon me. He tried all the tricks of the trade to overcome my difficulties, but without avail – and like the good friend he has ever been to me, he kept my secret.

The trouble rapidly reduced my repertory and the position became untenable. I ask you to accept this explanation of my action in retiring at the tender age of 60. I had quite hoped I was good enough for another five years, but I am sure you will agree with me that having preached the Gospel of the Viola for so many years, it was time to give up when I realised I could not entirely practise what I had preached. I found myself unable to give the viola my complete powers, such as they were, and my course became very clear. I felt I would rather renounce my calling than bring to it a hampered service.

I do not allow myself any pity. Indeed the pity would have been if I had gone on and made a mess of things. I alone know how little I have done. But I shall permit myself the joy of looking upon to-night's gathering as the seal of recognition of the viola as a solo instrument.

Telegrams sent by absent friends included tributes from Fritz Kreisler, William Walton, Arthur Schnabel, John Barbirolli and Joseph Szigeti. After the dinner Casals wrote to Tertis from Barcelona on 27 June (translated from French):

> My dear and much-admired colleague, I am sending you these few lines belatedly to congratulate you on the tribute which has been made to you by your friends, colleagues and admirers. I should have liked to be with you on this occasion to express, along with them, the sentiments that we feel for you, for the man and the artist. Only your decision to retire from your public upsets us all because this represents an irreparable loss to our art. We all hope that this good-bye will not prevent you returning from time to time. Forgive the delay but I would ask you to take into account the great preoccupations that absorb us all here.
>
> Your devoted, affectionate friend and colleague.
>
> Pau Casals

Messages of gratitude were also received from the members of the London Philharmonic Orchestra and the Royal Philharmonic Society.

At the end of the evening Tertis was presented with a book of signatures and a cheque. Among those present were: Sir Arnold Bax, Sir Adrian Boult, Harriet Cohen, Mrs Eugène Goossens, Julius Harrison, Ethel Hobday, Mr and Mrs Lauri Kennedy, Dr and Mrs Marchant, Mr and Mrs Robert Mayer, Mrs William Murdoch, Mr and Mrs Augustus Ralli, Mr and Mrs Felix Salmond, Mr and Mrs Albert Sammons, Dr and Mrs Sargent, Mrs Bernard Shore, Lady Maud Warrender, Mr Arthur Catterall, Mr B. J. Dale, Mr W. H. Reed.

One of the many thank-you letters Tertis wrote after the dinner was to his friend, the composer Vaughan Williams:

June 15th 1937

> My dear Ralph,
>
> How can I ever thank you for the more than generous things you said of me on Sunday. I am indeed a fortunate man. Coming from you, it will be a never ending source of gratification. I shall try not to be a useless hulk for the rest of my days, and perhaps in some way or other will hope to be of service to the musical profession.
>
> Excuse this very inadequate expression of gratitude to you, not only for Sunday, but for all you have done for me. The reaction of Sunday has reduced me to pulp.
>
> May I send my love to you both.
>
> Lionel.

Tertis wrote again to Vaughan Williams on 15 September, after hearing his Fourth Symphony on the radio the previous evening relayed from a Prom concert at Queen's Hall:

> My dear Ralph,
> Unfortunately we get a lot of interference on 'National', and we were horribly disappointed not to be able to hear the first part in comfort but thank goodness it was much better when you came on to conduct your symphony. It is a great master work and gets bigger every time I hear it. Thank you for the intense enjoyment we had. I have not been entirely idle – I have written a little book for string players on expressive tone quality, and shall be going to town one day a fortnight for eight hours teaching to eight professional violists! We hope you and Mrs Vaughan Williams are well and send our kindest rememberances [*sic*].
>
> Ever yours, Lionel
> Don't please trouble to answer this.

In the autumn of 1937 Frederick Riddle, then principal viola in the London Symphony Orchestra, received a telephone call from Tertis, who suggested he learn the Walton Concerto; and within a short time he was invited to record it on the Decca label with the LSO and the composer conducting. It seems likely that Walton had first asked Tertis to make the recording, but the unexpected retirement of the composer's favourite interpreter of his Concerto deprived future generations of hearing Tertis's reading. Happily Riddle rose to the challenge: his wonderful recording is still the benchmark against which all others are judged, and even after sixty years is still probably the best.

In an interview some thirty years after his retirement, Tertis took his mind back to that bleak year of 1937:

> ... after I gave up I ran amok, you know, at the dreadful disappointment of having to chuck up my profession when I was only sixty years old, which was the prime of life, and I went to live at a number of addresses all over the country, I couldn't rest anywhere and eventually I thought to myself, 'Well, I'll go and get as near as I can to Arthur Richardson, and start on the project of designing a viola' and we went to live in Bath; as I remember I used to go by car all the way to Crediton and back in the same day ... We talked a lot about it, and eventually he sent me a viola made according to my theories, which he'd put into practice.

❧ 10 ❧

The Richardson–Tertis Viola

Arthur Richardson and the R.T. Viola – orchestral playing in the UK
– working with Beecham – 'Beauty of Tone in String Playing'

WHATEVER Lionel Tertis did during his long and active life, he always gave everything to his task, and became impatient with others who, in his perception, did not have the same commitment and dedication. This trait sometimes led to misunderstandings and tensions that caused a strain on a friendship or a working relationship. A typical example was Tertis's association with the luthier Arthur Richardson of Crediton, Devon, a relationship in which passions on both sides often ran high. Now that the dust has settled on the disputes and disagreements, it can be seen that Tertis initiated a major contribution to the development of the instrument which in his words was 'the love and tyrant of my life'.

The viola is an inherently unstable instrument: if it were to be built in proportion to the violin and cello, it would be too big to play under the chin. Tertis used to say that if he could have his time again, he would play it cello-fashion, with the body of the instrument resting on his thighs. But as it was, he had to take the viola as he found it, and he spent much of his long life pondering what its ideal size and shape should be. He was always obsessed with having a good C-string sound at his disposal, and would have no truck with anyone who played a small viola.

Soon after he and Ada moved to Bath, he contacted Richardson about his ideas for a 'new' viola, and their great collaboration began. His wish was to develop an instrument large enough to produce a sonorous tone, yet with a manageable shape for ease of handling. He threw himself into the quest for the perfect size and sound with that single-minded enthusiasm of which he alone was capable. The collaboration was to secure Richardson's income for the rest of his life – at the cost, sometimes, of his peace of mind.

Arthur Richardson was born in Staveley, Derbyshire, in 1882. He started making violins in 1914 while he was living in Leeds and working as an ecclesiastical wood carver. In an essay written specially for this book, with the help of the late Ronald Roberts of Exeter, a luthier who worked with Richardson and author of *Making a Simple Violin and Viola*, Andrew Bellis continues Richardson's story:

He and his wife moved to Crediton in Devon after he had travelled to the area for a fortnight to collect some new gouges from a respected tool-maker near Exeter; they probably fell in love with the area, where the Richardsons lived for the rest of their lives. Carving and violin making were partners in the early days at the cottage (now demolished) in Park Street, but Arthur soon found fame as a luthier when he won first prize in the Cobbett Competition, London, for the best toned modern violins in 1919 ... In 1923 he was again a prizewinner but this time for a quartet of instruments, showing that by then he had made at least one viola (the quartet viola is dated 1921).

In a short biographical article about her father for the *Viola Research Society Newsletter* of 14 May 1981 Marjorie Baker wrote:

Leeds had an excellent library with a good section on Instruments which my father read avidly. It was the fine book by Hills, 'Antonio Stradivari, his Life and Work', which really captured his interest and on which he based all his future work. He was fascinated by the chapter dealing with Stradi-varius's development of the violin after the death of Amati when he began to work on his own account. ... Before ever making a musical instrument Richardson had taken many notes on the state of viola development and had earmarked this as a subject for exploration. However, the first instru-ments he made were violins and these were produced in sparetime hours on the kitchen table. Two were made in Leeds in 1914 and all subsequent instruments were made at Crediton in Devon ...

Early in 1937 Tertis retired from the concert platform ... [He] had the desire to develop a viola of a size large enough to give a sonorous viola tone and at the same time of a suitable shape to provide ease of handling. His intense energies ... were now diverted into perfecting the instrument itself. In Richardson he found the man with the skill and enthusiasm to join him in the task. My father was able to provide the knowledge of construction, design and measurements and Tertis the advice on tonal requirements and ease of handling. A period of great activity followed. My father was at work designing and constructing new violas. Whenever one was ready for playing, Tertis would come and give his opinion on tone and playability. The instruments were often opened up, readjustments made, and careful notes taken for future reference. Gradually a model evolved which went far towards satisfying the required qualities of tone, balance and ease of playing. During the next three years my father had only com-pleted ten instruments and his livelihood suffered a temporary setback accordingly.

The November 1939 issue of *The Strad* reprinted a letter from Richardson in which he explained the reasoning behind the development of the Richardson–Tertis Model:

> In the early days violas were made on a generous model. The Gasparo da Salo and early Amati violas were about 18" in length of body. These large violas proved distinctly unwieldy, and an opposite fashion set in and for a long time so-called small violas of from 15" upwards were produced which were in fact neither violins or violas and could not produce a semblance of real C string tone.
>
> In the last forty years a tendency to a more standardised viola has developed, thanks entirely to the propaganda and efforts of the celebrated viola soloist, Lionel Tertis, whose performances have done so much to draw attention to the quality of tone to be desired on the viola.
>
> As is well known, his viola by Montagnana was an instrument of 17⅛" in length and of generous dimensions in width and depth. From the playing point of view, perhaps a little difficult to handle, which only a virtuoso could overcome. Mr. Tertis ... conceived the idea that a viola could be designed, rather less in length, which would give greater ease and facility to the player, and at the same time possess a tone near to the ideal.
>
> To this end I have collaborated with Mr. Tertis and we have designed a viola of 16¾", the other dimensions in some respects similar to the full model of Montagnana, but having several new features to give a real viola tone and at the same time with a view of giving ease of manipulation.
>
> The scroll is of ordinary violin type, the angle of the neck and the arrangement of the fingerboard is such that very high notes on the instrument can be reached with comparative ease, enabling the player to cope with the difficulties of the most advanced technique. There are other special features which serve to eliminate undue weight for the left hand.

The Richardson family found Tertis very charming and friendly in their home, but he was a difficult man to work with, liable to explode in an alarming way. No doubt he was frustrated by having to rely on an intermediary to realize his designs physically in wood; but his outbursts deeply upset Richardson, who, like many dedicated craftsmen, was essentially a quiet, contemplative man. Marjorie Baker wrote: 'My mother, fearing for my father's health and livelihood, unavailingly begged my father to have nothing more to do with Tertis.'

A number of people have commented on periods of coolness between the two men and their many disagreements and misunderstandings. Marjorie Baker continues:

Basically, these differences arose because Tertis was not a practical man ... Although a perfectionist and genius in his playing, Tertis could not grasp the artistry of the maker's craft and the varying characteristics of timber. He thought it would be possible to produce drawings and measurements of an instrument to be strictly adhered to in the making, so that violas could be churned out like so many motor cars. My father, artist as he was, and always true to his ideas, would have nothing to do with this. Until this time the new-type violas had been labelled 'R.T.' (Richardson–Tertis) followed by the number. Tertis, without my father's knowledge, went to Lovett Gill with one of my father's instruments and got him to make drawings of it. These were printed and labelled simply 'Tertis Model'; the *Richardson* had been left out. Our family were up in arms at such injustice and at such underhand and unprofessional behaviour, but my father, although deeply hurt, was not interested in the advancement of his own finances or of his own image. He continued to make and experiment on instruments, both large and small, being only interested in musical instruments and music. ...

The total output of Richardson instruments, 526 in all, included 177 large violas, 30 smaller violas, 291 violins and 28 cellos. In 1961 Arthur Richardson was awarded the MBE for his services to music. Undoubtedly his outstanding contribution to music was his share in the creation of the larger R.T. model violas, which marked the most notable piece of original thinking in this field since the time of the later Italian masters of the 17th and 18th centuries.

But the Richardson model violas and the 'Tertis Model' instruments based on Lovett Gill's drawings were not the same. Andrew Bellis in his account described the distinction between the two:

All the instruments that Richardson made to his design were labelled Richardson–Tertis, or R.T., violas. When Tertis published what he thought was 'an accurate and detailed' viola plan (in 1950) the title had changed to 'The "Tertis model" Viola' ... Tertis had taken a Richardson viola to the architect Charles Lovett Gill ... and it was his plan that was the published and widely distributed one. But there is the difference ... the Gill drawing is not of a Richardson–Tertis model. There are several minor differences but one big one that first made me aware that there must be a story behind the two viola drawings. ... The main fault is in the string length of the Gill viola. Arthur Richardson knew that viola strings were made to perfectly suit an instrument having a string length of (in modern metric) 370 mm, under which conditions they would be correctly tensioned at modern pitch. Remember that the viola is a problem instrument anyway, in that the strings have to be fatter than they should be because the viola – even the largest model held under the chin – is too small for its pitch. The vibrating length of 370 mm is to this day the standard to the firm of Gustav Pirazzi who make Pirastro strings. Richardson put this string length on to his design which ensured that most players would find it comfortable, then he combined the outline of the Montagnana viola with the arching of the Maggini and careful development (with Tertis always willing to try the latest advancement) took care of the rest. On the Gill drawing, the string length increases to fifteen and three-sixteenths inches which is 386 mm, and means that for the same pitch the strings are now under increased tension. Richardson suggested Pirastro covered (apart from the A) gut strings, even stipulating the gauges (they are as a modern player would use apart from the D which is unusually thick ...) but by 1950 Tertis is advocating metal strings for the viola. Overstretching them may make a brighter sound at the expense of tone but the increase in string length, to me, renders the already large instrument unplayable. There are small remarks on the Gill drawing reproduced at the back of Tertis's first autobiography *Cinderella No More* saying 'revised May 1949 – further improved 1950'. I suggest that by making these 'improvements' Tertis took a perfectly good instrument – designed with great care by a perfectionist – and ruined it, in the process producing the exact opposite of his original idea. Since about 1970 it has been next to impossible to sell a 'Tertis Model' viola, but those 'in the know' who possess 'R.T.' violas (especially the early ones, I am told) are quite happy with them. There should be, barring terminal accidents, 178 'R.T.' violas made by Arthur Richardson in existence – not 177 as his daughter writes; Ronald Roberts, who assisted the luthier as his strength declined, remembered the making of number 178. ...

Tertis was honest and straightforward to the point of bluntness, and this trait did not endear him to some people. Those who knew him well spoke of him as a personality of infinite warmth, humour and affection. As a self-made musician, he had clear-cut ideas of what he liked or disliked at any one time, but he was constantly evaluating and reconsidering those ideas. His obsession with the R.T. viola brought out the best and the worst in him.

On visiting Glyndebourne in 1938, he showed R.T. Viola no. 4, which was unvarnished and packed in straw, to the London Symphony Orchestra's principal viola, Max Gilbert, who played on the instrument during the opera performance that evening. Gilbert overheard a lady in the audience say, 'Look darling, he's playing a nude violin!' – a reference to Noël Coward's currently popular play *Nude with Violin*.

Tertis asked the members of the LSO viola section if any of them played one of his violas. No one did and Tertis asked: 'Why?' Max Gilbert replied that when a diminuendo was played on an R.T. instrument there came a point where the sound suddenly disappeared. Tertis never spoke to him again. As it turned out, Winifred Copperwheat was to play on this very viola, R.T.4, for the rest of her career. In her article in *An Anthology of Viola Players*, she summarized its advantages:

> Owing to the fact that these new measurements have emanated from an executive artist, it is not surprising to learn that the 'player' has been very specially considered. For instance, the angle at which the neck has been set helps the player to reach the upper positions with greater ease; the weight of the instrument has been reduced to a minimum, having regard to its durability, and this greatly relieves the strain ...
>
> The special virtues of these instruments from the listener's point of view are the sonority and depth, especially of the beautiful C string, the wide range of dynamics, the clarity above the fifth position on all the strings – a weak spot on most violas – and the ready response both to speed and expression. A feature of this viola is its ability to cut through or stand out from an orchestra, with a true solo quality – an attribute which, up to now, has been missing in very many violas – and which in no way affects its natural characteristic of merging into the general harmony when desired. For this reason these violas are equally good as solo or chamber music instruments.

It has come to light that Tertis was also frustrated by the many inaccuracies in the Lovett Gill plans for the Tertis Model. A large correspondence survives between Tertis and George H. Smith of 12 Sewell Road, Norwich, who made violins, violas and cellos on an amateur basis from 1943. The letters show that Smith became variably and often quite intensively involved with some aspects of the evolving Tertis Model viola between 1945 and 1953. He produced some good instruments, and one of his violas was awarded a prize at the International Luthiers Competition in The Hague in 1949. Perhaps his greatest contribution to the Tertis Model viola related to his draughtsmanship and in producing a fine revised drawing which in Tertis's mind superseded those by Richardson and Lovett Gill, the latter of whose drawings received criticism from makers throughout the world for errors and carelessness.

George H. Smith's early career was in the shipyards, and from 1924 to 1964 he worked for the building firm of Boulton & Paul in Norwich. In 1928, after four years as a template-maker, he became a leading structural draughtsman; this involved him in working in the firm's London office. After the Second

World War he formed a training drawing office. In early 1945 the editor of *The Strad* suggested to Tertis that Smith might be willing to make a set of working drawings of the Tertis Model viola. Tertis wrote to Smith on 31 March 1945, suggesting that they met in London to discuss the matter. Three years later he wrote to Smith telling him that he would send him the drawings of the viola he had designed and asked 'meanwhile, I should be glad to know if you have sufficient really good wood to make the instrument. The size necessary for back and front being approximately 17½" to 18" – cut on the quarter.' Tertis sent a copy of the diagram to Smith on 24 April 1948.

The correspondence continued on 14 July 1948: Tertis told Smith of an important advance in the design of his model – a new neck length – and went on: 'Please also let me know how you progress and if it is at all possible for you I should much like to see the viola when it is finished – in the white.' On 30 July he added: '... the only thing I beg of you is to try and stick to the thickness and specifications as meticulously as possible and don't forget the new neck length.'

On 27 August 1948 Smith brought the new viola to Tertis's home. On 30 August Tertis wrote to him:

> ... There is one thing I forgot to discuss with you about the bass-bar. I think I told you that the bass-bar is a replica of the bar in my Montagnana viola, the dimensions and position of which were very successful after experiment. For a long time I have been thinking about this – from the point of view that the body length of the Montagnana is 17⅛" and the Tertis Model 16⅜" and therefore is our bar too heavy or deep?
>
> I have had this criticism from a maker in Norway who suggests the depth should not be more than 10 mm (a good ⅜"). As you mentioned that you had another piece of pine exactly like the top plate you have made, I am wondering whether you would be willing to try out this theory i.e. a lighter bass-bar? ... It seems to me a brilliant opportunity to have one with a heavier bar than the other. I have a feeling that the lighter bar would give us more resonance ...

In a further letter Tertis confirmed that the lighter bass-bar would be used in Smith's second viola, which was to be made from a piece of wood identical to that used for his first viola. Tertis went on '... but as you know, Lovett Gill's drawing is not absolutely accurate all through. One day perhaps I can persuade you to make me a diagram dead perfect! ... I think your idea of making the flutting [*sic*] deeper on your scroll is an improvement. There is plenty of time for the experimental bass-bar ...'

Smith produced a second viola which Tertis showed to one of the Voigt brothers. Tertis wrote to Smith after this meeting:

> I hasten to write to tell you that I have been to Voigt and directly he saw the back he exclaimed that one side was the wrong way up – which was the cause of one side appearing darker than the other according to the way you hold it.
>
> He proved it to me with two pieces of maple (in the white) when you split the wood you must be careful to keep them both in the same position (top to top and bottom to bottom) – if you turn one side upside down, you will see that one side appears darker than the other – ... even though the grain runs up just the same, and he says no amount of varnishing will put the matter right. He thought the pine was excellent and pleased with the tone ... They are such nice fellows – these brothers ...

The Voigt brothers were well-known British makers and restorers, from a family of violin-makers dating back to 1699, with a shop in Monmouth Street, Cambridge Circus, London. Their Tertis Model Viola was advertised in *The Strad* in 1950. Later, however, the Voigt brothers upset Tertis by designing a modified viola. Tertis was keen for George Smith to meet both the Voigts and Arthur Richardson, and to compare his first viola with the latter's instruments. Tertis had been very complimentary about the tone quality of Smith's viola when he had tested it in Norwich; having tried it out at his home for a few days he was more critical in a letter dated 23 September 1948, and put this down to Smith's not keeping to the exact thicknesses in the Tertis Model diagram.

A letter of 2 November 1948 complained further about the Lovett Gill drawing:

> The diagram is so full of inaccuracies, which is constantly being rubbed into me – (I have just had another complaint, this time from Paris, about the bass-bar) that I am beginning to feel rather sore about it, that Gill should have been so careless (this in confidence). My specification is in order and as Voigt has said to me, it is rather confusing for one thing (the specification) to say something different to the drawing.
>
> I am therefore writing to ask you whether you would undertake a diagram for me which I know would be accurate from you. The trouble is that I cannot contemplate any further great expense on my project (having been at it for eleven years), but if you could see your way to doing it for a nominal fee I should be grateful. My idea then would be to send it all over the world again to those makers who have received the faulty drawings.

It might be a good thing, also, to send it to the International Competition in Holland, as publicity.

Let me know if you think it possible for you to do this for me, and your lowest fee for the work.

By 1950 the correspondence had gone quiet. Bernard Shore wrote to Smith on 21 June 1950 to say how impressed he was with his viola and continued:

> I am sorry that Lionel Tertis seems to have cooled off as I should have thought that he would take considerable interest in these instruments ... You should also know that he has now slightly altered his measurements for the stop, and these have made remarkable differences in resonance due to slight differences in length of string.

Smith eventually completed his drawing in November 1953, and soon after that, the correspondence came to an end. Tertis then took an interest in another fine young professional maker, Wilfred G. Saunders of Nottingham (see Chapters 11 and 12).

Meanwhile letters of appreciation over the Tertis Model viola were coming in from Continental players. French violist Robert Boulay, professor of viola at the Paris Conservatoire, wrote from his home in Boulogne on 26 May 1949:

> My dear Maître,
>
> I am writing to you, not without emotion, you whom the violists of the entire world know and admire. But I think that they can also thank you when they know the viola built according to your design. I had already appreciated the exceptional qualities of a 'Tertis model' instrument in Edinburgh in August 1947, but since Mr. Vatelot, a Paris violin maker, was good enough to lend me one of the instruments made by him for a pupil of mine I have been filled with enthusiasm.
>
> This instrument has an incomparable fullness of tone on the lower strings, which are often so weak in the majority of violas, and thanks to the short length of stop it is playable by all violists.
>
> My pupil has already this year gained two successes in competitions, which were largely due to the Lionel Tertis model viola, which is beginning to be much talked about in Paris.
>
> I have myself ordered one from M. Vatelot and several of my pupils will follow my example ...
>
> I assure you, dear Maître, of my profound gratitude and I sign myself Respectfully and devotedly yours,
>
> Robert Boulay

William Primrose summarized Tertis's contribution to viola design in *Playing the Viola: Conversations with William Primrose* by David Dalton:

> There is no easy way around the disproportionate size of the viola for the range that it has to play. Tertis tried somewhat successfully to overcome this difficulty, he having played on a monstrous instrument vis-à-vis his physical stature. He was not a weakling in any way, but he was a small man with proportionately small arms, and he played on his very large Montagnana for years until the physical price exacted became too much. In order to overcome the difficulties and disadvantages of playing on what would be an oversized viola and to compensate tonally for what would be to him a less acceptable small instrument, Tertis ingeniously designed an instrument, the Tertis–Richardson model. He made a definite step in the right direction, it seemed, although I don't believe his model has taken over 'viola construction'.

Today it seems that the Tertis Model has had its vogue and has been relegated to an interesting historical development. Some of the fine instruments which were made to the Tertis pattern are still in professional use, but many of today's violists get wonderful sounds from instruments of various shapes and sizes, giving the player a choice that would have been unthinkable in Tertis's time. Nevertheless, the effort put into the Tertis Model was not wasted, as it created an enormous amount of interest in the whole question of viola size and shape. In many ways, today's luthiers (and, by extension, players) are indebted to Tertis, for opening up so many avenues of development for the instrument he loved.

Tertis also concerned himself with the working conditions of musicians. In October 1937 the *Daily Telegraph* published an article by him in which he set out ideal rules for the working life of an orchestra:

Rules for an Orchestra

We live in a world of overworked orchestras and under-rehearsed concerts. The following paragraphs tabulate rules for the conduct of a superior symphony orchestra. Whatever the difficulties in the way of realisation, these must be obeyed if the best possible results are desired.

1. The orchestra shall never give more than two concerts a week.

2. The best players the country produces, and the best only, must be engaged. This applies most particularly to the leaders of the strings.

3. The leader of each section of the strings and his associate leader or

understudy must be artists of accomplishment and prestige. Beauty of tone and temperamental feeling are essential qualifications.

4. Each string leader shall take his men for a sectional rehearsal of three hours for every concert.

5. All players shall be available when required individually by their leader for inspection of the condition of their instruments and for instruction in the improvement, when necessary, of their methods of tone production. This would particularly apply to players whose tone is poor through an inadequate vibrato.

6. Each leader shall edit all parts, with special reference to the fingering and phrasing of melodies. Note: A melody is impoverished if the same string is not used throughout the section.

7. Leaders shall finger the parts three months before the beginning of the concert season.

8. Separate parts shall be provided for each player, and it shall be a condition of their contracts that the players study the parts at home. Players to receive marked parts at the end of each week for the following week's concerts.

9. The orchestra's parts and scores to be kept exclusively for its use and to be shared with no other orchestra or conductor.

10. The leader shall see that all the instruments and bows in his section are good, that they are kept in good condition, and that good strings are used. Note: Dirty necks, fingerboards and strings are detrimental to string dexterity, and it is a common fault for too much resin to be allowed to accumulate on the strings.

11. Leaders of string sections shall meet once a week to co-ordinate their bowing marks.

12. No member of the orchestra shall belong to any other organisation whatever, whether of orchestral or chamber music; neither shall he teach at any institution.

13. Plan for rehearsals of two weekly concerts (Wednesday and Saturday): Monday, 10–1, preparatory sectional, taken by string leaders, while the conductor rehearses the wind, &c. Monday, 2–5, full orchestra. Tuesday, 10–1 and 2–5, full orchestra. Short rehearsal only (11–12.30) on Wednesday. Similar timetable for the Saturday concert.

14. No player shall accept any other professional engagement before the concert on the day of the concert.

15. No casual behaviour shall be tolerated. There shall be no crossing of legs at rehearsals. Violins, &c, shall not be left on chairs during intervals. The conductor's instructions, nuances, etc., shall be immediately entered in parts at all desks.

16. A thoroughly capable musician shall attend all rehearsals to criticise faulty balance.

Note: It is not possible for a conductor always to detect imperfect balance and clarity because of his proximity to the orchestra.

When he was guest of honour at the Musicians' Club in London on 28 March 1938 Tertis took the opportunity to express his views to an audience including Robert Mayer and Carl Flesch, as well as such artists as Isolde Menges, Howard Ferguson, Muriel Brunskill, Reinhold von Warlich and T. C. Sterndale Bennett, who provided the musical entertainment. The burden of his remarks was that orchestral musicians' schedules were far too exhausting, so that the quality of their performances suffered:

> Mr Tertis ... expressed regret that full advantage was not taken in England of the country's symphony orchestras. One reason which prevented our having a first-rate native orchestra was that while our orchestral players were second to none, owing to the conditions in which they worked they were producing quantity and not the quality which music-lovers desired of them. Their performance was one of mass production. They rehearsed in the morning, made gramophone recordings in the afternoon, and played at concerts at night, often under mediocre conductors. A weekly output of 30 hours of such work was more exhausting than 60 hours of manual labour. The BBC had in its grasp the opportunity of having a perfect orchestra, able to express itself triumphantly in the international language of music to the country's great good, and he deplored the apparent lack of interest in promoting the superlative musical talent which existed in the country. (*The Times*, 30 March 1938)

This broadside brought forth an instant reply from Sir Thomas Beecham, in a letter to the *Daily Telegraph*, in which he corrected Tertis's calculations and concluded that the average weekly output was in fact thirty-one hours, Tertis's ideal. He continued:

> Not much evidence here of slave-driving. And I should like to add that the

London Philharmonic Orchestra is not called upon to swell its working time by any of those little home studies which would be a part of the daily round of Mr Tertis's perfect machine.

With Mr Tertis's fantastic project to found a new orchestra to play four hours a week and rehearse 27 (not forgetting the home work) I do not propose to deal at length. It will not materialise for two obvious reasons; it is not wanted and it is so glaringly uneconomic that no one would be found to pay for it.

For the needs of the musical public as it exists to-day we have already in London all the orchestras we require. Their standard of performance is high enough to satisfy the demands of all the most critical intelligences save possibly a few virtuosi.

To these I should like to recall the wise old French proverb which should be written over the doors of most missionaries and enthusiasts: 'Le mieux c'est l'ennemi du bien.'

Their exchange of letters in the press went on for some time. A few months later Sir Thomas suddenly invited Tertis to lunch and greeted him thus: 'Hello – what fun we had in the *Daily Telegraph*!' Beecham invited Tertis to join audition panels in selecting new players for the London Philharmonic Orchestra, and soon afterwards asked him to attend his rehearsals and help correct the balance of tone and also edit the string parts. In his usual methodical way Tertis set to work concentrating on achieving unanimity in fingering and phrasing, an important factor in expressive string playing, especially in a section of players performing the same melodic line. Tertis suggested to Sir Thomas that he felt he could improve the expressive qualities of the viola section if he could be allowed to give individual help to each member, to which Beecham replied, 'My dear fellow, do what you like with them. Boil them if you like!'

Tertis was carrying out his duties at the Albert Hall when Kreisler was playing the Tchaikovsky Concerto. When Tertis suggested that the orchestra were much too loud in one place and that Kreisler should play up, Kreisler turned to Tertis and said, 'I agree', and then quite meekly, 'I will try – I will do my best'.

Some members of the orchestra saw Tertis's appointment as Beecham's assistant in 1938 as extraordinary. For one thing, the LPO acted as the Covent Garden pit band at that time, and Tertis's knowledge of the operatic repertoire was limited. Beecham asked him to bow and finger all the string parts. Bowing was, and still is, the job of the principal player in each section, and fingerings are always very personal. Many of the orchestral players found Tertis's fingerings idiosyncratic.

A rumour went around that Tertis suggested 'bugging' the orchestral pit with microphones so as to hear any critical remarks from the more rebellious members of the orchestra. An anecdote from that time tells how Tertis made an amazing howler at a recording session when he asked: 'Why can't the trombones all move their slides at the same distance and at the same time as it would look so much nicer?' The stage band for the Coronation Day performance of *Aida* were also far from pleased when they were told they must arrive one hour before the main rehearsal to be coached (on intonation) by Tertis.

Douglas Steele, who was Beecham's secretary and librarian in 1939, remembers that period when Tertis was bowing Beecham's parts:

> Beecham became exacting, formidable and quite ruthless. I was something to shoot at and abuse, a kind of whipping boy. He would roar for me, for Lionel Tertis, and for his librarian John Primrose (father of William) all over the theatre. Tertis and I would come from wherever we were (generally copying below stage), at the double.
>
> Beecham, whose sense of humour was notorious, particularly enjoyed discomfiting John Primrose. When he wanted to summon the harassed librarian he would yell 'Mr Daffodil!' or any other flower name he could think of. The orchestra enjoyed such scenes but disliked the marvellous system of part-marking which Sir Thomas and Tertis had devised. All bowings had to be exact in accordance with Tertis's system of bowing and there were hundreds of small details related to dynamics, phrasing and so on, which went into the parts in different coloured pencils. When I had marked them for a Sunday afternoon performance of Delius's Paris, which took place in Queen's Hall, the rehearsal revealed a series of shadings leading to the wonderful oboe melody, which did not yet absolutely satisfy Sir Thomas. We had spent hours transmitting into the parts, already heavily marked, indications for a slightly different tempo, and a series of complicated and most carefully graded diminuendos. Before the concert, we were summoned to Sir Thomas and given a mass of entirely new instructions, and there was a roar of abuse when the time factor was mentioned. Whatever happened on these occasions, Tertis would always say, 'No man has done more for British music than Sir Thomas'.
>
> And so we would get our coats off, and start again. The marking of parts was a ritual. Under the ground, within viewing distance of the Ring machinery, we toiled, often all night long. Tertis would come to me, and placing his great Richardson viola under his chin, say, 'Sir Thomas is worried about this little phrase in the slow movement of the Haffner'. He then played the adorable F sharp up to E, down a note to D, and back to F sharp, which I heard Sir Thomas rehearse twelve times that day, and continuing,

'Now, which bowing do you think makes the best sound – this, or that?'
I used to stand transfixed with delight and astonishment, mixed with some
fear, because it was a straight question, difficult to answer because of the
gorgeous sound he was making. I think we spent half-an-hour dealing
with the various kinds of bowing for these linking notes. At the performance it was the most tender and ravishing sound imaginable; and it was
then that all the struggle to serve Sir Thomas seemed utterly worth while,
and you became his slave again.

In 1937 Tertis wrote a small booklet entitled *Beauty of Tone in String Playing*.
The publication is preceded by a quotation: 'The gratification of interpretative
art lies in the fulfilment of its immense responsibilities.' Tertis corresponded
with Hubert Foss, then head of the music department at OUP, about the cost
of the book. Having completed the proofs, Tertis travelled from his home in
Bath to hear Kreisler give a concert in Bristol. When Tertis went round to the
artists' room during the interval, Kreisler immediately brought up the subject
of Tertis's retirement, and insisted that he should get around his handicap and
play again. The two old friends met for supper and Tertis took along a copy of
the proofs of his essay *Beauty of Tone*. Kreisler was keen to read it, and wrote
to Tertis on 13 February 1938 from the Piccadilly Hotel, London:

> I read your treatise with great interest and it seems to me that it con-
> stitutes a very valuable contribution to the pedagogical literature of our
> art. Based on years of study and proven beyond doubt by your own mag-
> nificent achievements, your observations will carry great weight with your
> colleagues and all students alike. It was good to see you again and I sin-
> cerely hope that you will reconsider your abdication and come back to
> public life. We need you!

The first two sentences of this note were included in the printed edition by a
proud Tertis. A review of the book appeared in the press on 30 April 1938:

Lionel Tertis on Vibrato

In a few words Lionel Tertis says much in his little treatise Beauty of Tone
in String Playing, just published by the Oxford University Press (2s). A
foreword by Fritz Kreisler declares it to be 'a very valuable contribution to
the pedagogical literature of our art.' With the 'acrobatics' of string playing Mr Tertis says he is not concerned. The essentials necessary to obtain
beauty of tone are his subject – just intonation, the vibrato, and the portamento in chief. 'The lack of any one of these will prevent the realisation
of the power to extract from the instrument an ideally expressive sound,
thrilling to the listener.'

The first section deals with true intonation – without which, says Mr Tertis, 'no one should be allowed to play in public', for 'utter carelessness' is the source of faulty intonation. The cure is expressed in one word – attentiveness. 'The certain road to never-failing perfect intonation is listening of the most concentrated kind.'

We turn a page and come to the question of vibrato. 'A perfect vibrato is indispensable.' A cantabile phrase played without vibrato is dead. The vibrato to be cultivated is neither too slow, for that means a sentimental effect, nor too quick, for an over-quick vibrato misses serenity and is nervously irritating. 'The vital thing about vibrato is that it should be continuous; there must be no break in it whatever, especially at the moment of proceeding from one note to another, whether those notes are in the same position or whether a change of position is involved. The vibrato in the note you are playing must go on to the very end of that note and must join the following note. In other words, keep your fingers alive!'

There are warnings against the abuse of portamento, which, however, 'is a most necessary adjunct to legato playing and can either enhance or mar beauty of tone'. Then there are a few pages on the right hand, with such hints as this: 'While playing on the one string you must, in preparation for crossing, get your bow as near as you dare to the string you are about to play upon.'

Finally Mr Tertis reminds the fiddler that to make an inanimate thing like a violin express the emotional sensibility of which he is capable he must bring into force all the vitality his body and soul possess. 'Your playing will reflect yourself. Therefore, to make your power of expression worth listening to, it is necessary to mould your life and action through life to all that is of the utmost sincerity.'

The little treatise in pamphlet form is an example of the fine printing of the university press.

After Ada's death Tertis found a copy of *Beauty of Tone* which he had given her in 1938; on a piece of paper attached to the front page Mrs Tertis had written, 'This copy very precious to me – his wife'. Tertis also inscribed a copy to Sir Henry Wood, who celebrated his golden jubilee as a conductor in 1938. During those fifty years, many composers and executive musicians owed their success to his early recognition and encouragement. The majority of orchestral musicians of that period were trained by him, including a number of generations of students at the Royal Academy of Music where he conducted the First Orchestra for so many years.

✂ 11 ✂

The Second World War

The 1939–1945 War – return to the concert platform –
the new viola – RCM – Dunhill's Triptych – NYO – BBC

WHEN WAR was declared on 3 September 1939 all theatres, cinemas and concert halls were closed by order of the Home Office. Even the BBC stopped doing anything at all creative, and filled the airwaves with news, theatre organ music and records, while the BBC Symphony Orchestra was immediately evacuated to Bristol. It can be seen with hindsight that this panic action was all mistaken, but at that stage, during the 'phoney war', no one was quite sure what horrors the Germans might perpetrate. The first musician to do anything positive was Myra Hess, who cancelled a lucrative American tour and, acting on an inspired suggestion by her pianist friend Denise Lassimonne, started organizing her famous lunchtime concerts. In common with other museums and galleries, the National Gallery in Trafalgar Square had been emptied of all its treasures, and it was there that the daily concerts began on Tuesday 10 October, with more than 1,000 people crowding in to hear Hess herself launch the series. (The Home Office had given permission for an audience of 200.) For the first few months the Tuesday and Friday programmes were repeated in the late afternoon, but eventually these repeats were discontinued. The concerts had an enormous effect on music-lovers' morale and Hess always considered them her greatest achievement.

Although Tertis was nearly sixty-three at the outbreak of war, he was desperate to do something to help the cause, and realized very quickly that he would have to go back on his 1937 decision never to play the viola again. Borrowing Eric Coates's Testore, he once again started to practise, with the aim of giving concerts for war charities. He announced his reappearance, and gave two recitals with William Murdoch at the Wigmore Hall on Saturday afternoons 4 and 25 November, using a Richardson viola rather than the Testore. The concert on 4 November was widely reviewed in the press. Ferruccio Bonavia had this to say in the December issue of *Musical Times*:

> There is no viola player like Lionel Tertis, and his return to the concert platform after an absence of two years was not less eventful because it took place not at Queen's but at the Wigmore Hall or because he played Sonatas and not Concertos. The programme consisted of three excellent

Sonatas by Dohnányi, Ireland and Brahms for viola and piano but, for once in a way, one had less thought for the music. Our ear delighted in the extraordinary beauty of the player's tone – beauty that one feared was lost when Tertis left us. He returns with powers absolutely unimpaired. In grace, finish, technical mastery, intelligence, he is what he has always been, that rare being who places all the resources of virtuosity humbly and unreservedly at the service of the composer. Admirably matched by the subtly-controlled piano-playing of William Murdoch, the performance made us feel deeply grateful for Tertis's decision to return to us at this critical hour. The new viola, made by Arthur Richardson of Crediton in Devonshire, served Mr. Tertis well. The resonance of the lower strings was particularly full and pleasing. What its tone will be in a few years it is impossible to predict, since time is an important factor in the development of new instrumental qualities. But one can say confidently that Mr. Richardson's viola promises well.

On 16 November Tertis also resumed broadcasting. This event aroused much interest, and he received a number of fan letters, one of which, from the famous piano teacher 'Uncle Tobs', read: 'My dear Lionel, We heard you on the wireless the other day. It was as great as ever. And it was a great happiness to hear you again. The new instrument came through most effectively, too. All love from Tobias Matthay.'

The new R.T. viola was provoking much interest. In January 1940 *The Strad* published a letter from Frank Ayliffe on the subject:

Dear Sir – It is certain that all viola players will have read with great interest your Editorial on the subject of the efforts of Mr Lionel Tertis, in collaboration with Mr Arthur Richardson, to evolve a Viola which, whilst of a length adequate for reasonable sonority from the C string, shall be so designed as to afford a maximum facility to the player. This latter feature is highly important, in that not only execution, but tone itself suffers if the instrument be unwieldy even though the player be a virtuoso.

I see that Mr Richardson claims that the new 16¾ in. model gives real viola tone; like as Pilate of old asked 'What is truth?' I would ask what is real viola tone? My notions as to this are well grounded and defined, but probably every viola player will hold equally well defined ideas, not only differing from mine, but also inter-divergent. For all that, an attempt may be made to determine certain features upon which, it is to be hoped, there may be some degree of common agreement.

First, the C string tone must not be tubby, but resonant, and then not hollow but strongly tending to the reedy. Withal it must not be such as refuses to match the tone of its neighbour G.

Then as to the A string. The French epigram 'le LA de l'Alto est toujours criard' must somehow or other be disproved.

The general tone throughout must be of a kind capable of a wide degree of dynamic range. Excessive reediness will reduce that range and if long maintained will pall upon the ear.

Another point, although lying outside actual tone quality, has an important bearing upon its determination; I refer to promptness of speech. It is a common defect in new violas that a lag occurs between the bow-stroke and the emission of the sound expected. This has a most disturbing effect upon the player and is thus inimical to fine and free tone production.

Let us now review our experiences, and examine how far Mr Richardson's new viola possesses these attributes. Probably Mr Tertis' broadcast on November 16th was given to display its qualities. What a pity it was that the B.B.C. did not allow the microphone faithfully to fulfil its functions. Instead the voice of this, the mildest mannered of the Strings family, was so pulled about, that what came over the air was an intense strident, nasal, high pressure tone, in volume enormously greater than any viola (thanks be to Heaven) has ever been known to produce. It was largely devoid of dynamics, was forte-fortissimo throughout, and most nearly resembled that which might come from a whole battery of basset horns. A non playing music listener remarked admirably that 'he never knew the viola was like that.' I could only reply that in very truth it never was. It seemed so sad that Mr Richardson's new viola should have been made thus to masquerade, and so convinced was I of foul play that I attended Mr Tertis' recital at Wigmore Hall on November 25th.

There, in the Brahms Sonata I really heard the instrument in all its splendour. Its tone was superb; strong, smooth and when required intensely reedy. Speech seemed as prompt as could be desired even in the quietest passages. The well nourished tone was such as can generally only be got very near the bridge, where, on most new instruments, the player dare not venture, but from the Hall the bow position vis à vis the bridge could not be seen clearly enough to settle this.

I am now left wondering how much of all that beauty was due to the magic of Mr Tertis' great attainment, and how much resided inherently in the new instrument as a result of Mr Richardson's skilled knowledge and craftsmanship and by virtue of the modifications in design. My three new English violas – 1926, 16½ in., 1930, 16½ in. and 1938, 16¾ in., the second and third by an eminent English maker, are all fine as regards tone, prompt speech and workmanship, but none of them will yet bear playing close to the bridge, for the production of the lovely reedy tone, of which Mr Tertis makes us so envious. ...

I hope that other viola players will record in your columns their reactions to the present important episode in the history of the viola.

Tertis wrote to Mrs Coolidge on 12 December 1939: 'I am playing again and after two years collaboration with a violin maker, have evolved a viola which is a true instrument. There are no good old ones to be had so now I have the satisfaction of knowing there will be some violas for future generations.'

In late 1939 Myra Hess invited Tertis to give three recitals in the National Gallery concert series. The first, on Friday 17 November, with Cedric Sharpe (cello) and William Murdoch (piano) consisted of Ireland's Viola Sonata, Goossens's *Rhapsody*, op. 13, for cello and piano, and Brahms's Piano Trio, op. 114. On Friday 1 December, with the veteran mezzo-soprano Elena Gerhardt and Myra Hess, it was an all-Brahms programme: the Sonata in F minor, op. 120, and Two Songs, op. 91, with viola and piano. The concert on Friday 8 December was given by the re-formed Chamber Music Players (Sammons, Tertis, Sharpe and Murdoch), and comprised two piano quartets – Brahms's C minor, op. 60, and Dvořák's E flat major, op. 87. The following day the *Star* newspaper reported: 'Twenty minutes before the advertised hour there were 700 people in the National Gallery and by one o'clock the audience numbered over 1,000, a wonderful memory of the musical public for a good thing. ... Ticket prices were a shilling, plus one penny for a programme.'

On 14 February 1940 Tertis joined the BBC Symphony Orchestra conducted by Sir Hamilton Harty in a performance of *Harold in Italy* at Colston Hall, Bristol. With Elena Gerhardt and Myra Hess, he gave a Brahms recital in the 'Monday Seven O'Clocks' series on 26 February.

The contralto Muriel Brunskill witnessed Tertis's London concerto comeback on 8 February that year at a Royal Philharmonic Society concert:

A concert was arranged at the Queen's Hall in aid of the Musicians' Benevolent Fund, in which the original 16 singers presented the 'Serenade to Music', and Albert Sammons and Lionel Tertis played Mozart's Sinfonia concertante for violin and viola. The Serenade was in the first part of the programme, so I went into the auditorium to listen to the second half. Never shall I forget the thrill of Mozart's pure music enfolding one; it was like coming into an oasis from an arid desert.

During the 1940 Bournemouth Festival, held at the Pavilion in February, Tertis and Sammons played the *Sinfonia concertante* with the Municipal

Orchestra. On 3 March Tertis was soloist in the Walton Concerto at a Hallé concert in Manchester conducted by Malcolm Sargent; later in the month he gave a recital in Glasgow with Sammons and a local pianist, Wight Henderson, in which they each played sonatas. The April issue of *Musical Opinion* reported:

A concert last month of the Glasgow Chamber Music Society was notable for bringing back to the concert platform the famous viola player Lionel Tertis. In association with Albert Sammons and Wight Henderson, he was heard in the Handel Sonata op. 2 no. 8 for violin, viola and piano, and with Mr. Henderson he played the F minor Sonata of Brahms. Other works in the programme were Ireland's Sonata no. 2 in A minor and the Sinfonia Concertante of Mozart. Mr. Henderson at the piano replaced the orchestra as well as it could be done.

It seems clear that, with his physical problems eased by his long lay-off, Tertis was once again able to attain the highest artistic level. His Brahms concerts with Elena Gerhardt and Myra Hess were acknowledged as being on a plane of their own. They performed on 18 February 1940 in one of the Palladium–National Sunday League concerts and again at a National Gallery concert on 21 June. The first concert was reviewed in the April issue of *Musical Opinion*:

Miss Hess and Mr. Tertis joined forces in the Sonata in F minor, and gave us some thoughtful and characteristically intimate playing, but some of the refinements tended to get lost in such a big auditorium; nor did the stage draperies help matters. Mme. Gerhardt, who contributed half a dozen songs in one group, and later 'Gestillte Sehnsucht' and 'Geistliches Wiegenlied' (obbligato by Mr. Tertis), was in much better voice than we have heard her for some time; in songs that suit her – such as these – she can give more artistic pleasure than most singers. We heard Miss Hess for the first time in the role of accompanist: we hope it will not be the last, for no singer could wish for a more sympathetic, adaptable and (when necessary) brilliant collaboration. For her own solos Miss Hess chose op. 119 complete (three Intermezzi and the E flat Rhapsody) which she played with her accustomed admirable artistry.

Tertis wrote to Mrs Coolidge on 19 March to let her know that: 'we are going to live at Worthing in Sussex with a niece of Ada's'. He joined the staff of the Royal College of Music in the summer term of 1940. Sir George Dyson, then Director of the RCM, was responsible. Tertis's appointment was reported to the meeting of the College's Executive and Finance Committee on 30 May, and also in the *RCM magazine*, vol. 35–6 (1939–40).

In the summer term two of Ernest Tomlinson's viola students at the RCM were told, by the powers that be, that Tertis had expressed a wish to teach at the college, and that he was to be given two students – Maxwell (Max) Ward and Livia Gollancz. Neither of them wanted to leave Tomlinson, who was revered by his students, but the college said the decision was irrevocable. This was not the best way to start with a new teacher, and Max Ward did not disguise his antagonism to the project. He and Tertis had terrible arguments, and by half-term he was allowed to return to his former teacher. Livia (daughter of the music-loving publisher Victor Gollancz, and soon to become a professional horn player) was only a second-study violist, and stuck it out for the whole term. Her memories of the lessons are that he taught her a very important element in practising – how to listen to yourself, not just to hear what your eye tells you. Both as regards perfect intonation and extraneous noises he was a hard task master. It was many years later that she realized the value of his insistence on intense listening. 'He opened my ears to myself.'

Tertis made three further appearances as soloist at Queen's Hall before it was destroyed by a German incendiary bomb. The first was on 9 July 1940, when he performed Walton's Viola Concerto with the London Philharmonic conducted by Charles Munch. The Battle of Britain was still raging, as the RAF's fighter pilots fought Hitler's Luftwaffe for control of the skies, and the Proms were in doubt until quite a late stage. Finally Keith Douglas of the Royal Philharmonic Society took over the promotion of what was billed as Sir Henry Wood's 'forty-sixth and last' Prom season; and, with the BBC SO out of the equation, the LSO was hired. On 10 August Tertis took part in the opening concert, at which Sir Henry conducted the *Sinfonia concertante*, with Sammons as violin soloist. Then the Battle of Britain ended, only for the Luftwaffe's night-time Blitz on London to begin. The Proms were disrupted almost every evening; and if it was deemed unsafe for the audience to go home, impromptu entertainments – often featuring Basil Cameron and Gerald Moore – continued after the concert, sometimes until 5.30 in the morning. In this atmosphere, Wood, Sammons and Tertis repeated the Mozart work on 3 September, four days before the government finally brought the curtain down prematurely on the Prom season. Sir Henry soldiered on after his 'last' season, almost up to his death in August 1944, although following the burning-out of Queen's Hall in May 1941 the Proms had to move to their present home, the Royal Albert Hall.

During 1940 Tertis gave five recitals in cathedrals in aid of war charities, accompanied on the piano by the cathedral organists. At Hereford, with Percy Hull, well over £100 plus a gold watch and a bangle was raised towards the Bomber Fund; at Gloucester, with Herbert Sumsion, it was money for Gloucester charities; at Winchester, with Harold Rhodes, the charity was the homeless in Southampton; at Exeter, with Alfred Wilcock, £50 was raised for the Lord Mayor of London's Distress Fund. The final recital in this series was at York, with Sir Edward Bairstow; among the works played was Tertis's transcription of the Haydn Cello Concerto in D, and Sir Edward played the Scherzo from his recently composed Organ Sonata in E flat. Tertis gave a recital with Gerald Moore in St Swithin's church, Lincoln; Geoffrey Kimpton, later to be a violist in the BBC Philharmonic Orchestra, was in the audience; to this day he remembers Tertis's beautiful tone. In Gerald Moore's book *Am I Too Loud*, Tertis's reply to the question: 'What do you do if the pianist plays too loudly?' was 'I play even softer'.

Tertis and Sammons were invited to play at a party at the Westminster home of Sir Arthur and Lady Colefax, who had frequent social occasions for painters, writers and musicians. They started their programme with the Handel–Halvorsen Passacaglia; no sooner had they started than they heard the sound of a siren in the distance giving warning of an air raid. They decided immediately to ignore all marks of expression and played double *forte* throughout. This effectively reduced the sound of falling bombs. Amongst the guests were Somerset Maugham and Ivor Novello, who both understood what was going on, and when the air raid was over the latter asked Tertis to play the Serenade from Delius's *Hassan*, muted, to bring calm after the storm.

Tertis was associated with other wartime concerts. The house of the pianist Harriet Cohen was destroyed in an air raid on London in 1940; shortly after this tragic event her friends Monsieur Bon and Victor Cazalet invited her to arrange weekly concerts in the Orchid Room at the Dorchester Hotel. Every week a collection was taken, and the proceeds shared between the National Gallery concerts and the Musicians' Benevolent Fund. Besides Tertis, the many distinguished musicians who participated were Maggie Teyte, Clifford Curzon, Louis Kentner, Léon Goossens and Oda Slobodskaya.

Tertis took part in a wonderful series of concerts in Reading that were a real boost for the cultural life of the town. These shilling concerts at the Olympia were organized by Sir Henry and Lady Piggott, influential figures at the Chelsea Music Society. Tertis appeared twice in 1940, and was reminded that he had played there nineteen years previously in a joint recital with Dame Nellie Melba, when he played works by Fauré, Kreisler, Wolstenholme and his own arrangement of the *Londonderry Air*. His recital with Gerald Moore on 8 March included the two Brahms Sonatas. He returned on Thursday 24 October with the pianist Muriel Bowman-Smith; one review described the occasion: 'Lionel Tertis as a viola player is unique. A Reading audience had a further opportunity of appreciating his great gifts ... He has a lovely instrument, and his fine sense of colour, impressive technique and complete sympathy were thoroughly demonstrated.' The programme included Beethoven's Variations on a theme of Mozart, Tertis's arrangement of Haydn's Cello Concerto in D and a group of short pieces by Szymanowski, Tartini, Delius and Marais.

After the destruction of Queen's Hall, where Tertis had given so many memorable performances, Eric Coates remembered how it looked in his mind's eye: 'It might be a picture of Ysaÿe and Lionel Tertis giving a performance of Mozart's *Sinfonia concertante* for violin and viola, Ysaÿe's towering frame, overshadowing the smaller figure of his companion, but whose tone could not compare with that of Tertis in his prime.'

In the autumn of 1941 Tertis approached Coates for a work for viola, and visited the Coates's home in Hampstead Village in November. In a letter of 1985 to Geoffrey Self, Austin Coates, the composer's son, remembered the occasion:

> Tertis ... came to lunch – we had a very serious conversation ... concerning some of the leading composers of [the] century. Afterwards, we went into the Drawing Room, and Tertis and my father played the work ['First Meeting']. It was quite a large room with a high ceiling and perfect sound. Tertis played it as if he'd known the work all his life – he was sight-reading. It was so beautiful I could never forget it. He was so delighted that he insisted on doing it again.

For some reason Tertis never played the piece again. A few years ago the English violist Michael Ponder resurrected the work, which he has also recorded.

In 1941, in Liverpool, Tertis performed both the Walton Concerto and Berlioz's *Harold in Italy* with the Liverpool Philharmonic Orchestra, conducted by Malcolm Sargent; the other work in the programme was Elgar's Cello Concerto, played by Beatrice Harrison. The 'Phil' had the reputation during the war of being Britain's finest orchestra; and it was packed with superb string players such as Henry Holst, Herbert Downes and Anthony Pini. Their concert series at the Coliseum was reviewed in the August issue of *Musical Opinion*:

> Under the auspices of Musical Culture Limited, Jack Hylton presented the orchestra, conducted by Malcolm Sargent, in a two weeks season of popular symphony concerts at the Coliseum, beginning on June 2nd. Sir Thomas Beecham once stated that the musical public of the metropolis amounted to no more than 3,000, yet we were informed that during the first week of these concerts 20,000 people paid for admission. So it would appear that apart from the more or less specialised Queen's Hall devotees, there does exist a large section of the public willing to pay for good music provided the fare is not too 'highbrow' and the prices reasonable. At any rate the series was extended for another week, till June 21st. The

programmes were on similar lines to the Proms, with a leavening of lighter works such as Eric Coates' 'The Three Bears' (conducted by the composer). The soloists included the following string players: violinists Ida Haendel, Eda Kersey, Albert Sammons, Thomas Matthews, Henry Holst, Lionel Tertis (viola) and the cellists Beatrice Harrison and Thelma Reiss.

On Sunday 16 February 1941 Tertis appeared in a BBC broadcast entitled 'The BBC Presents', which was recorded in Broadcasting House, Bristol on the same day. The programme linked up Tertis with the story of the viola, and told how he had championed the instrument and brought it into the limelight. The compère for the programme, Patric Curwen, presented it with almost a 'scrap-book' technique, including interviews, a dramatized scene between Paganini and Berlioz, and Tertis playing viola solos with orchestra and also with a singer. The programme included the *Londonderry Air* and the recording of a short discussion with Tertis and the composer B. J. Dale; this had been made on the new glass discs, which had the reputation of breaking very easily. Tertis's fee for this broadcast was £39 8s. 6d., which included £1 1s. 6d. fare from Aldershot to Bristol and two nights' subsistence of £1 12s. od. During the time of this broadcast Tertis was staying with Viscount Coke at Sowley House, Lymington, Hampshire. At that time Tertis was living at Montreal, Cargate Avenue, Alder-shot, Hampshire, but on 20 March he moved to Hereford, from where he wrote two letters to Sir Adrian Boult.

> On December 29th next if I am alive and kicking I shall be 65! and I am wondering whether perhaps the BBC would contemplate making it an occasion for a 'boost' for the viola.
>
> Forgive the liberty I take and the presumption for making such a pro-posal, but it seemed to me an excuse for a 'splash' for the viola if I could enlist the sympathy and help of the BBC ...

Tertis then went on to say that he had written to John Ireland and Walton about writing new works for the occasion. On 10 November he wrote to Boult again, this time from 4 Iverna Gardens, London W8.

> My dear Adrian,
>
> You were good to say in your letter of July 19th last that I was to keep you posted with regard to the compositions for viola and orchestra by Ireland and Walton – sadly – I have to report – no progress ... Walton's letter explains (mercifully he says he will do it later). As far as Ireland is con-cerned, I know he has made a start but I have heard no more from him ...

Tertis then listed a number of works which he thought would be suitable for his 65th anniversary, including the Bloch Suite ('never yet done with full orchestra').

> I know you will believe me when I say that my sole object is the cause of the viola and not glorification or personal advantage of any kind. As long as I can scrape a tune I want to do all I can for it, especially in the way of increasing its library. When I began there was – without exaggeration – practically no music for the solo violist ...

In a letter to Geoffrey Bush in 1942 Ireland wrote: 'I have been overworked lately – and am very behind with things. I am expected to do – (but never accomplish) – a work for viola and orchestra for Tertis to play in Portugal on a tour he is making for the British Council.' Sadly Ireland never composed the proposed work.

The BBC celebrated Tertis's birthday in a grand manner. The *Radio Times* of 26 December 1941 included a short article and photograph of Tertis in honour of the occasion, and on 29 December, the day of his anniversary, Tertis was soloist in Vaughan Williams's Suite with the BBC Northern Orchestra conducted by Julian Clifford, broadcast from the Manchester studios; on the same day he gave a broadcast recital from Manchester which featured his transcriptions of Handel's Sonata in F (first performance in this form), the Dale *Romance*, the Dvořák–Kreisler *Slavonic Dance* in G minor, Tertis's own *Sunset* and his arrangement of Schubert's *Allegretto*. The February issue of *Musical Opinion* reviewed the birthday concerts:

> Lionel Tertis celebrated his sixty-fifth birthday on December 29th (1941) by broadcasting Vaughan Williams's Suite for viola and orchestra, and also giving a solo recital later in the same evening. On January 2nd (1942) at the Gallery he gave a further recital in conjunction with Gerald Moore and Benjamin Dale. The programme consisted of Sonatas in D major and E major by Martini (arranged by Tertis), a Sonata in F major by Handel (arranged from the figured bass for viola by Tertis), Dale's 'Romance', and a miscellaneous group that included the Tartini-Kreisler Fugue, and Tertis's transcription of the Andante from Rachmaninoff's Cello Sonata. Both the Martini and the Handel were superbly played by Mr. Tertis and Mr. Moore. The 'Romance' dates from 1906 and is, therefore, approximately contemporaneous with the celebrated piano sonata, to which it is similar in idiom. The music, cast in a single spacious movement, is warmly lyrical, richly harmonised and expertly written for the two instruments. We hope, too, that the reception accorded to Mr. Dale at this concert will induce him to resume composition after his prolonged silence. Mr. Tertis lavished all the

resources of his art on the performance, and Mr. Dale, who has not been heard in the role of pianist for many years, proved a sympathetic coadjutor, well able to deal with his own music. With the exception of Casals, we have never heard a cellist equal Mr. Tertis's artistry, and perhaps, this is one reason why the Rachmaninoff Andante sounded to much better advantage than usual.

A short festival – March 9th to 13th (1942) – was given in the Bournemouth Pavilion by the London Philharmonic Orchestra. The conductors were Basil Cameron, Edric Cundell, Leslie Heward, Malcolm. Sargent and Sir Henry Wood; the soloists Ida Haendel, Moura Lympany, Moiseiwitsch, Solomon and Lionel Tertis.

Thomas Dunhill (1877–1946) dedicated his *Triptych, Three Impressions for viola and orchestra* to Tertis, who premièred it on 19 August 1942 at an Albert Hall Promenade Concert, broadcast live and conducted by Sir Adrian Boult. For many years Tertis had wanted to disprove the theory that varnish does not enhance the tone of an instrument, and on this occasion played on an unvarnished viola.

Between 1941 and 1942 Dunhill made entries in his diary concerning Tertis and the *Triptych* for viola and orchestra.

18th October 1941 – made some sketches for a possible viola and orchestra thing (for Tertis?); but didn't do very much.

24th October 1941 Sketching the projected viola thing for Tertis – but working very slowly.

25th November 1941 ... copied the ending? of the second curious viola piece. That virtually finishes my piano sketch – but of course I've done no scoring. I am very doubtful if this piece will do. I have an idea, in any case, it will need much revision.

2nd March 1942 Worked at revision and scoring Triptych. In afternoon, went to John Ireland's (both now at Banbury) ... and I played Triptych and showed him the score as far as done. He really seemed genuinely impressed by the work – and that pleased me and encouraged me enormously. He made one or two good suggestions in the scoring too. I was awfully bucked! I had half thought he wouldn't care for it.

15th June 1942 Went to RCM ... practised a bit there at the piano part of Triptych and Tertis came at 2, and we had a splendid 'go' at it. He is perfectly magnificent and makes it sound quite gorgeous!! We worked until about 3.30 ...

17th July 1942 Tertis came and we had another practice of the Triptych. He takes the last movement at a tremendous pace – and I couldn't play it at that speed! but it should be alright with orchestra.

18th August 1942 Henry J. was rehearsing hard and my piece didn't come on till after 12 – and then Boult just gave it a 'run-through' as he had to rehearse a Kodály Suite for to-night. He promises a proper rehearsal tomorrow. Tertis played on a new, unvarnished viola and caused a minor sensation in the orchestra with his ghostly white instrument! He says he's going to play on it tomorrow, too. It is certainly a magnificent instrument. Lunch with him at South Kensington.

The Strad published the following note in its October 1942 edition:

Mr. Arthur Richardson, the well known violin maker, has pointed out that we made no reference in our comments on the Promenade Concerts to the interesting fact that Lionel Tertis, in his first performance of Dunhill's 'Triptych' for viola and orchestra, played on a new Richardson instrument 'in the white'. It is not possible, of course, for our representative to be present at every concert in London, and our readers would not wish for his comments on a performance he had not heard. We understand that the experiment was a success and that Mr. Richardson's instrument had a powerful tone.

Two reviews of Dunhill's arrangement of the *Triptych* for viola and piano were published after the war. *Musical Opinion* in January 1946 wrote:

That Cinderella of instruments, the viola is now acquiring a fine repertoire, largely as a result of propaganda by its fairy godmother Lionel Tertis. At one time the viola player had little to turn to beyond arrangements of popular violin solos little suited to the character of the instrument. Certainly there was a splendid sonata by Rubinstein (now unaccountably forgotten) and a sonata and a few pieces by Carl Reinecke, the latter more suitable for cello. Dunhill's 'Triptych' bears every evidence of having been conceived entirely with technique and individual tone of the instrument in mind, and with no attempt to steal unsuitable acrobatics from its sister the violin. The three pieces are peculiarly English in character, and are an addition to real viola music. (5s. 6d. net.)

After Dunhill's death on 13 March 1946 *Musical Times* reviewed the work in its May issue:

Dunhill's Triptych was first heard with Lionel Tertis as soloist. My impression that the pieces were a little austere in character is confirmed by a study of the score. There is much to be said for an increase in the viola repertory, and these will be useful, although they are by no means easy of execution. Dunhill will be greatly missed, for he wrote so many things that were useful and needed, and always with such fine musicianship and clean workmanship.

One of the concerts Tertis played for the BBC in 1942 was given live from a studio in Evesham, Worcestershire. While he was performing the Bliss Sonata Frederick Riddle was broadcasting in an adjoining studio. When Tertis had finished his broadcast Riddle came into the studio and said, 'How the devil do you get up to the last bar in the Furiante?' Tertis replied, 'The Lord only knows.'

Tertis wrote to Ernest Newman from his home in Carshalton on 13 December 1942:

May I write to thank you for your recent articles concerning 'solo performers' which I have thoroughly enjoyed and have read with acidity. Although I suppose I am in the category of 'solo performers' (sounds like performing monkeys doesn't it? – and some of them are truly that!) I have often hoped for someone in authority to give them a good dubbing, in the hope of reducing their demeanour of 'almightiness'. The way certain of my fraternity strut on the platform like peacocks, and the devices some of them have of cultivating a lock of hair which can conveniently fall half way down their face at the first sforzando, makes one feel tired to say the least of it. These are only one or two signs in their platform behaviour which go to prove how much they are thinking of their own self-importance and how little they therefore realize of the music they are performing.

Tertis wrote to Newman again on 29 August 1943:

How I pester you with my letters, but I wish I had known of the Locheimer manuscript. I only saw this lovely melody in Karg-Elert's book and was so entranced that I not only took the liberty of making a little addition to the piano and viola parts but also had the effrontery to put some English words to it because to me the German words in Elert's book were so 'sick-making' (one of your potent expressions!). I would have given anything for you to have heard the Bloch Suite. I feel we got fairly near to the composer's wishes. I am trying to entice the B.B.C. to do it with orchestra. I have got I believe the only score in the country. It seems to have much more colour in the orchestral version. If it would interest you, I would love to send the score to you, in which case just let me have a post-card.

After the publication of Tertis's article 'Training for Virtuosity' in the August 1943 *Musical Times* (see Appendix 3) a correspondence occurred between Ernest Newman and Tertis. On 26 September Tertis wrote:

How very kind of you to send me a letter, and the Locheimer melody – how much more in keeping is the latter in the original. Thank you also for your kind reference to my article alas, I am sure it will have no more influence on the powers that be who musically misguide our country, than a 'drop in the ocean'. I have tried so hard to interest our educationalists of far greater effort and reform. I went to Allen when he was head of the R.C.M. – I have been to Marchant on the same subject, but all to no purpose. It was in one ear and out of the other as far as they were concerned. It is this sort of inaptitude and lack of conscience which seems to permeate the English musical profession. I long to see your article in the Sunday Times from your pen, on the meagre results we obtain from our music-making, and why! Only you could stir up the minds of our self-satisfied musicians – it would be a potent message, coming from you. Another of the things I should like to see after the war would be a mission sent to Russia consisting of a body of British musicians who had been through the mill and who were utterly sincere in their desire to raise the standard of our music-making and I feel something would come of it if you were part of that mission.

The Tertises moved back to Surrey during the war, and lived at Carshalton Beeches, but Ada was taken very seriously ill and entered a nursing home in Sutton. Lionel was keen to move her away from the bombing, and after much searching found a comfortable room for her in a nursing home in Malvern. He took accommodation nearby, and gave a recital in aid of the nursing home; in the audience was Miss Parke, who was Director of Music at Lawnside School, Malvern. The headmistress of this girls' school, Miss Winifred Barrows, believed that the arts should play an important role in the life of the pupils. Miss Parke was an accomplished pianist who regularly broadcast as soloist in recitals and with orchestra. A memorable event at Lawnside was when she joined Tertis in a recital on 24 September 1944; the next night they played for the Malvern Concert Club. Their programme on both occasions was Martini's Sonata in D, Brahms's Sonata, op. 120 no. 2, Szymanowski's 'Chant de Roxane', the Tartini-Kreisler Fugue, Verne-Bredt's Lullaby and Delius's Sonata no. 2.

The local *Malvern Gazette* reported on 9 August 1947 that two eminent musicians were honoured at the annual prize distribution at Lawnside School on 29 July; they were Sir Ivor Atkins, organist of Worcester Cathedral and master of choral singing at the school, and Tertis:

At the Lawnside annual prize-day gathering last week, Miss Winifred Barrows sprang a very pleasant surprise on the many parents who filled the
Winter Gardens, by inviting no less a personage than Lionel Tertis, that
master of the viola, to play to us. Although he played only three short
pieces, a melody of Couperin, Allegretto by Martini and the delightful
Serenade from 'Hassan' by Delius, they were sufficient to show he had lost
none of his artistry. Every time I hear him I marvel at the beautiful tone
he produces.

Tertis taught violin and viola briefly at Lawnside School from 12 May to early
June 1947, when he announced that he could no longer continue, as he did not
like to leave Ada alone at night. As a consolation Tertis, with Miss Parke at
the piano, gave a recital at the school – the first he had given since an accident
seven months before. One of his pupils there was Nancy Dibley, who auditioned and was selected for the original National Youth Orchestra.

Tertis recommended that a Miss Mundlack, a London-based musician,
should travel to Malvern to teach violin and viola, and this was agreed. On 27
November 1947 she gave a violin and viola recital with Miss Parke. Miss Mundlack used a new Richardson–Tertis viola; these instruments were featured in
a special article in the September 1947 edition of the *Picture Post*. Two years
later, on 2 November 1949, Tertis and Miss Parke gave a recital at the school in
the presence of Mrs Carice Elgar Blake. Their programme included the Brahms
Sonata in E minor, op. 38, Martini's Sonata in D, Wolstenholme's *Allegretto*,
Delius's *Hassan* Serenade, Marais's Rondeau and Delius's Violin Sonata no. 2:

In introducing Mr Tertis, Miss Winifred Barrows alluded to an article which
had been written after a recital he had given earlier in the year at the Royal College of Music to help in founding a viola bursary there:

> Not only has Lionel Tertis, by his own initiative and example, won rec-
> ognition for the viola as a solo instrument, but he has shown that in his
> sphere our country has led the world. 'With him it has always been the
> music that has come first and so it is today. His personality is so unassum-
> ing that he often gives the impression of doing something that is very easy
> and simple. This however, is deceptive. His art is so complete and vital that
> it contains innumerable shades of nuances, which he brings us, welded
> into one great whole. There is, moreover, such warmth and sincerity in
> his interpretations, that he carries us with him as if under a spell that is
> more compelling because while he never exaggerates, he never fails to
> reach the heart of the music.' It may be decades before we have another
> Lionel Tertis amongst us. Let us salute him today with our deep gratitude
> and admiration.

Tertis returned twice more to play at the Royal Dublin Society during the war. On each occasion he was partnered by Gerald Moore. On Monday 2 February 1942 they gave an afternoon concert: Handel's Sonata in F, Haydn's Concerto in D, with two original cadenzas by Tertis, Rachmaninov's *Andante*, Kreisler's *Valse*, Szymanowski's 'Chant de Roxane', Delius's Serenade, Tartini's Fugue for solo viola, and Brahms's Sonata in F minor. In the evening concert at 8.15 p.m. they played the Martini–Endicott Sonata in E, Beethoven's Variations on a theme of Mozart, op. 66, the Handel–Casadesus Concerto in B minor (with two original cadenzas by Tertis), Richard Walthew's *A Mosaic in Ten Pieces*, Wolstenholme's *The Answer* and *Allegretto*, Dvořák's *Slavonic Dance* in G minor, arr. Kreisler, Marais's *Rondeau* and *Le Basque*, and Grieg's Sonata.

Tertis and Gerald Moore stayed in Dublin from 31 January until 3 February, and were guests of Miss Griffiths at Rathmines Castle. One of the concerts was reviewed by Harold White, the music critic of the *Irish Independent* on 3 February 1942:

> The genius of Tertis has not only encouraged younger players like Bernard Shore and Primrose seriously to study the instrument, but has inspired composers such as Benjamin Dale and York Bowen to write sonatas for viola and piano. It is unfortunate that the repertory of music for viola is so limited. It was noticed that the majority of the pieces at the recitals were arrangements by Tertis himself. Even the Brahms Sonata, op. 120, no. 1, was originally composed for the clarinet, yet eminently suitable for the viola. With Gerald Moore at the piano we had all that friendly converse, that playfulness as well as the lyrical beauty which the composer intended to portray. The Handel Sonata in F and the Haydn Concerto in D were both effective on the viola and the latter work was enhanced by the two cadenzas interpolated by the player, both artistically preserving the spirit and mood of the music. Tertis played an unaccompanied fugue by Tartini, and in the evening a delightful Martini Sonata as well as a Grieg Sonata and a number of short pieces.

Tertis and Moore returned a year later to the Royal Dublin Society on Monday 8 February 1943, once again playing two concerts in the Members Hall, Ball's Bridge. At 3 p.m. they played arrangements by Tertis of Martini's Sonata in D, Bach's Chaconne, John Ireland's Sonata (originally for cello) and Grieg's Sonata, op. 45. At 8 p.m. their programme was Beethoven's Sonata in G minor, op. 5 no. 2 (originally for cello), Delius's Sonata no. 2, Brahms's Sonata in E flat, op. 120 no. 2, and Tertis's arrangement of John Ireland's Violin Sonata no. 2 in A minor.

On 31 March 1943 Tertis premièred Richard Walthew's *Mosaic in Ten Pieces* in the version for viola and orchestra in a concert conducted by Clarence Raybould, which was broadcast by the BBC on 10 July. The work was reviewed in the August issue of *Musical Times*:

> Tertis was a joy, one day. He played Walthew's 'Mosaic' in ten little pieces. Originally written for clarinet and piano in 1900, we were told, the music has been scored for viola and orchestra. It is the work of a happy craftsman, genial, jesting (so few composers joke now). In a slow movement Walthew is at his serene best. Brahms would have enjoyed the Valsette, and Elgar have beamed upon other parts. Tertis's phrasing is the best lesson I can imagine for any young musician. Even the bounteously baroque cadenzas in Casadesus' arrangement of a Handel Concerto were ripely joyous. I think this was the best hour of solo artistry I have enjoyed for many a year.　　　　　　　　　　　　('Round About Radio' by W. R. Anderson)

Tertis and Clifford Curzon gave two recitals at the Wigmore Hall on Monday 24 May and Monday 28 June 1943, assisted by Maggie Teyte. The first programme included sonatas for viola and piano by Martini, Bliss and Brahms (op. 120 no. 2), the Bach *Chaconne* and Beethoven's Piano Sonata 'Les Adieux'. In their final recital the programme consisted of Bax's Sonata, Bloch's Suite, songs with viola and piano (Fauré's *Dans les ruines d'une abbaye*, Fifteenth-century melody (anon.) 1460, Duparc's *Phydilé*) and Brahms's Sonata, op. 120 no. 1.

Tertis resumed his duo partnership with Solomon, whom he described thus: 'Time was when Sergei Rachmaninov represented my ideal pianist; but he has been eclipsed, in my opinion, by Solomon – for me the greatest of pianists – as technician and musician.' They gave two recitals together at the Wigmore Hall in aid of King George's Fund for Sailors, assisted by Maggie Teyte.

Benjamin Dale died suddenly on 30 July 1943, after a rehearsal of his *The Flowing Tide* at the Albert Hall. At the memorial service Tertis, accompanied by York Bowen, played Dale's Romance for viola and piano. The service was reported in the November issue of *Musical Opinion*:

> Benjamin Dale's memorial service was perfectly arranged, and perfectly given. Dr. Cunningham was at the organ, and the choir of the Royal Academy of Music sang the Principal's beautiful 'The Souls of the Righteous'. After the 23rd Psalm and the lesson, the Griller Quartet played the Andante from Beethoven's op. 59 no. 3. Three prayers followed, and the hymn 'Praise to the Holiest in the height' was splendidly sung by the congregation. After the blessing, we had Dale's lovely Romance from the Suite

for viola and piano played by Lionel Tertis and York Bowen. The Royal Academy of Music did full honour to its late Warden with the best it had to give, – and that was good indeed.

Tertis's writings were nothing if not controversial. The following article, 'Not Wishful Thinking', appeared in Hinrichsen's *Musical Year Book* of 1944, *Music in Our Time*, subtitled 'Some Revisions and Reforms for Post-War Musical England' and included 'a ragbag of suggestions ranging from the wisely prescient (on occupational injury), to the wildly old-fashioned (on style of hair) and impractically élitist (on the super-orchestra)':

It is time musicians used a little exertion to put their 'musical house' in order. My suggestions to this end will probably be considered Utopian – but even were this so (with which I hasten to add I most vehemently disagree) none can gainsay that to strive toward perfection is to envisage a desirable goal, and cannot but help raise the status of our music-making. We are leagues behind what we might accomplish. We are content to plod along in our academic stereotyped fashion, utterly without conscience as to our obligation to further the progress of our Art.

I make the following tentative 'after the war' suggestions, in the rather sanguine and optimistic hope that they may arouse us from our musical somnolence.

I Would Like to See:

FOR SOLOISTS

A system of specialised training for outstanding talent. The Russians have evolved one, and we could benefit by their experience. We should send a mission to Russia consisting of a body of British musicians who have 'been through the mill' and who are completely sincere in their desire to improve our standards.

Notes: 1) Our music students should be provided with a sound general education, and executants especially should have included in their curriculum some knowledge of anatomy.

2) Most performers at some time or other during their professional careers are particularly prone to suffer from Neuritis, Fibrositis, Scoliosis, or any of the other 'isises' through ignorance of the science of anatomy as it effects them, and of the essential measures for counteraction to reduce the effect of such occupationally influenced afflictions, i.e. massage, relaxation, correct stance, easy breathing etc., etc.

3) Long hair and locks over the right eyebrow are sick-making to look at, and entirely useless in furthering musical capability.

For Conductors

They should be caught young. Included in their special course would be their training, over a score of years, in a general practical knowledge of the various musical and unmusical contrivances employed in the orchestra.

Notes: 1) 'Yes Men' in the profession will say 'A little practical knowledge is dangerous'; but there are always exceptions to the rule, and this is one of them.

2) Violent acrobatic gesticulations on the part of the conductor are distracting and disturbing to the audience, and are superfluous for orchestral players.

The Orchestra

Our best orchestral players are interspersed among numerous organisations. We ought to possess a Super-Orchestra, and it could only materialise if it consisted – as it should – in a concentration of our best players in every department, without any exceptions. (One player not quite up to standard in any one section is sufficient to mar that body).

Notes: 1) Our academies and colleges should provide facilities for specialised training of orchestral players (especially string instrumentalists). They are generally taught as if they were all going to be soloists, and can perhaps give a fairly respectable performance of a concerto or two, in which they have been instructed and which they have practised, but very few, if any, have studied and have been individually taught the intricacies, difficulties, and subtleties of the performance of orchestral music. They should receive instruction from an experienced and competent orchestral player, who knows the orchestral repertoire and can therefore pass on all the 'tricks of the trade'.

2) In several auditions which I undertook for Sir Thomas Beecham, I heard scores of capable instrumentalists; but almost without exception they were a dismal failure when called upon to tackle orchestral music.

The B.B.C.

The B.B.C. is the organisation which should run the Super-Orchestra mentioned in the previous paragraph. Such an orchestra can only exist if relieved of the anxiety of the commercial aspect. It would not operate in opposition to our other orchestras. It would give two concerts only per week, and so allow time for sufficient and meticulous rehearsal. One of these concerts could be given in the Studio and one in public – the profits from the latter to go to the funds of our outside orchestras. On certain occasions the B.B.C. Orchestra would give propaganda concerts abroad. The members of the Super-Orchestra should not work more than six days a week. Attached to the orchestra there should be an experienced overseer, whose duties, among others, will be to see that all instruments and their accessories are always in perfect condition.

Notes: 1) I wish the B.B.C. would thoroughly probe the unsolved problem of the seating position of the various sections of the orchestra. Better tonal quality and quantity would certainly follow, if thoughtful experiment could be made with a full symphony orchestra for a few sessions for this specific purpose only. (An expensive procedure, but well worth it). For example, improvement is particularly needed to combat the inequality of tone quantity, as between the 1st and 2nd violins. Another thing to be tackled is the subduing of the always too prominent timpani (when on the air), etc., etc.

2) I wish the B.B.C. could also provide further research for the possibility of improvement in the acoustical properties of its studios. It is a great help to the performer to feel that what he is producing is being freely disseminated over the air. It is demoralizing and distinctly detrimental to performance to make music in a room that is practically without resonance. (A major fault it produces is the tendency to force). If the B.B.C. engineers could overcome this difficulty the result would be considerably enhanced performances.

BRITISH COMPOSERS

It should be possible for concert promoters to include one native work in every programme (i.e., when the whole of the concert is not taken up by a single composition).

Note: The assertion, often heard, that this would detract from box-office takings, is fudge.

THE STATE

The State should make possible equality of opportunity for the best musical training, for those worthy of it, in a State-aided Music School.

TEACHERS

Do not let us drift into insularism. It would be of distinct value to us to be able to welcome to the profession a few foreign teachers of outstanding accomplishment.

THE CONCERT HALL

The post-war concert hall should be built with particular attention to the seating of the orchestra, and with due regard to satisfactory conditions for the audience.

Notes: 1) Concert-hall platforms large enough to hold an orchestra have been built with very little consideration for the convenience of the players, and generally contain an abundance of obstructions.

2) Seats in the Auditorium are usually uncomfortable, the hall is either draughty, ill-ventilated, or over-heated, and little thought is given to other amenities, such as adequate refreshment facilities and cloak-room provision.

APPENDIX

'Music here is too much a business and too little an Art.'

'Our lethargic profession needs a very stiff dose of Honesty of Purpose.'

'The Art of Music is the nearest approach to Nature. Wielded properly it is a most potent influence on Humanity, and is a universal language.'

POSTSCRIPT

I shall probably be accused of being presumptuous in my criticisms of the many branches of our music-making. But in defence I claim the right to criticize by reason of my many years of observation and my ardently patriotic desire to further the cause of our much neglected music-talent and music-effort. I submit that the suggestions and proposals in this essay are constructive, and therefore worthy of consideration.

The article was reviewed in the August 1944 issue of *Musical Opinion*:

> Mr Lionel Tertis, in his article, 'Not Wishful Thinking' maintains that our music schools and academies in no wise pull their weight in supplying the urgent need for competent orchestral players producing hundreds of would-be, but rarely efficient, soloists. Sir Thomas Beecham, on the other hand, in his book, 'The Mingled Chime', draws attention to what he considers greatly improved standards in orchestral aspirants for symphonic work, attributing this to the intelligence of the training now available in English schools of music.

During the early 1940s there were some dissenting voices in the BBC regarding Tertis's standard of performance around this period. On 1 September 1942 Tertis wrote a letter to St George Philips at the BBC, suggesting that he might play his transcription of John Ireland's Cello Sonata with the composer at the piano. In a BBC memo dated 2 September Herbert Murrill asked for guidance, questioning the wisdom of broadcasting the sonata other than in its original form. In reply to Murrill's memo, a note on behalf of Julian Herbage on 23 September stated: 'D.M. (Director of Music) agrees the combination of Ireland and Tertis justifies our including this in programmes in spite of the fact that Tertis is not on the top of his form nowadays; Ireland himself feels that now [Antoni] Sala is no longer available there are no cellists who can really do the work justice, which seems at least some reason for the transcription being performed.' The first broadcast of the viola version, with the composer at the piano, was on Monday 14 December 1942 – Tertis also played his arrangement of Ireland's *The Holy Boy*.

Tertis wrote to Arthur Bliss, Director of Music at the BBC, on 2 August 1943:

> ... I am also very conscious and grateful for all the B.B.C. have done in giving a continuous strong helpful hand in my life-long campaign for the Viola, but the fact remains, that my professional engagements are few and far-between (for the usual reason, that the Viola Soloist is not a box-office draw) that I have only had two B.B.C. engagements since December 14th 1942, and I have been asked more than once, why am I so rarely on the 'air' – that I have to live, that my playing still seems to give satisfaction, and that if I cannot look to the B.B.C. for a certain amount of professional work, to provide the where-with-all, what am I to do? I have sacrificed my life for the Viola (and if I had another life, would do so again) but I feel my efforts are at least worth a hand-to mouth existence. Forgive this outburst – but the B.B.C. is the only institution to whom I feel I can air these views (views, probably not realized by anybody).

Tertis wrote to Julian Herbage on 10 April 1944 about a forthcoming broadcast of the Bloch Suite:

> I was so delighted to get the news concerning the Bloch Suite and I write to thank you. I am really looking forward to it, and I am so glad I am to play it with Sir Adrian. I should very much like to consult him about some slight alterations. About 20 years ago when I was giving a number of recitals I roped in a very few strings and some wind instruments, and played the Bloch at the Wigmore Hall – Eugène Goossens conducting – but this was a travesty with so few players, and therefore May 1st (1944) will really be the first performance in England with full orchestra. By-the-way I think it ought to be advertised as a suite for orchestra and viola (not viola and orchestra) – the orchestra is such a wonderful part of it ...

In 1944 Tertis changed his agent for a short time from Ibbs & Tillett to a Mr E. A. Michell.

During August he gave a recital in aid of the Malvern Hospital, where his wife Ada had been a patient. A number of his former students attended, including Winifred Copperwheat, then Professor of Viola at the Royal Academy of Music. Norris Stanley, a well-known Midlands-based violinist and leader of the Birmingham Orchestra, and pianist Albert Webb joined Tertis in his arrangement of the Bach Double Concerto. Brahms's F minor Sonata, Bach's *Chaconne* and shorter pieces such as Delius's Serenade and the *Londonderry Air* completed the programme, which Tertis played on a new Richardson–Tertis Model viola.

In February 1945 Tertis and Solomon recorded the Brahms Sonata in E flat, op. 120 no. 2. Tertis was very unhappy with the reproduction of the viola sound at these sessions; he felt it was pinched. In fact he was so annoyed that he put his viola away and refused to finish the recording. The first movement of the Brahms is missing, but the other movements exist, along with the Martini–Endicott filler, the best-played side of all from the violist's point of view.

At the Wigmore Hall on Wednesday 22 November 1944 an unusual concert was given by Harold Bauer and friends, including Albert Sammons, Cedric Sharpe and Tertis. The programme included the Bloch Suite and the Brahms Piano Quartet in G minor and was prefaced by the following:

> This concert is given by Mr. Harold Bauer and the Eminent Artists, who are so whole-heartedly co-operating with him, for the pleasure of making music together as comrades, and it has no object beyond that. It is not intended to provide a musical sensation, nor is it given for financial profit, for none of the participants receive any remuneration. The proceeds will be devoted to an object of general musical interest subsequently to be decided upon.

When Casals returned to London on 26 June 1945 to play a concerto at the Royal Albert Hall, his old friend Tertis was one of the first visitors after the concert to congratulate his coeval.

On Friday 1 March 1946 Tertis and York Bowen gave a recital at the National Gallery, forty-two years after their first concert together in 1904. Clifton Gray-Fisk reviewed the concert in *Musical Opinion*:

> It was very refreshing to hear these admirable artists again in partnership after a lapse of many years, since in technique and temperament they are exceptionally well matched. The Martini, a slight but charming piece, was superbly played and the Beethoven was treated with more care and respect than it actually deserves as it is a dull, trivial and quite uninspired

work. These items, however, really served as a warming-up practice for the most important part of the recital, the exquisite, haunting Romance of B. J. Dale (perhaps a trifle long even in the abbreviated version) which reminded us yet again that his untimely demise was a grievous loss to British music and also showed us how tragic it was that he could not, for economic reasons, devote himself entirely to composition. Few works of comparable quality have been written for the viola by any composer and none at all by the contemporary 'clique'. The performance was genuinely re-creative and could not have been bettered. Ireland's splendid virile Sonata, which has so well withstood the test of 30 years, sounds equally well on the dark colour of the viola. Indeed Mr. Tertis's warm, vibrant tone and Mr. Bowen's perfect piano playing combined to produce the most satisfying reading of the work we have yet heard.

A month later, on 3 April, Tertis and Bowen returned to the Royal Academy of Music to give a lunchtime recital as part of the Academy's Review Week events, repeating the programme they played at the National Gallery.

Not long before Sir Hamilton Harty's death in 1941, Tertis wrote to tell the conductor that he was thinking of arranging Mozart's Clarinet Concerto for viola. Harty replied: 'I am interested about the Viola Concerto. It ought to make a good piece for viola. Good luck to it. I think you might suggest a few possible cuts especially in the last movement. It's rather long.' Tertis set to work on this dubious enterprise and premièred the arrangement at the Three Choirs Festival in Hereford in 1946. There was very little press interest – in fact, the only review, by Ralph Hill, appeared in the *Daily Mail* under a prominent headline: 'Mozart knew best'. Tertis was severely criticized for making his arrangement. A few days later the critic Ferruccio Bonavia invited him to a Press Club lunch; there he met Ralph Hill who humorously said: 'I suppose you'll be having me up for slander.' Tertis replied: 'On the contrary, I am grateful beyond words for the publicity you have given the viola, moreover I don't at all mind being "second best to Mozart".' The guest of honour at the lunch was indisposed, so Bonavia approached Tertis, and without preamble, informed him that he would have to replace him. Tertis, realizing he would have to make a speech, lost his appetite and spent the time thinking what he might say. When the time came he stood up and said: 'Gentlemen, I feel like the lamb in the lions' den! But I say to you – I am an obstinate customer. For the last twenty years or so I have hurled vituperations at the press for their audacity in upbraiding me for my so-called crime of making arrangements from the classics, etc. for solo viola. Moreover I am impervious to pin pricks and the more you go for me, the more I shall do it ...'

At the time Tertis made his viola version of Mozart's Clarinet Concerto he had no idea that Toscanini's brother-in-law, the Italian violinist Enrico Polo, had made such an arrangement for Ricordi in 1927. Recent research has brought forward another transcription, published by André in 1802 – 'arrangé pour l'Alto par un Amateur'. The identity of the person responsible is unknown, but it has been suggested in some circles that it could have been Beethoven. This version, edited by Christopher Hogwood, was published by Bärenreiter in 1999.

Meanwhile Tertis's wife Ada was still seriously ill. Harry Danks remembers her as 'a typically homely lady, charming with a strong personality, who was dedicated to Lionel'. Ada Tertis had to spend periods of time in a nursing home and Lionel had to give her a lot of care and attention when she was at home, so when Harry went for a lesson he often used to cut the lawn and do gardening for Tertis.

Gilbert Shufflebotham, principal viola of the City of Birmingham Orchestra, also had some lessons with Tertis shortly after the war. On 17 November 1947 Shufflebotham was the soloist in the Walton Concerto in a concert promoted by the BBC to celebrate the orchestra's Silver Jubilee, with Sir Adrian Boult at the helm. Owing to the busy schedule, as was often the case, time did not allow for a pre-rehearsal day – on this occasion an hour was found in Bristol to run through the concerto in preparation for the following day's concert. The *Birmingham Post*'s critic praised Shufflebotham's playing: 'Expression was sensitive and beautiful, intonation impeccable.'

Tertis gave a concert at the Wigmore Hall on 2 October 1946 to raise funds for a new prize at the Royal Academy of Music for viola compositions. He was assisted by the Zorian String Quartet and York Bowen in a programme that featured his *Variations on a Four Bar Theme of Handel* for two violas, which he played with Winifred Copperwheat. The critic in the *Daily Telegraph* referred to it as a 'memorable evening':

> After Lionel Tertis's magnificent performance of his transcription for viola of John Ireland's second violin sonata last night at the concert he gave at Wigmore Hall for a viola prize at the Royal Academy of Music, a violinist in the audience who had played the work in its original form declared the transcription to transcend the original. Clarinettists are not so likely to approve Mr. Tertis's transcription of Mozart's clarinet concerto. But it has ample justification. The viola player is now endowed with a fine classic. It sounded divinely beautiful.
>
> At the end Mr. Tertis, in a speech, supported a suggestion I made in The Daily Telegraph on Saturday, by saying that if he had his time over again

he would play the viola not under his chin but between his knees, cello fashion.

Gordon Jacob helped Tertis to select the winners in the competition, and found him 'much more broadminded and tolerant than he had been before'. Jacob came to know him quite well in the 1930s and 1940s, when they lived not far apart in Surrey: 'He was then keen on encouraging young composers to write for the viola and realized that they could not be expected to write in the style of his earlier contemporaries such as Thomas Dunhill, Benjamin Dale and York Bowen who had written excellent music for him in the past.' The Lionel Tertis Prize was awarded to the South African composer John Joubert for his Concerto for viola and chamber orchestra.

Owing to a severe recurrence of fibrositis during the winter of 1946–7, Tertis had to withdraw once again from music-making. Having time on his hands, he indulged his penchant for inditing letters to the press. With the founding of Walter Legge's Philharmonia and Beecham's Royal Philharmonic, London now had five permanent symphonic ensembles – not to mention such freelance bands as the New SO and National SO – and Tertis wrote to the *Daily Telegraph*, complaining that 'the present-day mushroom growth of orchestras in London is ridiculous'. After a period of rest and treatment he was once again able to resume playing, and managed to conceal the shortcomings in his bow arm. In 1947, when he was seventy years old, he recorded two short pieces for HMV – 'Come, Sweet Death' by Bach, which he arranged for viola and Sonata in E major by Martini. The BBC recorded him playing the Brahms E flat Sonata with Ernest Lush but the discs appear to have been destroyed.

The following poem was written by Alan Denson after a performance that Tertis gave of *Harold in Italy* at a Royal Albert Hall Promenade Concert on 19 August 1947.[1]

Lionel Tertis

Within Berlioz' marvellous score
Evoking 'Harold in Italy'
Your viola's voice intoning
Every phrase has filled my mind
With modulated grace and fire;
Eloquence sublimely free
From rhythmic eccentricity.

Great heart, great artist, what you gave
Was an example to us all

Mere listeners, and executants
For your faultless pitch disposed
All listeners to model life
At every level on your scale;
Your quest for perfect form, vivacity.

The concert was reviewed in the *Daily Telegraph* next day:

Last night 70-year-old Lionel Tertis gave an exceedingly fine performance of Berlioz's 'Harold in Italy' at the Albert Hall Proms. Mr Tertis is a great stylist among violists. With all the necessary romantic fire his playing has subtleties as remarkable as the tone, which, even when reduced to a bare minimum, penetrates to every corner of the Albert Hall. Mr Tertis was valiantly aided by the orchestral playing under Basil Cameron ...

In the audience at this concert was the fifteen-year-old Norman Kent, who was later to distinguish himself as a violist in the Liverpool Philharmonic and BBC Symphony Orchestras. He 'could not believe the amount of sound Tertis made – though I did think it sounded more like a saxophone than a viola'.

In 1947 Ruth Railton had the idea of forming a National Youth Orchestra. Her enthusiasm was boundless, and, before the idea had come to fruition, Malcolm Arnold, then a young trumpet player in the London Philharmonic Orchestra, had agreed to write a new work for the fledgling ensemble. Railton contacted some of the leading instrumental teachers of the time – she was determined that each section of her orchestra should have the best tutors available. Douglas Cameron (who had been in Tertis's chamber-music class in the 1920s) had established himself as a fine cello teacher at the Royal Academy of Music, and was the first to agree, followed by that fine Danish violinist Henry Holst. With trepidation Railton then approached Tertis, 'and with what nerve I asked the great Lionel Tertis to teach my beginners on the viola'.

Railton insisted on a number of rules right from the beginning:

1. It was important to establish an atmosphere of courtesy and appreciation for the distinguished musicians who were coming to tutor the orchestra.
2. Good discipline in the rehearsal rooms.
3. Punctuality for all rehearsals – and no running in corridors when carrying instruments.
4. Right from the start it was stressed that the young musicians selected had always to be on their best behaviour as they were representatives of their country.

She was keen that every student should have both individual help on their own instrument, plus theory and some choral training, and that they should all take part in the end-of-course concert.

None of the tutors had taught at this level before, but Railton had a good response. Douglas Cameron reported: 'They may be beginners but they're so quick, so keen.' Tertis was full of astonishment: 'All this young talent on the viola! But they all need individual attention every day before they can play in an orchestra', and he advised all those who played instruments smaller than 16½" to 'put them on the fire'.

An unforeseen visit from the national press and some administrative problems caused difficulty between Tertis and the course director. Railton remembered: 'I had been unable to see L.T., who had some problems with his timetable. When he left at lunch-time he handed in a note. He thought I had ignored him that morning ... so he was saying goodbye and wouldn't be coming back again.' That evening, however, Miss Railton received an apology and flowers from Tertis.

Shortly after Tertis's departure Ruth Railton received an unexpected telephone call from his former student Bernard Shore, formerly principal viola in the BBC SO, but now HM Chief Inspector of Music. He happened to be in the area, and asked Miss Railton if he could come and see work in progress. Her answer was: 'Yes please; you're needed to take over the violas at the five o'clock rehearsal.' Shore, after this initial visit, had hoped to stay on as the regular viola tutor of the NYO, but in his position as HMI it did not seem right; however, he continued to support the aims and objectives of the orchestra for the rest of his life.

The first course of the National Youth Orchestra of Great Britain was held at the Bath Assembly Halls in 1948. Margaret Major and Christopher Wellington, both later to distinguish themselves in the music profession, were the front desk of the viola section, and both were convinced that they were the first principal viola in the orchestra. Margaret Major was accepted for the National Youth Orchestra the day after her sixteenth birthday, and went to the first course with all the other excited young players. Christopher Wellington was inspired by Tertis's recordings when he took up the viola at Bryanston School. After a successful audition he was invited to join the NYO for their first course. His recollections of the occasion differ from those of Ruth Railton:

In April 1948 the National Youth Orchestra of Great Britain met for the first time – and an anxious Douglas Cameron picked up a baton wondering whether this newly assembled bunch of boys and girls could play anything resembling Weber's 'Oberon' Overture. It turned out they could

– although hurrying somewhat, which was characteristic of that first
Orchestra. Lionel Tertis had been persuaded by Ruth Railton to coach
the violas – and on the second day of the course was introduced to an
awe-struck viola section. Our knees soon knocked even more vigorously
as Tertis proceeded to give each of us in turn a 5-minute audition. As Principal I stood up first – and unwisely launched into the Brahms F minor
Sonata – Tertis had me playing E–A flat–G for 2 minutes – and didn't
consider it in tune even then! Margaret Major, then 16, was already as
able a player as many professionals, but neither she nor any of the others
found any favour with the great man. Tertis collected up his belongings
and marched off to announce to Ruth Railton 'They're all quite hopeless
– I can't do a thing with them!' – and went home.

With hindsight one can see that Tertis, who can rarely have had contact with
players less advanced than top RAM standard, could not foresee that this over-
awed bunch of children would reach a viable performance standard in a few
days' time; he may even have been concerned that the whole orchestra might
fail – to the dismay of his immensely high standards and even to the detriment
of his reputation.

Christopher later had some lessons with Winifred Copperwheat, and
acquired a particularly good Tertis Model from Arthur Richardson (R.T.
no. 101), which was fitted from day one with gut strings (in spite of Tertis's own
predilection for metal).

Throughout his life Tertis always regretted that he started playing a string
instrument so late, and in consequence lacked a natural technical ability. He
always found it necessary to practise very hard before any public concert – 'and
the prospect of a public performance – whether before an audience of two or
two-thousand, and whether I was playing but once a week or seven times – was
a call upon every ounce of courage I possessed, like the prospect of undergoing
a surgical operation.' When he had a difficult passage or work to play (e.g. the
Bach *Chaconne*) he would practise in a very heavy overcoat; this made it so
much easier when he had to perform in an ordinary suit or evening dress.

In August 1948 the BBC appointed a number of well-known musicians as
'outside assessors' on their audition panels; these experts would sit in listening
rooms connected to the studio by microphone and loudspeaker. The musicians
who auditioned never knew the identity of the panel, and vice versa. Among
the names of those who agreed to serve as assessors were Dame Myra Hess,
Louis Kentner, Albert Sammons, Roy Henderson, Arthur Bliss and Tertis. On
5 September 1948 Tertis wrote to Sir Steuart Wilson who was Head of Music at
the BBC:

... I don't know what the procedure is at the auditions (this being the first I shall have attended) but as you say in your letter of April 13th last, we, – the adjudicators must remember the vast difference as between a broadcasting standard and a mere diploma examination. Therefore, in view of this importance, forgive my presumption in suggesting that the written adjudgments on the different candidates be a strictly private one of each adjudicator ... so that when the results come up for discussion on the 21st October the reports of those present at the auditions, whether BBC music staff, or adjudicators, shall have been entirely uninfluenced.

I should so like to see you one day if you can possibly spare the time, it concerns my not having broadcast for a h–l of a time. I know I am an 'old horse', but I flatter myself I am still able to 'deliver the goods', and I am keen that the world should not look upon me – just yet, as being defunct. My paramount reason for this is to keep my name alive a little longer as a protagonist for the viola while I am developing my scheme connected with the viola I have evolved, by which, I hope to interest violin makers to provide decent violas for the present and future generations of violists. The diagram and specification in English and French, as enclosed, has gone practically all over the world and the resulting correspondences from foreign craftsmen (so far 21 different countries) is distinctly encouraging.

Tertis wrote to Kenneth Wright at the BBC on 9 July 1949 regarding the auditions:

Dear Kenneth,
May I be forgiven for this botheration but I write to you as chairman of the meetings held subsequent to auditions. I believe I am right in saying that I have now attended three times as a member of the listening panel and each attendance has revealed a low standard of accomplishment for the purpose of broadcasting. It seems to me that there must be something wrong in the procedure for selecting candidates for these important auditions – a teacher's opinion, – or a questionnaire as to – 'when did you last appear in public, and where' etc. is of no real value. The requirement that should be necessary for qualification for an audition proper – in my opinion – ought to be a preliminary one, by an expert of your staff, by his or her attendance at a public performance given by the applicant, in which the programme was evidence of importance. When one thinks of the reserve in high standard and capability demanded by a broadcast – as opposed to a mere public appearance – I feel a preliminary 'try out' such as I suggest is imperative and might give some chance of the 'pudding being proved

in the eating' – and so save a lot of waste of time in these major auditions. Forgive my presumption in offering these opinions – at the same time – if it is possible – I should be glad if Sir Steuart Wilson could be acquainted with what I have ventured to propound.

This letter resulted in the following reply from Steuart Wilson on 27 July:

Dear Lionel,
Thank you very much for putting your point of view so strongly about the standard of qualification.

There are two points of view here. One is the apparent waste of your time in hearing an unknown performer who does not in fact make good. The other side is the advantage which we now have of having at last satisfied the Music Profession that there is a free and unobstructed passage towards an audition. When they get it they are heard under conditions which create no prejudice, and when it is all over they get a straight answer.

The difficulty of giving public concerts is so great as to make it impossible that we should insist on it as a prior condition. A further difficulty of receiving an engagement for a public concert is that unless they broadcast, access to that market is getting more and more restricted.

I am afraid that it may be possible that you have had a bad run and have been unlucky. Anyway, we do appreciate both your presence and your patience on this difficult job.

The Carl Flesch Medal was competed for at the Guildhall School of Music and Drama on 5 November 1948; Tertis was among the adjudicators, with Edric Cundell (Principal of Guildhall), Basil Cameron, Max Rostal and David Wise (leader of the London Philharmonic Orchestra).

In 1949 Tertis wrote to Phyllis Ebsworth, the viola player of both the Ebsworth and Macnaghten String Quartets:

Dear Madam,
With the permission of Sir George Dyson I am giving a Recital on June 14th at 5.30 p.m. for the purpose of raising funds to provide prizes for Solo Viola composition at the Royal College of Music. (Prizes for this purpose already exist at the Royal Academy of Music). The library of Solo Music for Viola is still meagre and the necessity of increasing it is of importance to the progress of this neglected medium of expression. I shall have the privilege of being most generously assisted at the recital by Ruth Fermoy (piano), Max Rostal (violin) and the 'Copperwheat String Quartet'.

The programme will include

Chaconne (for viola alone)   Bach
Sonata in E flat (viola and piano)   Brahms
Double Concerto in D minor (violin, viola and string quartet)   Bach

I am avoiding the idea of giving the recital at one of the usual Concert Halls in order to reduce expenses to a minimum and I am glad to say the Royal College of Music is generously helping me in allowing me the use of their Concert Hall free – but this means I cannot sell tickets. I therefore take the liberty of enclosing two invitation tickets in the hope that it may be possible for you to help me in my project by joining my list of Patrons with a donation however large or small. I already have 25 guineas but would like to gather say another £100 in order to make my scheme a workable one.

I should be most grateful to be able to publish your name as a Patron.

Yours sincerely,

Lionel Tertis

On 24 November 1949 the Executive and Finance Committee at the Royal College of Music reported that the sum of £408 15s. 6d., raised by subscription, had been received from Mr. Lionel Tertis 'to institute prizes for solo viola compositions at the college for such time as this amount and any interest thereon shall last'. (Nearly six years later the same committee noted: 'Now that the Tertis Prize money is almost all spent, Mr. Lionel Tertis has agreed that the Director should hand the balance to one or two worthy students in need of help.') Professor John Paynter remembered the concert fifty years later:

It also reminded me of Tertis who was such a wonderful musician and around that time helped to found the viola composition prizes at the Royal College of Music to encourage composers to write more for the viola. I remember a magnificent recital which launched the prize fund – Tertis and Max Rostal gave a stunning performance of the Bach Double Violin Concerto (Rostal, of course, playing his beautiful Guarneri violin but Tertis playing the other violin part on the viola. Two such renowned players, clearly united in their thinking about that work, created a very highly charged atmosphere, as you can imagine.

The soloists were accompanied on this occasion by the Copperwheat String Quartet with that wonderful violist Winifred Copperwheat in the unusual role of first violin, with Maureen Flynn (2nd violin), Marjorie Lempfert (viola) and Norina Semino (cello). The ensemble played Schubert's *Quartettsatz* op. Posth. in C minor in the concert and Tertis and Ruth Fermoy started the proceedings with the Sonata in D by Martini.

The printed programme included a long list of distinguished musicians who had already subscribed to the prize fund, including Casals, Kreisler, Solomon, Myra Hess, Bax and a number of fellow violists such as Watson Forbes, James Lockyer, Nannie Jamieson, Jean Stewart, Lena Wood, Sydney Errington, Paul Cropper, Eric Coates, Bernard Shore and the complete viola section of the BBC Symphony Orchestra, whose principal was Harry Danks.

Tertis met Lady Fermoy – a lady-in-waiting to the then Queen, an amateur pianist of professional standard and a former pupil of Cortot – at Holkham in the 1940s. They often made music together, both privately and at the King's Lynn Festival. (After Tertis's death, as Ruth, Lady Fermoy, she became President of the Lionel Tertis International Viola Competition.) Another aristocratic friend of Tertis, the Earl of Leicester, whom he had known since the First World War, died on 21 August 1949; at the funeral service at Holkham church Tertis played his arrangement of Bach's 'Come Sweet Death'. One of the last times the Earl and Tertis met was during the winter of 1946–7, when a severe recurrence of fibrositis temporarily forced Tertis to withdraw from music-making, and he complained to Lord Leicester that he was beginning to feel old. His Lordship exploded: 'Good gracious, Lionel, what stuff and nonsense, you are in the prime of life!' and on a following visit presented Tertis with the following poem.

> Age is a quality of mind
> If you've left dreams behind
> If hope is cold
> If you no longer look ahead
> If your ambitious fires are dead
> Then you are old.
>
> But if from life you take the best
> If in life you keep a zest
> If love you hold
> No matter how the years go by
> No matter how the birthdays fly
> You are not old.

1 Lionel Tertis's father,
Alexander Tertis

2 Lionel Tertis's mother,
Phoebe, née Hermann

3 The Royal Academy of Music, Tenterden Street, *c.*1895

4 Sir Alexander Mackenzie, Principal of the Royal Academy of Music, *c.*1896

5 Royal Academy of Music medallion for sight-singing, presented to Tertis, 1897

6 Hans Wessely, Tertis's violin professor at the Royal Academy of Music, 1895–7

7 Sir Henry Wood, conductor of the
Queen's Hall Orchestra

8 Arnold Bax, *c.*1904, when he
composed his Concert Piece for Tertis

9 Fritz Kreisler, Tertis's inspiration, and
later colleague and friend

10 William Wolstenholme, blind
organist and composer

11 Eric Coates, violist and composer, who studied with Tertis from 1906

12 Frank Bridge, outstanding violist and composer

13 York Bowen, *c.*1905, who wrote many pieces for Tertis, including a Viola Concerto, and was also his accompanist

14 B. J. Dale, *c.*1905, who wrote three major works for Tertis's campaign on behalf of the viola

15 Tertis's first wife, Ada Gawthrop, whom he married in 1913

16 Eugène Ysaÿe, the great Belgian violin virtuoso

17 Tertis with the composer Cyril Scott, discussing the latter's *Fantasia*, *c.*1912

18 A group of musicians, including Tertis (*right*) and Ysaÿe (*left*),
visiting the Belgian Front, 1916

WIGMORE HALL
WIGMORE STREET, W.

Wednesday,

Oct. 31st, at 8.15

LIONEL

TERTIS

AND

WILLIAM

MURDOCH

VIOLA AND PIANOFORTE
Sonata Recital

CHAPPELL GRAND PIANOFORTE

Reserved Stalls 7s. 6d. (Tax 1s.). Reserved Area 5s. (Tax 9d.)
Unreserved Area and Balcony, 2s. 6d. (Tax 6d.)

Telephone—5564 GERRARD.
Telegrams—" MUSACEOUS LONDON."

L. G. SHARPE, 61, Regent Street, W. 1.

Vail & Co., Printers, E.C.1.

P.T.O.

19 Programme for a sonata recital by Tertis and William Murdoch,
Wigmore Hall, 1917

21 Adrian Boult c.1918,
a lifelong friend of Tertis

20 Rebecca Clarke, distinguished
composer and former viola student
of Tertis

22 Albert Sammons, the outstanding
British violinist of his time, a great
friend of Tertis and his colleague in
The Chamber Music Players

23 Tertis playing his wonderful Montagnana viola

24 The first time William Primrose and Tertis made music together,
at the Salle Pleyel, Paris, 30 May 1928

25 Dame Nellie Melba,
with whom Tertis appeared on her
farewell tour of 1926

26 Harriet Cohen, Tertis's accompanist
on a number of European tours

27 Tertis with Phyllis McDonald, Adna Ryerson, Winifred Copperwheat and Joan
Mulholland, at the time they performed all the Haydn String Quartets, 1928

28 An early picture of the Griller Quartet: (*left to right*) Philip Burton,
Jack O'Brien, Sidney Griller and Colin Hampton

29 Tertis and Solomon, who premièred the Sonata by Arthur Bliss

30 Bernard Shore, principal viola in
the original BBC Symphony Orchestra,
a former student of Tertis, 1930

31 May Harrison (violin),
with whom Tertis played Delius's
Double Concerto

32 Harry Danks, principal viola in the BBC Symphony Orchestra
for thirty-two years, student and friend of Tertis

33 The Chamber Music Players, c.1935: Lauri Kennedy, Albert Sammons, William Murdoch, Tertis

34 Tertis, *c.*1937, at the time of his retirement

35 Tertis with Sir Thomas Beecham and Fritz Kreisler at the Royal Albert Hall, 1938

36 Tertis with luthier Arthur Richardson, Crediton, c.1948

37 Thomas Dunhill, John Ireland and Tertis, *c.*1941

38 Tertis and William Primrose, c.1950: a unique photograph of two of the world's greatest viola players

39 Tertis with Ann Glock and Sándor Végh
at the Dartington Summer School of Music, 1955

40 Lillian Warmington, who became Tertis's second wife

41 Lionel and Lillian Tertis, with sculptures by Henry Moore
which they found in the garden of their Wimbledon home

42 King's Lynn Festival: Lady Fermoy, Laurance Turner (violin), Lady Barbirolli (Evelyn Rothwell, oboe),
Sir John Barbirolli (cello), Sydney Errington (viola), Tertis, Julian Bream (guitar)

43 Tertis with Ralph Vaughan Williams and the conductor Herbert Menges at a rehearsal of Vaughan Williams's *Flos campi*, 1958

44 Tertis and Ralph Vaughan Williams, 1958

45 Tertis and Pablo Casals, 1961

46 Sir John Barbirolli greets Tertis at the King's Lynn Festival, 1968

47 Portrait of Tertis by Derek Hill, commissioned by Lady Sylvia Combe

48 Tertis's 90th-birthday photograph

49 Tertis with Artur and Nela Rubinstein at Tertis's home in Wimbledon,
7 September 1972

50 Tertis with Sir Adrian Boult at Tertis's home in Wimbledon

51 Lionel Tertis, 1974

52 Lionel and Lillian Tertis with the composer Edmund Rubbra, 2 July 1974

Promoting the Tertis Model Viola

*CBE – promoting the T.M. – Wilfred Saunders – death of Ada
– move to Devon – Dartington – Lillian Warmington*

I N JANUARY 1950 Tertis declared himself 'greatly honoured' when King
George VI appointed him Commander of the Order of the British Empire
(CBE) 'for services to music, particularly in relation to the viola'. Sadly Ada,
who had been ailing for some six years, was in a nursing home at the time, and
could not accompany him to Buckingham Palace to receive the honour from
the King. Tertis therefore asked Charles Lovett Gill to go with him. Later in
the year the committee of the Musicians' Benevolent Fund conferred an award
on him that also proved dear to his heart; Tertis received the news in a letter,
dated 30 October, from the chief critic of *The Times*, Frank Howes, chairman
of the fund:

> It gives me pleasure to write and tell you that the Executive Committee
> of this Fund has nominated you for the 'Kreisler Award of Merit'. Certain
> monies have been placed at our disposal for the making of these awards,
> which bear the names of those who have been eminent in music and
> helped our Fund in its ordinary work. Plunket Greene and Myra Hess are
> other names which are attached to these awards. We think that for you,
> who have done so much for string playing, it is appropriate that the award
> should be the one bearing Kreisler's name. I enclose a cheque for £250,
> the normal amount of these awards, with the hope that you will do us the
> honour of allowing us to inscribe your name upon our roll of honoured
> musicians.

On 4 January 1950 Kenneth Harding's Divertimento for four violas was
broadcast on the BBC Third Programme by the composer and three colleagues
in the BBC Symphony Orchestra – Harry Danks, Jacqueline Townshend and
Stanley Wootton. The performance was reviewed in the April 1950 issue of *The
Strad*:

> Mr Harding has written very suitable music, which exploits the intellectual
> and distinctly unsentimental character of the viola. The balance, both as
> regards quality and volume would hardly have been so good with instru-
> ments of different dimensions. As it was, all four players were using the

model worked out by Lionel Tertis in collaboration with Arthur Richardson of Crediton, Devon.

Not everyone was convinced by the Tertis Model. Whereas the Swiss player Albert Bertschmann of the Basel Quartet and the Busch Chamber Players swore by it, and made three trips to Crediton – buying a new Richardson viola each time – the luthier Clifford Hoing was violently opposed to it: even to mention it to him was like a red rag to a bull. Hoing had his own baby, the 16¼ inch 'Diploma model', and his acrimonious debate with Tertis about the ideal size for a viola went on for years in *The Strad*. It would seem that both men, being rather self-opinionated, simply could not resist having a go at each other.

On 4 December 1950 Tertis arranged a concert at the Wigmore Hall to demonstrate the qualities of the Tertis Model viola. The artists taking part included William Primrose, with Ernest Lush at the piano, in Brahms's Sonata in E flat, op. 120 no. 2, in which Primrose played on four different Tertis Model violas; he played the first movement on one by Pierre Vidoudez of Geneva, the second movement was shared by an instrument of E. & P. Voigt of London and one by C. Lovett Gill. In the finale Primrose played on a viola by Arthur Richardson, one of seven used in the concert. Tertis's arrangement for two violas of the slow movement from Mozart's Duo in B flat, K424, featured Winifred Copperwheat and Jacqueline Townshend; Harry Danks, Stanley Wootton, Jacqueline Townshend and Kenneth Harding premièred Kenneth Harding's Concertante for four violas dedicated to Tertis, and also played the composer's Divertimento, which had already received three performances since its première in a live broadcast. The quartet were joined by Winifred Copperwheat and Hope Hambourg in B. J. Dale's *Introduction and Andante*, op. 5, for six violas. The highlight of the concert was the first performance of Tertis's transcription for three violas of Beethoven's Trio, op. 87 (originally written for two oboes and cor anglais), played by William Primrose, Harry Danks and Stanley Wootton. Harry Danks remembered that they were able to have only one rehearsal, but *The Strad* critic commented: 'A most interesting afternoon closed with a fine performance of one of Mr. Tertis's most successful transcriptions.' Tertis gave the following address to the audience:

> The design of the violas to which you are listening today has been conceived, first, as a result of the scarcity of violas and secondly because of the deficiencies of small and large violas still in circulation. These deficiencies have continually confronted me during my fifty-seven [*recte* 54] years of viola playing. The small violas have insufficient air space and therefore lack viola sonority. The large ones with their cumbersome features effectively

prevent ease of manipulation, (as my colleague William Primrose once pungently remarked with regard to the very large viola, – 'The viola is difficult enough without having to indulge in a wrestling match with it'). The many different sizes of violas in circulation make it difficult for a player to go from one viola to another, as is possible with the more or less standardized violin, and it is this lack of standardization in the viola which we are trying to rectify and which has hitherto been an obstacle to its progress. Now that the viola has obtained and is consolidating its rightful place on the musical map, more than ever necessary is the provision of good instruments, of which there is a great scarcity the World over; there are nothing like enough for the growing army of efficient and discerning viola players. The 'Tertis Model' we think will help to correct these shortages and defects. It is 16 ¾ inches long and this I consider to be the maximum length for playing under the chin and at the same time the minimum from which we hope for a really satisfactory sonority. In this model we have been fortunate in our arrangement of air space, and also incorporated are other features, resulting from practical experience, which make it, for its size, easy to handle. The fact that from 1938 approximately a hundred and thirty of these violas have been made, mostly by eminent professional craftsmen, here and in other countries, and that the vast majority of these instruments are in the hands of professional viola players, speaks for itself. The standardization of the viola for which we are striving though as yet by no means achieved, is well on the way, and I think will prove to have a most beneficent influence in furthering the cause of the viola.

I should like to pay tribute to the violin-maker Arthur Richardson, – I am particularly indebted to him for the many experiments which he made towards realizing my theories with regard to the ideal viola from the player's point of view, and I venture to suggest our collaboration has not been in vain. Mr. Richardson enjoys the unique distinction of being the first man in the history of fiddle craftsmanship to have made nearly one hundred violas, – to be precise, ninety-six. I want also to thank Mr. C. Lovett Gill, eminent architect and amateur violin-maker, for his fine drawing of the design of this instrument. These drawings are in use in many parts of the Globe. Mr. Gill has made seven of these violas, one of which you have heard today. On my own behalf I should like to add that neither in the viola nor the scheme have I any financial interest whatsoever. Not a few of my friends have accused me of being an altruistic duffer, in not accepting financial reward for my part in the development of this viola. But if I had, this would have sent up the price of the instrument; and we viola players as a class have never been and, I fear, never will be particularly affluent;

and further, I would not have my endeavours for the viola in this direction tainted with monetary gain, – my satisfaction lies in the fact that I have helped to provide the present and future generation of viola players with a fine toned and manageable instrument.

From the very beginning of my campaign for the viola in 1895 [*recte* 1896] I have found that anything, however slightly unorthodox, that tends towards progress, has generally met with violent opposition, and I know that some craftsmen and violin dealers resent the idea that a mere instrumentalist should dare to lay down the law as to the design of the viola, but I have had much experience of being up against prejudice, and I am impervious to pinpricks. I know that I am not a violin-maker, nor am I a scientist, nor do I understand the secrets of acoustics, – but I say to the violin-makers that I have kept my eyes and ears open for well over half a century and have put two and two together, in other words, the design is simply an amalgamation of all the good points in the many instruments I have seen, heard, and played plus anything that I have learned that makes for ease in manipulating the larger dimensions of the viola. As you will see from your programmes, there are eminent violin craftsmen in various countries who have welcomed my ideas and who are making these violas.

There are one or two other matters I want to mention, – first my gratitude to my colleagues who have given their artistry for this demonstration; and I want specially to thank William Primrose for undertaking my job today. I am sure I am speaking on behalf of all viola players when I say that we rejoice in the magnificent work he is doing for the cause of the viola. I conclude with the hope that today's demonstration will result in still wider publicity for this Viola, which it is pleasant to feel has emanated from England.

Around this time Tertis was approached by the music publishers Bosworth & Co., with a request that he arrange some of Ševčík's celebrated violin studies for viola. Tertis agreed, on condition that Bosworth & Co. publish his arrangement of the Beethoven Trio. Both sides were happy, and violists gained two useful additions to their repertoire. Ševčík's Studies, op. 2, parts 1, 2 and 3, *The School of Bowing Technique*, transposed and edited by Tertis, appeared in 1957, and his introduction to Ševčík's op. 8 change of position exercises is worth quoting.

Remember!

1) The first consideration in string playing, is the attainment of perfect intonation. This can only be achieved by the most intense and concentrated

listening, (not superficial listening). Never pass a note that is the slightest degree out of tune.

2) Hold and keep your fingers down on the strings in all these exercises, whenever and wherever it is at all possible.

3) Attention must be paid to accurate note values. Be particularly careful when there are two notes with separate bows, immediately followed by two notes of the same value in one bow, or one note separately, followed by three notes of the same value in one bow etc. etc. No matter how varied the groupings, every note must be of exact equal value.

4) When practising these exercises slowly lift your fingers high and feel you are doing so from the knuckles and bring your fingers down hard on the fingerboard, – when practising them rapidly, do not lift your fingers high and put them down lightly on the fingerboard.

5) Divide the bowing up so as to, first, practise the exercises slowly and play them in tune. When you can do this efficiently, use the bowing as indicated, or as many notes in the one bow as possible.

In 1950, at the age of twenty-two, the violin-maker Wilfred Saunders set up his own workshop. Progress was slow, and he had to rely on word of mouth, believing that reputations were made by what players said to each other about instruments, and not by flashy publicity. He had one or two lucky breaks; there was an article in *Picture Post* about the Tertis–Richardson Model viola in 1947. It was supposed to be the perfect viola, with narrow upper bouts, extra wide lower bouts and short corners to facilitate playing in the higher positions. Saunders sent for the plans and made a viola from them. He did not follow the design to the letter but made slight alterations. Tertis saw the resulting viola and asked Saunders to make one, sticking more closely to the model:

It was one of those that came out just right and Tertis used it for the next ten years. But what a taskmaster he was! He could be utterly charming and he could be totally intractable. There was no arguing with him. I remember once going down to meet him at the Sesame Imperial and Pioneer Club in London. My train broke down, so I was late for the meeting. He was so furious that I knew nothing was going to be right about the viola, and indeed he ranted about the position of the soundpost and insisted on my following his exact instructions. I went away and left the viola completely untouched in its case. When I returned next morning he took it out, played a few bars and expressed complete satisfaction adding: 'There you see, why can't you get these things right in the first place.' He wasn't easy to work with and in the end I couldn't sustain the demands he made on me.

Tertis nevertheless put Saunders on the map. The Israel Philharmonic Orchestra ordered seven Tertis Model violas, of which Saunders made three, and many other commissions flowed from that.

In 1949 Noel Cox went to Nottingham as the first Music Adviser to the city, and very shortly afterwards met an amateur flautist by the name of Saunders who was a railwayman. He told Cox about his two sons, one who was hoping to be an architect and the other a cabinet-maker. The latter was Wilfred, who soon gave up cabinet-making and started making violins. Wilfred and his wife Janet lived in West Bridgford, a suburb just south of the River Trent, quite near to Noel Cox. In the early 1950s Cox received a phone call from Wilfred Saunders, saying that Tertis was going to visit him to look at some violas, and asking if he would like to come round to meet Tertis and play the piano for him. Cox was naturally delighted at the great opportunity, and when he arrived at the Saunders' house there was the Grand Old Man surrounded by instruments; very soon they were playing Brahms Sonatas together. 'Needless to say these are not something you can do without plenty of prior practice (particularly the F minor) and I think I probably played very badly', Cox remembered. However, Tertis was very kind. Noel Cox's lasting memory of the occasion is of seeing Tertis put down the viola when there were a few bars rest, and picking up another, playing all the time.

Wilfred Saunders received many letters from Tertis during the years he made Tertis Model instruments, including a long letter in April 1955 and two short ones from the following year. The examples that follow show the two sides of Tertis's personality; the one dated 24 April 1955, as Saunders says:

> ... shows how impossible he could be. His viola plans and instructions had the soundpost ¼" outside the bridge. This idea he thought gave him a certain type of tone on one viola Arthur Richardson had made some years earlier, so according to Tertis all violas had to be fitted up like this. With the soundpost position like this a bump would appear on the outside of the belly, and the belly could crack. He was ignorant about the structure of the instrument. I had written him a long letter explaining how wood could withstand sheer pressure along the grain, but not across the grain. I did him careful drawings telling him different forces – compression, tension, sheer etc.
>
> A complete waste of time! So I thought my idea would help to strengthen this point of the belly. He played the viola for several weeks with complete

satisfaction until he poked about inside with his mirror and found my veneer.

The following letter gives some idea of what Saunders had to put up with at that time:

> Edgmoor, Middlemoor, Tavistock, Devon Sunday 24th April 1955
>
> Dear Saunders,
>
> I have your letter of yesterday. It is perfectly true that you mentioned something to me about the strengthening of the belly and veneer, – but you did not mention the word soundpost. If you had given me the slightest impression that the veneer was on the belly where the soundpost stands!! why I would not have countenanced it. Naturally, in the short time I was with you, I did not look at the post with the mirror for I would not have dreamt of a post being fitted on to a piece of veneer – and on a new fiddle! No doubt a depression does occur in an old fiddle but one puts up with that and fits a sound-post accordingly. A sound-post is an extremely sensitive part of the anatomy of a fiddle and any obstruction between it and the plates is nothing but an obstacle harmful to tonal quality. Apart from this any decent fiddle craftsman or player would immediately jump to the conclusion that there was some sort of blemish or even a crack under that piece of veneer! I think to say the least of it, you should have consulted me first before doing such a drastic thing. In doing this you have not only violently deviated from my specification of my 'Tertis Model', but you have also made a most vital mistake in the width of your f holes. They should be as per my drawing $^{11}/_{32}''$ and yours are considerably narrower. Richardson made innumerable experiments with the width of f holes and I have in conjunction with George Schlieps of New York, – to the extent of my playing in between (his use of the knife) of every shaving he took off the f holes in a viola in the white, – ruining two plates in the process, and we all three came to the definite conclusion that a width of $^{11}/_{32}''$ gave us the best tonal quality. Now I am taking all this trouble in writing this long letter, because I think so extremely well of your most careful and fine craftsmanship and for that reason I am only too willing and prepared, and glad to further your interests but, my viola must be made according to my specification and drawings. After all, I don't think I am asking much, when as I say in the preamble on my specification, – to craftsmen, – to be loyal to my dimensions etc. I give my life's experience together with drawings and specification per gratis, and I think I have a right to expect that the drawings etc. should be followed meticulously.

When you mentioned about veneer at our short meeting at Carlos Place, my mind went back to our meeting at Cocker's when we had the discussion on the trouble of the fingerboard sinking, and one of the suggestions was thickening the top plate around the region of the block and upper part of belly, and I thought you had put veneer there!

I have shown your viola to Richardson, and he paid many compliments on your work, but entirely agreed with me about the veneer, and narrow f holes. I also showed your viola to my pupil Harry Danks but fortunately did not know then about the veneer on the post. I had intended playing on your viola at my lecture recital at Cambridge on May 5th but I can't do this with your viola in its present condition. Of course at Carlos Place, as the room there is outrageously resonant everything sounds extremely well, but in the ordinary normal hall or room the Cocker had much more subtlety of tone qualities and I put this down to your two deviations (post and f holes). Now I can't go on writing for ever, but as I have said I take this trouble because of your talent. It therefore amounts to this:– that I must ask you to take off the top plate of your viola and remove the veneer, and widen the f holes at widest point to $^{11}/_{32}$", otherwise I cannot use it. I know this is a great trouble for you, but you will admit it is not my fault. As I have said I am ready to help you all I know, and I don't hesitate to say you deserve it, but it can only be, providing you put these points right and providing you stick to my specification and drawings.

I shall be glad if you will let me have an answer to this immediately, in order to enable me to play on your viola at an important affair at Norwich which I want to do and I shall probably be playing on the Continent and America in the autumn where I should also be glad to take your viola, but I must have time to 'break it in'.

Yours sincerely,
Lionel Tertis

The other side of Tertis's personality shows in letters of 3 July and 17 November 1956:

Dear Mr Saunders,
I play upon your no. 8 'Tertis Model' viola which you made for me with great satisfaction and I much admire your fine craftsmanship and the meticulous care you have taken in making the instrument.

Yours sincerely,
Lionel Tertis

P.S. You are at liberty to use this testimonial if you wish.

Dear Wilfred,

Here is further repercussion of my U.S.A. visit. I feel it is very important that only the best of your tonal successes should go there (to the USA). Primrose not only heard no. 8 but played on it and said it was the best tone of any 'T.M.' he had seen or played.

L.T.

Three works composed for the viola, which were awarded the 1950 Tertis Prize at the Royal College of Music, were premièred at the College on Friday 19 January 1951. They were Ronald Tremain's Concertino for viola and orchestra, soloist Cecil Aronowitz, Bridget Fry's Concerto for solo viola, wind quintet and string orchestra, soloist Kenneth Essex, and Dorothy Franchi's *Rhapsody* for viola and orchestra, with Herbert Downes as soloist. The three concertante works were accompanied by a section of the London Symphony Orchestra conducted by Richard Austin. The Suite for viola and piano by William Harris was awarded the Lionel Tertis Prize at the Royal College of Music in 1952, and was published by Oxford University Press the following year.

The first Lionel Tertis Viola Prize Competition also took place at the Royal College of Music in 1951. The winner, Margaret Major, was awarded a Tertis Model viola made by Arthur Richardson.

Ada Tertis died late in 1951. Lionel had been looking after her as best he could; but on six occasions since 1944 she had had to enter a nursing home. Gerald Moore looked back on their marriage and their last years together:

In all his struggles, or at least since he was in his middle twenties, Lionel had been encouraged and inspired by his wife Ada, herself a violist, and her failing health from 1944 onwards pushed his viola into second place. His devotion and solicitude were touching to behold. One observed the little man's surprising strength as he lifted her from her invalid chair. 'I have been taught the expert way to do it.'

After her death Lionel went to live with his nephew Harold Milner in Carshalton Beeches, Surrey, for about a year. Tertis did not always see eye to eye with Milner's wife Doreen, and finally moved into digs in Sutton for a short time. Harold Milner remembered Lionel doing his daily practice in his bedroom; on one occasion he heard the Bach *Chaconne*, which Tertis had not played in a concert for a number of years; the playing was so beautiful that Milner went up to his room and said: 'If you don't play that in public again, I'll spit in your eye.' Some years later Tertis played the work in a major London concert hall with all his old fervour and control. When Milner went to the artists' room afterwards, Tertis took off his glasses and said 'Spit.' Milner said 'What for?' 'I didn't play it properly, Tertis replied. Milner said that Tertis was always his own sternest critic.

Tertis finally left Sutton and was invited to live in Devon with relations, Brigadier and Mrs Shaw and their two children, Vicky and Anthony; his great-nephew Anthony Shaw remembers:

Many people who knew him realise that Lionel Tertis was two apparently quite different men – professionally a lion, prepared to battle to the death for his own very high standards, a terror to his luthiers, an exacting and occasionally ferocious teacher and even colleague, though very loyal and loving to his professional friends; and in private life a mild and gentle person, devoted to his first and second wives, a charming and undemanding guest, happy to make his contribution in the household and very little trouble to anyone, though his health did give him some trouble at different times.

It was mainly the second of these Lionels that I got to know when he was living with us from around 1953 to 1958. He stayed with my (maternal) uncle Harold and aunt Doreen and family in Carshalton after his first wife died, but he didn't altogether fit in there, although my uncle was devoted to him, and left after a year to come and try his luck with us. Edgmoor, in the tiny moorside village of Middlemoor (near Tavistock, Devon), is a somewhat rambling house, which started as a small cottage, now the dining room, with my parents' room immediately above it, and was then built on to over the years, with outbuildings, and is now a house with 6–7 bedrooms, having just undergone its latest partial conversion, with the outbuildings also recently converted into a delightful self-catering cottage. A house beloved of children – I remember my horror when we were to leave it after the war and move to a house in the village – we were saved only by the death of the pre-war tenant, who was due to return after the war (my parents soon afterwards bought the house); again, how my four nephews loved to stay there on holiday from Tanzania, and their unwillingness for it to be sold for something more practical and easier to maintain.

I see Uncle Lionel in the old dining-room, partly below ground level, with the little windows, cosy with reddish curtains from the yacht of a friend, and with a view over the flowerbed, and a picture (among others) of Anton Rubinstein on the wall (via my maternal grandmother, to whom it had been left by Tobias Matthay, in whose teaching room at 96 Wimpole Street my mother remembers it hanging), maybe a fire, sitting at the large polished mahogany dining table at his voluminous correspondence, patiently concentrating in spite of the intensive efforts I must have seemed to be making to drive him crazy, practising my clarinet and piano (both jazz and classical), occasionally Scottish dances on the accordion, and so on. I remember once when I was attempting, in the drawing-room across the hall, with doubtless truly appalling crudity of technique and inspiration, to improvise in the style of Mozart, his coming in and inquiring politely which piece I was playing, and actually appearing quite complimentary – not his leonine professional self I am sure. Once, when I was messing about with the accordion, he came in and asked me whether I couldn't put in a bit of vibrato. I answered, no doubt with all the untroubled arrogance of youth, that one didn't do vibrato on an accordion, whereupon he lay on his stomach on the floor (aged almost 80, I imagine!) and demonstrated how it might be done! I think something similar happened when I was learning classical guitar. He said polite, and not entirely insincere things to my mother about me, but certainly never suggested I should study music!

Sometimes (perhaps increasingly over time?) he was practising the viola, particularly the Bach Chaconne, which I think he played almost every day, then (probably at different times) the Elgar concerto, Flos Campi (for King's Lynn) and his own piece Blackbirds. This dining room was really 'his' room, though it was used as a dining room when we had guests and parties. He was very tolerant, even when he came in and found me 'courting' in his armchair – he discreetly apologised and withdrew, perhaps secure in the feeling that I was away (school, university, abroad) most of the time anyway. He also had the largest bedroom upstairs, but it was never the cosiest of rooms, though it has a very pleasant view over the garden and fields to the church and the top of the village of Whitchurch.

He must have had to exercise great tolerance, as he sometimes had to put up with different music in every room – perhaps my mother, who was a professional musician, trained at the Matthay School where my grandmother was also a teacher, giving a piano lesson, my sister practising in another room, and me playing the clarinet in my bedroom ('That there A'th'ny Shaw belly-aching again', as one passer-by was clearly heard to remark ...).

He was always very much part of the family, and of course joined us for all meals and parties, and insisted on doing his bit by washing up after family meals, a function in which I was loath to usurp him. He was very concerned with what was going on in the family, and my sister particularly remembers his sympathy and anger when she complained (probably not too seriously!) about her music exam, and how concerned he was that 'she shouldn't keep her young man waiting' – that advice bore fruit, though he is now quite used to waiting! – He often used to tell us anecdotes during meals about his musical life, of which I recognised most in his two autobiographies: but it is pleasant to recall him telling them in his slightly high pitched voice, with a little tinge of Cockney thrown in here and there: it must have brought the world of the great musicians closer to us all. I don't remember any of them visiting, though one or two may have while I was away (most of the time). But he used to go away from time to time to London or other places, and participated several times in the Dartington summer school. I remember him coming back talking about the new discoveries of the year – Dietrich Fischer Dieskau, Julian Bream, and probably others – 'very clever young chap' was the usual somewhat understated description. As far as I can recall, he spent most of his time at that period experimenting with and campaigning for the Tertis Model viola – I particularly remember his pride (I suppose then, but perhaps later) when the Israel Philharmonic Orchestra acquired a number of his violas. I have already mentioned his ferocity with his viola-makers. My sister tells me she once accompanied him on a visit to Richardson in Crediton, and was dumbfounded by his explosive reaction when he learned that his measurements had been varied by a millimetre or two; she had never seen him like that before. I myself remember a visit from a viola maker, who may possibly have been Richardson or perhaps his successor, but, mercifully, no fireworks. But I do remember Uncle Lionel muttering wrathfully about his makers from time to time, and also, occasionally, discovering another 'clever young fellow'.

He very occasionally played his viola with my mother and other friends, but my mother thinks this was very rare, though my sister also remembers helping him practise for a concert and singing the soprano part with him and my mother. My sister also thinks that he practised with my mother somewhat more often than she remembers.

Apart from his viola, he had several occupations. He used to go for a walk over the moors every day for an hour or two, not alone, but accompanied by our beautiful and captivating bearded collie, Laddie (an escapee from Dartmoor prison, where he had apparently been abandoned by a warder on posting to a less dog-friendly environment). Edgmoor is truly on the edge of the moor, and he just had to walk about 50 yards up the lane from the back gate to reach it; then, if it was not too wet, on up over the moor across the stream (there was then a little bridge, since collapsed), flattening out a bit after a few hundred yards, though still uphill for a mile or so, then over the golf course (happy memories of his earlier golf-manic days – he nearly gave up the viola for golf at one point, he used to say) and down between the gorse-bushes to the most idyllic spot where a beautiful stream meanders along the valley, down from the upper moors, and under a small bridge, before disappearing a bit later off the moors and between the fields – a place he apparently referred to as the Lido, though we knew it quite incorrectly as Pennycomequick (which is actually some distance away). Occasionally he used to disappear off to Plymouth to his favourite restaurant or cafe, where he had allegedly won the heart of a waitress, who used to help him with the crossword, I am told. And occasionally he would go off to take the waters for his various ailments in Bath.

I well remember – who wouldn't? – the moment when I learned that he was planning to remarry. I was playing clarinet in a traditional jazz group at Cambridge, the Riverside Seven, of matchless repute, and we were staying in the pleasant country house of our trumpeter and leader for an outside engagement. When I came down to breakfast one day, I happened to glance at the tabloid newspaper lying on the table – huge banner headlines – '82-year-old musician to wed', or something on those lines. The thought of Lionel never crossed my mind, but when I idly started to read what followed, I suddenly saw his name – my knees almost folded beneath me as I read on that he was to wed a lady around half his age! Although the lady in question had visited him at Edgmoor, together with her mother, and I had met them both, the question of marriage had never entered my head, nor indeed had it occurred to my parents, who were as astonished when the press started to storm their telephone (yes, even in those days!) as I was on reading that newspaper.

My wife and I paid him a couple of short visits in Wimbledon after his second marriage, where he and Lillian were kind and welcoming. My main memory from these visits (probably more taken up with chat about our experiences with the British Council than with his life) was when he showed us his newly executed portrait (by Sutherland? or whom?), which seemed to us an excellent likeness, and with which I think he was well-pleased.

Altogether the experience of living day-to-day with a world-famous musician taught me, among other things, that it is possible to combine in one person the steel necessary for great achievements with a very simple life-style and a charming and unassuming presence.

Julian Herbage paid tribute to Tertis on his seventy-fifth birthday in the BBC Home Service programme *Music Magazine* on Sunday 30 December 1951. The following is an extract from the editorial of the programme:

Yesterday Lionel Tertis celebrated his 75th birthday. Well, I'm not quite old enough to go back 50 years and to tell you what viola playing was like in England in the early 1900s – but in those days, from what I have heard, anyone who couldn't make the grade as a violinist was perfectly safe at the viola desk.

Tertis has devoted his whole life to changing that situation. As an executant he has done for the viola what Haydn had done for it as a composer – he made it an instrument in his own right, and furthermore he made it a solo instrument, persuading composers like Bax, Bliss and Vaughan Williams to write sonatas and concertos for it. And not content with setting a standard of performance, and of achieving a repertoire for the viola, Tertis set about designing an ideal instrument, so that one can truly say that as a designer, an executant and as a musician, Tertis has given his life to the viola, and given it an equal status with that king of instruments, the violin. That is a fact of musical history.

Nowadays, I suppose, Tertis is mainly in evidence as a teacher – and as a teacher we will certainly remember his giving birth to the Griller String Quartet, and nursing them through their infancy until they became an ensemble of international reputation. But today I don't want merely to catalogue Tertis's achievements – I would rather you heard the beautiful tone that he brought to his instrument. Can you imagine, without Tertis's tone and technique, that the Serenade from 'Hassan' could ever have sounded like this on a viola? It's Tertis's arrangement, of course. [Tertis's recording of Delius's *Hassan* Serenade is then played.]

Tertis was taken seriously ill in 1952, and during March underwent a major operation at the Sutton and Cheam hospital. During his stay in hospital he received a letter from George Willoughby, orchestral manager of the BBC Symphony Orchestra, inviting him to join Sir Malcolm Sargent at auditions for members of the orchestra's viola section not heard on a previous visit. Owing to a slight setback after his operation Tertis reluctantly had to decline. Frank Thistleton, secretary of the Musicians' Benevolent Fund and an old friend of Tertis, persuaded him to convalesce at the Society's home in Westgate-on-Sea. Tertis made a complete recovery and was able to take part in the King's Lynn Festival in July, where he was invited to play during the morning service at Sandringham Church in the presence of the Queen Mother and Princess Margaret. Tertis was greatly moved by this occasion, and H.M. showed an interest in the design of the viola he was using.

During the festival Tertis heard Sir John Barbirolli's transcription of Bach's choral prelude 'In our Hour of Deepest Need'. Barbirolli sent Tertis a copy of the published score with the following inscription: 'For my very dear friend Lionel Tertis who In our Hour of Deepest Need restored the viola to us. John.' Harry Danks remembered a meeting between Tertis and Pierre Monteux:

He loved to listen to the orchestra in rehearsal and during the 1950s spent many hours in the BBC Maida Vale studios listening to the BBC Symphony Orchestra at work. The famous conductor Pierre Monteux was spending a few days with us and Lionel was keen to renew their old friendship; they had not met for many years. Typical of Lionel's modesty, he wondered if Monteux would remember him and asked me to stay at his side when they met. At the mid-morning break Monteux walked straight over to Lionel and without saying good morning or any form of greeting said: 'Do you still play my instrument?' Monteux of course played the viola and until quite late in his life loved to sit in a string quartet. There was a twinkle in Monteux's eye as he said this which Lionel did not miss and it was quite moving to watch the two elderly viola players renew acquaintance.

I have often been asked to describe Lionel Tertis, and what I have to say of him never varied over the years I knew him, with the exception of growing older which in my opinion he did with grace and charm. He could show irritability if displeased, which was not often in my company, although during some of my early lessons he did not spare me a quick rebuke, but then no doubt I deserved it. Equally when pleased he could express his pleasure beautifully, and in my experience he meant what he said. Hypocrisy was not in his character.

Tertis had many different interpretations and approaches to works he played. I have four copies of the solo part of the Walton Viola Concerto that belonged to him, each one containing different ideas. Tertis's fingerings brought out what for him were the true sonorities of the viola. Some violists think he over-fingered his music but according to those who knew him in his prime he was continually searching for beautiful and varied tone and wide range of expression for every work he performed.

However, relations between pupil and teacher were not always smooth. The following passage by Danks demonstrates how Tertis could fall out even with his close friends if they didn't agree with him:

For years I played on a Tertis Model viola which always proved satisfactory up to a point, but there was something missing. In spite of Lionel Tertis supporting me in everything to do with the viola, I was never completely happy with the sound produced, in spite of the hours I practised. Everything was reasonably in place and I was successful in my profession, but I felt that quality of sound was lacking. It was no use talking it over with Lionel. He was adamant that his model had everything and, apart from his former Montagnana, he had little time for the old master-craftsmen – at least those who made violas.

W. E. Hill & Sons of Bond Street, London, where Harry was a customer, invited him to try two violas by Gasparo da Salò and one by the brothers Amati; he chose the latter. Harry said:

When I told Lionel of my change he was furious with me and refused to look at the Amati, at the same time ridiculing me for being so stupid. We parted on a broken friendship for many years. I thought he had acted quite wrongly; he was firm in his views and did not change them (although we became friends later on).

Prior to this upset, Lionel had spent many hours in the Maida Vale studios of the BBC, always listening to the morning rehearsal, having lunch with us all in the canteen and talking to many old friends, but this ceased.

It was several months before he appeared once more. This happened when Sir Adrian Boult was conducting a new work for string orchestra by Alan Rawsthorne, which contained a cadenza for solo viola. I was playing on the Amati and, when we came to the moment of the cadenza, I did my best, having previously looked at it.

At the end of this work we broke for coffee. Lionel came across the large studio floor bursting with praise, at the same time saying, 'You were playing on the Tertis model, weren't you?'

I am afraid my feelings towards him were not kind and I said, 'No, I was not, I was playing on that instrument you said had no sound.' Sir Adrian, who was close enough to hear our remarks to one another, was very cross with me for my attitude towards Lionel. Lionel himself walked away and out of the studio, and it was months before we resumed the friendship which had begun in the mid-1930s.

In the summer of 1953 Elizabeth Watson won the Lionel Tertis Viola Prize Competition for students from the leading colleges, at the Royal College of Music. The adjudicators were Tertis, Harry Danks and Sir Thomas Armstrong, then principal at the Royal Academy of Music. Watson remembers: 'I played the whole of the Bloch Suite (1919), and gave it lots of positive phrasing which seemed appropriate. On walking to the platform I heard Tertis saying of my old German viola, "small, small". Elizabeth Watson said that at the end of the competition Tertis was full of praise and exhortation to play the viola, to promote it, to commission and arrange works – and to let him know when she was playing.

The prize was a Tertis Model viola made by Lawrence Cocker of Derby. Tertis sent her a card saying that she should use Prim strings on the Cocker, and that she could get them at Hills in Bond Street; Watson was a student of Frederick Riddle, who insisted that all his students use gut strings. In the early autumn of 1953 Elizabeth telephoned Tertis to say she would be playing in a quintet concert at St Martin-in-the-Fields, and the other violist would be Christopher Wellington, who would also be playing a Tertis Model. Watson then told Tertis that she had put gut strings on the viola and hoped he didn't mind. Tertis replied forcefully and told her she had no right to change them, as the instrument was designed for Prim strings. His vehemence was such that Elizabeth had to hold the telephone away from her ear. Tertis attended the concert and was charming to the violinists and cellist. He said to Christopher Wellington 'so you use these gut strings too'. Elizabeth was obviously not in favour, but insisted that she liked the sound of gut strings.

Wellington's student quartet from the Royal College of Music played Vaughan Williams's String Quartet no. 2 in A minor, which the composer dedicated to the violist Jean Stewart, and gave the viola the leading voice throughout. The other work in the programme was Vaughan Williams's *Phantasy Quintet*, in which they were joined by Elizabeth Watson. Wellington's memory of the concert was as follows:

> I suppose I should not have been surprised when I sat down to play the quartet and found Lionel Tertis sitting in the second row. I can't imagine that that did much for my nerves; at any rate, when Tertis came round to see us afterwards all he said to me was 'It's very difficult, isn't it?!' I recollect being amused rather than dismayed – but again the incident demonstrated that Tertis's superlative standards made no concessions at all – the best result imaginable would be only just good enough!

Some months later Elizabeth Watson heard that the British Council were offering six scholarships for further study. Her dream at that time was to study in Vienna. She needed two references; her chamber-music coach at the RCM, Cecil Aronowitz, agreed immediately to her request; she then approached Tertis. He had moved to Devon, but the British Council suggested she put Tertis's name provisionally on the form while awaiting his reply. His reply was that people were always taking his name in vain; he could not remember Elizabeth's playing, and it might have changed anyway. He would be in London in January and might be able to hear her play and consider a reference then. Alas, all too late for the British Council.

Elizabeth came across Tertis again two or three years later, when she was in Zermatt attending a summer course of masterclasses by Casals, Sandor

Végh and other wondrous musicians. In the middle of a class Végh suddenly announced 'Ah – here is the Casals of the viola' – and there was Tertis. Elizabeth had no wish to revive a problem, so avoided him. A day or so later she was sitting in the hotel foyer waiting for a lesson with Végh, with a copy of a Brahms Sonata, edited by Tertis, on her lap, when Tertis came by. She swiftly turned the music over but Tertis came up to her and said: 'Aren't you the American cellist who played so beautifully in Casals' class?' 'Sorry, no.'

Two years after Ada's death Tertis's short memoir was published (1953) entitled *Cinderella No More* – the book ends with a beautiful tribute to his wife: 'She was more to me even than the viola.' He received a letter dated 14 August 1953 from Sacheverell Sitwell:

> Reid's Hotel, Funchal, Madeira
>
> Dear Lionel Tertis,
>
> I so much enjoyed reading your book – also, meeting you again at King's Lynn. As I told you, I well recall hearing you and Kreisler playing the Mozart Sym. Concertante. An unforgettable experience, and one of the memories of youth.
>
> I was most touched by your account of your childhood. Never a word of hardship or complaint. You have had a wonderful life, I am sure you will agree.
>
> I miss dear Violet (Gordon Woodhouse) so much, and shall never forget how she played Bach and Scarlatti, and the 'Midsummer's Night's Dream.' What an artist! Did you ever hear her play Desdemona's song from Otello (Verdi)? I have the Galuppi piece in my ears at this moment.
>
> Your book has a very special touch to it. And the impression of your personality.
>
> I send you my best wishes. This is a beautiful place. A sort of Elysian island without Americans!
>
> Do remember to look at Rameau. The suite arranged by Mottl is very beautiful. Rameau is much deeper than most Frenchmen.
>
> Yours ever,
> Sacheverell Sitwell

Richard Capell reviewed the book in the January 1954 issue of *Music & Letters*:

> Rarely has one man changed the course of musical history; yet it just is such a story which is unfolded in the small book called Cinderella No More – Lionel Tertis's autobiography. One calls it an autobiography, but it deals only secondarily with Tertis himself. In nearly every chapter the

premier place is held by the viola, 'the love and tyrant', as he calls it, 'of my life'. No doubt it would have occupied that position everywhere had he become acquainted with that instrument in his earliest years. He did not, however, meet it until 1896.

By the pupils he has taught ... he has founded the school of viola playing as truly as Corelli did that of the violin. And finally, by his scientific researches, united to his acute aesthetic perception, he has established what would seem to be the best model on which to build the violas of today and the future ...

... But I can touch on only two more matters. One is the beautiful tribute to his wife ... The other is the imponderable, unwritten element in his life which he himself, perhaps, could not explain but which grows ever clearer to the reader as the simply written, intensely sincere narrative proceeds. What were the instincts, the intuitions, the inner sources of power which enabled a boy trained as a pianist to begin playing the violin at an age so late that it would have seemed impossible for him to acquire the real string player technique; to triumph over inferior tuition in the early stages of his violin-playing career; to pass to the viola and to realize, almost in an instant, that here was his destiny, and to make himself the greatest player of the viola in the world? ...

In July 1953 Charles Kreitzer, a young South African violist, and his violinist wife Lucy left Cape Town on the *Arundel Castle* for a three-month vacation in the UK and Europe. On arrival in London they attended many Promenade concerts. Charles had always been a great fan of Tertis and possessed many of his recordings. In London they found a copy of *Cinderella No More*, and after reading it were determined to meet its author. Through the principal violist of the BBC Symphony Orchestra, Harry Danks, they learnt that his former teacher was now living in retirement in Devon. Kreitzer hoped that a meeting with Tertis might lead to some lessons with him. Within a few days he and his wife took the train from London to Tavistock. They booked in at the small Bedford Hotel, and contacted Tertis by phone. At first he was a little wary of the two strangers who had arrived without warning. The Kreitzers' first impression of him, then seventy-seven years old, was of a frail, sad little man with a subdued but compelling personality.

Tertis agreed to give Charles some lessons, beginning with the Elgar Concerto; these lessons often lasted for over three hours. Other works which Kreitzer played to Tertis were the Walton Concerto, Bloch Suite and the Concerto by the South African composer John Joubert. Tertis was very complimentary about Kreitzer's talent and tried to persuade him to make a career in England.

Charles and Lucy told Tertis that when they performed the *Sinfonia concertante* in Cape Town they played his cadenzas. Tertis replied: 'It is quite impossible for anyone else to have played them', however he was intrigued to hear of how their friend Blanche Gerstman had 'copied' the cadenzas from the Sammons–Tertis records.

During their visit to Devon the Kreitzers visited Arthur Richardson in Crediton where they purchased R.T. no. 115 from him. On leaving Tavistock they invited Tertis to come to South Africa one day to spend a holiday with them. They left for London thinking they would never see him again. (Little did they know!)

Bernard Shore was in touch with Tertis regularly throughout the 1950s, and on 26 March 1954 he received the following letter:

> My dear Bernard,
> When you read this don't say 'but this is so sudden!' but just say! 'Yes darling!' Will you do me the honour of joining me in a duet (unaccompanied) in some variations I have concocted on a Passacaglia of Handel. I am just revising them with a view to performing them and other items at a recital (at the Wigmore Hall I hope) in June. I think I have only done the two viola stunt once before in public. If you'll say yes, I will send your part along as soon as I have finished it. Keep this confidential until I know definitely that it is coming off.
>   Love to you both, Lionel

The concert took place at the Wigmore Hall on Thursday 24 June, and was advertised as a Demonstration Recital on the improved Tertis Model viola, in aid of the Musicians' Benevolent Fund. All three violas used in this concert were made by Lawrence Cocker of Derby. Tertis spoke to the audience briefly before the first item:

> Since I embarked on this project of a standardized viola in 1937–38 I have concentrated on making this maximum-sized instrument (that is maximum size for playing under the chin) as easy to manage as possible. The length of the viola has not been altered but I have made some six revisions, most of which tend to make it easier to play upon than the previous model, and any advance in this direction is a great asset to the player.
>   It would take too long to enter into the technical details of the alterations but all these improvements are included in the drawings of which Messrs. W. E. Hill & Sons are the sole distributors. I shall be playing on two examples and shall change from one to the other between movements and during movements whenever the opportunity occurs, to show that

good tone quality is not confined to just one viola, and also to show the advantage of standard size which permits one to change violas without interfering with one's intonation and without being nonplussed by variations in measurements. I might also mention that the viola on which I shall play the Bach Chaconne is only five weeks old.

With Ruth Fermoy he played the Martini–Endicott Sonata in D, Ireland's Sonata no. 2, Brahms's Sonata, op. 120 no. 2, Galuppi's *Aria amorosa*, Szymanowski's 'Chant de Roxane' and finally one of his own compositions, *The Blackbirds*. Bernard Shore joined his master in Tertis's Variations on a theme of Handel for two violas. Shore wrote of the Tertis Model violas:

> The Tertis Model instruments, I'm convinced, have had a most important influence because students nowadays can play on a fine instrument at reasonable cost. The small instrument is quite unable to produce the volume of sound from its lower strings, where it is terribly disappointing, even though it can be quite satisfactory in higher registers. It is owing to Lionel Tertis that we can now have the ideal instrument for size.

Christopher Wellington remembered the occasion:

> 1954 saw another concert to demonstrate the Tertis Model also at the Wigmore Hall. This time Tertis played a recital in which he was accompanied by Lady Fermoy. Tertis apologized for playing sitting down – but as he perched on a double bass stool and was short in stature anyway it made little apparent difference. He used three different Tertis Model violas to show how readily he could change between them explaining that the one he was using for the Bach Chaconne was only a matter of weeks old. I recall a Sonata by Padre Martini with which he started, the Chaconne of course, and John Ireland's A minor Violin Sonata. Among smaller pieces I remember Tertis's piece The Blackbirds and the Allegretto by Schubert (his arrangement of the Trio from the Scherzo of the great G major Quartet op. 161).
>
> Although Tertis was 77 years old by then (and had officially retired some sixteen years before) my major impression of his playing was of the enormously powerful tone he generated – it seemed like the sum of five players put together. It struck me that his intensively expressive style of playing was best suited to the biggest works – the Bach (an impressive performance at any age) and the Ireland. The Ireland Sonata was rather effortful at times – with the great player choosing the violin register – well above the treble stave which he had never been shy of using.

There was undoubted charm in his approach to the smaller pieces – but he could scarcely help being a giant player – though so small in stature. I was very pleased to have heard Tertis in person, but I confess I found my ear had become a bit overwhelmed by the end of the afternoon – the power and richness of sound was just too unceasing.

In her diary entry dated 24 June 1954 the young British violist Veronica Leigh (Jacobs) was also inspired by Tertis's Wigmore Hall concert:

A recital I shall never forget – Lionel Tertis playing on three different specimens of the improved Tertis Model. Such breadth of tone and variety of colour ('A' string slightly nasal) and although Tertis seemed an old man he had an impeccable technique. He sat down to play everything but the Bach Chaconne. It was an astonishing feat of intonation and double stopping and such a wonderful tone – am I committing a sin suggesting that it sounded better than when it is played on the violin? Also he played Variations on a theme of Handel for two violas with Bernard Shore (whose right hand has only index and little fingers) and it sounded like a whole army! The Brahms E flat Sonata which he played with Lady Fermoy was marvellous.

In a letter dated 6 July 1954 Tertis wrote to Bernard Shore from Edgmoor, saying he would be in Town (London) on the 14th (afternoon), 15th and 16th (the latter for the RCM prize which he had asked Harry Danks to adjudicate). He mentioned that on the way to London he would be going to Cheltenham to hear Danks play the Whettam Concerto, and that he had written to the Swedish makers of Prim about a problem with their strings. 'P.S. I am also interviewing Natali of Cathedral Strings. They ought to be able to do as well as the Swedish people.'

Harry Danks, playing on a Richardson–Tertis viola, premièred Graham Whettam's Viola Concerto at the Cheltenham Festival in 1954 with the Hallé Orchestra under Sir John Barbirolli. Tertis and Richardson both attended, but they were not at that time on speaking terms, since Tertis started calling the model viola the 'Tertis Model' rather than the 'Richardson–Tertis Model'.

On Tuesday 3 August 1954 Tertis presented a programme on the West of England Home Service; it was no. 11 in a series called *In the Gramophone Library*:

Tertis: I hope your wireless sets are properly tuned, for I want you to feel thoroughly satisfied with the records I've chosen. At this moment I am trying to imagine that at least the whole of the West Country are gathered around their radio-sets, wondering why on earth an antediluvian viola-player should have been chosen for this gramophone session and what sort of chap I am! By this time I am sure you will have noticed one characteristic about me, and that is, my pip-squeak of a voice, – that's not my fault – indeed, my high-pitched counter-tenor has more than once led to embarrassing situations! For instance, if I ring up a departmental store, and ask the lady operator for gentlemen's underwear, or for the ladies lingerie department, she invariably replies, 'Yes, Madam'!

Having led you up the garden-path, so to speak, I'll now get along with my job and introduce you to my choice of records, which I am certain will interest you. One, I venture to say, will make you positively hilarious! It is made by a Frenchman whom I consider a genius. When I first heard this record many years ago, I was convulsed! I have often listened to it since, and it still has the same effect upon me. I have decided to put it on last of all, in the hope that I have so aroused your curiosity that you will be inveigled to listen to my machinations to the bitter end.

The first record I have selected is a piano piece entitled 'The Musical-Box' played by that superb artist, Solomon.

By way of contrast now listen to Solomon in a display of prodigious technique, in Liszt's 'Hungarian Fantasia' for piano and orchestra.

A most striking aspect of that record is the dramatic playing of both pianist and orchestra – especially noticeable is (the veritable sinuosity of) Solomon's chord playing, his wonderful facility, so consistent in its accuracy, indeed, his control of the keyboard is absolute, but, it is always the servant of the music. No matter who the composer is, he captures his idiom, be it classical or otherwise, and he portrays it with the deepest sincerity.

I want you now to listen to a part of the last movement of Schubert's great D minor string quartet known as 'Death and the Maiden'. Now I am going to be naughty with regard to this record, and have it played at a greater speed than the actual recording. I'll give you the reason for committing this offence after we've heard it.

I once played this work with a world-famous Czechoslovakian string quartet – the Bohemian Quartet. (I presume they had not recorded it for I could not find it in the BBC Gramophone Library which after all is the largest in the world) so I was obliged to utilize another Quartet's recording of it, and step up the pace, for the Czechs played it at break neck speed. Fortunately I knew the work well and so could fall in with their ideas.

Whenever I hear this Schubert quartet, it reminds me of an episode, which to say the least of it, was somewhat irregular! My association with the Czechs was the result of an urgent appeal. Their viola player, Nedbal (who was a very fine artist), I was told, had been suddenly taken ill, and I was called upon at a moment's notice to fill the gap. At the end of the tour I eventually discovered that the remarkable and devastating reason for their viola-player's disappearance was, that he had not, in point of fact, been ill at all, but had run off with the first violinist's wife!

The next disc I have chosen – far removed from string-tone, is a record on the harmonica, better known as a mouth organ. Of course you all know who it will be, and you are right – that great artist – Larry Adler. Here is a record he made of Kreisler's Caprice Viennoise. It will show his lovely quality of sound, the extraordinary variety he gets in tone-colour, and his amazing technique on that tiny instrument which his hand practically conceals. He does such curious things with the rhythm now and then – he slithers – bites off chunks of it so to speak, and plays all sorts of tricks, but all the time he cleverly contrives to imitate the string playing of it. It is really great fun. You must excuse the scratch on the record because it is a well-worn one.

I have digressed a bit. Before I leave the story of the viola I want to try to illustrate its attractions by playing it myself and by means of recorded sound.

So now for a breath-taking one by a wonderful viola-player who is keeping the flag of the viola flying. It displays most amazing technique, and refutes, that once-upon-a time assertion, that the viola is slow-speaking and mournful, and quite incapable of being skittish. It is played by William Primrose. The record is entitled 'La Campanella' by Paganini.

Wasn't that quite wonderful! By way of contrast here is a record of a song by Brahms, called 'Minnelied' arranged for viola and played by 'yours truly'. It was made some 30 years ago when the technique of record manufacture was not so advanced – even so, it is not too bad for it does show the characteristic tone-quality of the viola which I feel, is more human in sound than the nerve-piercing violin. Here and there you will notice slight indiscretions in the record – or shall I say, over-indulgence in portamenti, but then, I was younger when I made it.

I am now going to give you the quality of the viola – when muted. It is a little bit out of an 18th century piece by Galuppi. No record of this has been made, so I am going to play it myself. (Lionel Tertis plays aria 'Amorosa'.)

And now for the last record and a bit of fun – we've been serious long enough! I have been impatiently waiting to put on this last one – you will remember by the Frenchman I spoke of, at the beginning of this session.

It is a record he sings to represent different nationalities in supposed languages, which in fact, are no language at all!

I call that real genius, don't you? And I hope you've enjoyed him as much as I have. Well, good night and I trust I have been able to interest you.

Tertis's admiration for William Primrose was reciprocated. William Primrose dedicated his arrangement of Beethoven's Notturno, op. 42, for viola and piano 'To Lionel Tertis, with affection and esteem'. This was published in 1952 by Schott & Co.

Bernard Shore, then fifty-eight, was playing *Flos campi* at the Three Choirs Festival in 1954, and went to Tertis for advice on 24 August. Tertis wrote to him from Dartington Hall.

> My dear Bernard,
>
> Thank you for your more than kind letter. It is good of you to think so much of my efforts and I can assure you it is a real happiness to me if I feel I can be of help to any of my brother and sister viola players. I know you are going to play better than you have ever done at the Three Choirs and I wish I could come to hear you.
>
> Much love to you both, Lionel.

Shore returned Tertis's part of *Flos campi* to him, and in a letter from Edgmoor dated 16 September 1954 Tertis thanked him and said how happy he was to know that the performance went so well, and that David Willcocks (conductor) was so good. In his P.S. Tertis wrote: 'I understand the fault in the Prim strings has been rectified.'

In 1954 Tertis contacted the music committee of the Society for Cultural Relations with the USSR regarding the possibility of a visit to promote the Tertis Model viola. Copies of the plans of his viola had already been sent to the Union of Soviet Composers through the British Embassy in Moscow. However, in mid-December Tertis was beginning to have second thoughts about the visit; in a letter to the composer Alan Bush, a member of the music committee, he wrote:

> I feel my visit would not serve its purpose unless I was prepared to give a major performance, such as a concerto with orchestra, or a full-blown recital, and I am beginning to think at this stage in my life, I am not in a position to promise to fulfil such an undertaking to my satisfaction, so therefore please forgive my doubts about the possibility of my going to Moscow.

On 10 February 1955 Fritz Kreisler sent Tertis a postcard saying: 'Dear friend Lionel Tertis! Thank you for your birthday greeting. It is deeply appreciated. Your old friend! Fritz Kreisler.'

Tertis often wrote to Shore, and said how difficult it was to decipher his letters. For example on 19 January 1955 he wrote: 'Please always type in the future, hitherto it has taken me usually two or three days to read your writing – at two hourly intervals – so as to avoid eye strain and brain-fever!!!' (Interestingly, Tertis's letters of this period are not always easy to decipher!) In his P.S. Tertis says he has to write hundreds of letters but was feeling better, and had just been for a five-mile walk over the moor with the dog that morning. In April and May Tertis travelled to London more than once to help Shore with his interpretation of the Bliss Viola Sonata.

With Ruth Fermoy at the piano Tertis played for the Norfolk and Norwich Music Club at the Assembly House, Norwich on 25 June. In the first half they played Sonatas by Delius (no. 2) and John Ireland (A minor). After the interval Tertis gave a talk entitled 'Some Reflections of a Musician'. This covered a wide range of subjects, including chamber music, orchestras, conductors and modern music.

Around Christmas time 1955 Christopher Wellington wrote to Tertis to express his thanks for Tertis's great playing and his appreciation of the design of the Tertis Model viola. (Wellington was then playing Arthur Richardson no. 101.) He had hoped to meet Tertis to talk about his career and viola subjects in general, but discovered that Tertis was now living in Devon, and the meeting never took place. Tertis was still campaigning for his design of viola, and was disappointed to hear that Wellington was the only member of the Sadler's Wells Orchestra using his model. Christopher Wellington has always been conscious of Tertis's achievements and influence. In his school days he first heard the 78 rpm recordings of Tertis and Harriet Cohen in the Brahms F minor Sonata and the Delius Sonata no. 2 with George Reeves, and these became Wellington's benchmark for how the viola should sound. 'I only have to hear a few notes of Tertis's playing to picture that small but powerful fanatic of the viola who did so much to raise awareness of his chosen instrument – by his playing, by causing new music to be written and by his interest in instrument making.'

At the Royal Academy of Music on 25 July 1956 a panel, including Sir John Barbirolli, Tertis and the accompanist Gerald Moore, heard five young instrumentalists compete for the Suggia Gift. Gerald Moore described the occasion in his book *Furthermoore*: 'I sat with Lionel Tertis on a jury listening to young 'cellists ... and can still hear the nonagenarian [*recte* octogenarian] Lionel Tertis as he listened to a boy of ten, hissing furiously in my ear "This boy is asleep."

Half an hour later Lionel was unrecognisable, he was wreathed in smiles as a little girl with flaxen hair played to us, nay, attacked us. She was hardly as tall as her instrument. It was his, and my, introduction to Jackie.' The eleven-year-old Jacqueline du Pré was given the award towards private lessons with William Pleeth, on condition that she devoted at least four hours daily to private practice.

In 1954 Tertis was informed of the Dartington Summer School of Music held at Totnes, Devon. He was curious, and enrolled as a student; William Glock, the Director, was amazed to see the great Tertis as one of his students, and within a week invited him to coach the more advanced chamber-music players. For the next few years he became a member of staff and coached chamber music for a month each summer.

After his first experience at Dartington, Tertis was invited to lunch with Glock and his wife, and on 29 August 1954 wrote to thank them:

> I thoroughly enjoyed my week at Dartington and my eyes have been opened to the great good that is being done at the summer school. I should also like to say how much I appreciate your suggesting and wanting me to participate next year, and if it could be brought about that one or two teams of really capable players could be provided – preferably professionals, – nothing would interest me more, for the coaching of string quartet playing is absorbing to me, and a task in which I have confidence of being able to be of use.

Penelope Howard, who was leader of the Arriaga Quartet for thirty years, recalls lessons with Tertis at Dartington:

> He looked like a diminutive Father Christmas, with startlingly bright blue twinkling eyes and a comically high voice. I was aware, even at 18 years old, however, of the enormous privilege of being his only pupil every morning for a whole week because I knew he had performed Mozart's Sinfonia concertante with my idol, Fritz Kreisler. ... A man of galvanic energy even in his eighties, he was bored out of his brains with no work to do and as there were no viola players at the Summer School that year, a minion was sent to my room at some ungodly hour (I was often still asleep) to order me to come and play to the maestro. ... I will always be deeply grateful for the hours and hours of fastidious attention to phrasing, dynamics and tone control which he lavished on my unworthy self. And in my head I can still hear his squeaky voice shouting, 'Go back to the score, Penny, go back to the score! You're not doing Bach's phrasing!'

Jeremy Wilson, who was stage manager during Tertis's visits to Dartington

Summer School, has memories of being present in the Great Hall when Tertis was coaching the Zorian Quartet: 'I recall the whole rehearsal session seemed to be devoted to intonation. He was merciless, and I cannot remember them playing any more than the opening bars at all.' Wilson also recollects Tertis coaching three amateurs in Beethoven's Trio, op. 87, for two oboes and cor anglais, the latter part being played on the viola. 'I was playing second oboe, and whilst he spared us the intonation torture, I do remember his concentration on the quality of sound we produced. As to musical insights, I really can remember nothing. I do remember not being at all scared, so I think he must have been gentle with amateurs and students.'

A report of the 1957 summer school appeared in the November issue of *The Strad*:

> Dartington Hall Summer School dealt nobly with its string section this year. Szymon Goldberg, visiting for the first time, gave master classes for advanced violinists and was heard in a memorable recital. The International Cello Centre was again invited to participate and Maurice Eisenberg's master classes and concert appearances were regular and welcome features throughout the entire course. Lionel Tertis, emerging from his retirement, and Bernard Shore, took charge of viola teaching and Mr Tertis, André Mangeot and Sybil Eaton shared the ensemble coaching. Notable chamber music concerts were given by the Amadeus and Hollywood String Quartets and the Haydn Trio. The four weeks also brought a unique opportunity, to enjoy a short but comprehensive Stravinsky Festival in the presence of the composer.

Veronica Leigh Jacobs remembers how, as a student at the Royal Academy of Music attending the 1958 Dartington Summer School with fellow students from the Academy, she was coached every day by Hans Keller in Haydn Quartets:

> His musicological approach was interesting and provoked much discussion during the lessons. Towards the end of the week we were asked to have some coaching with Lionel Tertis and I remember how he brought my attention to the phrasing of the slow movement of the 'Emperor' Quartet by showing me a more adventurous fingering in the viola variation. He also disapproved of the viola I had borrowed from the RAM because it was 'too small – no tone on the C string'. After our performance in the student concert, Cecil Aronowitz (the well-known South African-born violist) told us that the music coached by Tertis was more alive and less dry than the interpretations of Hans Keller.

At the 1956 Dartington Summer School the director, William Glock, invited the American cellist Maurice Eisenberg to give masterclasses; one of the cellists who participated was one of his English students, Lillian Warmington. Tertis was keen that year to coach a piano trio, and Maurice Eisenberg suggested Miss Warmington as a possible cellist. With a Norwegian violinist and an experienced British pianist they received regular coaching from the great man. Tertis was very taken with the cellist, whom he found very musical; and it would not be long before their paths crossed again.

A PERSONAL NOTE

During the last twenty-five years I have visited Mrs Tertis's beautiful home many times. On each occasion she told me stories of her time with Lionel. This is her account of their first meeting:

> In August 1956 I went down to Dartington Summer School to attend and play at the Master Classes of Maurice Eisenberg, who had been my teacher for many years ... After a few days I was suddenly asked if I would join a trio which was going to be coached by Mr Lionel Tertis. ... I had been told that Mr Tertis was very strict but I thoroughly enjoyed the classes with him. ...
>
> In 1957 I again went to Dartington and played the Handel Sonata in G minor for two cellos and piano to Mr Tertis (the other cellist was Antonia Butler), which was subsequently included in one of the afternoon concerts. At the same time I was working on the Elgar Concerto for the master classes. Next day I went down with a very bad cold and stayed in bed, but Mr Tertis came to see me in the morning and afternoon ...

The rest is history ...

∞ 13 ∞

Return to America and Eightieth Birthday Celebrations

Return to America – 80th birthday celebrations –
Soloist with the Hallé – Hoing–Tertis correspondence in The Strad

I N OCTOBER 1956 *The Strad* announced that 'Lionel Tertis, the veteran British violist, is emerging from his retirement to fly to the United States. The object of his visit is to introduce and demonstrate the Tertis Model viola.' He was invited to stay with friends in New York – Dr and Mrs Fairchild. Mary Fairchild had studied viola with Tertis in London and, though small in stature, was an advocate of the 'T.M.' viola. Tertis's visit included lecture-recitals, talks, cocktail parties, sightseeing and much more, from 10 a.m. until well after midnight most days. He opened his American visit by promoting his new viola in front of an illustrious audience at the Mannes School of Music; those present included Louis Persinger, Joseph Fuchs, William Primrose and the luthier Rembert Wurlitzer, who, having heard Tertis play and inspected his Saunders viola, was so enthusiastic about the instrument that he ordered one from Saunders in England. Wurlitzer also gave Tertis a list of 300 violin-makers in the USA; Tertis sent copies of his drawings of the viola together with specifications to all these. Within a few years more than sixty had produced Tertis Model violas.

The entertainments Mary Fairchild organized for Tertis included tea with the pianist James Friskin and his wife, the violist and composer Rebecca Clarke. These two English musicians had both studied at the Royal College of Music, and many years later had settled in the USA and married in middle age. James was also a composer; his Elegy for viola and piano was published by Stainer & Bell in 1915. Rebecca Clarke, who had studied with Tertis before the First World War, had virtually given up composing, and was completely forgotten by her former public. Only after her death would her fine viola sonata, piano trio and other compositions be rediscovered.

The Violin, Viola, Violoncello Teachers' Guild Incorporated, as part of their sixteenth season, invited Tertis to give a demonstration recital of the new Tertis Model viola, which was in such demand in England and on the Continent. This was followed by a short question period.

On Monday 5 November 1956 Tertis gave a lecture-recital on string quartet playing to the Society of Chamber Music Associates at the Brooklyn Academy of Music. This was the first of what were described as 'Five Music-in-the-Round workshops in ensemble playing by well known professional artists'. In a letter of thanks after the event, Blanche Schwarz Levy, President of the Violin Teachers' Guild Inc., wrote: 'Your gracious personality and your great artistry were a great joy to all present. I doubt if there were ever so many violists assembled at one time and your performance will always be a wonderful inspiration to us.'

During his visit he met his old friend Fritz Kreisler for the last time. The eighty-one-year-old violinist, long retired, used to spend many of his days at his publisher Charles Foley's offices in mid-town Manhattan, to keep out of the way of his formidable wife Harriet. Seated in a comfortable old black leather armchair, he would hold court in the outer office, and it was no doubt there that Tertis met him. They reminisced about old times, and Kreisler ran his fingers over Tertis's viola, commenting on how easy it was to reach the upper positions. Kreisler then said: 'Do you know that at our first rehearsal of the Mozart Sinfonia concertante here in New York, when you took your instrument out of the case (the 17⅛" Montagnana) its enormous size positively frightened me!'

Samuel and Sada Applebaum, who had heard Kreisler and Tertis perform the *Sinfonia concertante* at Carnegie Hall in 1924, had corresponded with Tertis a number of times since the end of the Second World War. Dr and Mrs Fairchild invited the Applebaums to their home in New York City to meet Tertis and to interview him for their forthcoming book *The Way they Play*. They remember him as 'a gentle person, compact and smallish in physical size, with a mild manner and rather high-pitched voice. His cheeks are ruddy. He rather resembles Rudyard Kipling, we thought as we talked with him. He is a little ceremonious, precise and positive, with towering absorption in his subject, which is the viola, and specifically his own model of viola.'[1]

Harold Coletta, the American violist, remembered meeting Tertis during this visit and shared the following story with the author:

> Although Lionel Tertis was close to eighty years old when I first heard him perform in person, I had for years admired his recordings. I went backstage after his performance to congratulate him and shake his hand. I asked him if he might have some time while in New York City to hear me perform and give me some constructive criticism. He answered politely that he had too much to do during his brief stay here. A lovely lady overheard this quick exchange and must have seen the deep disappointment on my face. She said quietly to me, 'Lionel is staying with us and I'll try to arrange for you to spend some time with him.' Charming and gracious Mrs Mary Fairchild had just returned from London where she had had six months of study with Tertis.

Mrs Fairchild telephoned the next day to say that Lionel Tertis could see me the next afternoon. He greeted me cordially and we went right to work. His highly intelligent criticisms and recommendations were given to me with warmth and kindness. At one point, after covering two major works, Mr Tertis sat down, waved his arms toward himself and said, 'Please ask anything.' I was deeply touched by his sincerity and generosity. I asked, among many other questions, 'In learning a piece, do you play phrases over and over again?' He smiled and said, 'Yes, until I am green in the face!'

Apparently, he was pleased with my immediate responses to his suggestions (at one point complimenting me after I played a phrase by saying, 'You're lightning quick!'), and he offered me his last afternoon in New York before flying back to London. His kindness and sensitivity as a person made a deep and lasting impression on me.

As Tertis grew older he had increasing trouble with his eyesight, and eventually became nearly blind. Photographs of him as an old man show him carrying a white stick. While he was in New York he consulted two eye specialists.

On 8 October 1956 Tertis sent a letter to Eric Warr at BBC Yalding House, London.

> Dear Eric,
> I reach the prime of life (80) on December 29th and I must say it would be a great satisfaction to me and a 'leg-up' for the viola if the BBC would contemplate my giving a recital with a short talk on the viola on that date. I am giving 3 demonstration-recitals in New York of the 'Tertis Model' on 21st, 25th, and 29th and flying back on October 30th arriving I hope at my club (Sesame, 47, Grosvenor St. W1) on October 31st, when I will ring you up at Yalding House if I may. Would you be so kind as to put this idea before Maurice Johnstone and tell him he can give me an audition if he likes so as to see whether I can still scrape a tune decently.
> With kindest remembrances to Mrs. Warr and yourself,
>   Yours sincerely,
>   Lionel Tertis

A joint tribute to Casals and Tertis was given on the eve of their eightieth birthdays on the BBC Home Service on Friday 28 December 1956 from 10.00 to 10.30 p.m. (This was a supplement to *Music Magazine.*) Julian Herbage, in his introduction to the Tertis part of the programme, said:

> If he were living in the first Elizabethan era, Tertis would long ago have been given the title 'Father of the Viola'. An extremely active parent he is,

too, and like all good fathers, his main interest today centres in his prog-
eny. In other words, he has put all his great experience towards perfecting
the design of the viola itself, and encouraging makers all over the world to
adopt his plan for an ideal instrument.

Tertis then spoke briefly about how the Tertis Model came about, and gave
a few illustrations on the instrument; the first, a section of a melody on the
G string, was followed by a few bars on the C string, showing the sonority
of the lowest string. Alvar Lidell sang two songs with viola obbligato – John
Dowland's 'Come again, sweet love' and a fifteenth-century folksong, 'The birds
are silent in the trees', which had the addition of the piano. Finally Bernard
Shore paid homage to his former teacher, and put Tertis's achievement in its
proper perspective:

> To all viola players, and indeed countless string players all over the world,
> the name of Lionel Tertis conjures up the whole line of great virtuosi – from
> Paganini to Kreisler and the modern giants like Menuhin and Heifetz.
>
> But whereas violinists have always had things their own way, Tertis for
> years had to fight a continuous battle on two fronts – to convert his audi-
> ences to a love of the viola, and to persuade composers to write music for
> it. That we are doing honour to him on the eve of his 80th birthday, and
> that his name is being coupled to that of Casals is pretty good evidence of
> how well he has fought his battle and won.
>
> Artists often dazzle our ears with miraculous dexterity, but too often we
> are actually left unmoved in our innermost feelings. With Tertis, some-
> thing always lay behind the surface, and the sheer grandeur of his tone,
> contrasted with exquisite delicacy, was merely the means of an extraor-
> dinary power of expression, that invariably touched us. His playing has
> always been intensely individual – and that quiet, rugged personality on
> the platform, utterly devoid of showmanship, was typical of his perform-
> ance.
>
> You could never say that he came from any particular school of playing
> – as there was none – he made it himself.
>
> He began his career as a pianist and violinist, but immediately he
> touched the viola everything else went by the board, and while still a stu-
> dent at the Royal Academy of Music, we find his composer friends coming
> under his spell, and one after another writing their finest music for him.
> York Bowen, Benjamin Dale, Arnold Bax, Holst, Vaughan Williams are
> among the great number who have written for him.
>
> He retired far too early owing to trouble with his right arm, but indomi-
> table as ever he turned his fiery energy into perfecting the new design of

viola which you have heard, and which is now creating interest amongst makers all over the world.

Nevertheless it is as a great artist that we most revere him. By his supreme example, viola players are now filled with hope for their beloved instrument, and the title of his autobiography – 'Cinderella No More' – might well serve as the signal of his triumph.

Tertis wrote to Shore from Edgmoor on 29 December 1956 (his eightieth birthday)

My dear Bernard.
Only a short note, I am simply overwhelmed with letters and telephone calls, everybody so good and kind to me. First, I nearly fainted when I saw your beautiful writing – how did you do it. I am delighted and now – how can I thank you for the lovely things you said about me – the eulogy of my humble little efforts in life.

Thank you again with all my heart and thank your dear Olive for your letters of congratulations and love – but Bernard, did you hear, such an appalling bad balance between viola and voice! I might have been playing on a half-sized violin in a remote corner of another room! The balance was perfect when Lidell (Alvar) did it with me. It was small, heart-breaking and didn't give a semblance of the qualities of the viola. Now we are at the mercy of those fellows who control balance and tone …
L.T.

The radio programme was pre-recorded on 12 December; at the same time he recorded the Brahms E flat sonata with Ernest Lush. They spent from 2 to 5 p.m. on the Brahms, and Tertis was quite content with it, but when it came to the *Music Magazine* extracts he was not so happy. In a letter to Wilfred Saunders he wrote: 'I was so tired with three hours of nervous tension that although I only had to do bits and pieces I was horribly dissatisfied. Listen in if you can and let me have your and your wife's candid opinion!'

On 29 December 1956 he wrote to Leonard Isaacs at the BBC:

First and foremost I should like to send my grateful thanks and express my deep appreciation of the honour and kindness the BBC have done me in so generously broadcasting such a handsome tribute of my humble efforts in life on the occasion of my eightieth birthday, but, may I be forgiven when I say I was bitterly disappointed with the astonishingly bad balance that came over the air, of the songs with viola obbligato. Just before we did this, I had said in my script, 'I will now illustrate with the collaboration of Mr Lidell, the viola as obbligato to the voice, which is a very neglected medium! Not only was Lidell's beautiful singing amplified in these two delicately woven songs, but the viola sounded like a half-sized violin, played in a remote corner of another room. Even I, who knew the obbligato so well, had the greatest difficulty in recognizing and hearing harmonies and phrases I myself had written. Everybody here, and there were quite a number, both musical and unmusical, commented on the extraordinary distant sound of the viola.

I am grieved more than I can say in the knowledge that such inexcusable faulty balance must have done serious harm to what I have fought for all my life – the cause of the viola!

Yours sincerely, Lionel Tertis

Leonard Isaacs replied on 1 January:

I had been going to write today in any case to tell you how very much I enjoyed your playing last Friday evening, and now it seems more than ever necessary that I should write because of your letter. I was aware of no bad balance at all. I listened on a set with VHF reception and the quality of the viola was absolutely magnificent. In the two little excerpts which you played to illustrate the instrument's tone (the second on the C string only) it was as rich a sound as I have ever heard on any string instrument, and as for your disappointment with the obbligato I can only assume that some atmospheric freak caused reception to be bad in Devonshire because I heard every note you played beside Mr Lidell's voice. Of course a broadcast or a record is two-dimensional whereas in the presence of the performance one's two ears give a three-dimensional depth for what is heard. This is an allowance which one has to make in listening to all music over the air. I am most distressed that you should have been disappointed but I think you listen with the hyper-acute nerves of one who has not only made the recording but has some other thing very much at heart. I should be very surprised indeed if you do not receive a great many congratulatory letters and I can only conclude by saying that my wife and I were enchanted both by your playing and your personality over the air. It was a great joy to hear you again and I am only sorry that I shall not be in the country when your Brahms sonata is broadcast. With very kindest wishes and greetings for 1957,

Yours sincerely, Leonard Isaacs

A fulsome tribute to the octogeniarians Casals and Tertis appeared in the December 1956 issue of *The Strad*, extracts from which appear below:

Students of astrology might do well to look up the old charts of the year

1876 and examine the positions of the stars and planets on December 29. Would this reveal anything of special significance or was it by coincidence that in towns as far apart as Vendrell in Catalonia and West Hartlepool in Northern England two babies were born that day who were destined to change and enhance the status of two stringed instruments to such a degree that they enriched the lives of countless music-lovers? Furthermore, is it merely a matter of chance that today both men are still amazingly active, each approaching his eightieth birthday with the appearance of agelessness despite strenuous work over many epoch-making decades in which triumphs were achieved not only as the result of supreme talent but also as the fruits of determined idealism translated by relentless purpose and continuous effort into new instrumental idioms? ...

The effect of Tertis' influence was the more pronounced because his emergence coincided with a musical resurgence in England, the first since the days of Purcell that led to the expression of a genuine creative spirit. Many members of what was then known as the rising British school, uplifted by Tertis' vision and encouraged by his need for original viola music, chose his instrument as the medium for some of their noblest works. Concertos were written by Bax, York Bowen, Dale, McEwen, and later by Walton and others, while the list of attractive compositions for viola and piano is still expanding. ...

The example of these two great veteran artists is an inspiration to all. May they long be spared to generate their beneficent influence personally.

In March 1957 there was a correspondence between Tertis and Bernard Shore, who was keen to borrow Tertis's copy of the Bax *Phantasy* that he was to broadcast in the same month. On 9 March Tertis wrote that he could not find his copy, but wished Shore every success, and felt sure he would give a grand show of it. He told Bernard that his BBC recording of the Brahms E flat Sonata with Ernest Lush (piano) was to be broadcast on the following Friday, 15 March. He wrote a letter of congratulation to Shore on his performance of the Bax *Phantasy* on 13 March:

My dear old Bernard.
I am very proud of you. You played splendidly as I knew you would and the viola sounded magnificent, not the orchestra – as usual far too loud ... L.T.

He wrote again to Shore on 21 April, explaining that he was very busy, including daily visits to his masseur in Banstead. In another letter he wrote: 'I am still not

100% fit but hope to get through my two weeks at Dartington – Edgmoor will be empty for a week 1–8 September so I am going to Bath that week to spy out the land with a view to spending the winter there.' His letter of 24 August 1957 reported on his Dartington visit: 'Well, we have got through the scrimmage of one week and I expect to get through the next in likely manner. Although so far, those that I have had in my class are not very good at fiddle-playing, they are very enthusiastic, which is a great stimulant.' He then went on to say that he was delighted that Bernard had arranged the Brahms D minor Violin Sonata for viola: 'It is splendid of you to enlarge the library as you do.' Tertis continued to have regular massage during this period.

Bernard Shore's daughter, Jane Nicholas, remembers Tertis: 'Lionel was a dear – I always called him Uncle Lionel and my sister Christine remembers her embarrassment whenever she answered the 'phone because he had such a high-pitched voice, she thought he was Mrs Tertis!'

At the beginning of his eighth decade, and at Sir John Barbirolli's instigation, Tertis was invited to be the soloist at two concerts during the Hallé Orchestra's Centenary Festival. The previous occasion he had played under Sir John's baton was 11 January 1931, when he joined Antonio Brosa in a broadcast perform-ance of the *Sinfonia concertante*. The initial invitation was that Tertis should be soloist in *Harold in Italy*. However, there was a change of plan, as Tertis described in a letter to Sydney Errington (at that time principal viola in the Hallé Orchestra).

Edgmoor, Middlemoor, Tavistock
12th May 1957

My dear Sydney,

... Perhaps you have heard that I have had to give up the idea of playing 'Harold' with Sir John. It would have been a wonderful experience for me but my eyes have become faulty and I came to the conclusion that I dare not try my share of this magnificent work from memory. By-the-way, if you are playing it during the Halle Festival would you care to have my ideas of phrasing and fingering. I have played it a good many times during my life and if you will forgive my presumption, I would go through it with you con amore, in case my editing was any help to you ...

Yours ever, Lionel

Instead of *Harold in Italy* Tertis substituted Dale's *Romance* in the composer's version with orchestral accompaniment. Tertis wrote to Shore from Sidmouth, Devon: 'It was my privilege to have you play the piano for me, and how wonder-fully you did it.' Tertis also said that he was having further massage for his 'old back'. He was preparing for two performances of the Dale with John Barbirolli and the Hallé.[2] 'The Romance gets more and more difficult as the fatal day of Manchester draws near! I have had an invitation to spend the winter at Cape Town, would you go if you were me?!'

These two concerts took place at the Free Trade Hall, Manchester on Wednesday and Thursday 30 and 31 October 1957. Michael Kennedy in the *Daily Telegraph* on 31 October wrote:

> Lionel Tertis, emerging from semi-retirement at the age of 80, was the viola soloist at last night's Halle concert conducted by Sir John Barbirolli ... He played the Romance by Benjamin Dale ... This is no milk and water idyll but a work of considerable imaginative power which emphasises our loss from Dale's failure to achieve full maturity as a composer. Its opening theme is perfectly suited to Mr Tertis's famous dark tone, which age seems to have robbed of hardly any of its former strength and lustre.
>
> Here indeed was an experience to treasure, and when he played with velvety smoothness, the soft return of the main theme stood still and the audience listened spellbound.

The concert was also reviewed in the *Daily Mail*:

'Father' of Viola keeps a pledge

> The modest little man with the look of an elder statesman walked briskly on to a concert platform last night to fulfil 'my one great ambition before I die'.
>
> Lionel Tertis ... had come out of semi-retirement to play as a soloist with an orchestra ... and no-one in the audience knew he was playing with an arm still racked with the arthritis that forced him to retire from the concert platform before the war.
>
> But he was determined to keep the promise he made to Sir John Barbirolli earlier this year. He told him: 'John, I've one ambition left before I die – to play with the Halle under your baton' ... Last night Tertis held the audience spellbound with his playing of Benjamin Dale's Romance ... said Sir John afterwards: 'He is still the father of all viola players'.

Tertis paid tribute to Barbirolli's masterful accompanying when he remembered the occasion: 'At the second concert I was more in the mood and played better. I indulged, in the inspiration of the moment, in most audacious changes of rubato, phrasing and nuance, and whatever unexpected liberties I took, John was with me, on the dot every time.'

Shortly before these concerts Tertis received two short pieces for viola and piano from Alan Bush (*Dance Melody* and *Song Melody*, op. 47), who wrote: 'It would give me the greatest pleasure if you would accept the dedication of these pieces.' Tertis accepted the dedication by return of post. Unfortunately, owing to his failing eyesight, he never played them, and sent the music to Bernard Shore in the hope that he would première them.

During the winter of 1957–8 Tertis suffered from a severe bout of bronchitis. On 9 January 1958 he wrote to Shore: 'I have been working at Flos Campi and think I've got the hang of it.' On 6 February he sent a postcard to Shore from Edgmoor: 'I hope to come to town (London) on Wednesday, and sail for the South of France on 17th. If there is a chance of you playing the score of Flos Campi with me I should be so grateful.'

Tertis sent the Shores two postcards on 28 February and 12 March 1958 from the South of France. He stayed at La Vieille Maison, Saint-Paul, Alpes-Maritimes. In a further letter he said he would be leaving for London on Saturday 29 March, and asked Shore if he would get him a ticket for Vaughan Williams's Symphony, which was being played on 2 April. Tertis planned to stay at his club from 31 March to 3 April; he asked the Shores if he could visit them on the afternoon of Sunday 30th and wondered if Bernard would once again play the piano part of *Flos campi* with him.

On 25 March 1958 William Primrose and Paul Doktor presented a two-viola concert at the Mannes School of Music in New York City. A special feature was the first American performance of Tertis's Variations on a Theme of Handel. Primrose sent Tertis a copy of the programme, on the back of which he wrote: 'We had a fine concert and many converts to our instrument.' Harris Goldsmith wrote in the May *Musical Courier*:

> A viola recital is far from a commonplace occurrence, a recital of viola duets an absolute rarity. Before this concert, I was unaware of the fact that any literature for the instrument in pairs existed, aside from the Bach Sixth Brandenburg Concerto. It seemed to me that a novelty concert was going to be presented, but no two performers could be better qualified to give the viola its deserved dignity than Messrs. Primrose and Doktor. Technically and musically, both are masters, although their styles differ greatly. Primrose's sharp, straight lines of sound were balanced by Doktor's plushy, round tones.
>
> The program opened with three moving Fantasias by the sixteenth-century composer Orlandus Lassus. With the soloists' superb delineation of the pieces, it immediately became evident that this was to be an evening of considerably more than simple novelty. Karl Stamitz' Duet no. 3, a pleasant piece, was played with wit and polish. The twentieth century was represented by Alexander Wunderer's Duet in G major and Lionel Tertis'

Passacaglia on a theme by Handel, both in their U.S. premieres. Wunderer, a noted Viennese pedagogue, who died in 1956, has written a piece that utilizes the sounds of the two violas to great effect, without being music of great stature. The work is strongly derivative of Richard Strauss. Like Wunderer, Tertis, the twentieth century's grand champion of the viola, has produced a work specifically designed to get maximum tonal results from the instruments, although his opus is in a more severe vein. There is no startling inventiveness displayed, but rather a craftsmanship that is the result of prying into every sonic corner of the viola's potentialities. The performances could not have been more accomplished. ...

I sincerely hope that this is not the last to be heard of viola duets, as the results can be, and most assuredly were, with Messrs. Primrose and Doktor, immeasurably gratifying.

After the concert Primrose and Doktor wrote to Tertis:

My dear Lionel,
We both wish you had been here tonight as you were so vividly and presently just over a year ago. As our dear friend and colleague, Harry Berly, used to say, it was 'jolly decent, old boy!' We had a fine concert, a fine public and many converts to our instrument. Hope to see you when I am in England next month. God bless you William.

Dear Mr Tertis,
I was ever so happy that we had a chance to play your wonderful and effective Passacaglia. I copied the parts and return your music by same mail.
Most cordially, Paul Doktor.

Tertis was very upset by a letter from a Cheshire violist, Derek Vaughan, which appeared in the March 1957 edition of *The Strad*:

Large Size Violas

It is extremely gratifying to hear of the success in Moscow of an English viola which is built on sane proportions. This is really a double-success for the maker, Mr. Hoing; the highest possible praise from the Russians, and further recognition of the fact that it is correct proportions and design which make for quality of tone, not size.

Viola players have had so much propaganda forced upon them concerning the alleged virtues of the over-sized viola, that it would be very interesting to make a short survey of the whole position.

It was stated in the columns of The Strad some years ago, that of all the violas in this country, those with the finest tone are in the region of

16¼in. However, somehow or other Mr. Tertis has got several makers in this country turning out large violas of 16¾in., and now estimates that there are about 200 of these in England alone. When one considers that most of these have been made by expert craftsmen, then I think we should be able to expect some very fine instruments. But the results are very disappointing. During the past few years I have played upon seven Tertis model violas; two by Richardson, two by Voigt, one by Lawrence Cocker and two of forgotten parentage. The workmanship of these instruments was of a very high order, but none of them had any sort of tone quality, and their chief characteristic was a tendency to 'boom', particularly on the C string. It is rather significant to note that each of these seven players now has another viola. I remember Mr. Tertis once quoting that you can't get a quart out of a pint pot, but to take the saying a stage further, if you put a quart in a three-pint pot, you are going to have a lot of unnecessary wasted space, like the over-sized viola.

No, the over-sized viola is not the answer. What we want are violas of fine tone quality, and this means working in the direction of those violas which have proved to be consistently good, no matter what size they may be, and not by being biased one way or the other.

Derek Vaughan, Bromborough, Cheshire.

Tertis promptly wrote to Bernard Shore:

> Sesame Imperial & Pioneer Club
> Wed. 6th March 1957

My dear Bernard,
Here is the cutting from the Strad. An absolutely untrue and uncalled for attack. Hoing and the fellow who wrote the letter must have put their heads together. For the good of our cause I shall try and reply in no uncertain manner ... L.T.

Also in March 1957 Tertis wrote to Sydney Errington during a train journey to Tavistock:

My dear Sydney,
I've been 'under the weather' since the middle of December and am just going home after a course of treatment in London, feeling somewhat better ... The reason for this letter is that I have just spotted this letter in this month's Strad! It looks like a conspiracy between Hoing (Clifford Hoing – viola maker) and the fellow who wrote it and is so untrue and uncalled for that I feel, for the good of our cause, that I must answer it in no uncertain manner. I wonder if you have time to refute this scandalous statement.

A letter from you, as leader of the Halle violas, would be very influential, saying what you think of your Cocker viola and the others that are played in the Northern orchestras.

Yours ever, Lionel Tertis

On 11 March Errington wrote from his home in Leeds to the editor of *The Strad*. (This was included in the May edition.)

Dear Sir,

I have just read with amazement in your March issue, a letter in which your correspondent seeks, with a few strokes of his pen, to 'liquidate' all the years of work and experiment Lionel Tertis has devoted to improving his beloved instrument, the viola.

Six of us in the Halle use the L.T. model (3 Richardson, 3 Cocker) and I would like to put it on record that we are satisfied and happy with our instruments and have been for years (myself since 1943). There are also many more being used by professionals and amateurs in the North. Are we all the dupes of skilful propaganda? We don't think so.

To say that L.T. violas have not 'any sort of tone quality' is ludicrous in the extreme and an insult both to Lionel Tertis who developed these instruments and to the players who use them.

Yours faithfully,

Sydney Errington, Principal Viola Hallé Orchestra.

Another former Tertis student, Lena Wood, wrote:

The eulogies passed by the Russians on the Hoing viola would have been more gratifying if a Tertis model viola had also been tried in Moscow at the same time. Mr Vaughan wholeheartedly accepts the praise given to a solitary instrument, yet he himself condemns unequivocally seven Tertis models (also English) – and he ends his letter by saying one must not be biased one way or the other!

One would prefer to have a Russian opinion on a Tertis Model before accepting the 'unbiased' opinion of Mr Vaughan.

Lena Wood, Stourbridge, Worcestershire

Wilfred Saunders replied to Vaughan's letter from the maker's point of view:

Many players use fine old Italian violas measuring around 16¼ inches because they must have an old Italian instrument at any cost, and violas in this class are mostly either 16¼ inches or under, or well over 17 inches … When Stradivari decided to make a real viola for his own satisfaction, he made it 18⅞ inches. Mr Tertis has not somehow or other got we makers to turn out 16¾ inch violas. We make these T.M. violas for exactly the same reason that the old Italian makers made violins and cellos, that is, we can sell at a price which makes it worth our trouble, about three times as many of these instruments as we can make; 90% going to professional players all over the world. Almost every critic of the T.M. viola states rather lamely that the C string booms! Would one of them please explain more exactly what this 'boom' is? When a player has grown accustomed to a small viola with a C string which only croaks when one treats it roughly in a forte passage, he finds a free, resonant C string – which you can really force to obtain a tone of maximum volume and of good round quality is rather a surprise, and it takes many hours of playing before one can do justice to such an instrument. To play a few notes and then dismiss the viola as booming is silly and proves nothing ... To conclude, can Mr Vaughan give readers an account of his experience and qualifications for putting his opinions on this matter into print? For myself, the opinions of players like Bernard Shore, who has and plays a T.M. viola by Lawrence Cocker and Harry Danks, who plays a Richardson, is conclusive evidence that this viola is sound, and what many players really want.

Tertis's reply was also included in the correspondence column of the May edition of *The Strad*:

I should be grateful if you could find space in your valuable columns to enable me to reply to a letter by Mr Vaughan ... No one would gainsay the wonderful accomplishments as an executant of that eminent solo-violist, William Primrose, who, having played on more than one 'Tertis Model' viola, has acclaimed them 'as the answer to every violist's prayer'. We may justifiably be permitted to ruminate on the qualifications of Mr Vaughan either as violist or critic. With what authority does he pronounce that, 'some years ago it was stated in the columns of the Strad that of all the violas in this country, those with the finest tone were in the region of 16¼ inches'. In this connection, all will agree that the C string sonority is the distinguishing feature of the viola. Nevertheless, I recall that Mr Hoing advocated an even smaller instrument, which, in addition to it being incapable of giving a semblance of C string sonority, would be neither violin or viola. The 16¾ inch 'Tertis Model' viola, which is neither too small or too large, possesses this all important C string sonority as well as fine tonal quality on its other three strings, in addition to several features in its design which makes it easy to manage.

That great authority, the late Alfred Hill, of the famous house of W. E. Hill & Sons, advocated and insisted that 16¾ inches was the ideal size for a viola. To the expert craftsmen, Arthur Richardson, Lawrence Cocker and Paul Voigt, who Mr Vaughan states I have somehow or other got them turning out the 'Tertis Model' viola, he can now add that fine craftsman, Wilfred Saunders, of Nottingham, all of whom have orders for the 'Tertis Model' from professional players at home and abroad.

The 'Tertis Model' is also being made by professional craftsmen in North and South America, France, Germany, Scandinavia, Switzerland, Australia, Canada and other countries. In the USA alone, so far, thirty-nine professional violin makers have the drawings and specifications of the 'Tertis Model' viola and are making them. Is it likely that all these expert craftsmen, both at home and abroad, would go on producing them, if, as Mr Vaughan suggests, the quality of tone in them is so lacking. More important still, is it conceivable that demands for the 'Tertis Model' would be so insistent from professional players all over the world.

Mr Vaughan is the victim of a slight misconception. The boom to which he refers is not in the C string, but in the world-wide demand both by violists and viola makers for the 'Tertis Model'.

In all, some 300 of these instruments are already in existence and it is significant, that after seeing and hearing one at a demonstration recital I gave recently in New York, before a distinguished gathering of instrumentalists, that famous connoisseur and violin maker, Mr Rembert Wurlitzer of New York, has ordered one from Saunders of Nottingham.

As most people are aware, my source of satisfaction is, that as result of my experience as a solo violist, for over sixty-three years, I have been the means of providing a fine-toned viola for my brother and sister viola players. I would like to reiterate that I have no financial interest in the 'Tertis Model' viola. Mr Vaughan speaks of the gratifying success of the undersized viola in Moscow. I am prepared to leave Russia and all it stands for to Mr Hoing and Mr Vaughan with their undersized violas, and to rest content with the approval and the approbation of the civilized world.

Lionel Tertis, Tavistock, Devon.

Lewis Harris, a representative of the Israel Philharmonic Orchestra based in London, contacted Tertis in March 1958, and asked if he could arrange for seven Tertis Model violas to be sent to the orchestra as soon as possible. Tertis asked Arthur Richardson and Lawrence Cocker to make two violas each and Wilfred Saunders was asked to make three. The violas were duly sent to the Israel Philharmonic, and Tertis received a letter from the principal viola dated 1 December 1958:

Dear Maestro,

We have now received the seven violas and are playing on them with great delight. I consider myself lucky in having secured a Saunders instrument. I might mention that the other day – for the first time in my experience – the conductor said, 'the violas are a little too loud'! This will show you how sonorous is the tone.

We are very proud and happy that you, dear Maestro, should have taken all the personal care and trouble to ensure that the Viola Section of the Israel Philharmonic should obtain these fine instruments and on behalf of my colleagues and myself, I wish to express to you our warmest gratitude and thanks. We consider it an honour and a privilege that Lionel Tertis should have interested himself on our behalf.

As usual, we have a busy schedule of concerts with full halls and are enjoying the music making since the conductor is that fine musician, Jean Martinon, and the soloist is the remarkable young pianist, Glenn Gould. Then, at the beginning of the new year, we expect Carlo Maria Giulini with whom we are always happy to play.

We hope, dear Maestro, that you are well and wish you long continuance of health and activity.

Again with sincere thanks,

Very cordially yours,

Marek Rak

Principal Viola of the Israel Philharmonic Orchestra

Arie Israeli (Viola Principal), Chaim Bor, Yehudith Borochoff, Zeev Steinberg, Reuven Tottenstein, Daniel Benjamini.

Second Marriage and Last Appearance

*Flos campi – Manchester Concert – South Africa –
marriage to Lillian – 85th birthday tribute –
Royal Philharmonic Society Gold Medal – last appearance*

A T   T H E   1958 King's Lynn Festival Tertis was the soloist in Vaughan
Williams's *Flos campi*, which he had premièred in 1925. With the conduc-
tor Herbert Menges he visited RVW at his London home, 10 Hanover Terrace,
and had a further rehearsal at Mahatma Gandhi Hall (Morley College) with
orchestra and chorus (the Linden Singers), which Vaughan Williams attended.
The *Sunday Times* of 29 June 1958 had a front-page photograph of Tertis and
Vaughan Williams at rehearsal, and on page 5 there was an article entitled 'Mr
Tertis's Philosophy':

> Lionel Tertis, Britain's outstanding viola player, who at eighty-one is busy
> rehearsing a lengthy work for the King's Lynn Festival, accepts the difficul-
> ties of an arthritic arm and a burdensome myopia with what he calls the
> Beecham philosophy of playing till you drop.
>
> Because he can read the score only by poring over it, he has had, he says,
> to cultivate his faculty of memorising an entire work a phrase at a time.
>
> Characteristically, Mr Tertis is more ready to talk of the three young
> viola-makers he has discovered in this country than of himself. When he
> was severely crippled by arthritis in 1936, he spent his time designing a
> viola, then an instrument hard to find anywhere at any price. From this
> design instruments have gone from England all over the world, made by
> the three young men in their own homes and in their spare time. Some of
> them are of a craftmanship which Mr Tertis reckons the finest he has seen
> anywhere.

The performance took place on 1 August in St Nicholas Chapel, a large and
beautiful fifteenth-century church, in the presence of the Queen Mother, who
told Tertis how moved she had been by his playing of *Flos campi*. The Queen
Mother's Lady-in-Waiting, Ruth, Lady Fermoy, founded the King's Lynn Festival in 1951 and was the guiding spirit for a number of years.

Some time before the concert, Tertis wrote to Lillian Warmington,[1] inviting her to attend his performance of *Flos campi*, which she happily accepted.
During the festival many of the artists, including Gerald Moore (who had on

occasion played piano quartets with Sammons, Tertis and Cedric Sharpe), Herbert Menges and Lady Fermoy, stayed at a country hotel a few miles from King's Lynn. Tertis and Lillian Warmington were also guests there for the duration of the festival and afterwards travelled together to Bournemouth, via London, where Lillian and her mother had invited Lionel to stay with them for a holiday. During his visit Lionel proposed to Lillian. Their engagement was unofficial, and it was arranged that an announcement would appear in the national press the day after the three of them were on their way to South Africa.

Paul Cropper heard his former teacher play for the last time at a Manchester Tuesday Midday Concert on 2 December 1958; two eighteenth-century sonatas and a group of three solos supplemented the main work – the Brahms F minor sonata. Cropper remembers: 'It was all great playing at the age of eighty-one.' Colin Mason wrote in the *Manchester Guardian*:

> Lionel Tertis, who gave yesterday's Midday Concert (dedicated to the memory of Edward Isaacs) in the Lesser Free Trade Hall, Manchester, is 81. He played sitting down from memory (because his sight is failing), and on an enormous viola of the size that he introduced in his younger days, such as would stretch the elbow of a baboon. Mr Tertis, by the way, is a small man, and his hands by no means reach his knees. The claims for the supposedly superior tone of the larger instrument are not really proven ... And the general richness and colour of the tone is at least as likely to have been due to Mr Tertis's playing as to the instrument. The only evidence to the ear that it was not a young virtuoso that was playing was the lifetime's wisdom and experience in the phrasing – an experience that was not an old man's substitute for energy and quickness, but was combined with a vivacity of style that the youngest player might despair to match.
>
> With the minimum of effort, moving the point of his bow with scarcely more pressure than its own weight, backwards and forwards in centimetres on the muted strings, he produced full silvery notes with finely differentiated accents that carried each phrase in one effortless movement from up-beat to cadence, or through any other arc the melody might describe. And when Brahms F minor Sonata took him beyond the tonal range of the elegant eighteenth-century pieces by Martini and Galuppi, he deepened his colours and his tone with equal ease of style and no more exertion than a slightly ampler bow. The recital was a model of the art of string playing, which many violinists as well as viola players might have listened to with profit. Mr Tertis's responsive and excellent partner was Ruth Fermoy ...

Charles and Lucy Kreitzer of Cape Town had been corresponding with Tertis regularly since the time Charles had lessons with him in Devon; in fact, they had had a reunion during the intervening years in London. In 1958 the Kreitzers received a letter from Tertis, asking if their invitation made in Tavistock to visit them in South Africa still stood, to which they replied immediately, inviting Tertis to stay with them in their home in Cape Town. On 16 December, in a letter to Bernard Shore and his wife, he wrote: 'My dear Olive and Bernard, We, Mrs Warmington, Lillian and I, are just off. Our boat 'City of Exeter' leaves Tilbury early tomorrow (Thursday) ... Look in Saturday's paper!' Lillian Tertis remembered the sea voyage: 'The purser said that he had never seen such a rough sea during forty years. Neither Lionel nor my mother were troubled by this at all, in fact they went up on deck to watch the gigantic waves while I remained in bed in my cabin feeling very ill.'

At Christmas time Charles and Lucy Kreitzer were at Cape Town docks, where they met a sprightly and vigorous eighty-two-year-old violist, helping an elderly lady and her daughter with their luggage. They were greeted on arrival at the Kreitzer's home by a very excited maid, who was keen to show everyone her engagement ring. Tertis shook the young lady's hand warmly and said, 'My dear, I am so happy for you. Now you can congratulate me, for I, too, have just become engaged.' The Kreitzers immediately thought he was referring to Mrs Warmington, the elderly lady on the ship, but to their surprise and delight his fiancée was in fact the lady's daughter, Lillian. Mrs Warmington and her daughter stayed at the York Hotel, Green Point, Cape Town.

Tertis was interviewed by Beatrice Marx, who had known him in his student days in London, for an article she was preparing for the *Cape Times*. During the interview she asked him if he would be the soloist in a concert to be given by the local orchestra in the City Hall in aid of the Ellie Marx Scholarship Fund on Monday 16 February. The visiting conductor that year was Charles Mackerras, who was happy to be associated with the legendary violist in the first performance in South Africa of Vaughan Williams's *Flos campi*. A number of well-known singers from the Cape Town area gave their services to make up the chorus. The Kreitzer's friend Blanche Gerstman arranged an orchestral accompaniment to Galuppi's Air which Tertis played as an encore, by all accounts with 'charming simplicity and ravishing tone'.

Lionel recorded a short programme for the South African Broadcasting Corporation in the Concert Hall of Broadcasting House in Cape Town on 2 February with the pianist Arthur Woodland. These items were later included on one side of an LP record, Pearl ILP 0111185.5 (Wolstenholme, *Allegretto*; Dale, *Romance*; Galuppi, *Aria amorosa*; Martini, *Allegro*).

On 20 February, at the invitation of the South African Broadcasting Corporation, Lionel and his fiancée pre-recorded a joint recital before an invited audience in Cape Town Studios, broadcast on 4 March. Arthur Woodland was the pianist. The programme consisted of Toccata for cello and piano by Frescobaldi, Sonata in E for viola and piano by Martini, Elizabethan melody for viola and cello by Dowland, a Sonata movement for viola and cello by Beethoven and a fifteenth-century folksong for viola, cello and piano.

During their three-month stay Tertis and Lillian joined Elsie Hall, also in her eighties, in a chamber concert in the City Hall on Friday 27 February. The programme included both the Brahms sonatas, which were separated by Tertis's arrangement of the Elizabethan melody and the Beethoven duo.

One of the pleasures of Tertis's stay were his evening walks with Charles Kreitzer along the beach to Moville Point lighthouse and back. There were also moments of hilarity on sightseeing trips in the Kreitzers' car. In her book *Taking a Bow* Lucy Factor Kreitzer tells the following story:

With the engaged couple sitting in the back of our car, Charles mischievously turned the wheel sharply while taking a corner, causing our distinguished guest to tumble towards Lillian. Delightedly, he called out, 'Oh Charles, do that again!' From then on, this became a ritual at the traffic island and we were all in hysterics on the occasion when Charles decided to circle it again and again and again!

Lionel and Lillian returned to South Africa on a number of other occasions, and on 29 December 1967 he celebrated his ninety-first birthday at a huge party at which Derek Hudson, the director of the Cape Town orchestra, proposed the toast. The last time the Kreitzers spoke to Tertis was on 29 December 1974, when they phoned to congratulate him on his ninety-eighth birthday.

Back in England, a wedding had to be organized. Tertis wrote to Bernard Shore from Bournemouth: 'I am coming to the Sesame [club] for a few days tomorrow to arrange everything (in double quick time for our wedding day on April 25th). I don't know how we shall encompass everything in such a short space of time, but we must see you somehow if at all possible. Much love Lionel.'

On 25 April 1959, three weeks after their holiday in Cape Town, Tertis married Lillian Florence Margaret Warmington, daughter of Mr and Mrs Harold Warmington, at the Musicians' Church, St Sepulchre's, Holborn. The historic building is the largest parish church in the City of London, incorporating the musicians' chapel, which contains many memorials to famous musicians, including a number of Tertis's former colleagues and friends; Henry Wood, who was assistant organist at St Sepulchre's when he was fourteen, is buried in the church, which contains a stained glass window in his memory. Dame Nellie Melba and John Ireland are also remembered, and the musicians' book of remembrance includes well over a thousand names.

Frank Thistleton, secretary of the Musicians' Benevolent Fund and a long-time friend of Tertis, was best man. The choir of St Paul's sang the setting of Psalm 121, 'I will lift up mine eyes unto the hills', by Ernest Walker, who had accompanied Tertis on a number of occasions at concerts in Oxford. The organist was Sir William McKie, who played Bach's Prelude and Fugue in B minor during the signing of the register. Tertis and his bride then took the unusual step of playing at their own wedding; three short duets for viola and cello – Psalm 23, 'Crimond', Elizabethan Melody by John Dowland and an anonymous folksong with organ accompaniment.

There were about a dozen photographers in the church during the ceremony. The following press report appeared the day after their wedding:

Sweet Wedding Music ... by the bride and groom

An Elizabethan Melody, with Lionel Tertis, viola, and Lillian Warmington, cello, accompanied at the organ by Sir William McKie ... An ordinary enough item in a concert programme but this, yesterday, was a London church, St. Sepulchre's, Holborn, and the violist and 'cellist have been married just five minutes ... The 'concert' – they played three pieces together – was, said the 82-year-old groom and his bride, 39, a 'little thanksgiving from us both to the Almighty'.

The 'world's greatest violist', a widower, who retired from the concert platform in 1937, and his bride met a year ago as teacher and pupil. 'I hope to persuade him back to the platform now for duet recitals', she said.

Leaving for the Mayfair reception for the 150 guests who had listened to a unique wedding concert the groom joked, 'I don't feel a day over 52.'

Lady Fermoy hosted a reception for them at her London home and from there Mr and Mrs Tertis embarked on a three-week European honeymoon visiting Brussels, Berne, Geneva, Lausanne, Paris, Rome, Milan, Rimini and Venice. During their stay they visited every violin maker in each city, taking the opportunity to demonstrate the T.M. viola and giving them copies of diagrams.

The following is Lillian Tertis's recollection of their honeymoon:

During three days in Paris we met friends including my Portuguese friend who gave me away at my wedding. We also visited a violin maker called Vatelot and Lionel showed him his viola. On the fourth day we flew to Rome and from there went by train to Rimini on the coast and visited a famous violin-maker Capicchioni from whom I borrowed a cello and tried it all morning and the next day but decided against it in the end. Our next port of call was San Marino, a famous rock town, and then on by bus to Venice where we arrived at 7 p.m. in a gondola. We explored the tiny streets next day and eventually found a violin-maker whom we brought to our hotel and showed him the Tertis-model viola and gave him the drawings.

On 10 July 1959 Tertis wrote to Bernard Shore from 10 Branksome Wood Road, Bournemouth:

> My dear Bernard, Lillian is writing this for me as my eyes are bothering me a little – she is giving a recital in aid of the Musicians' Benevolent Fund at the Wigmore Hall on 2nd November and would so much like to end the programme with the C minor Brahms piano quartet.
>
> I have written to Brosa (Antonio) to ask if he can play the violin; Lady Fermoy would play the piano – and Lillian, the cello part and it would be lovely if you could play the viola.
>
> It is a favourite work of mine and I have some pet fingerings for the lovely tunes which I should like to show you.
>
> Now, if you could possibly do this, would you be an angel and send a P.C. to the following address before the 18th. Greythorne, Bonaccord Road, Swanage. I hope the answer will be 'yes'.

Brosa was unable to do the date, and Lady Fermoy had to go to America, so the Brahms had to be cancelled.

Tertis wrote again to Shore from Bournemouth on 31 October, saying that he had not been well; his doctor recommended that they should go abroad and that he and Lillian would be flying to the South of France on the following Thursday. This meant they would miss Shore's recital on 12 November; Tertis hoped he would have a roaring success.

At the Danish State Radio studios in Copenhagen on 11 June 1960 Lionel and Lillian recorded a programme of duos for viola and cello, including the 'Eye-glass' duet by Beethoven, which was later included on the Pearl LP. Later in the year they accepted an invitation from Dr Gioacchino Pasqualini, the president of the Association of Violin Makers in Italy, to attend the first ever exhibition devoted entirely to new violas; more than 150 instruments from sixteen countries were exhibited. Lillian Tertis wrote an article about their visit which was originally published in *The Strad* in October 1959 and also appeared in *My Viola and I*.

After his marriage he developed the idea of designing a cello along similar lines to the Tertis Model viola, which could be constructed at a reasonable cost. The L.F.M.T. (Lillian Tertis's initials) cello was made by the luthier Lawrence Cocker, and was first played by Lillian Tertis at 'An Invitation Recital' at the

Wigmore Hall on 31 May 1960, in which she was accompanied by Norah Newby in Couperin's *Pièces en Concert* arranged by Bazelaire, followed by Bach's Third Suite in C for solo cello; finally she joined forces with Lionel in a group of duos for viola and cello – Sonata movement by Beethoven, Tertis's arrangements of Variations on a four-bar theme of Handel, followed by Dowland's Elizabethan Melody and the Tartini–Kreisler Fugue. At the conclusion of the recital a collection was taken on behalf of the Musicians' Benevolent Fund.

Lawrence Cocker first became interested in the Tertis Model viola when he obtained copies of the plans from Arthur Richardson. The two men met for the first time at the Wigmore Hall in 1950 at the demonstration concert of the Tertis Model viola. Tertis was always impressed by Cocker's very high standard of workmanship and the meticulous care he took over details.

In 1959, when Tertis turned his attention to the possibility of a Tertis Model cello, he invited Cocker to make the first instrument, followed by a second two years later. Cocker eventually built twelve Tertis Model cellos. Under the auspices of the British Council, demonstration recitals and broadcasts were arranged in Scandinavia and Spain to introduce the Cocker cello. When Tertis put his mind to a Tertis Model violin, Cocker made two which were used in the RAM concert in 1962 (see below). Cockers's quartet of Tertis Model instruments was on exhibition at the King's Lynn Festival in 1963. Lillian was so delighted with her two Cocker Tertis Model cellos that she eventually sold her fine Testore instrument and never regretted it. In 1978 Cocker gave his comments regarding the Tertis Model:

> I work on both an inside and outside mould, and make my violas to a model I've developed myself, through trial and error, although I was steeped in the Tertis Model for a long time. I did the drawings for Lionel, for the Tertis Model cello and violin, and he put me in touch with some of the top players all over the world. But the Tertis Model viola being so large and cavernous tended to have a big booming C string at the expense of the upper register, excepting the occasional instrument. I made Tertis Model violas for him as well as Tertis Model cellos and violins, which some describe as having a tone half-way between the plush and the bright!

In July 1960 Winifred Barrows retired as headmistress of Lawnside School after thirty-five years service; a number of notable musicians and men of letters and the theatre took part in a concert as part of the school's annual prize-giving, held in the Winter Gardens, Malvern. Sir Barry Jackson, a great friend of Elgar and Bernard Shaw, gave a number of recitations, Léon Goossens performed a group of oboe solos, and Lionel and Lillian Tertis played Dowland's

Elizabethan Melody and the Tartini Fugue. A pupil at the school, Margaret Gill, thanked Mr and Mrs Tertis, saying: '"Killing care and grief of heart" do indeed fall asleep under the spell of lovely music, and we are so deeply grateful to you both.' Winifred Barrows said a few words before the two duets: 'Mr and Mrs Tertis are wonderful friends of Lawnside, Mr Tertis is the Prince of Viola Players by which title he is universally known.' She then went on to say how once upon a time he came to the school's rescue and actually taught viola and violin to some lucky, lucky girls. 'What an honour for Lawnside!' she added.

Tertis was a proud man, but more for the viola and his life's work of propaganda and evangelism than for himself. On one occasion, hearing a viola being practised in a nearby room in an Amsterdam hotel, Tertis knocked on the door and introduced himself to the violist of the Smetana Quartet, Milan Škampa: 'You won't know me, but my name is Tertis ...' Škampa felt it was like meeting God and almost went down on his knees before the great man.

With renewed vigour and the support of Lillian, Tertis continued his promotion and development of the Tertis Model. They visited Scandinavia in 1960, giving broadcasts and demonstrations in Denmark, Sweden and Norway. During the following year they went to Spain, where Lillian introduced the Tertis Model cello. Their first recital was given in Madrid on 17 January 1961. It was reviewed in *The Times*:

> The recital took place in Madrid's fine old Conservatory of Music with the object of enabling Spanish professional musicians to hear the fine tonal qualities of these Tertis models ... Their programme (presented from memory) included a Sonata movement by Beethoven and Variations on a theme of Handel written by Mr. Tertis.
>
> Playing without accompaniment, the duet of the 84 year old Lionel Tertis and his wife revealed the remarkable qualities of their two instruments.

On 19 January they travelled to give another demonstration-recital in Barcelona, where they played two days later at the Conservatorio de Musica de Barcelona. On 30 January they left for Cannes for a short vacation.

Casals and Tertis, the heavenly twins, had made music together on a number of occasions. In August 1960 the Tertises visited Casals at his summer school in Zermatt; another visitor that year was Elisabeth, Queen of the Belgians, whom Tertis had first met during the First World War. Lionel and Lillian played some of their duo repertoire to the Queen and Casals. During lunch Casals said to Tertis: 'You and I must play a duet together on our ninetieth birthday.' Casals conducted a performance of his oratorio *The Peace* at the Royal Festival Hall in 1962; at a reception afterwards he was joined by two old friends, who first met in Mrs Draper's 'cellar' fifty years earlier – Tertis and the conductor Pierre Monteux.

Mr and Mrs Tertis moved to 42 Marryat Road in Wimbledon on 5 October 1961. Harry Danks was a regular visitor there, and Lionel always enjoyed hearing and keeping up to date with music profession gossip. On one of Harry's visits the viola-maker Maurice Bouette was present, having brought an instrument for Tertis to hear; another visitor was Peter Lewis, a member of Harry's viola section in the BBC Symphony Orchestra. When Harry arrived, Tertis was impatient to hear the new viola; everyone was seated and Harry played one of Tertis's old favourites, the *Allegretto* by Wolstenholme. As soon as Harry finished Tertis came over to him, and in a quiet voice (unheard by the others in the room) said: 'Harry, your vibrato is a lot better' and did not mention the viola. Tertis still cared about his former pupil even though Danks was now a highly respected member of the music profession, and not the unsure youth who had travelled from the Midlands in the mid-1930s.

Frank Thistleton, who had been Tertis's best man when he married Lillian in April 1959, was the Appeals Organizer for the Musicians' Benevolent Fund. In February 1962 he wrote to Lionel:

My dear Lionel, Some of your friends have suggested to me that they would like to show their warm appreciation of all that you have done for viola players and also for the instrument itself, by having a little luncheon at which they could be present. This would also be an opportunity of celebrating your 85th birthday.

As you know, I should be delighted and only feel too privileged to help in any way I possibly can. I have 'phoned up the Connaught Rooms and I find I can get a suitable room on Friday, May 11th at 12.30 for 1 o'clock. ...

Have you yourself any wishes in regard to speakers? You might like Bernard or Ruth Fermoy to say a few words, but you may have others in mind and I should be most grateful for your suggestions. Do please let me know and I will write and ask them. I will keep you informed and let you have full particulars later on.

I do so hope that the date will be quite convenient to you and Lillian.

With love to you both from Gypsie and me,

Ever your affectionate friend, Frank

Tertis having agreed to attend, Frank Thistleton sent out a further letter, dated 16 March:

A Luncheon in honour of Lionel Tertis is being arranged at the Connaught Rooms on Friday, 11th May, at 12.30 for one o'clock. The price of tickets will be 25/- excluding wines. It is surely not an overstatement to say that Mr. Tertis has done more for the encouragement of viola players than any other musician in this country. In this brief letter it is impossible to even begin to outline the importance of his work, so that this tribute to him is indeed long overdue especially since this is his 85th year. What he has done is one of the most remarkable achievements in the history of viola playing for he has brought the viola back to its rightful place, not only in this country but in many famous orchestras throughout the world. The Chair will be taken by Dr. Wilfrid Greenhouse Allt, and Sir John Barbirolli and Mr. Bernard Shore will be among the speakers.

The dinner was attended by 132 friends and colleagues, including Erich Auerbach, Sir John Barbirolli, Mr. E. H. Barnes, Leslie Boosey, Alan Bush, Douglas Cameron, Harriet Cohen, Winifred Copperwheat, John Denison, Phyllis Ebsworth, Lady Fermoy, Sir Eugène Goossens, Rachel Goundry, Norman Greenwood, Mrs Greenwood, Mrs F. Haase, Mrs Hope Hambourg, Julius Harrison, Roy Henderson, Dr Gordon Jacob, Louis Kentner, Sir Robert Mayer, Sir William McKie, Yehudi Menuhin, Countess of Munster, Ivor Newton, Gwendoline Parke, Ernest Read, Frederick Riddle, Max Salpeter, Bernard Shore, Derek Simpson, Frank Thistleton, John Tobin, Wilfred Van Wyck, Mrs Warmington, Mrs Ralph Vaughan Williams and Olive Zorian.

The speakers were Dr Wilfrid Greenhouse Allt, Sir John Barbirolli, Ruth, Lady Fermoy and Bernard Shore. Barbirolli spoke of the many years that he had known Lionel: viola players in almost every orchestra in this country had benefited by knowing him and, in numerous cases, by being his pupils; he had remarkable sympathy and understanding in dealing with young and, all too often, impecunious students. Lady Fermoy mentioned the great admiration she had always had for Lionel, and spoke warmly of the happiness and pleasure she had enjoyed through playing with him on many and various occasions. Bernard Shore related how Tertis had done more for viola players than anyone in the country and possibly in the world; the standard of playing the viola in orchestras had improved beyond all knowledge, and there was not an orchestra in this country where his famous Tertis Model viola was not in use today, as well as in numerous other orchestras in America and other parts of the world. He stated that Tertis's viola playing had a quality entirely its own and akin to the unique violin tone achieved by Kreisler. Tertis replied:

Embarrassment is a word totally inadequate in which to describe my feelings as I listened to the kind things spoken on my humble little efforts in life. Would that I could live up to them.

Now I have a confession to make. When last February I received a letter from the Musicians' Benevolent Fund suggesting this luncheon, my first reaction was to try and escape such dazzling limelight and say 'No', but my dear wife pointed the way and then I realized that it would be ungrateful and ungracious to shirk this delightful ordeal.

Now I want to say a very few words in reply to my friends who have just spoken. It is a great privilege of mine to know Lady Fermoy, and a further joy to have made music with her in public on very many occasions. Lady Fermoy is a most instinctive musician in ensemble playing, indeed she senses how you are going to interpret a phrase almost before you do yourself, and you know what a source of inspiration that means in music making.

As for Sir John Barbirolli, why he could play my head off when he was eleven and a half years old. At that tender age he gave a most amazing performance of the Saint-Saens Cello Concerto. His playing of it will live long in my memory as being quite wonderful musically and technically. He was a prodigious prodigy; and now as our greatest conductor, I am so proud to have him here.

Bernard Shore, between you and me, is a fan of mine. We viola players owe him a debt of gratitude for lecturing and preaching the gospel of the viola as a solo instrument up and down the country, and in so doing has done immense good for the cause.

I want to thank Dr Greenhouse Allt for the honour he is doing me in presiding at this luncheon. Trinity College of Music, of which he is the principal, was the first institution I entered as a student of the piano and violin. I gained much benefit and musical enthusiasm during my studentship, but Dr Allt will know little of this for when I entered the college it was long before he was born.

Now I want to say something about the vicissitudes of the viola in the early days, but my vision and memory being rather faulty I shall have to try to read it, otherwise I may get stuck, and many a time put the cart before the horse with the result that neither you nor I will know what I am talking about. Don't be alarmed at these numerous pages. The words are written large to give me a chance to see them, in any case I promise you it will all be over before tea-time.

Seventy years ago I was apparently the only enthusiast endeavouring to raise the viola out of the rut. Many could have done the job better, but interest in the viola as a solo instrument was practically non-existent. The general public hardly knew what a viola was. I remember taking a lady into dinner and she suddenly turned to me and said: 'What is a VOILA?'

On another occasion I heard two people conversing, one saying to the other: 'I believe the viola is a peculiarly-shaped brass instrument.'

In 1892 the viola was the 'scullery maid' of the orchestra, or, as Berlioz more aptly put it 'The Cinderella of the string family.' Today it is a solo instrument and enjoys a place in the sun.

In 1895 [1896] when I began to play the viola as a solo instrument, prejudice and storms of abuse were my lot, also for endeavouring to enlarge the meagre library of viola solo music by making arrangements. But I was an obstinate customer – the more they went for me the more I did it. Not so very long ago I arranged the Mozart Clarinet Concerto for viola and orchestra and gave the first performance of it at a Three Choirs Festival at Hereford. The next day, out came a long tirade in the Daily Mail at my effrontery at making this arrangement, with large flaming headlines which read 'Mozart Knew Best.' Two days later I met at a press luncheon the critic who wrote the article whom I knew personally – the late Ralph Hill. He came towards me and said: 'I suppose you will have me up for slander?' and I replied 'Not at all, your article was a fine piece of publicity for the viola; in it you mentioned the word 'viola' at least 30 times, and moreover I don't at all mind being second best to Mozart.'

I'd like to tell you of two more incidents in which I was involved – I had a good deal of contact with Sir Thomas Beecham in the early days, and on one occasion I remarked to him that the tone quality of the viola section in his orchestra was rather poor. I asked him if he would mind if I gave them some help in tone production, the players being willing, and his reply was: 'BOIL them if you like.'

The other story concerns a visit I made to New York about five years ago. I was making music there and among my activities was a lecture on string quartet playing to a vast gathering of amateur chamber music players. At the conclusion of my paper I was plied with questions for quite half an hour until I thought I'd never be able to answer another one, when suddenly a man got up at the back of the hall and said: 'Say, Mr Tertis, could you give me the recipe for longevity?' For a moment I was completely knocked off my perch but recovering replied: 'I don't drink, I don't smoke, but I'm not quite a saint.'

To conclude, I want to say a big thank you to the Musicians' Benevolent Fund for arranging this luncheon for me. We all know what a magnificent organisation it is and what wonderful humanitarian work they encompass on behalf of poor musicians.

As for my dear friend Frank Thistleton, I am not the only one who knows that he is an angel in disguise. He has been a moving spirit since the inception of the M.B.F. A more wonderful organiser does not exist. I am sure had he been asked to organise British Railways, it would have been a paying concern by now.

Last, but not least, I want to thank you all for your overwhelming kindness in coming here today. It is a happy memory I shall keep with me to the end of my days.

Following the speeches Dr Allt presented Mr Tertis with a gold half-hunter watch and 'Albert' together with a gold pencil, a gift from members of the music profession and many music-lovers.

Tertis received many letters and messages, including two from Italy. The first of these came from the violinist and quartet leader Pina Carmirelli:

> Roma 4 Maggio 1962
>
> I am terribly sorry for not being able to be present to the meeting of May 11th when the musical profession will pay a tribute to Lionel Tertis.
>
> I have the greatest and deepest admiration for this wonderful artist (a great mind and a great heart) – and for the countless contributions of beauties he has given to the world of music in the 85 glorious years of his life.
>
> I send to him from the deep of my heart my most sincere and affectionate wishes for his birthday, ardently hoping that for many many years to come he may spread among us the treasure of his great artistry and of his great soul.

Tertis had met the members of the Carmirelli Quartet on one of his early visits to the King's Lynn Festival, where, much to his surprise, he had discovered that they were all playing on Tertis Model instruments made by the Rimini maker Marino Capicchioni. The Quartet was closely associated with another famous Roman ensemble, the Quintetto Boccherini, which Pina Carmirelli and Arturo Bonucci had founded. By the time Tertis met the quartet, only Bonucci and the violist Luigi Sagrati were still playing in the quintet – although the Spanish second violinist, Montserrat Cervera, would later return as leader. The Carmirelli ensemble played most beautifully in a typically Italian style, but, alas, made only a handful of recordings.

The other Italian missive was from William Walton:

> San Felice, Forio D'Ischia 27.4.62
>
> I am so very sorry that I am unable to attend the luncheon given in your honour. All the same I should like to pay tribute to your genius, not only as a superlative virtuoso on the viola, but also for having elevated that somewhat despised and neglected instrument to the high position it now

holds, largely through your teaching and guidance, and I doubt if there is a violist present who has not benefited by your inspired example and musical integrity.

Composers also owe you a debt of gratitude in that you encouraged them to write works for the viola, very often written specially for yourself.

So all in all I hope that you can look back over the years of your long career with considerable satisfaction at your great and enduring achievement.

Tertis also received telegrams from Solomon and Artur Rubinstein.

At the Royal Academy Recital Diploma examinations for strings in the summer term of 1962 the two external examiners were Tertis and Paul Beard, who for many years was concert-master of the BBC Symphony Orchestra. Three viola students had reached the final round of this demanding examination; Graeme Scott, Simon Whistler and myself. As I entered the hall, which was full to capacity, Beard turned to Tertis and in a loud voice said: 'Another small viola'. At that time I was playing on a 16¼" Hoing instrument, and one of the works I performed on that occasion was Milhaud's First Concerto. (Years later Sidney Errington told me that Tertis had no time for Milhaud's music, so I was doomed on two fronts before ever playing a note!) Scott, a fine player, was awarded the major viola prize that year, and appropriately played on a Tertis Model viola; later he became Principal Viola in the BBC Symphony Orchestra.

In 1962 the International Cello Centre in London hosted a special reception in honour of Casals, at which Tertis presented his old friend with a copy of his Variations on a theme of Handel for viola and cello, in the hope that they might play these on their ninetieth birthday: alas, this never materialized, as Tertis gave up public performance in 1964.

On 23 July 1962 the BBC recorded Tertis's interview with Roy Plomley for a forthcoming edition of the ever popular programme *Desert Island Discs*, in which the castaway chooses eight gramophone records and in between talks about his or her life and work. The programme went out on the BBC Home Service on Monday 13 August. Roy Plomley asked Tertis if he had a plan in choosing his records and Tertis replied, 'Yes. It is because most of the records you're going to hear are by personal friends of mine, with whom I have made music and listened to very often. And I thought it would help me to visualise them and assist me in my loneliness as a consequence'. Tertis's friends featured in the programme included Sir John and Lady Barbirolli (the oboist Evelyn Rothwell), Solomon, Artur Rubinstein, the Carmirelli String Quartet and Fritz Kreisler. Interestingly the signature tune for this programme is Eric Coates's

By the Sleepy Lagoon. Tertis's choice of luxury was a large portrait of his wife, and the book was a collection of works by Rider Haggard, Conan Doyle and Jules Verne.

David Oistrakh wrote to Tertis on 26 February 1963 from Kiev:

Dear Mr Tertis,

I received your kind letter on return from a concert tour which lasted many months. This accounts for the somewhat long delay in replying.

I am most grateful for your warm words on the Bach concerto which we have finished with Yehudi Menuhin and I am taking this opportunity to say that I have valued and admired your considerable art over many years.

With best wishes, Yours, David Oistrakh.

(Translation – British Council)

During my last term as a student I was one of a large audience when on Friday 21 June 1963 Tertis returned to his Alma Mater, the Royal Academy of Music, for a concert to demonstrate the tone qualities of the complete string quartet of Tertis Model instruments. The Carmirelli String Quartet performed Boccherini's Quartet in A, op. 39, and the first of Haydn's op. 76 quartets. They used two new Tertis Model violins made by Cocker of Derby in July 1962, a cello by the same maker which was completed in 1961 and a viola made by Saunders of Nottingham in 1955. Lillian Tertis and Antonia Butler, accompanied by Sir Thomas Armstrong, performed the first two movements of Handel's Sonata in G minor for two cellos, both made by Cocker; Lillian played her husband's arrangement of an Adagio from Bach's *Easter Oratorio*, with Sir Thomas Armstrong at the organ. Pina Carmirelli received high critical praise for her performance of Bach's *Chaconne* on a Cocker violin that she had had for only forty-eight hours.

The concert was held to raise funds to purchase a Tertis Model viola (value £100) to be competed for by students from the major music colleges. The competition took place at the Royal Academy of Music on Wednesday 4 December 1963; the test piece was the first and last movements of Brahms's Sonata in F minor, op. 120 no. 1, and the adjudicator was Tertis. John Graham, a Canadian-born student at the RAM, was awarded the Tertis Model viola. Another competitor was Rusen Günes, a student of Frederick Riddle at the Royal College of Music. After Günes finished playing he was asked what instrument he had used; Günes replied: 'A Turkish viola' – Tertis immediately said: 'That's not a Tertis viola!'

Millie Stanfield's article 'Lionel Tertis and the Future', published in *The Strad* in August 1963, is devoted mainly to an interview she had with Tertis after the concert at the Academy on 21 June. Her opening paragraph is worth quoting:

> If a cross section of string players in this country was asked to name the English artist who had done most during the last sixty years to influence posterity in this field, an overwhelming majority would probably reply: 'Lionel Tertis.' Not only did his readings inspire thousands to reach higher standards in their own musical attainments but his enthusiastic and unceasing sponsorship of his chosen instrument, the viola, completely changed its status: from being the neglected 'poor relation' of its popular sister, the violin, it became a much loved solo instrument with an entirely individual character. This has long been universally acknowledged as has its effect in encouraging our composers of the early twentieth century to write beautiful and effective works for the viola, thus helping to enhance the prestige of British music throughout the world.

Miss Stanfield asked Tertis when he became interested in the problems of obtaining good instruments to meet the needs of the growing numbers of players and the origin of his undertaking. He replied:

> Already in 1900 my pupils used to complain: 'What is the use of my playing the viola? It is so hard to find an instrument. The old masters are too expensive for me and even those are either too big and unmanageable or have been cut down with the result that they are neither violin nor viola.' That set me thinking and I resolved that one day I would design a viola for I was beginning to have certain theories as to what might constitute a standard viola.

Throughout his life Tertis always took a keen interest in the education of young musicians. He was a great supporter of the Yehudi Menuhin School, which was opened in 1963, and the first viola player at the school was Nicholas Logie, who had occasional lessons from Tertis.

In 1963 Lionel and Lillian Tertis were guests at the King's Lynn Festival, at which Lillian performed Lionel's arrangement of the Adagio from Bach's *Easter Oratorio* for cello and organ during the Festival Service at St Margaret's Church. They attended two concerts given by the Hallé Orchestra conducted by their friend Sir John Barbirolli.

Tertis in his memoirs said he was proud that he missed only two King's Lynn Festivals through illness. In his book *Farewell Recital* Gerald Moore remembered Mstislav Rostropovich's visit to the King's Lynn Festival in 1965. With a section of the London Symphony Orchestra he directed and played three concertos by Vivaldi and one each by Tartini and Boccherini. This was a tremendous coup for Lady Fermoy, director of the festival. Moore writes:

> small wonder that Lionel Tertis, King of the Viola, very much a member of the Fermoy coterie, was determined to make the journey from London specially for the occasion. But alas poor Lionel! He caught a severe cold and in his ninetieth year, was forced to stay in his hotel room. After the concert we took Lillian (Mrs Tertis) to meet Rostropovich, who at once asked, 'Where is Lionel?' I explained why he could not be there whereupon he asked if he could go and see him.

Tertis in his own memoir continues: 'he (Rostropovich) burst into my room, where he found me enveloped in a dressing gown and with a temperature – in spite of which he embraced me! I had never met him in my life but I can only presume he must have known me through broadcasts or records.'

The BBC honoured both Casals and Tertis in a special edition of *Music Magazine* on their joint eighty-seventh birthday – 29 December 1963. The programme, entitled 'Pablo Casals and Lionel Tertis: a birthday greeting by Arthur Jacobs', was relayed at 10.30 a.m. on the Home Service.

Tertis and William Primrose had great affection and respect for each other. Tertis had been concerned about Primrose's health in 1963 as the following short New Year's greeting illustrated:

> 42 Marryat Road London SW19 January 1st 1964
> Dear William, I was delighted to get your message in Paul Doktor's letter and to know from him that you are better, we can ill afford to do without your wonderful playing. Don't forget to let me know as soon as you contemplate coming to England. I should love you to put your bow on the new instruments. My wife joins me in sending our best wishes to you and your wife for 1964.
> Ever yours, Lionel

On 22 April 1964 at a Royal Philharmonic Society concert given by the Hallé Orchestra and Sir John Barbirolli at the Royal Festival Hall, Tertis was presented with the Society's Gold Medal. Just before the interval Sir John said: 'Little did I think in 1917 when I joined the Royal Philharmonic Society Orchestra, that one day I would be presenting the society's gold medal, music's highest honour, to a man then already established as the first British virtuoso of the viola, Lionel Tertis.' The music critic of *The Times* also noted: 'it is extraordinary that this great musician was not awarded the medal several decades ago when he was regularly playing in public ...' Sir John Barbirolli, in presenting the medal, referred to Tertis as: 'A unique figure in our musical life, revered as the greatest viola virtuoso of our time.' After the presentation Tertis replied:

I must confess it is somewhat unnerving to find myself in rather an extraordinary situation tonight. Here I am on the platform at the Royal Philharmonic Society concert, being awarded the highest musical distinction, and getting away with it without scraping a tune! Be that as it may, I do so want to express my gratitude to the Royal Philharmonic Society for the honour they have done me, and I'm sure my fellow viola-players will allow me to speak on their behalf as well as my own in saying how much we exult in the fact that the Society's Gold Medal has given a further tremendous uplift to the importance and status of our beloved instrument, and as a consequence it now has a real place in the sun.

Christopher Regan remembered his father's comments at the time when there was an element on the Royal Philharmonic Society committee and management that felt honorary membership would have been more appropriate for Tertis, but a majority, which included Leslie Regan, were determined that only the Gold Medal would do. Leslie Regan wrote to Tertis on 20 April 1964:

My dear Lionel,
I cannot tell you how sad I am that next Wed. I shall be thousands of miles away in Canada which will prevent my being present at THE great occasion.
    That you are being honoured at last gives me more joy than I can possibly express. Nobody could be, or is more worthy of it and how I should have loved being on the same platform with you to join with John in voicing the sentiment we feel from our hearts. But you may be sure I shall be thinking of you, and on my return we must have a celebration of our own. I hope all will go well and that it will prove to be a happy day and one you will always recall with great happiness.
    Love to you both, Yrs ever, Leslie.

Tertis received the following letter after the presentation:

Gardiner's Croft, Bambers Green,
Takeley, Nr Bishop's Stortford, Herts

My dear Lionel,
For me last night was indeed one to remember. I am, within my capacities and my opportunities, a confirmed Shakespeare lover, and have a particular delight in his gargantuan and lovable old rascal – Falstaff. Barbirolli and

the Halle last night introduced me to Elgar's magnificent study and what a work it is and what a performance it received!

Then, undaunted by the effort it must have been to bring it off, he came back and said just the things about you which should be said, with a sincerity and affection which was obvious, in spite of his physical difficulty at times in saying them.

Then you spoke in just the way you should have spoken – simple, lovable, single hearted man that you are.

In the audience one could feel the affectionate response and just in front of us there was a handsome young man who clapped his hands sore every time you mentioned the viola. Doreen whispered to me 'I'm sure he's a viola player'.

Naturally apart from my thoughts and feelings about you, two others were very much in my mind – my father and mother – and I said to Doreen 'If only this could have happened when it should have, thirty years ago when Micky and Mother could have been there and would have been so proud and joyful!

I went out and watched the river for a few minutes during the rest of the interval and thought about the three of you and the joy I have had from you, all in your different ways. And I thought also of dear Aunt Ada.

Before the concert I had an amazing encounter. Doreen and I had a quick meal in the Buffet at the Festival Hall and a most pleasant and humorous old gentleman and his attractive and charming wife came and sat at our table. We got into conversation, which was very amusing, and eventually, through a chance reference by a young woman who came over and spoke to them, a suspicion grew up in my mind and eventually I asked him a direct question. I said 'Are you Mr Ernest Read?' 'Yes, I'm Ernest Read' he said. 'Good God' said I, 'I'm Lionel Tertis's nephew'. You can imagine what followed then. He spoke of you with great affection and, indeed, with reverence of your artistic eminence. Amid all of the hundreds of people eating there it seemed extraordinary that the man who should bring his wife to our table should be one who knew you before I was born!

As you said, with your usual self-effacing devotion to the 'beloved tyrant', it was 'a red letter day for the viola'. The audience, however, with the sympathetic ripple of laughter with which they greeted this remark, were clearly replying 'Yes, but who made it so'?

And – though this is a matter of very small moment – it was a red letter day for

Your very affectionate nephew, Harold [Milner]

P.S. I have not forgotten and will not forget that you have promised that you and Lillian will come to our little cottage in the summer. I am going to keep you up to this, for though we have not seen each other for some years – to my shame – you have never been neglected in my thoughts.

P.P.S. I liked Barbirolli's phrase 'undiminished equality'. I was there when it was Fritz Kreisler and Tertis. I think, of that occasion at any rate, I would have said 'undiminished equality and complete union of minds'. I shall never forget it. Forty years ago this year?

During the spring of 1964 Tertis, in his eighty-eighth year, made his last public appearance with his viola at a London Philharmonic Society's club meeting, when he gave a short lecture demonstration of the Tertis Model instruments. He was joined by his wife in a group of duos for viola and cello, and Antonio Brosa and Leonard Hirsch played Bach's double concerto on two Tertis Model violins. Tertis's talk at this occasion is given in full in Appendix 3.

TV Profile and Ninetieth Birthday

Orchestral Seating Plan – TV Profile – 90th birthday

LIONEL Tertis's restless mind was forever evolving solutions to musical problems – usually concerning sound and tone quality, which was one of his lifelong obsessions. In the early 1960s he returned to a scheme he had devised forty years earlier, for what he deemed to be the ideal orchestral seating plan. His goal was to improve the blend and balance between the different sections within the ensemble.

One of his acoustic discoveries had arisen from the supposedly primitive pre-electric method of making recordings. When he had to play into the recording horn in the Aeolian-Vocalion studios, Tertis found there was a considerable difference in the tone quality of the disc when he played in different positions. The result was much more convincing when he played with the scroll directly facing the horn, than when he held the viola in the usual position at right angles to the horn. He also noticed that when a solo violinist or violist playing a concerto with orchestra faced the audience at right angles (the acceptable way), the tone was not as convincing as when he played with the scroll directly facing the audience. His other observation regarding the accepted method of seating the string players in an orchestra was that the sound holes (f holes) of the instruments faced in many different directions on a concert platform. Tertis's idea was that generally there would be a better tone, blend and balance throughout the orchestra if all, or nearly all, the string players faced the public with their instruments.

At the Free Trade Hall, Manchester, on 2 May 1964 Sir John Barbirolli gave the Tertis seating plan a trial. Tertis's idea was that the orchestra should play short excerpts from the repertoire, in the old and new seating positions. Owing to a misunderstanding, the occasion was advertised as an invitation concert in which Berlioz's *Roman Carnival* Overture and the tone poem *Don Juan* were played, first in Tertis's seating plan and then, after the interval, in the more conventional manner; according to Tertis, this 'made it impossible to form an adequate judgement owing to the long interval between the two seating arrangements'. Differing opinions appeared in the press. Michael Kennedy of the *Daily Telegraph* felt that 'with modification Mr Tertis's ideas certainly seem to be worth consideration'. Other critics thought Tertis's plan gave an extra brilliance to the violins, generally at the expense of the lower strings.

In June 1964 Tertis was very enthusiastic to hear from William Glock about his idea for forming a BBC Training Orchestra, which came to fruition shortly afterwards. Tertis had always been a keen advocate of proper orchestral training in our musical institutions, and believed strongly that every week young viola students should have special classes to learn the orchestral repertoire. This, he felt, would be far more beneficial than so much playing through. He found, and the problem still exists today, that many talented young players lack a knowledge of the large and often difficult orchestral repertoire.

A short TV profile of Tertis was shown on an arts programme of the time, *Monitor*, on 21 November 1964. Huw Wheldon introduced the programme, which was written and directed by Melvyn Bragg. It was shown as the third of three items in this edition of the programme, and there was no billing in the *Radio Times*, as it had been put in at very short notice. Lionel and Lillian Tertis had been led to believe that a whole forty-five-minute programme was to be devoted to him. In fact filming took place not only at the Tertises' home but at Yehudi Menuhin's, where Menuhin played and commented on the Tertis Model viola, and in the workshop of the violin-maker Lawrence Cocker in Derby. The file for the programme gives details of what was included: Tertis was shown in his home in Wimbledon, when he described his first public performance as a pianist, then he and his wife Lillian played an arrangement for viola and cello, after which Tertis spoke about his work as a designer of violas. Lawrence Cocker was shown making a viola to Tertis's specifications, and Tertis told how the instrument was used in fifteen countries and explained various points of the new model. The programme ended with Lillian Tertis joining her husband in a performance of Galuppi's *Aria amorosa*. Yehudi Menuhin spoke about Tertis's gift for the viola, and Lawrence Cocker demonstrated how he went about making violas. This was probably Tertis's first and only television appearance.

The Royal Philharmonic Society, after their Annual General Meeting, arranged a second demonstration concert of Tertis Model string instruments at the Royal Academy of Music on the evening of Thursday 26 September 1964. The Martin String Quartet (David Martin and David Stone, violins, Eileen Grainger, viola, Bernard Richards, cello) performed two quartets on Tertis Model instruments, and a short movement by Haydn, played first on their own instruments and repeated immediately on the four Tertis Model instruments. Lionel gave a short address on the construction of the new instruments.

Tertis was invited to be a member of the jury for the BBC Violin Competition in March 1965; the first round was held on 1–3 March, and the latter stages on 9–13 March. His colleagues on the jury were his former student Sidney Griller and Alfredo Campoli; the chairman was a member of the BBC staff, Eric Warr. Tertis had always admired Campoli's playing, and in his memoir *My Viola and I* he wrote about a performance of the Elgar Violin Concerto that the violinist gave with the BBC Scottish Orchestra under their conductor James Loughran: 'Among the numerous times I have heard this wonderful work, so full of lyric moments that stir one to the depths, this performance of Campoli's was certainly the best I have ever heard.'

Tertis was very taken with the competition, and afterwards, in a letter to the *Daily Telegraph*, praised the level of the British violinists who took part: 'It would be a splendid move towards encouraging British embryo virtuosi if further competitions on the same lines could be instituted by the BBC for the various other solo instruments.'

A BBC viola competition was organized by Watson Forbes when he was Head of Music for BBC Scotland. His colleagues on the jury were Frederick Riddle and William Primrose.

At the instigation of Yehudi Menuhin and Yfrah Neaman, viola players were able to compete alongside violinists in the 1970 and 1972 International Carl Flesch Violin Competitions. In the first of these, violists were awarded the second and third prizes and, much to Tertis's joy, in the 1972 event the first two prizes were awarded to viola players: alas, violists have never been invited again. In the 1970 competition, although the first prize was awarded to the twenty-four-year-old Bulgarian violinist Stoika Milanova, the spotlight nevertheless was on the second-prize winner, Luigi Alberto Bianchi, a fine young Italian violist.

Both prizewinners were featured in a concert as part of the City of London Festival in Southwark Cathedral. Milanova and Menuhin gave a performance of the Bach Double Violin Concerto and Menuhin and Bianchi joined forces in Mozart's *Sinfonia concertante*. The latter was warmly received by the critics, though the performance was halted at the end of the slow movement when the cathedral's lights failed. After a short pause the concert continued in the twilight. It was after this concert that Bianchi encountered Tertis.

I met Lionel Tertis, who was accompanied by a lady (his wife Lillian) because he was quite blind. But he was very alert with his ears; he was very nice with me and Menuhin showed a great respect and admiration for this very old man. He asked me about my Capicchioni viola, if it was a Tertis Model (it was in fact a Strad model) and he pointed out the powerful tone I produced in the vast venue and was amazed about the failure of the electricity and also asked me who was my teacher. I told him my last teacher was Renzo Sabatini in Rome. Tertis told me he had heard him play the viola d'amore in London in the mid 1950s but seems to me that he never met him personally.

Csaba Erdélyi was awarded first prize, and Atar Arad second prize in the 1972 Carl Flesch Violin Competition – the third prize went to the best violinist that year. After the announcement of the prizewinners, a Festival Hall concert was cancelled because the organizer felt that a viola soloist would not be a box-office draw, and a top London agent told Erdélyi that if he had been a violinist he would have been able to get him concerts on five continents, but as a violist he would have to look after himself.

In the previous year Erdélyi played the Walton Viola Concerto at a BBC Henry Wood Promenade Concert; Tertis, then well into his nineties, had promised to attend the concert. Just before Erdélyi went out onto the platform he was told that Tertis was unable to come to the concert, but would listen to the performance on the radio, and invited him to go to his home in Wimbledon the following morning so that they could discuss the performance. Erdélyi was amazed when next morning Tertis told him every fingering he had used in his performance. Tertis then offered him alternative, very personal, fingerings which involved many shifts but were all musically superior to the ones he had used. Erdélyi remembers: 'He sat down with the score and from memory told me every finger I used – his hearing was that acute.' After this Tertis spent a considerable amount of time on Erdélyi's intonation, getting him to listen more intently!

On 15 July 1966 Trinity College of Music conferred Honorary Fellowship (Hon. FTCL) on Tertis.

Sidney Griller arranged for the young Alberni String Quartet (Dennis Simons, Howard Davis, John White and Gregory Baron) to go and play to Tertis in October 1966. Howard Davis recalls the occasion vividly:

Recollections of a visit to Lionel Tertis forty years ago remain very clear – the coaching itself, the man himself and the sense of being, as it were, in touch with the last quarter of the nineteenth century. Tertis was small; as he sat in front of our quartet, seated on a dining chair, his feet did not reach the floor. The intensity of the coaching was something never to be forgotten, even by a quartet accustomed to rigorous sessions with Griller, and perhaps the most memorable element in a playing sense was the way he dragooned four young players into creating a true pianissimo whilst still projecting with great clarity. The reviews of our Wigmore Hall recital the following week all commented on this aspect of our playing – pure Tertis. Historically, his account of playing with the Bohemian Quartet sixty years earlier was fascinating – not least for the throwaway comment that Josef Suk (the second violin): 'was a gentleman – the others spat every-where.' Tertis moved house frequently; when he finally moved with his second wife Lillian into their new home in Wimbledon the terrace was completely overgrown and, when it was cleared, two 'modern' sculptures were uncovered. These were not at all to Tertis's liking – but were discovered to be two early Henry Moores, long forgotten but worth more than the price of the house ...

The work the Alberni Quartet played was Haydn's unfinished quartet, op. 103; the session lasted about three hours without a break and only finished when Tertis, then nearly ninety years old, said he had to stop because they were expecting friends for dinner. The quartet were exhausted!

Tertis's ninetieth birthday was celebrated in style; the BBC broadcast the following programme in mid-afternoon and Tertis introduced each work: Mozart's *Sinfonia concertante* (the Columbia recording with Sammons and Tertis and the London Philharmonic Orchestra conducted by Sir Hamilton Harty); Harry Danks and Lillian Tertis playing Lionel's Variations on a Four-bar Theme of Handel; and Margaret Major, Cecil Aronowitz and Harry Danks in a performance of Beethoven's Trio, op. 87, arranged by Tertis for three violas. The broadcast ended with the well-known recording of Tertis and Ethel Hobday playing the Preludium and Allegro by Kreisler.

David Stone, the producer of the BBC programme which celebrated Tertis's ninetieth birthday, remembers going to visit Tertis at his Wimbledon home to discuss what might be included in the time available. In particular Tertis wanted his arrangement for three violas of the Beethoven Trio for two oboes and cor anglais. This was to be performed by three eminent violists of the day. Stone was somewhat taken aback to find the heat aroused among the players involved as to which of them was to play the top part. In fact the high exposed viola part is very difficult throughout, and it is likely that all three players involved were so busy professionally that they would not have had the time required to master the part in the time available. David Stone also recalls that Tertis's eyesight was failing, and, as he was to speak, the actual script had to be written in large capital letters.

During Stone's visit Tertis played him a number of his old recordings. One of these was his arrangement of the well-known *Liebestraum* by Liszt. As they listened to the record Stone was somewhat surprised to see Tertis's eyes filled with tears; it must have had a particular memory for the old man. Stone's earliest memory of Tertis was a concert in which he played the *Romance* from the Suite by Benjamin Dale, with the composer at the piano; Stone still remembers, sixty years later, the ardour which Tertis brought to the music.

EMI also celebrated Tertis's ninetieth birthday by issuing an LP record in their Great Instrumentalists series, which included the Sammons–Tertis–Harty performance of Mozart's *Sinfonia concertante* and pieces by Brahms, Delius, Handel, Kreisler, Liszt and Mendelssohn. Bernard Shore contributed the sleeve note.

In the evening the Royal Philharmonic Society marked the occasion by organizing a dinner on 29 December 1966 at the Connaught Rooms, Great Queen Street; Tertis was guest of honour. The impressive guest list included Sir John and Lady Barbirolli, Antonia Butler, Christopher Bunting, The Marchioness of Cholmondeley, Phyllis Coates, Harriet Cohen, Winifred Copperwheat, John Denison, Harry Danks, Sybil Eaton, Gwynne Edwards, Lady Fermoy, Léon Goossens, Sidney Griller, Mrs Ralph Vaughan Williams and Miss Seymour Whinyates.[1] Sir Thomas Armstrong was in the chair, and gave the following address:

> As we think today of Lionel Tertis we may well be aware of the sense of continuity that one feels in our profession, for his long career stretches back into an epoch of great masters, with some of whom he lived and worked in close cooperation: influences from many sources flowed into the stream of his musicianship. Among his early intimates, for instance, was Ysaÿe, pupil of Massart, who was a pupil of Kreutzer for whom Beethoven wrote the sonata: and anybody who worked with Tertis was soon aware of the effects of this tradition and discipline, which showed in every aspect of his own playing and his teaching.
>
> It was probably his single-mindedness that marked him off from other more ordinary people, and made him not only one of the great string-players of all time, but also a visionary who was able to create a new place in music for his instrument. Younger musicians can hardly understand what he did for the viola. When he began to play in public the Mozart Concertante was a virtually unknown composition, and it was hard to find a soloist for 'Harold in Italy'. Beecham recalled that the viola section had been 'the despair of conductors, the diversion of the audience, and the perpetual exasperation of the Press, or at least of that section of the Press that knew what a viola was': and it was Tertis's achievement to change all that, and to place the viola side by side as a solo instrument with the violin and cello. But he began by perfecting his own performance. 'From the first bars', wrote Arthur Rubinstein, 'I became aware of a new element in the ensemble, a sonority I had never heard before … He was the greatest glory of England in the way of instrument players.'
>
> It is noticeable that the word 'passionate' is often used in connexion

with Tertis's playing. Vaughan Williams spoke of his 'passionate utterance and eloquent phrasing', and all who remember Tertis's performances of Flos Campi will understand this comment. It is certain, moreover, that only a passionate nature could have attained the single-minded concentration that dominated Tertis's career in all its stages, and lay behind his determination to accept no personal profit from the work that he did in later life. Plans and drawings of his viola were at first freely given to any craftsman who was interested: and when the demands greatly increased, and profits could be made, these were given, like Handel's, to the Royal Society of Musicians. Passionate also was his devotion to good craftsmanship, wherever it was to be found; and it is not fanciful to see in this respect for craftsmanship an aspect of the integrity that lay at the heart of his own work and outlook, and amounted almost to a religious experience.

About Tertis's personal life little can be said without intrusion into private grief: but we all recognize that after a time of desolation and discouragement joy and purpose were brought back into his days by Lillian Tertis, who shared his labours and his triumphs. Beecham noted, as early as 1937, that you could discern nothing of Lionel's inner life from the tranquil façade of his countenance; but performances like his could not have emerged from a placid and uneventful nature, and it was in his playing that the heart of the man was publicly revealed.

Behind the tranquil façade that Beecham described, however, there lay unseen forces of strength and inspiration, forces that enabled Tertis to do great things and inspire others to attempt them: and something of these forces is allowed to appear in a few words of his own. 'Do not forget', he wrote, 'that your playing will reveal your innermost self. Therefore ... mould your mind and action through life to all that is of the utmost sincerity.' 'The interpreter of music in its highest form must rise in his music-making above the levels of the everyday world, its commonness and its vanity, and hold himself apart in an atmosphere of idealism.'

Sir John Barbirolli and Sir Edward Boyle MP also gave speeches, and Sir Thomas read the following poem he had written especially for the occasion:

> Tertis, whose viola, with noble sound
> Carries as far as thought can reach
> Music that yourself have found
> And were the first to teach,
> We greet you! Friends and colleagues gathered here
> Join with a thousand others, far and near,

In salutation. Long may you enjoy
The affection and fame
That glorify your name,
Oh! happy nonagenarian birthday boy!

Ardent for truth, and living truth alone,
Truth in design, in craftsmanship, and tone
Quick to sustain a rhythm's beating heart
And, with expressive art,
To guide a noble strain towards its dying fall.
Often we lesser men have sought
With scant success or none at all
To reach your summit of integrity
Of skill, of patience, and tenacity
Of clear constructive thought.

Thrice thirty years have borne away
Many who in their day
Have charmed the multitudes and given to men
Foretaste of heaven.
Singers, composers, players, hearts on fire
To tell of life and death, of hearts's desire
Of love rewarded or of faith betrayed
Of gallant wooer, or forsaken maid
To quicken hearts that languish, and declare
Hopes that the prophets dimly have discerned
And only music can portray.
Yet, though there pass away
Even as I speak, this very day
Many from whom we learned
All that we know and are,
Yet are there with us still
Leaders as true as those whom we recall
In former years.
Of these is Lionel, nor indeed the last
Of the unending line of pioneers
And master-singers all
Who link the present with the past
Pointing us to the triumphs yet to be
And music still un-heard that talent may foresee
And only genius fulfill.

Tertis; and Casals too, though far away
In distant Pyrenees, yet still tonight
In thought amongst us here –
Born, by some strange star-confluence of the skies
Upon the self-same day
He shares an equal honour with his peer
In our festivities,
Wearing by right
With him the laurel and the bay.

Greetings to both! and even though
No word of mine can fitly match
The task of praise, yet this we ask:
Accept our homage. Take the love
Of all whom music's power can move
Of all who now recall
The magic of your bow
Bringing to life anew
The truth that long ago
Old Browning's abt Vogler knew
The truth of the elect, the chosen few,
Whom God may whisper in the ear
To let them hear
Those deep and solemn harmonies
Whose echoes, ever sounding in the skies,
Entranced poets faintly may discern
Yet cannot fully learn,
And we musicians know.

Tertis was overcome with emotion, but in his reply he thanked the Royal Philharmonic Society for inviting him on so many occasions to play at their concerts, beginning with the première of York Bowen's Viola Concerto in 1908. He also reminded Sir Thomas Armstrong that it was when he was a student at the Royal Academy that he started playing the viola – the recipe for a long and active life! Tertis then turned to Sir Edward Boyle, a talented amateur musician, and said he often wished he could be an amateur so that he could play what he liked, when he liked, or not at all. Sir John Barbirolli and Tertis had known each other for many years, and Tertis was particularly touched that Barbirolli had not only come to the dinner but also given a speech on the night before his visit to the Soviet Union with the BBC Symphony Orchestra.

Telegrams arrived from all over the world, including one from the mayor of

West Hartlepool (Tertis's birthplace), the Queen Mother – 'Warmest congratulations on your 90th birthday I hope you will have a very happy day' – and from
Artur Rubinstein in New York – 'Dearest Lionel accept my heartfelt wishes for
your glorious anniversary … To one of the greatest musicians of my life-time
and my dearest friend.'

∽ 16 ∽

Final Years

South Africa – Elgar birthplace – Rubinstein – Primrose –
96th birthday – My Viola and I – death

I N 1967 Lillian and Lionel Tertis went to South Africa to take a holiday and to promote the Tertis Model. In a letter dated 17 October from Radnor Hotel, Green Point, Cape Town, to Bernard Shore and his wife, they described their outward journey:

> This boat is very fine and modern in every way and we have a delightful cabin, but the people on board make us think what it must be like at a Butlin's Holiday Camp! and there are over 700 of them, not including ourselves. The food is less than mediocre although they produce a magnificently long menu which takes a ¼ hour to peruse. We shall certainly try to get another shipping line coming home or shall fly back with our orchestra of 'Tertis Model' instruments.

In Cape Town they were again guests of the Kreitzers. Among the gifts Tertis brought his friends was a copy of the BBC tribute marking his ninetieth birthday and the newly issued long-playing record from EMI, including a selection of his recordings made after the First World War. One side of the record was taken up by the Mozart *Sinfonia concertante*, with Sammons and Tertis as soloists. After supper one evening they were all listening to the slow movement when the Kreitzers' youngest daughter suddenly left the room crying; her mother immediately went after her to find out what the problem was. The girl finally explained to her mother that she found it unbearably moving to see the expression on Tertis's face as he listened to himself playing many decades earlier.

The Kreitzers organized a party in their music room on the occasion of Lionel's ninety-first birthday on 29 December 1967, and the toast was proposed by the musical director of the Cape Town Orchestra, Derek Hudson.

Tertis was very keen that a South African craftsman should make Tertis Model violas. He was astounded that there was not one professional maker in Cape Town, and wrote a letter on the subject to the *Cape Times*, which appeared on 24 November 1967:

Fiddle-maker needed

From Mr Lionel Tertis (Humewood Hotel, Green Point)

I am enjoying a happy holiday in Cape Town. At the same time, it is a 'busman's holiday', for I attend rehearsals of the Cape Town Orchestra under the direction of Derek Hudson, whose fine conducting I much admire. These rehearsals are a great pleasure to me.

There is however, one thing sadly lacking. There is not an expert violin craftsman in Cape Town – so vitally necessary to an orchestra and a college of music, to say nothing of the amateur string players here. If anything goes wrong with their instruments they have to send them to Johannesburg, Durban or London, with all the dangers of transit to these distant parts, and consequent delay in repair. A talented young South African woodworker should be sent for a course of instruction to the world-famous school of violin making in Mittenwald, Germany. He would return an expert fiddle-maker, able to attend to all the wants of string players in Cape Town and thus fill a most important gap.

The South African Broadcasting Corporation paid a generous ninety-first birthday tribute to Tertis; it was written and presented by Charles Oxtoby, who said in his introductory remarks:

1876 – it seems a long time ago doesn't it? Well of course it is a long time ago, but when you meet Lionel Tertis today it seems utterly impossible to believe that he was born for instance a mere five years after H M Stanley's dramatic meeting with Dr Livingstone at Ujiji ...

A few days ago Mr Tertis called in at the studios and we chatted about a number of matters musical and otherwise. For instance, he mentioned that he remembered the first motor cars which could literally be driven only at walking speed – a man carrying a red flag walking in front of each!

The programme followed a similar format to the BBC tribute a year earlier; excerpts were included from Tertis's recordings of the Kreisler 'Pugnani' *Preludium and Allegro*, Liszt's *Liebestraum* and Mozart's *Sinfonia concertante*.

Back in Britain in 1968, the Tertises' energies were channelled in another direction. During a visit to Malvern to see their old friends from Lawnside School, Miss Winifred Barrows and Miss Parke, Lionel and his wife visited Elgar's birthplace. They were so overcome by what they saw that Tertis penned a letter to the *Daily Telegraph*, published on Saturday 2 November 1968, supporting the appeal for contributions towards the upkeep of this museum in memory of the composer, with whom he had made music on a number of occasions:

Sir – One of the great treasures of Britain is the birthplace of Sir Edward Elgar at Broadheath, near Worcester. Recently, on a visit to this modest home, I was truly moved and overjoyed to find it filled with all the manuscripts, letters, decorations and all manner of precious belongings spanning the life of this great composer – all of untold value to the nation. This home should be preserved as one of our most important national monuments.

As long ago as 1934 The Daily Telegraph initiated an appeal under the chairmanship of the late Sir Landon Ronald to found the Elgar Birthplace Trust, which resulted in raising some £2,500. Just over a year ago the appeal was 'revived' by my colleague Yehudi Menuhin. For this donations and subscriptions are still being sought so that ultimately the sum of £25,000 may be achieved which would serve to maintain Sir Edward's home for all time. I therefore humbly venture to make the following suggestions toward the realisation of this goal:

1. All students of our academies and colleges of music both here and in the Commonwealth, all my orchestral colleagues in the symphony orchestras of the world and indeed all music-lovers would, I am sure, be interested and find it possible to express their interest in donating the small sum of 5 shillings, and those who felt so moved, and could afford it, multiples of that amount.

2. If their respective rules permit, might not the Arts Council, the Royal Society of Musicians, the British Council, the Performing Right Society, the BBC and other institutions contribute towards this incalculably important project?

3. A reminder – by the Tourist Information Centre (and their offices overseas) to our American, Commonwealth and other overseas friends who all but invariably visit Shakespeare's birthplace at Stratford-on-Avon – that Broadheath is but a very short distance away. Could not this be stated in their literature?

A suggestion which has, by coincidence, reached me simultaneously from two friends of mine – Sir Arthur Bliss, our Master of the Queen's Musick, and Miss Winifred Barrows, retired headmistress of 'Lawnside' in Malvern – is their wonderful idea of the publication of a postage stamp depicting Sir Edward and issued on the birthday of the composer, June 2, next year. May I as a nonagenarian selfishly implore the Postmaster-General to perform some miracle of rearrangement which would enable him to give this issue priority, in the hope that I may have the chance of seeing it in circulation next June?

Yours faithfully, Lionel Tertis

Tertis set an example in fund-raising by donating his instruments to be sold at Sotheby's in August 1972, the proceeds to go to the Elgar Birthplace Trust. The press reported on the sale:

> Lionel Tertis's own playing instrument, the large Tertis model Saunders of Nottingham brought £290, the attractive pair of violins also his model and especially made for him by Laurence Cocker of Derby went up to £75 and £85, while the two heavy violin bows that had served him throughout his entire playing career posed problems for buyers. On the one hand they were bows that had long satisfied the greatest and be it added the most loved viola player of our time ... on the other they were unnamed bows of no identifiable school with ordinary nickel mounts. They sold for £26 and £32.

Sir John Barbirolli and Tertis kept in touch regularly, and they met annually at the King's Lynn Festival; in 1968 they were photographed together for the last time. Tertis wrote in the folder where he kept this photograph: 'For dearest Lillian – This picture which I treasure, for I think it does show two fairly aged musicians who I suspect adore each other.'

Barbirolli telephoned Tertis in early June 1969 to tell him he was leaving in a few days for Puerto Rica, where he was to conduct at the Casals Festival. He wondered if Tertis might like to write a few lines to his old friend Casals. On 23 June a letter arrived from Puerto Rica, addressed to Maître Lionel Tertis:

> My dear friend,
> How happy I was to receive your dear letter! Many times I think of you and of the times we made music together. It was always a joy and a privilege for me to play with you. I wish so much that we may meet again! ...
> I hope that you are keeping well and that you continue to make music, I have wonderful reports about your health and I pray God that you may continue to enjoy it for many years with your good wife ...
> With my affection and admiration
> Pablo Casals

The sudden death of Barbirolli during the summer of 1970, in his seventieth year, was a shattering blow to Tertis: 'The magic of his baton has ever been a source of inspiration to me, and his memory will never fade. He has been one of the greatest ambassadors for music that England ever possessed. ... the most significant thing for me was his extraordinary power to draw forth the lovely warmth of expression and tone quality from whatever orchestra he conducted.'

As Tertis grew older he was seen less and less at London concerts, but he always insisted on attending any recital by Artur Rubinstein. Tertis commented:

> During the course of my life ... there has never been a pianist for me who can extract so much poetry from this percussive instrument as my dearest friend Arthur Rubinstein does. Indeed, the extraordinary method his fingers employ in gliding over the keys literally makes the piano sing, which is nothing short of a miracle and on more than one occasion has brought tears to my eyes. An added feature of his performance is his unmatchable balance of tone between the ponderous masculine bass and the feminine treble in all circumstances, be it pianissimo or fortissimo. It has been my good fortune to have had the privilege and honour of his friendship for some sixty years, during which we have made music together on many occasions, and it is a deep gratification and joy for me to be able to join in paying homage to this wonderful man.

The last time he heard his old friend was on 15 June 1970; Rubinstein, then eighty-two, was in top form. When they met after the concert Tertis was astonished to hear about the hectic international schedule Rubinstein was still undertaking When Tertis asked him where he got his energy from, Rubinstein replied: 'Well, it's better than twiddling my thumbs!'

Some six months later Tertis was unable, through ill-health, to attend Rubinstein's next London concert. Shortly afterwards Rubinstein telephoned Tertis from Paris, saying that he was going to fly over specially on 7 December to visit Tertis at his home in Wimbledon. Rubinstein realized that the Tertises had an out-of-date stereo record-player, and after his visit he contacted Harrods, asking them to deliver a new model and a large selection of his recordings – this generous gift gave Tertis much happiness during the final years of his life. On a photograph which took pride of place on Mrs Tertis's grand piano, Rubinstein wrote: 'To my dearest Lionel – the great artist and the most lovable man – in memory of our lifelong, true friendship – devotedly. Arthur Rubinstein.'

Sue Branch, now resident in New Zealand, remembered as a star-struck teenager meeting Tertis at one of Rubinstein's concerts:

> My grandmother was a friend of Arthur Rubinstein and used to take me to his recitals and concerts, and to meet him afterwards. On one such occasion he remembered that I had started the viola at the time of our previous meeting (what a memory he must have had!) and said: 'Mayme, Lionel is just outside in the passage – why not introduce your granddaughter to him?' I was a very ignorant sixth former who happened to learn the piano – but I had heard of Lionel Tertis somehow, and could barely believe I was

meeting him. He looked, to a schoolgirl, small, frail and old! He asked me how long I'd been learning the viola and it was about one and a half years. He told me that if I'd been learning just a few months, it might have been worth starting again with the viola upside-down on my knee, so I could play a really large instrument such as he was now designing.

As far as I know, that suggestion has never been made elsewhere, nor have I seen the viola played that way. However my impression, right or wrong, that he was implying the viola could be played like this has influenced me thus – when playing long pizzicato passages, particularly when less visible, e.g. in the 'pit', I often play that way and find greater strength in my left hand fingers, an ease of appropriate vibrato, and a wider variety of right hand angles to pluck. I wonder if anyone else does this, even all the time including with bow?

With the love and support of his wife Tertis continued his work on his autobiography *My Viola and I*. Shortly after he celebrated his ninety-fifth birthday, in the early weeks of January 1972, he was invited by the Prime Minister, Edward Heath, to a dinner in honour of Sir William Walton. Unbeknown to Tertis, one of the guests was HRH Queen Elizabeth, the Queen Mother, whom he was delighted to meet again. Tertis related a most unusual story which happened at the dinner table; owing to his failing sight, his wife always sat near to him so that she could organize the food on his plate. On this occasion she was talking to the guest on the other side of her and did not notice that her husband had started to try to help himself from a hot plate that had been put in front of him with what he thought was a small portion of food on it. He began attacking the 'food' with his fork when suddenly his wife turned to him and quietly said: 'For Heaven's sake put your fork down! There's nothing on your plate … you are digging at the coat of arms!'

In his time as Prime Minister, Edward Heath often arranged concerts at 10 Downing Street or Chequers. On 29 March 1972, Walton's seventieth birthday, he arranged a special evening at no. 10. To mark the occasion Heath commissioned some works in honour of his guest, as well as performances of some of Walton's compositions. Herbert Howells contributed a grace; Sir Arthur Bliss wrote *An Ode for William Walton* to witty words by Walton's friend Paul Dehn; the Martin Neary Singers performed Walton's *Set me as a Seal upon Thine Heart*; Alvar Lidell narrated ten movements from *Façade* with David Atherton and the London Sinfonietta. In a sixtieth-birthday interview Walton had been asked if there was any work by another composer he would have liked to have written; without hesitation he said, 'Yes, Schubert's B flat Trio!' As midnight struck, John Lill, John Georgiadis and Douglas Cummings began what was to be a wonderfully spontaneous and fresh performance of this work in front of a galaxy of celebrities from the arts including Lionel and Lillian Tertis.

During 1972 the following correspondence took place between the two great violists of the twentieth century, Tertis and William Primrose:

Indiana University, US

February 6 1972

Dear Lionel,

I recently returned from Japan where I conducted a series of Master Classes in Kobe, Osaka and Tokyo. I want to report to you that the standard of viola playing I heard was startling and hard to credit. I don't wish to suggest that we have no superior players here in the States, or on your side in Britain and the Continent.

But, I must emphasise standard! the over-all quality of playing. I encountered a number of surprising things: I did not realize before I went there the great number of violists and viola enthusiasts in Japan. There is a 'Society of Japanese Violists' which numbers several hundreds ... mostly young men, which I find encouraging. I have been invited to teach for one year or more starting next September at the National University of Music and Fine Arts. Now, the one critical problem (and it will come as no surprise to you) is the lack of good, or even, adequate instruments.

I was informed that there are some good fiddle makers in Japan, particularly in the Nagoya region. If, when, I return I could take with me a set of the Tertis Model designs, introduce these to the various makers the problem, I am disposed to believe, would readily be solved.

One more matter, dear Lionel, I have recently finished writing a book, a sort of quasi-biography along, or rather, with the help of a former student Dr David Dalton of Brigham Young University. Needless to say, the Lionel Tertis chapter is of imposing length, and there are frequent references to you throughout the others. But, I don't have a picture of you to include among the illustrations! May I have one, please? I so much like the photograph on the cover of your recording, the Long Playing one of a few years ago.

I do hope to hear from you and to receive the photo and the viola designs. (How grateful these wonderful Japanese youngsters will be to you).

My most affectionate greetings,

William Primrose

42, Marryat Road, London. S.W.19

February 12th 1972

My dear William,

Your letter with its information has delighted me beyond words. The knowledge that you are, and will be, spreading your influence – in that wonderful nation Japan – will, I am sure be a magnificent up-lift for the solo Viola.

Before I go further, I know you will be sorry to hear that I have been 'hors de combat' in my bed with heart trouble and bronchitis for a month. I am not complaining really for the cause of it is Anno Domini. However, yesterday was the first time I have been allowed to sit up fully dressed – and while there is breath in my body, I want, like you, to do all that is good for the viola our beloved instrument – for which you have done and are doing so much.

With regard to the drawings of the 'Tertis Model' (which includes a minute detailed specification from scroll to tail piece button) they are not in my hands now and are copyright. But I am proud to say, and with intense gratification – that Messrs W. E. Hill & Sons of 140, New Bond Street, London W.1. have most generously undertaken to be sole distributors of these drawings, and through their generosity I have been able to donate all profits therefrom to the Royal Society of Musicians Samaritan Fund (which is devoted to down and out musicians) – so far to the sum of some £100. ...

I am enclosing a copy of the photograph that is on the L.P. record for your book. I trust it will be suitable for your purpose.

One other project I have in hand is the disposal of my 'Tertis Model' viola (made by Saunders of Nottingham in 1955) which you personally heard at the Mannes School in New York when I gave that lecture recital in 1956.

Not only is it a fine specimen of craftsmanship, but has one of the best tone qualities I have ever played upon and which I used exclusively in the last 14 years of my public professional career. I am hoping to put this instrument in one of Sotheby's sales perhaps sometime in April or May, the proceeds of which will be donated to the upkeep of the Elgar Birthplace which is grievously and sorely in need of funds. I am sure everyone, especially musicians will see the necessity of keeping this modest little home of our immortal composer in perpetuity.

Again I want to repeat – I am delighted with your news.

Yours affectionately,

Lionel

August 15th 1972

Dear Lionel,

A few words, and a request, before I leave in one week from now to associate myself with all these wonderful violists at Tokyo University, about whom I informed you in my previous letter. Regarding the request, it is as follows: Having been requested by the editor of the ASTA (American String Teachers Association) to contribute an article to their magazine, published every quarter, the concernancy, if I may borrow from the late James Agate, being viola, and violists; and having been instrumental in amalgamating this ASTA with JSTA (Japan String Teachers Association), I would be honored to contribute a tribute to you, co-incident with your birthday on December 29th. But, away beyond such a tribute, would encourage all of us violists in America, and in Japan, to have a message from you, no matter how brief, to tell us how Lionel Tertis engendered the Crusade. I am well aware how grateful we would all be to you.

My most affectionate greetings,
William Primrose

Tertis replied on 24 August, promising to send some material for the article, and adding: 'If you see Dr Suzuki please tell him of my great admiration for the wonderful miracle he has accomplished for the young string players of Japan.' On 11 September Tertis reported: 'I am not very well – having just completed the exhausting task (at my age) of my autobiography. My doctor, finding me at my desk strewn with papers etc has warned me to do nothing more and ordered a complete rest for two or three months – hence – with apologies my brief word, knowing you will understand … and wishing you all success in the splendid task you have undertaken in Japan.' The 'brief word' he had promised William Primrose was enclosed in the same letter, and is reproduced in full in Appendix 3. The article appeared in November 1972 with the following introduction:

> By the time this article greets the reader the great Master and pioneer of the viola, Lionel Tertis, will have celebrated his ninety sixth birthday, an event which took place on December 29th last. No one has yet attempted to 'canonize' him, and I am persuaded that any such attempt he would regard as unseemly; and no one has made a career out of him, so far as I know. If anyone should be sensible of some pointed allusion in these remarks there is not much I can do about it. I sharpened the barb myself! In commemoration of his birthday, and for the immense value of all he has done to make life admissible and tolerable for all of us violists, I have asked him to write a few lines, a message of sorts, to be published in the

A.S.T.A. magazine. He graciously assented, and without further preamble I offer it.

During the summer of 1972 the BBC relayed a special programme about Solomon; Tertis gave an interview to the producer, and was deeply upset to hear that it would not be used.

Tertis discussed with Harry Danks the possibility of a unique viola concert. After much thought Danks talked the idea over with the members of his section in the BBC Symphony Orchestra, and they agreed to join their principal in an afternoon concert at the Wigmore Hall on 29 December 1972 – Tertis's ninety-sixth birthday. The entire proceeds were donated to the Royal Society of Musicians Henry Wood Fund. Harry Danks started the proceedings with Max Reger's Suite no. 1 in G minor for solo viola; this was followed by Tertis's Variations on a four-bar theme of Handel for two violas (Harry Danks and John Coulling), Beethoven's Trio, op. 87, transcribed for three violas by Tertis (Harry Danks, John Coulling and Eric Sargon), York Bowen's *Fantasie* for four violas (Harry Danks, Norman Kent, Michael Duffield and James Swainson). After the interval Harry Danks, John Coulling, Peter Lewis, David Melliard and Sheila Spencer played Concertante for five violas by Kenneth Harding and the concert ended with a performance of B. J. Dale's *Introduction and Andante*, op. 5, for six violas (Harry Danks, John Coulling, Eric Sargon, Barry Townsend, Gerald Manning, Jasmine Kara). The works by Bowen, Harding and Dale were all written for Tertis. A review in *The Strad* noted:

> The Tertis event seemed intent on breaking some records. It was the first time viola music only has been permitted to fill an entire bill, with not so much as a piano keyboard visible to intrude an alien non-violistic note, also these were all works written for viola long ago, and left on the shelf simply because even today works for multiple violas do not spring to the mind of concert givers ... This was a highly successful concert. The hall was full ...

William Mann in *The Times* wrote:

> Lionel Tertis, to whom all the musical world is in debt for his triumphant proof that the viola is as agile, expressive and colourful a soloist as any instrument in the orchestra, celebrated his ninety-sixth birthday yesterday. In his honour the viola section of the BBC Symphony Orchestra trooped to the Wigmore Hall and gave a remarkable concert of music ... almost all of it the creative result of Tertis's persuasive labours ...
>
> Mr Tertis was there too and he made a speech at the end. He called it his 'piece for solo voice marked Adagio con espressione', but it was cheerful,

firmly delivered and very much to the point. He thanked his colleagues and fellow members of the audience, described orchestral musicians as saints and the salt of the earth, reminded us that Harry Danks and his colleagues had given up their afternoon, between the morning's rehearsal and the evening's Promenade concert, to 'bring the viola into the lime-light'.

Tertis received a telegram from Tokyo from William Primrose and all his students wishing him happy birthday. Tertis replied on 6 January:

Dear William,
Grateful thanks for your cable with all the names of your students. The concert was a great 'leg-up' for the viola. Give my best wishes to all your students and congratulate them from me on being coached by you.
   Forgive more, am snowed under with letters, telegrams etc. etc.
Much love to you both from us both
   Lionel

As a tribute to Tertis on the day before his ninety-seventh birthday the BBC broadcast the programme 'Wrap Him in Gold' (reputed to be a comment made by Louis Zimmermann, concert-master of the Concertgebouw Orchestra after Tertis had rehearsed with them) presented by Bernard Keeffe. After the introductory music (Tertis's recording of his arrangement of Brahms's *Minnelied*, op. 71 no. 5), there were a few short memories from some of his friends. Gerald Moore said: 'I never think of Lionel without picturing him with a viola under his chin, and his viola, his tone, had a quality, a characteristic, a personality, such as you'd find in a singer's voice'. Sir Arthur Bliss's contribution was that 'Tertis raised this Cinderella into a Princess'. Artur Rubinstein said: 'He is the greatest glory of England in the way of instrument or players'. Near to the end of the programme Keeffe asked Tertis whether he thought his life's work on behalf of the viola had been crowned in the way he wanted. Tertis replied: 'Not crowned in the way that I wanted, for the simple reason that there are far fewer soloists now, because of the economic situation of every country ... they have to get into orchestras now, those that would like to be soloists, to earn the wherewithal to live, you know what it costs to live now and there's no time for solo playing. And they couldn't exist on solo playing now'. He went on to say that it was much worse than a few years ago: 'I think it's because of the pace of life, it's such a terrific high pitch, you've no time to breathe really, no matter what walk of life you're in, you are so to speak prodded in the back from the moment you get up until you go to bed. And I'm afraid this will go on until the world perhaps will become more sensible and more prosperous as a consequence'.

Tertis expressed his views on live performance and mechanical reproduction in an article published in 1973.

Bow and fiddle! The mind of man through the ages evolved these music-making instruments of such elegance, such resources, such power of expression, such possibilities, so enormously, tyrannically exacting, and at the same time so rewarding. Some of the scientifically minded of our time suggest that hand-made music is a passing phenomenon; they say that music of the future will be something utterly different, produced in a mechanical laboratory and transmitted by means the radio has made familiar. Conductors, orchestras, soloists, concert rooms and conservatoires, according to these people, will be superseded and looked upon as no less primitive than the Vikings who sailed their way from Norway to Labrador. I would have no wish to live, with these scientific friends, in that so-called 'brave new world' ... no radio, no tape-recorder, no gramophone, however well they are manipulated can compare with music performed in the flesh. The overcoming of difficulties, the struggle with the recalcitrant instrument, the wringing of beauty from contraptions of wood, hair, gut and metal – all this is something that makes life worth living. Music loses its vital personality when it is nothing more than a commodity obtained by turning a switch ... The music we value as the real thing has to be struggled for, missed, and struggled for again.

A second LP devoted to Tertis was issued by EMI in 1974 in the HMV Treasury series. Lovingly compiled and transferred from 78 rpm discs by Bryan Crimp, it featured his recording of the Brahms F minor Sonata in which the pianist was Harriet Cohen. In his sleeve note Michael Kennedy quoted Tertis designating the two late sonatas by Brahms as 'bread and butter' and 'the bible' of the viola player – 'physical and spiritual nourishment'. He paid tribute to Tertis the artist: 'His style of performance and actual quality of the sound are as unmistakable and individual as are those of Casals, Kreisler and Rubinstein in their respective fields and it is in their company he belongs'. The record also included the second Delius Sonata, two movements from Handel's Sonata in F and a group of shorter pieces. A note was appended which showed Tertis's justifiable pride in his articulation on the acoustic Vocalion recording of Kreisler's *La Chasse*: 'Lionel Tertis recommends the listener to La Chasse to turn up the volume and ignore the surface noise. Only in this way will it be possible to hear the double-stopping on the two lower strings of the 17⅛″ large viola on which it was played.'

Tertis wrote to Bernard Shore from Wimbledon on 1 June 1974 in reply to an earlier letter from Shore:

My dear Bernard,

I am dictating this to Lillian – I am so pleased to hear your pupil is doing well and is so enthusiastic.

Of course I should be glad to hear how he has progressed, but alas, I cannot do so at the moment. I am rather poorly just now and my doctor has sternly warned me to go slow for a bit.

Impress on Mr Chase to go and hear great instrumentalists at any and every opportunity and grab everything he likes that they do – and turn a deaf ear to whatever he doesn't like. I personally have always found this the greatest of incentives ...

Lionel Tertis

Roger Chase was subsequently taken by his teacher Bernard Shore to meet Tertis at his Wimbledon home. 'I went along and played the Dale Romance to him. He was a really diminutive figure by that time. He stood at my elbow and for twenty minutes he made me play just one shift – I can remember it now, D flat to G flat. He kept saying: "Sing, sing, sing!"' Chase played on two Tertis Model violas during his studies – one by Charles Lovett Gill, the other by Maurice Bouette. He stoutly defended these violas: 'I have never understood why people knock the Tertis Model. I think all the gibes at them are unjustified – they are a magnificent compromise. I can see what Tertis was trying to do and I can sympathise with his ideas. The Tertis Models are 16¾" and they have a stop anyone can get around.'

Throughout his career Frank Stiles, as both composer and violist, had been aware of the debt owed by viola players to Tertis, and he would have loved to write a work for Tertis to play. This was not possible, so as a consolation he wrote his second Viola Concerto in honour of Tertis's ninety-eighth birthday; it was premièred by Michael Ponder at a special concert, 'A Tribute to Lionel Tertis', held at the Purcell Room on 29 May 1974. The programme included Mozart's *Sinfonia concertante* (with Tertis's cadenzas) and Tertis's arrangement of Kreisler's Preludium and Allegro. The orchestra was the Priory Concertante, conducted by Barry Dix, who, like Frank Stiles, studied the viola with Winifred Copperwheat; a further link with Tertis was that Ponder was a student of Gwynne Edwards.

My Viola and I, Tertis's autobiography, was published by Paul Elek in 1974; it includes some material from his brief memoir *Cinderella No More*, written in the late 1940s. Besides covering the remaining very active thirty years in the new book, Tertis gives a much more detailed account of his early life. The book contains an updated version of his 'Beauty of Tone in String Playing' and three further articles – 'The Art of String Quartet Playing', 'Hints to Composers' and 'The Tertis Model Viola'.

A select gathering of close friends met at his home to celebrate the book's publication. Among the guests were Ruth, Lady Fermoy, Michael Kennedy (music critic and author), Desmond Hill (of the violin-makers W. E. Hill & Sons), John Whittle (manager of the classical department of EMI records), Muriel Williams (Director of the Musicians' Benevolent Fund), Gerald Mac-donald (Consultant Administrator of the Fund), Paul Elek (the publisher of *My Viola and I*) and Tony Wood, who edited the book for publication. Lillian Tertis read a speech on behalf of her husband, who told how he had recently complained about 'Anno Domini beyond repair' to a friend who immediately replied: 'No – Anno Domini indestructable!' Tertis also referred to the fact that all his life people had complimented him on his rubicund complexion, even when he felt poorly. Now, whenever he told people how fragile he felt, they would immediately reply: 'But your cheeks are so full of colour!'

The book received many complimentary reviews, both in the national press and musical journals. In a long critique in the *Daily Telegraph* Martin Cooper ended with the following paragraph:

> Mr Tertis's standard for himself and for every other artist, is expressed in his foreword, which is also a confession of his musical faith. 'The music we value as the real thing', he writes, 'has to be struggled for with all the power of the will, all possible concentration of the mind, struggled for, missed and struggled for again'. No wonder he succeeded in his crusade.

Robert Lewin, reviewing the book in *The Strad*, wrote:

> The test of an autobiography is what it reveals to us of the essential person himself and Lionel Tertis' life story has one predominating theme, his immense lifelong dedication to the viola. The centre-piece of this book is not Lionel Tertis, it is the viola, one suspects L.T. would not choose to have it otherwise, and in all musical history no instrument has been fortunate enough to find a more persuasive ambassador. ...
>
> Lionel Tertis once used the name Cinderella as a synonym for the gross neglect of the viola. Cinderella however is a grand story – a writer once said it is the only story, all others being variations on that same theme. Tertis' own life story is Cinderella too, a real life romance of a historic figure whose humble beginnings only serve to highlight the unique position he has attained. For all the generous tributes Tertis pays in his book to the viola stars of today, those players themselves would be the first to acknowledge Lionel Tertis' own stature as the supreme master. Yes, Lionel

Tertis, the viola is indeed a marvellous instrument, but never quite so wonderful as when in your hands.

Bernard Shore in his review for *The Gramophone* wrote:

This will not only become the bible for all viola players, but a historic document for all musicians and music lovers, covering as it does three-quarters-of-a-century of music-making all over the world ... Despite his utter dedication to the viola, he also succeeded in inspiring the love of two devoted women. His first wife (Ada) who died in 1951, and after many dark years he married Lillian, to whom the musical world will always be indebted for bringing Lionel Tertis to his 98th year in peace and comfort, and it is to her the book itself is dedicated.

In these pages Lionel Tertis comes to life, as they read just like the man himself, with all his difficulties and triumphs, but still a very simple and uncomplicated man, imbued with a central passion – that his beloved viola should at last be fully recognised and studied with as great a love as any dedicated artist for his instrument or voice.

Shore described his final meeting with Tertis:

After meeting Tertis in the large drawing room of his home, one feels less astonished that a man who was born in 1876 should still have sufficient energy and enthusiasm to be adding to his writings. A small, frail figure, barely able to see, but nevertheless standing quite erect; and the moment the talk turns to music his face is alight. His mind is prodigiously active and he speaks with precision, vehemence and humour, criticising the latest broadcast solo viola performance, commenting on his own old 78 recordings.

Lionel Tertis died on Saturday 22 February 1975. The effect of his death on the music profession was eloquently expressed by Bernard Shore in an obituary published in the Summer 1975 issue of the *RAM Magazine*:

The death of Lionel Tertis marks the end of an era: those glorious years when Kreisler reigned supreme over the violinists, Casals over the cellists, and Tertis himself was the greatest viola player of all time ... It was an era in which sheer individuality and the personal magnetism of the artist played a far bigger part, before the techniques of recording, broadcasting and television developed a new electronic way of life ... Tertis's virtuosity held one spellbound, by the pure magic of his playing and power of his personality ...

He had to develop an entirely new technique; overcome the peculiar problem of tone production which the viola presented; increase the range of the instrument by about one octave; and be able to do anything the violinists and cellists could! He had to solve the difficulty of playing a large viola, and be able to climb about all over it with consummate ease. His marvellous production of tone, which he could colour with as many shades as the painter can contrive from his palette, was something quite unique, whilst his ability to express himself with such ease and conviction was so magnetic that the listener seemed to become part of the music itself ...

Then, the effect of his teaching brought a new look to the study of the viola and countless recruits. None of us who have studied with him will ever forget that appalling acute ear of his for faulty intonation, his everlasting search for beauty of tone from his pupils, and the demands he made for expressing themselves. We can remember that high falsetto voice exclaiming: 'That's no use your fingers are all dead – bring them to life, or you'll kill that lovely phrase'! Then would follow the inimitable demonstration, and one would go home with those gorgeous sounds ringing in the ear, and want to practise, practise, practise to try and get things right for the next lesson.

There were many obituaries, one including a tribute by Ralph Vaughan Williams at an earlier dinner in honour of Tertis: 'The golden tones, passionate utterances and wonderful phrasing will always remain in the memory of those who have heard him and those who have not heard him will live richer because he has played.'

Lillian Tertis received many letters, including one from Solomon: 'Lionel has been a dear friend of mine through most of my life – we always managed to meet whenever possible even during our busiest years. It was a great joy to play sonatas with him and we never disagreed musically – I miss him very much – Solomon.' The following moving tribute from William Primrose was dated 12 March 1975:

Dear Mrs Tertis,
It is with some hesitation I sit down to write these lines of condolence concerning the doleful news I received a day or so ago concerning Lionel. At this remove I run the danger of touching a wound that may be in the process of healing, as time does heal all grief. I had been travelling throughout the Continent during the last month and hardly saw an English written newspaper, other than the Paris edition of the New York Tribune (and that seldom), certainly not a London paper, and was, therefore, quite unaware of the dreadful loss you had sustained and, for that matter,

the whole musical world had sustained, until the day before I left Geneva to return to Australia. I had dinner with my old [*sic*] Frederick Holding, who knew Lionel well in the old days when he, Holding, was a very well known violinist in London. It was after dinner that Frederick directed my attention to a news clipping from an English paper. The news was a great shock. One comes to believe that people like Lionel Tertis will be among us for ever. As indeed he will, but only in the form of his great spirit and his great dedication to the crusade he initiated so long ago. As I have written elsewhere none of us violists could possibly have pursued our dream had not Lionel, with his indomitable courage, blazed the trail for us. I now ask you to forgive, in the circumstances I have hinted at above, what must have appeared to you as downright callous and insensitive behavior. I trust, having brought your kind understanding to bear, you will believe how grieved I am and how much I feel for you in these solemn days, and recall with Spenser 'Sleep after toil, death after life does greatly please'. And toil he did. May his death award him peace.

Sincerely yours, William

Lillian Tertis replied on 3 April:

Dear Mr Primrose,
It was so good of you to write me such a delightful letter and I did appreciate hearing from you.

As you can imagine my very dear Lionel has left a terrible gap and I miss him more every day, but I try to console myself in thinking that he did have a wonderful life and I shall always feel privileged to have had the care of him in his latter years. I am also grateful beyond words that he lived to see his autobiography published and another L.P. record issued. He was always so interested in your work in Japan, and delighted to hear that there were so many keen viola players there. I wonder if you are going back?

I imagine you will not be coming to England in the near future as you have so recently been in Europe, but in case you did come, there is to be a memorial service on May 22nd. How nice it would be to see you then.

Meanwhile I do thank you so much for your kind sympathy.
Yours sincerely, Lillian F. M. Tertis

A memorial service was held at 12 noon on 22 May 1975 at the Church of the Holy Sepulchre, Holborn Viaduct, London, with Canon Richard Tydeman officiating. The lesson was read by Alvar Lidell and the address was given by Sir Thomas Armstrong. Artur Rubinstein came specially from Paris, and as the music ended he was seen to shake his head in sorrow and his hand came up to brush away the tears. Further along the same row sat the crippled Solomon. The service was reported in the July issue of *The Strad*:

> There was a large attendance at the service with almost every music society in the country represented, also other organizations including the BBC, the Elgar Society, EMI, W. E. Hill & Sons, and many others. ...
>
> The service was a moving occasion and it was appropriate that music of Elgar – Tertis's affection for Elgar was emphasized all through his long life – was played and also sung by the choir of St. Paul's Cathedral. After the service some of Lionel Tertis' records were played – a fitting coda to this farewell to a very great man whose name will always be associated with the viola. Not only his reputation lives on, this was a reminder that through the medium of the gramophone we can re-live the Tertis memory – that mixture of nobility and sweetness that makes up the Tertis sound, the music of the master viola player himself.

Tertis's legacy has been summarized by William Primrose in his *Walk on the North Side: Memoirs of a Violist*:

> Tertis was an indomitable man. He initiated all this viola business and set the string world on its ear. He was the first person to attempt to persuade the public at large to listen to the viola as a solo instrument and in so doing upset many apple carts. He knew very well that he was not going to get anywhere in his crusade unless he stormed and battered the citadel of apathy that held violists and the instrument in the deepest dungeon of low esteem and regard. And storm and batter he did! It was a heroic battle. For those of us who followed in his train, our task was rendered all the more easy and rewarding because of him. He was the first to insist that the viola was an instrument distinct from other string instruments, that it had a personality of its own. To suggest to him that performance on it was no more than playing the violin a fifth down was to commit the sin of sins and to evoke his sweet and devastating wrath ...
>
> During the early part of his career Tertis was reviled – not looked upon as a 'downstart' (pace G.B.S.). Although a small man he was a feisty warrior and wouldn't take no for an answer at any time from anybody. He had the deepest faith in what he was doing and an unquenchable love for the viola – for what he felt and realized he was capable of. Gradually he forced recognition of the instrument on the concert-going public ... Here was something new, to which they had to listen ...
>
> He made a perfect pest of himself to composers, more or less sitting on

their doorsteps and insisting they write for him. These days it is somewhat different. Composers will respond to a commission; a nice cheque fluttering before their eyes usually cajoles them into writing. In Tertis's day, however, that was demonstrably not the case, at least not for him. Consequently the works he was able to wring from reluctant composers are in a way even more important than those we commission today. Most of those who wrote for Tertis were minor British composers – but good ones. Like minor poets they can be engaging. He had to convince them that he offered a worthwhile way of communicating their musical thoughts. And, of course, he was convincing. ...

Tertis's name has been kept alive by the Lionel Tertis International Viola Competition and Workshop, which since 1980 has been organized at Port Erin on the Isle of Man. (See Appendix 8.) Initially the competition was held every four years, but it was soon made triennial.

A comprehensive reissue of all Tertis's recordings was released in 2006, along with four albums of his transcriptions for viola and piano.

Every year, somewhere in the world, the congress of the International Viola Society takes place, and Tertis's name is always mentioned. Indeed, wherever violists foregather, his name is bound to come up, as he is universally recognized as the father of modern viola playing. In many ways he can be seen as the father, or at least the midwife, of the modern viola itself, as his experiments with the Tertis Model brought the whole question of viola design into prominence. That the viola sections of today's British orchestras play with such superb tone, and that the violist of a modern British string quartet is often the strongest of the four players, can also be traced back to Tertis's influence through his coaching.

He would be amazed to know that today at least a dozen top-flight viola soloists are among the élite of the musical jet set, and that audiences no longer look askance at the presence of a viola concerto on a concert programme. The foundation for this healthy state of viola playing was laid by Tertis and Tertis alone. It was largely owing to his seven decades of bullying, cajoling and buttonholing conductors, composers and concert presenters that the viola was finally taken seriously. Others contributed, not least William Primrose, but the main thrust of the argument always came from Tertis. It was no small achievement for such a long life, a life which began in the same year that Brahms wrote his first symphony and ended in the year of the Soyuz–Apollo test flight.

⬿ Notes ⬾

Chapter 1: The Tertis Family

1 The synagogue had been founded in 1862 by a group of Polish immigrants who lived in Spitalfields, under the leadership of Jacob Davidson, a bootmaker who lived at 15–16 Princes Street. In 1870, 18 Princes Street (off Brick Lane) was leased and converted into a synagogue. In the early 1890s the building required considerable repairs which were carried out following a public appeal. The newly repaired building, with an altered façade, was opened in March 1893. In June the name of the street was changed to Princelet Street and the synagogue became the Princelet Street Synagogue.

2 B. M. Carrodus was the third and best known of five musical sons of the Victorian violinist John Tiplady Carrodus (1836–95), a Yorkshireman who changed his name from Carruthers. Born in 1866 B. M. Carrodus was a third-generation violinist, named Bernhard Molique after his father's teacher. He started lessons at six with Carrodus senior and made a momentous solo debut at the Gloucester Festival seventeen years later: while he was playing Hans Sitt's Second Concerto, his E-string snapped, and his father, who was leading the orchestra, passed him his violin. B. M. Carrodus played by command with his father for Queen Victoria, and toured with Sims Reeves, Emma Albani and Sir Charles Santley. At the 1894 Hereford Festival all five brothers played in an orchestra led by their father, four of them turning out for his jubilee the following year. B. M. Carrodus taught at Trinity College, where one of his pupils was Lionel Tertis, and around the turn of the century led a quartet in which two of his brothers took the inner parts. Deafness brought an early end to his career. He retired in 1905, and died on 1 December 1935. His violin was a Stradivarius. His published compositions included two mazurkas, a *Scottish Rhapsody*, a Romance in G, four Miniatures and various studies.

3 Percy Hilder Miles was a child prodigy, composing a number of works in his childhood and was the soloist in Beethoven's Violin Concerto at St James's Hall when he was thirteen. He was elected ARAM in 1899, and taught at the RAM, where he proposed to one of his students, the seventeen-year-old Rebecca Clarke. Clarke was immediately withdrawn from the Academy by her father and subsequently studied with Stanford at the RCM. Percy Miles was an inveterate traveller and a great champion of British music.

4 This famous concert series was established in 1878 to present regular events at South Place chapel on the north-east corner of the City of London. For many years there was no admission charge, and a collection was made to cover the cost of each concert. When the lease of the chapel expired in 1928 the concerts transferred to the Conway Hall in Red Lion Square, Holborn, London, home of the South Place Ethical Society; to this day, chamber music concerts are given there for at least six months each year.

5 Holbrooke added the 'e' to his surname in his youth; much later he changed his Christian name to Josef.

Chapter 2: Early Career

1 William Wolstenholme was born in Blackburn on 24 February 1865. He attended the Worcester College for the Blind from the age of nine, where he studied with Dr Done, the organist of Worcester Cathedral. During that period he had violin lessons from Edward Elgar, who also acted as his amanuensis when Wolstenholme sat his Bachelor of Music examination at Oxford University. Hawley and Tertis eventually found an organist's post for Wolstenholme at the Norfolk Square church in Paddington. He lived and worked in London until his death on 23 July 1931.

The *Romanza* and *Allegretto* were originally composed for viola, and first copied into conventional notation by Frank Park, the viola player of the Catterall String Quartet. Wolstenholme afterwards arranged them for organ solo. Altogether he composed five works for viola and piano, the others being *Canzona*, *The Question* and *The Answer*. Tertis often played these pieces in his concerts and, with the exception of the *Romanza*, he recorded them for Vocalion and later Columbia.

2 On 27 March 1909 Tertis and his colleagues in the Zimmermann Quartet gave a concert in the Aeolian Hall, when Lena Ashwell recited to the accompaniment of music composed by Stanley Hawley. Hawley studied at the RAM, where he played Grieg's Piano Concerto in the presence of the composer. He was a famous accompanist, a composer of some repute and quite a power in the musical world in the early years of the century: he was very helpful to Tertis and many other young musicians. *The Strad* in May 1909 reported: 'a recent performance of Beethoven's "Harp" quartet, played by the London String Quartet, Messrs. Louis Zimmermann, Horace Fellowes, Lionel Tertis and Jacques Renard (an excellent organisation this), at their concert at the Aeolian Hall. They also played some quartet movements, such as Mr. Frank Bridge's "Three Idylls" and the "Interludium in modo Antico" of Glazounov.'

3 'This proved a significant work. The opening movement is rhapsodical in character, the changes in sentiment being sharply made after the Hungarian fashion, but the music holds the attention by its picturesqueness and romanticism. The second number is built on a beautiful melody replete with tenderness and grave earnestness. For the third and last movement, a return is made to the style of the opening of the sonata . . . and the treatment of the themes forms an effective conclusion.' (*Daily Telegraph*)

4 Edwin York Bowen was born in 1884 and entered the Royal Academy of Music in 1898 to study piano with Alfred Izard and later Tobias Matthay. His recordings show that he was one of the best pianists of his time, with a colossal technique which he kept into old age. He was also an accomplished horn and viola player and could play most other instruments. Myers Foggin, an ex-student of Bowen, gained the impression that playing the viola gave him the greatest joy. He remembered Bowen playing the Franck Violin Sonata on the viola from the original violin part, and it seemed to present no difficulties to him.

5 The first orchestral concert of the Beecham Symphony Orchestra, with whom Thomas Beecham gave a magnificent series of concerts and opera performances, included Berlioz's Te Deum and *Roman Carnival* Overture plus Delius's *Sea Drift*.

6 Benjamin Dale ('B.J.D.' to his friends) was born in North London in 1885. He learnt piano, harmony and organ from an early age and made such excellent progress that he was allowed to enter the Royal Academy of Music at the age of fifteen. He studied composition with Frederick Corder (1852–1932) and his creative talent developed rapidly.

7 The composer Joseph Holbrooke said, 'We have to go to the sextets, symphonies and variations of Brahms to find anything so lovely', and Edwin Evans found it 'One of the most polished examples of pure Lyric form in chamber music since the great classics'. Sir Henry Wood commented: 'I wish Dale's output was larger because I so admire his Viola Suite he wrote specially for Tertis. It is a work of first rank, the solo part being beautifully laid out and the scoring perfect.' H. Osmond Anderton, writing about B. J. Dale in *Musical Opinion* in April 1922, said: 'Dale's op. 2 was the Suite for viola and piano, which I heard Tertis play at the R.A.M., at the time of its production. The writer's relations with this wonderfully fine player were, no doubt, a controlling factor in his exploitation of the instrument ... The Suite is a wonderfully fine work, having not only a true feeling for the genius of the two instruments but nobly imaginative qualities. It is not a work for tyros; but players with adequate technique will find it amply repays study ... Dale has scored it, and it has been performed by Tertis in London, under Nikisch, at The Hague under Mengelberg and at Glasgow under Ronald.'

8 Dale's *Introduction and Andante*, op. 5, was eventually published by Corda Music (1996), edited by John White.

9 The first time Bowen and Tertis collaborated was in 1904, when they played Bowen's Romance in D flat at the Bechstein Hall. They gave two further recitals at the Bechstein Hall in 1905. On 30 October they included Bowen's C minor Sonata, and their second appearance was on 11 December. They premiered Bowen's Second Sonata in a concert arranged by Frederick Corder in conjunction with the Royal Academy Musical Union; this took place in the concert room at the Academy on 3 February 1906; they gave a further performance of the new sonata at the Aeolian Hall on 26 February that year. On their return from Germany in November 1907 they played works by Ernest Walker, W. H. Bell and B. J. Dale at Broadwood's Hall. The critics, although full of praise for the playing of the artists, were divided in their opinions of the compositions.

10 John White has edited the Bowen *Fantasie* for four violas (this edition remains unpublished).

11 The Society of British Composers was formed in 1905 with the object of safeguarding and promoting the interests of British composers. Tertis claimed that his persistence, with the support of Stanley Hawley, had played a part in its establishment. Frederick Corder was chairman, and J. B. McEwen Hon. Secretary.

12 James Lockyer had originally planned a business career. He had some violin lessons with Hans Wessely, who who suggested he should take up the viola. Within a month he was awarded the Ada Lewis viola scholarship to study at the RAM. As a pupil of Tertis he was awarded all the major honours, and twice won the coveted Rube Prize.

13 York Bowen's Viola Concerto in C minor, op. 25, edited by John White, is published by Josef Weinberger. It was first recorded by Lawrence Power (viola) and the BBC Scottish Symphony Orchestra, conductor Martyn Brabbins (Hyperion CD A67546, issued 2005).

14 Bax's music was inspired by his love for the west coast of Ireland and the writings of W. B. Yeats. In the programme note for the first performance of the *Concert Piece* in 1904, Bax wrote: 'It will be observed that a Celtic element predominates, free use being made of the flattened seventh, the falling intervals of the pentatonic scale and the features peculiar to Irish music.' The *Concert Piece* was published for the first time in 1999 by Marlow Music (now published by Corda Music), and has recently been recorded by Martin Outram on a CD of the composer's music (Naxos, 2006).

15 Sir Ernest Palmer established the Patrons' Fund in the early years of the twentieth century with the aim of promoting the music of new national composers.

16 The ISM was founded in 1882. The goals of the society were many; it took the lead in the organization of music teachers, provided a forum for discussion and leadership in the performance of British works at conferences.

17 Other works in the programme were: Ernest Guiraud's Serenade, Alfredo d'Ambrosio's *Andante*, Wolstenholme's *Allegretto* and Henri Vieuxtemps's *Saltarello*.

18 On leaving the RAM Dorothy Jones became the violist of the Egerton String Quartet, and in 1920 joined the Kendall Quartet, whose other members were violinists Katherine Kendall and Marjorie Clemens (replaced by Dorothy Brook) and cellist Edith Hanson. They were the second ensemble to broadcast for 2LO, and later gave the inaugural concert at the Victoria and Albert Museum. In 1925 they toured Ceylon (Sri Lanka), Malaya, Australia and South Africa, playing 110 concerts in ten months and travelling 40,000 miles.

19 Phyllis Mitchell was awarded the Ada Lewis scholarship to the RAM in September 1906 (to study with Tertis). She took part in several RAM student chamber concerts at the Queen's Hall between 1907 and 1911, and was awarded the Lesley Alexander gift for viola playing in 1909. She played in the premiere of Bowen's *Fantasie* for Four Violas (1908).

20 Holbrooke's Nocturne 'Fairyland' is available in a number of versions, either for piano, viola and oboe d'amore (with an alternative part for oboe, violin, flute or clarinet), or small orchestra.

21 Ernest Walker wrote his Viola Sonata for Alfred Hobday in the 1890s. Tertis edited it for publication in 1912. Walker studied classics at Oxford; in 1890 he joined the staff at Balliol College, where he was Director of Music for twenty-five years. 'This work, both in mood and execution, reveals a freedom of invention and melodic fluency

possessed of attractions which do not recede. We find appropriate harmonic variety without a corresponding complexity. Rhythmically the music is very much alive. It is rare to find a composer with such an assured aptitude for proper treatment of the viola as a solo instrument. The temptation is to think of it, tonally, in terms of the violin. Dr. Walker shows that his comprehension extends to every potentiality which reason demands; and in the security of his technique the poetry is not neglected.' (Robert Hull, *Musical Opinion*, July 1931)

22 'Other new music recently heard includes Mr. T. F. Dunhill's Phantasy Trio for piano-forte, violin and viola, played at the last of the composer's concerts at the Steinway Hall. Mr. Dunhill has learnt the art of writing most effectively in the true chamber music style, and if this work does not reveal any ideas of outstanding force, it is eminently pleasing, and one would think, grateful to play. It was performed by the composer himself, Miss Marjorie Hayward and Mr. Lionel Tertis.' (*The Strad*, April 1912). The Trio was largely written in Tintagel, North Cornwall, in 1911, for the Cobbett Competition, and was published in 1912. It was one of the first British chamber works to be recorded (in an abridged version on Vocalion, by Sammons, Tertis ('eloquent') and Frank St Leger).

Chapter 3: The First World War

1 Artur Rubinstein wrote in his autobiography: 'In later years my manager Sol Hurok used the h-less "Artur" for my publicity, but I sign "Arthur" in countries where it is common practice.'

2 Joseph Jongen was director of the Royal Brussels Conservatory, as his brother Léon was to be later, but his career was not limited to this position, one that he held brilliantly as a successor of Fétis, Gevaert, Tinel and Dubois. He was also a virtuoso pianist, a brilliant organist, and a chamber musician of the first rank. As a composer he tackled every genre except opera.

3 The Steinway Hall, Lower Seymour Street, which was used as a concert hall from 1878, had previously been the Quebec Institute and the Marylebone Literary Institute, during which time both Dickens and Thackeray gave readings from the platform. In 1925 it was taken over by a new company and renamed the Grotrian Hall. Acoustically, it was absolutely perfect. Mr Gordon Selfridge acquired the site in 1938.

4 Later Bowen gave the manuscript of his arrangement of the *English Dance* to his student Monica Watson, who in turn gave it to the author, who has recently edited it for publication.

Chapter 4: The Chamber Music Players

1 In suggesting the group's name, Ada Tertis may well have been aware that in 1913 Sammons and Cedric Sharpe had played in an ensemble called the British Chamber Music Players.

2 Hurlstone acquired a fine reputation as a student at the RCM, and later taught there, but died in 1906, aged thirty.

Chapter 5: American Tours

1 This is the only mention of a recording of the double concerto by Bach. One can only presume that it was not suitable for issue.

2 Thelma Bentwich, a dedicated pupil of Casals, emigrated to Palestine the following year and, under her married name Yellin, became one of the foremost pioneers of music in what is now Israel.

3 Williams, who still played the cello without an endpin, as his teacher Robert Hausmann had done, had emerged from his ordeal in Ruhleben with a permanent tremor which made it difficult for him to play in public. Not long after this concert he retired to teach and coach chamber ensembles, although he continued to play chamber music privately.

4 Beckwith, one of Britain's best violinists, was to die prematurely in 1928, aged forty-one.

5 C. M. Loeffler was born in Alsace on 30 January 1861 and studied the violin under Joachim and Massart. He moved to North America, where he became the co-concert master of the Boston Symphony Orchestra (1885–1903). On his retirement from the orchestra he devoted his time to composition. He died at Medfield, Mass., on 28 May 1935.

6 Goodson, a pupil of Leschetizky, taught at the RAM, where one of her students was the young Clifford Curzon.

7 Edward Kreiner, Polish-born violist, was principal viola in Fritz Reiner's Cincinnati Symphony Orchestra in 1923. By all accounts he was a strong personality, in one case forming a string quartet and paying his younger colleagues less money than himself.

Chapter 6: Return to the RAM

1 Bernard Shore was born in London on 17 March 1896 and educated at St Paul's School and the Royal College of Music. He intended to become an organist; however, during war service in France he was severely wounded in the right hand by a bombing accident. As he was carried into a field dressing station, he told the surgeon: 'I want you to preserve every eighth of an inch you can'. He was left with enough of the hand to grip a bow, and so concentrated on his second instrument, the viola. He resumed his studies at the Royal College of Music in 1919, winning two gold medals. He was appointed principal viola in the newly formed BBC Symphony Orchestra in 1929. He was a forthright advocate of the Tertis Model viola, and demonstrated it vigorously at the first Lionel Tertis International Viola Competition and Workshop

on the Isle of Man in 1980, when he was eighty-four years old but still producing a sonorous tone. He died in 1985.

2 William Voller (1854–1933) and his brothers Alfred (1856–1918) and Charles (1865–1949) were well-known violin repairers/restorers in London. See John Dilworth, Andrew Fairfax and John Miles, *The Voller Brothers* (British Violin Making Association, 2006).

3 Tertis often spoke to Danks about one of his students, Harry Berly, the finest talent he had ever worked with; he had high hopes that Berly would become one of the greatest players of his time. Sadly, after a fatal motoring accident in which Berly's girlfriend was killed, the young man took his own life. Even at the end of his own life, Lionel Tertis still talked about Harry Berly with affection and admiration.

4 Tertis had appeared annually at the Newcastle Chamber Music Society as a member of the Allied String Quartet and the Chamber Music Players. In a varied programme which included piano solos and two groups of songs performed by Elsa Murray-Aynsley accompanied by Edgar L. Bainton, Tertis played Bach's 'Komm, Süsser Tod', Kreisler's *Prelude and Allegro*, Tertis's *Sunset*, Marais's *Le Basque* and Wolstenholme's *Allegretto*, with Bainton as his accompanist.

5 This superb performance has its own niche in gramophone history. Not long after it had been deleted from the catalogue in 1930, a schoolboy called Patrick Saul wanted to hear it. He was appalled to discover not only that he could not obtain the two discs himself, but that no official body had preserved copies. This occurrence led to Saul's lifelong campaign for the preservation of recordings, which resulted first in the setting up of the British Institute of Recorded Sound and eventually in the establishment of the National Sound Archive at the British Library.

6 In the dictionary of Australian colloquialisms, Melba is commemorated in the phrase 'to do a Melba', which means to make a habit of returning from retirement in a number of farewell performances.

7 Mary Stewart, a student of Tertis, was violist of the Boris Pecker Quartet, and also played in a piano quartet with Jessie Grimson, Herbert Withers and his pianist wife.

Chapter 7: The Elgar and Walton Concertos

1 Although he did not perform it, Tertis was certainly aware of Cecil Forsyth's Viola Concerto; he was a good friend of Émile Férir, who premièred the work, and in 1912 it was included in a list of new viola repertoire on the back of one of Tertis's programmes.

Chapter 8: BBC Orchestra and New British Works for Viola

1 Reeves was then one of the most accomplished accompanists in London, and was later to make a career in America.

Chapter 9: A Shock Retirement

1 Cyril Rootham was music director of Cambridge University Music Society and exerted a strong influence in cultivating the art of music at the University, where he was a lecturer in music.

2 Eight letters written between 15 September 1932 and 22 September 1934 relating to a 'Poem' for viola and orchestra by Eugène Goossens (1893–1962) from Lionel Tertis to the composer, are now in the British Library.

Chapter 11: The Second World War

1 Reprinted by permission from Alan Denson, *Personal Inflexions* (Aberdeen: Oliver Alden, 1981).

Chapter 13: Return to America and Eightieth Birthday Celebrations

1 The Applebaums' son, Michael Tree, is the violist of the Guarneri Quartet.

2 Barbirolli invited Tertis to join a panel to find a new leader for the Hallé Orchestra after Laurance Turner retired. The auditions took place in June 1958 at Morley College, London. Martin Milner was the successful candidate and Tertis was to see more of him at the annual King's Lynn Festival. Milner participated in a chamber concert, with Lady Barbirolli, at the first Lionel Tertis International Viola Competition and Workshop on the Isle of Man in 1980.

Chapter 14: Second Marriage and Last Appearance

1 Lillian Florence Margaret Warmington, born 1 May 1915, daughter of Harold Henry Warmington (solicitor), was educated at Godolphin School, Salisbury. She studied the cello with Diran Alexanian at the Cortot–Thibaud–Casals School. During the war she was chief of the ambulance section at one of the Civil Defence depots in the Midlands. She joined the Entertainments National Services Association (ENSA), and was in one of the first companies to take classical music to HM Forces. Later she gave concerts in Holland, Belgium and Germany, being often near the front line in the early days. After the war she gave recitals and broadcasts in London and the provinces, and appeared twice as soloist with the Bournemouth Municipal Orchestra under Rudolf Schwarz.

Chapter 15: TV Profile and Ninetieth Birthday

1 In reply to the invitation to the Royal Philharmonic Society Luncheon in honour of Tertis, Harriet Cohen wrote: 'As I was this great master's solo pianist for over five years, visiting the foremost European cities in Recital Tours with him, you can imagine with what pleasure I accept your invitation to be present at the occasion to honour my dear old friend.'

APPENDIX 1

Tertis's Violas

The following is a list of some of the violas used by Lionel Tertis.

1896   His first viola was loaned to him by the Royal Academy of Music; he described it as '... a small instrument, incapable of a true C-string sonority'

1897   A fellow student loaned him a Guadagnini.

c.1918   He owned a 17" viola by Carlo Antonio Testore (Milan 1735), which he sold to Mr Tom Brannard for the sum of £175 in 1934. This viola is now in the possession of Thomas Riebl, the Austrian violist, who has served on the jury for the Lionel Tertis Viola Competition. Riebl: 'It is the most wonderful instrument I have come across so far and I feel very privileged in playing this viola with such a great history.'

During this time Tertis also owned an Amati.

from 1919   After the 1914–1918 War he often borrowed a viola from Mr Chetham-Strode. Once attributed to Mariani (1645), more recently it has often been ascribed as a Maggini (1600). He used this for some of his earliest Vocalion recordings.

1924   From the Paris dealer, Maucutel & Deschamps, he bought the Domenico Montagnana viola (c.1727), which he used for most, if not all, of his Columbia recordings of 1924–33.

1928   He bought a 17¾" Gasparo da Salò (c.1590) from Silvestre in Paris, which he described as '... the finest viola in existence'. It was known to both European and American connoisseurs and many tried to buy it. Tertis played it for the first time at a concert in Bournemouth in May 1928. He soon, however, returned to his beloved Montagnana.

1939   He borrowed a Testore from Eric Coates.

Afterwards he used two R.T. Model violas by Arthur Richardson (nos. 10 & 32), and a Tertis Model viola by Wilfred Saunders (no. 8).

The Tertis Model Viola

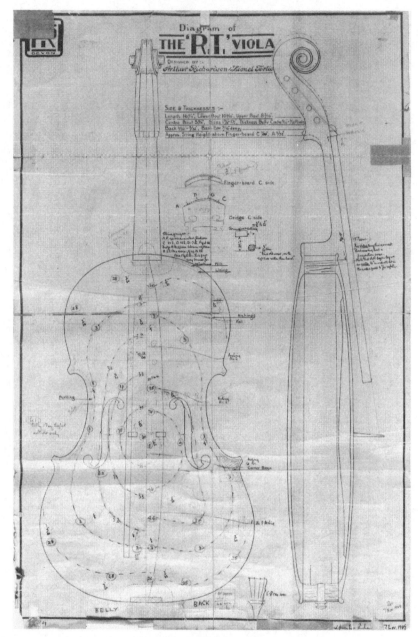

1 The 'R.T.' Viola, designed by Arthur Richardson/Lionel Tertis 1949;
plan drawn by Arthur Richardson

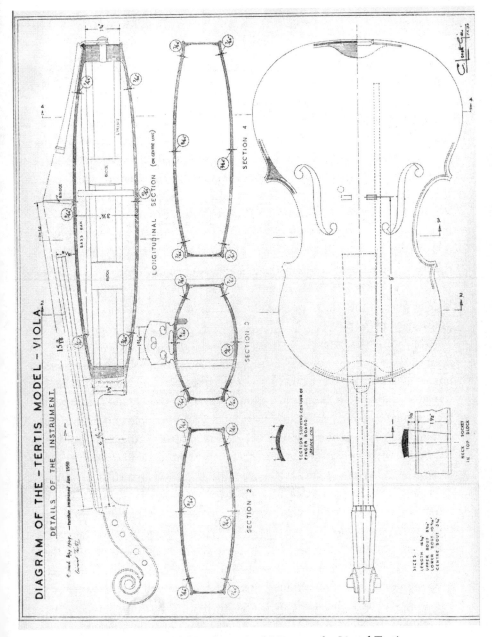

2 The Tertis Model Viola, revised May 1949 by Lionel Tertis;
plan drawn by C. Lovett Gill, FRIBA

Tertis's Writings and Talks

'Training for Virtuosity', *Daily Telegraph*, 1937

The musical talent of our country has never been given the encouragement it ought to receive. This lack of interest and consideration is due to the indifference that the State has always shown towards music.

The following facts concerning this important matter are the result of practically sixty years' experience as an ambitious instrumentalist, always fighting against impossible odds. The careless neglect of our national effort in the art of music not only concerns our executants, but applies to other branches of our music-making. It is, however, natural that I should confine my comments to the executant, for in that province my life of musical activity has been most concerned, and my observations and experiences during those many years qualify and enable me to say indubitably that British talent in the sphere of Music is the last of the arts to receive a helping hand in our country. The State has never realized the power of music, except perhaps in war time, and then there is very little to offer in the way of propaganda, owing to lack of encouragement and preparation in the past.

Music is an international language; it is therefore important to produce executants of the greatest possible lustre, for in their accomplishments we should possess eloquent speakers able to gain the sympathies and good will of most foreign countries. The exceptionally musically gifted child of our future generation should be given by the State every facility for developing his talents. The continental artists of high repute receive correct musical guidance from early childhood, with every advantage and encouragement, generally from the State; and the State in consequence reaps good dividends, for the resultant great artist is a real asset to his country, as a musical ambassador. How different is the treatment meted out to the children of our land who early in life show exceptional musical propensities! We may be justly proud of our outstanding executants (easily counted on one hand) in their achievements, and of what they have accomplished in spite of lack of specialized training and other very necessary conditions. Take, for example, our own Albert Sammons. If ever there was a natural born violinist, surely he is one. He has had practically no guidance in the study of his instrument. He had to begin earning his livelihood at a very tender age, in the atmosphere of the café, with very little time for study; and in spite of all these damning conditions, he has risen to his present eminence.

Had he received the specialized training and general schooling to which he was entitled, he would have been second to none, past or present. In most other countries such genius as his would have been fostered and given every encouragement. Another example is Laurie [*sic*] Kennedy, the fine Australian 'cellist, of immense natural talent, who from early childhood had to earn his living in various ways, with no guidance or time to develop his musical gifts.

In further defence of my arguments, I consider it necessary and expedient that I should give a *detailed* account of the early struggles and difficulties which I personally encountered in the pursuit of my musical ambitions, as another illustration of what happens here to a child of decided musical talent. I was born at West Hartlepool in December 1876; began to show decided interest in music at the age of three; learnt to play the piano at five; at six, appeared as an infant prodigy at a public concert at Highbury in North London. From then I continued my furious study of the piano (I was practising eight hours a day by the time I was twelve years old), though with inadequate guidance, and I remember that all through those early days I was convinced that the piano was too mechanical for my taste. I wanted to discard it for the violin, for which I had a yearning and a passion – but alas! This ambition was not realized until too late in life. My parents' means were very limited: moreover conditions did not exist (as they still do not exist) for specialized training. My general education, such as it was, occupied in all about five years at an East End Board School, including a short time at Cowper Street School, which I left at a very early age. When I was thirteen [*recte* fifteen–sixteen] I entered Trinity College of Music as a piano student, playing concertos with the College Orchestra, for by then I had acquired quite a respectable technique. But my studies did not last long; funds had run out, and I had to start earning my living. My first professional appointment was as a musician-attendant at a lunatic asylum at the age of fourteen. Another engagement was as a member of a Hungarian band (dressed for the part), of which all the members were British! On another occasion I was part of a seaside pier orchestra; and so on. From these miscellaneous jobs I managed to provide a little money for further spasmodic study. On the occasion of my first professional engagement, I received a letter from Prof. Bradbury Turner, who was Principal of Trinity College at that time. In it he said: 'I am glad to hear you have got the appointment, and I trust it may be the means of helping you to realize what you wish and that you will be able to push on with your studies. You are very young and it is a pity you are taken away so early from the necessary course, but we have to do the best for ourselves under such conditions.' My spasmodic study continued until I was sixteen, and meantime I had managed to obtain a few violin lessons from one who, I afterwards realized, must certainly have been the world's worst teacher! However in those last two years I contrived to accumulate the wherewithal to go to Leipzig for a six-months' course at the Conservatorium. But I found during my short visit that this once famous institution had very much deteriorated in its efficiency and methods, and I learnt precious little. After this short course at Leipzig, I was an intermittent student at the Royal Academy of Music, London – intermittent for the usual reason: lack of funds. I persisted in my ambition of trying to play the violin, ignorant of the fact that it was already too late in life to become a first-rate executant. However, by good fortune, somewhere about 1893–94 [*recte* 1896–7] I became interested in the viola (at that time little played and rarely heard as a solo instrument). Entranced with its tone-qualities, I resolved to try and become a propagandist for its right to be heard much more frequently as a solo instrument. I had some lessons from my Royal Academy violin profes-sor, who knew very little about the viola. I studied it principally by myself. At the time I came across the neglected viola no serious efforts were being made to champion its cause as a solo instrument; and owing to my having the field practically to myself, my lack of early specialized training, with the consequent deficiency in my technical equipment, was not deeply felt; and so, being for-tunately possessed of natural musical ability, I was enabled to pursue my idea of spreading recognition for the Cinderella of the string family. I conclude this lengthy résumé of my own case, with the certain knowledge of how much bet-ter a job I should have made of it if I could have enjoyed the same facilities that the musical educationists of foreign countries are able to provide. We do not possess a specialized course or method of training for the embryo virtuoso, and so fail to make the most of the youthful player of exceptional promise.

The talented child should begin to specialize between the age of five and seven. A perfect technique is acquired only by those whose training is under-taken seriously at that age, when joints and sinews are still in the making and can be conformed and directed to the tremendous tasks they will be called upon to accomplish. The biographies of all the great executants convey this moral.

The title of this article, and the emphasis I have laid on the importance of technical proficiency must not give the impression that nothing else is nec-essary in the make up of a first-class executant. On the contrary, a true and natural musical feeling – a God-given attribute, I maintain – is the *first* consid-eration. I assert that this true musicality is sufficiently discernible in the very early life of children to warrant its encouragement and development. Never-theless, outstanding acrobatics is a necessary adjunct and can be obtained only by application (and plenty of it) from a very early age.

The curriculum of our leading schools is well suited to the requirements of would-be composers, and admirably organized for the production of well-equipped all-round musicians – the general practitioners of music, so to speak. What is needed for the training of the specialist is a distinctly organized course of study.

I do not consider myself competent to suggest a definite plan for the development of the budding virtuoso, but I think that the study of the Russian system would provide this.

One of the essentials I visualize for the convincingly talented child is his virtual adoption by the music school, which would undertake his vitally important general education, always bearing in mind that the child's vocation should command first consideration. The virtuoso-to-be should not be submitted to the full curriculum of the music school. He has not the time for it. However gifted a child is, there *must* be plenty of time available for application. Scholarships should be offered throughout the British Isles and the Empire for the outstandingly talented child of between the age of five and seven. A further point of importance is that the child should be given frequent opportunity of hearing the greatest artists. This, I hold, is of momentous consequence to his progress and cannot be too highly stressed.

I hope the facts I have stated will meet the eye of those who have the power to help, and *will* help to provide propitious conditions for the training of our future specialist executants, and so give rightful opportunity and encouragement for the young musical interpretative talent of post-war England.

'An English Viola', *The Strad*, February 1945

For fifty years or more, my object in life has been to further the cause of the viola. My plan of action to give it 'a place in the sun' began in 1893 [*recte* 1896] – with a fierce fight for it as a solo instrument and so to combat its relegation to the position of being principally only an accompanying medium. My reinforcements to this end have been and are, firstly, my pupils, who now also 'preach the gospel', and secondly, the extensive library of solo viola music which we now possess, thanks to our composers, and the numerous arrangements I have made, and that other viola players are making. Thirdly, in addition I have given a good deal of thought to the question of the design of the instrument itself.

I foresaw many, many years ago that as viola players become more numerous, the few good violas in existence would in no way be sufficient to meet the demand, and it was imperative, if we did not want the viola to lapse into the comparative obscurity of fifty years ago, that someone should make an effort to try and bring about the production of an instrument capable of giving that distinct and satisfying sound that only a fine viola can give.

Some fifteen or twenty years ago, a well-known violin maker – Arthur

Richardson of Crediton – called on me at Bideford (where I was giving a recital) and expressed a desire to take a template of my Montagnana (1717) viola. The conversation we had on that occasion rather impressed me, and I made a mental note that I would make further contact with him later on. The opportunity occurred some seven years ago when I retired (as I thought for good) from the concert platform. I migrated to Bath, with the express intention of being nearer to Richardson, and we agreed to collaborate in an effort to design a viola which would possess particularly a really sonorous C string – usually lacking in the majority of violas, and especially so in so-called violas of sixteen inches or under.

In many instances they are violas which have been cut down or built to that size. Such undersized instruments should be consigned to the rubbish heap. They cannot emit true viola sound, and those who play them are therefore not viola players. It is not too much to say that by reason of this collaboration between Richardson and myself (begun in 1937) viola players will be provided with a viola which possesses big depth of tone coupled with fine quality from the moment it is made.

The design is not what would be called quite orthodox. Among the points in its make-up are, besides the true viola tone, a light-weight yet very strongly made instrument, large but manageable (sixteen and three-quarter inches, which I consider is the ideal size viola, especially for solo playing), an instrument with an abnormally big air space (or sound box), and one wherein meticulous consideration has been given to the great importance – from the player's point of view – of what I would call 'ease of handling' – I make bold to say that these seven years of collaboration between maker and professional performer have produced a viola to be known as the 'R.T.' (Richardson–Tertis), which will hold its own with most of the comparatively few famous old instruments in both quality and quantity of tone.

I have used quite a few of them for my professional work, and the present one that I am playing is just over one month old. Some of my pupils play on the Richardson viola in preference to their old Italian instruments.

A week or two ago I was able to arrange an interesting test of two of these violas. One was twelve months old and the other my present instrument. The test was attended by my old pupil and friend Mr. Bernard Shore, and a young Canadian professional violist, now in the country with the R.C.A.F. [Royal Canadian Air Force], whom I invited at the suggestion of the Editor of this journal, who was also present. Mr. Shore kindly loaned me his Montagnana, which, in my opinion, is one of the finest toned violas in the world. This was formerly my own concert instrument, and on which I made many of my recordings and broadcasts. I played numerous short passages on each of the instruments, and all present were surprised at the volume, reserve of power, and true viola tone quality of the two new instruments, especially the latest of the two, which embodies one or two minor improvements, the principal one being the increase of the width of the middle bouts by an eighth of an inch, adopted by Richardson and myself during the past twelve months.

The measurements of the latest 'R.T.' viola are: Length of body, 16¾ inches; Upper bouts, 8³⁄₁₆; Middle bouts 5¾; Lower bouts 10⁹⁄₁₆; Ribs (upper), 1½, (lower), 1¾; Depth over centre of plates, 3⅜ (approximately); String length, 14¹¹⁄₁₆.

I would here hasten to say that I have no financial interest in the production of the 'R.T.' viola, and would under no circumstances ever wish to have. My reward is the fact that I have been instrumental in helping towards providing an instrument worthy of the name V I O L A for the present and future generations of viola players.

I have had nothing to do with the actual making of the instrument – that is Richardson's craftsmanship, but I do take to myself the satisfaction of having contributed quite considerably to its design and also particularly as to the 'manœuvrability of handling' from the player's standpoint. Our numerous experiments over the long period of seven years have been a test of patience, and I pay tribute to Richardson's dogged and persistent efforts, which could only come from a man with his artistic ideals.

> Correspondence related to this article appeared in later editions of *The Strad*.

Dear Sir, – I have been reading with interest Mr. Lionel Tertis' article on the new viola, which claims that the problems connected with this instrument have now been solved. This is interesting news. But it must be observed that the claim is made for an instrument of 16¾ inch back. Smaller instruments, of 16 inch and under, must be 'consigned to the rubbish heap.' The question then for some of us must be: is the new viola suited to persons with small hands? Even on my 15½ inch viola I found some double stopping in the first position decidedly difficult. On a larger instrument I should have to use a mixed fingering. Perhaps this is intended? What is the practice on these big violas?

Like Mr. Tertis and the maker of the new viola, I have myself regretted the defectiveness of the viola in respect of the fourth string. This led to some experiments and research work alluded to in a letter printed in The Strad a good many years ago. I am not a violin-maker nor a skilled mechanic, only an amateur and a bungler in my methods. Nevertheless my work led to some interesting results, both theoretically and practically, the latter especially in another branch of tonal acoustics.

My experiments were made on a 15½ inch viola, of good material, I should say, but poor in tone, and fairly new. I succeeded in making a most astonishing improvement, noticeably on the fourth string, which I was able to reduce to a thickness intermediate between a thin C and a G string. In spite of the reduced tension, the tone was quite powerful, and the string as easy and responsive as the best violin G. Noticeably, also, I was able to secure evenness of response on all stops of all strings.

Unfortunately, I was not content to leave the instrument thus. Though so responsive and powerful, the tone lacked mellowness. There followed some experiments with varnish, which detracted from the good results obtained. None the less, I had for many years an instrument with a C string well superior to the ordinary run. Now, after fifteen years, I have found the tone of this instrument to have gone all to pieces, and so conclude that my method does not lead to permanent results.

There I must be content to leave things, at least for the present. The strings are not my chief interest in music. I can afford to leave the field to others. What I have demonstrated, however, is that it is possible for a small viola of 15½ inch back to possess a fourth string as easy and responsive as the G on the best violin. Of course, I realized from the first that if a viola were made large enough, the trouble with the C string would not arise. There is, it seems, a right ratio of length to weight and thickness of string, which is required. When bowing the fourth string on an average viola one can feel that energy is being wasted, and the motion of the bow is being transformed only partly into sound, the rest going into scrape.

My experiments recorded certain results which I have not seen anywhere alluded to. I found that a loud spot, or a weak spot, on any string in the first position, would be generally repeated a fifth above on the same string. The rule, however, is not absolute, and sometimes there is a discrepancy of a semitone or a tone. Also I discovered that every individual stop in the first position is related to a certain area on the lower half of the table. Like Mr. Walker, your American correspondent (Sept 1943) I had decided that, all else being in order, tone and responsiveness depended on the finish of the surface prior to varnishing all over the instrument (the scroll only excepted, but not the peg-box!), but especially the table (not so Mr. Walker), and most of all its lower half. I suspect Mr. Walker of having a secret here – in the finish. Let me add that I was very interested in this gentleman's letter, and also that from Mr. Lavender, who slighted the idea of putting a plug in one's ears when playing the fiddle. Has he tried it, I wonder? Even a good violin may disclose a certain amount of scrape when played so close to the ear, Cotton-wool hides this scrapiness and is not a bad idea, it seems to me. Does your correspondent, Mr. Lavender, know that cotton-wool is used to mellow the tone of the free reed in the harmonium? And it does mellow it, in a remarkable degree.

Let me conclude by saying that I hope Mr. Walker's new methods of fiddle-making will prove as successful as he hopes, and lead to permanent results; and also that he will not wait until after the war to give his new violin to the musical world, as I understand was his original intention.

As for Mr. Tertis and his collaborator, Mr. Richardson, if their claim is fully justified, even in respect of the larger instrument, they are certainly to be congratulated on the results of their patient co-operation.

Yours faithfully,

A. Arundel.

Caernarvonshire

Dear Sir, – Is it not rather too drastic to condemn all violas of 16 inches and under 'to the rubbish heap', as Mr. Tertis put it, and to call them bastard fiddles as your correspondent does? With admiration for his well-written and well-reasoned letter, and with due respect for his views, one would like to venture the opinion that true viola quality exists in some small violas, if shortness of length is compensated by other factors: breadth, depth of sides, scientific modelling – probably the wood used and the varnish also count.

A few months ago, a viola by Mantegatia was illustrated in The Strad. Were I the fortunate possessor of this instrument, I should hate to hear it called a bastard fiddle because it measures a mere 15 inches, and surely even a 'true viola lover' like your correspondent would hesitate to condemn it to the rubbish heap.

One might as well say that because Clara Butt, six feet tall and built in proportion, had the biggest contralto voice of her generation, contraltos of only five feet four should be discouraged from learning to sing. Had this been so, the musical world might have been the poorer, bearing in mind Kirkby Lunn (see what Sir Henry Wood said in his book about her!) and other contraltos of fewer than seventy-two inches.

The violins of Guarnerius del Gesù are not despised because he seldom if ever exceeded 13⅞ inches. On the contrary. For sheer power, let alone quality, his violins are probably the greatest in the world, with the finest G string tone.

This question of large v. small violas crops up at intervals. One recalls that when a virtuoso of the 'viola-alta' became conductor of one of our leading orchestras, it was observed that his viola section took to large violas. But are these same players still using the same instruments? One doubts it. One suspects that many a fine orchestral player cherishes a lovely little Banks viola, or a Charles Harris or a cut-down Testore, and would hesitate to exchange for a big viola merely on account of its size, though if all big ones were as splendid as the 'R.T.' viola they might be willing and even anxious to do so.

As your correspondent truly says, present-day makers should get busy. England will indeed be lucky if her future viola-makers prove to be worthy followers of Mr. Richardson. But don't let us run away with the idea that all small violas are unworthy of the name. Some are very fine.

Yours faithfully,

W. James.

Wolstanton, Stoke-on-Trent

Talk at London Philharmonic Society club meeting, spring 1964

When I began playing the viola about 70 years ago, in the 1890s, I found that the comparatively few really good old violas were excessively large, clumsy, and most awkward to play. Not only that, but they were of vastly different sizes. Indeed, the body-length of these violas was anything between a good 17 and 18 inches, making them practically unmanageable. Some of them had been mutilated, and cut down to 15 or 16 inches long in order to make them easier to play.

The result was that the reduced air space did not, and could not, give us any semblance of the real C-string sonority which, after all, is the vital tone-quality of the viola. One of my objects, therefore, was to standardise the size, so that the player could go from one viola to another without any difficulty; and now I feel that this standardisation is well on the way.

'Wrestling Match'

I remember a colleague once remarking to me, about the very large instrument: 'The viola is difficult enough, without having to indulge in a wrestling match with it!'

In due course I came to the conclusion as to what the maximum size should be for playing under the chin; and eventually I decided that the ideal body length should be 16¾ inches; and this is the minimum from which to expect a rich tone quality. What I aimed to do was to obtain the same, or more, air space in them as was contained in the large instruments, hoping that the result would be a smaller and much more manageable viola but still with the characteristic C string sonority. I began by making the arching of the plates continuous, like a railway bridge.

This idea first came to me when I was a special constable in the First World War and one of my duties was patrolling under a railway bridge. The incessant heavy traffic going over this bridge brought home to me the great strength of continuous arching.

More Air Space

The usual contour of the plates of the violin, the viola and the cello is this: it begins by being flat for about half an inch or more. Then it rises to the centre, and follows the same procedure on the opposite side.

In my design the arching began immediately from the purfling; and in this way I gained extra air space all around the sides of the instrument, from both front and back plates.

With the same object in view – the gaining of more air space in this short-ened body length – I made the lower bouts abnormally wide – 10⅝ inches; and the centre bouts are also wide – 5¾ inches. In this way I gained quite another chunk of air space.

To the same end, I made the width of the ribs, at lower bouts, one and three quarter inches. This width tapers regularly to one and a half inches, which is practically normal at top bouts, so as not to impede the hand. Thus once again I increased air space.

In the old-master violas, the necks and fingerboards were very wide, making it unnecessarily difficult for the fourth finger to reach the C string. I therefore designed a neck and fingerboard as narrow as that of the violin – if violinists can play with that width of fingerboard, why shouldn't we viola players enjoy the same advantage?

The width of the nut at the top of the fingerboard I made identical with that of the violin – fifteen-sixteenths of an inch.

I also incorporated in the design another idea, making the insweep of the shoulder right up to the neck, so that the thumb could get well into the neck, allowing the player to reach the higher positions with greater ease. The old violas also had very long scrolls, and this I shortened, reducing leverage and weight – I reduced weight in the instrument wherever I could do so without affecting stability. For the same reason I used violin pegs as well.

In the bad old days the general opinion was that everything connected with the viola had to be heavy – even the bows were like broomsticks. Personally, I never used anything but the lighter violin bow, with a very strong stick. In my design the blocks inside the viola are semicircular. The bass-bar and sound post are further apart than they normally are, thus giving less congestion to the plate at the centre bout. I was able to do this because of the great strength achieved by the arching of the plates.

Made in 14 Lands

This is a brief survey of my theories and plans which led to the first Tertis Viola being made in 1937. There are now well over 600 of these violas, made by professional craftsman in 15 countries – in America, Canada, Australia, France, Denmark, Finland, Spain, Sweden, Bulgaria, Czechoslovakia, Germany, Holland, Italy, Israel and the UK – and played mostly by professionals.

Having come to this point with the viola, I said to myself: 'Why not a cello and violin on the same lines, but of course in proportion?' With the aid of my violin maker, Lawrence Cocker, I was able to put these ideas, too, into practice. The first cello was made in 1961, the second in 1962, followed at the end of that year by two violins.

These violins were first heard in public in June of last year, and since then both the new cello and the new violin are being made in six countries so far – in Italy, Denmark, America, Canada, Germany and South Africa.

Fraction of Antique Cost

My satisfaction with what has been achieved lies in the knowledge that string players can now obtain instruments with tone quality that will content them, at a fraction of the cost of antique instruments made by the old masters. I want to emphasise that I am not a violin maker, nor am I a scientist, nor do I know anything about acoustics – who does? But as a result of my 70 years of solo playing, during which I have handled a number of old master instruments, and from observation of them over this long period, I simply put two and two together, and eradicated some of their clumsy features.

I feel that the distribution of air space inside the instrument is the major influence on their tonal qualities, and apparently I have been very fortunate in achieving it.

Tertis's 'brief word', sent to William Primrose for publication

It was quite by chance that I became a Viola player. I was a young violin student at the Royal Academy of Music, London in the early 1890s when a colleague of mine there (an excellent violinist) who was very keen to indulge in quartet playing, asked me if I would take up the viola. There was no such 'curiosity'! as a violist at that time among the string players studying there.

The Academy possessed a so-called viola (extremely small) which I borrowed and worked at it for about three weeks at the same time learning to read the alto clef. At the end of that time in conjunction with my three fellow students (1st violin, 2nd violin and cello) played the Beethoven op. 18 no. 1 to the then principal of the Royal Academy of Music – Sir Alexander Mackenzie. After we had played the work to him in the concert hall of the RAM he came to the platform and asked me how long I had taken up the viola, and when I told him – three weeks, his reply was – 'In my opinion you will never regret it' and I never have. I loved the timbre and pitch of the instrument the first moment I played on it.

May I therefore offer the following advice to good violinists – Take up the viola. There are not enough good viola players. They will find themselves, if they do so, in much greater request. There are more than enough good violinists but not nearly enough good viola players. I would like to add that William Primrose once called himself a 'disciple' of mine, it happened thus:– Primrose in his younger days was a brilliant violinist and he was asked by Sir Thomas Beecham to join me in the Mozart Sinfonia Concertante at a concert in Paris with the Lamoureux Orchestra which Sir Thomas was conducting. After the concert William told me he was struck with the warm quality of the viola and as a consequence he discarded his violin and took up the viola. We all know the result – his world-wide reputation as a magnificent viola soloist.

I would like to add one word of warning to those who take my advice. Have nothing to do with so-called small violas. They do not possess, through lack of air space, a semblance of characteristic C string deep sonority which is one of the principle attractions of viola sound.

Other thoughts which I want to proffer are:
1) That it is the duty of all viola players to inveigle their composer friends to write for the viola.
2) It is also the duty of viola players to raid the repertory of the violin, cello or any other instrument and arrange and transcribe works from their catalogue suitable for the viola, and so enlarge our library.

∽ APPENDIX 4 ∽
Tertis's BBC Appearances

21 DECEMBER 1924
'Daily Express' wireless concert from the Chelmsford station,
including Maggie Teyte, Edna Thornton, Ben Davies,
Frederick Ranalow, John Goss, Lionel Tertis and George Reeves.

8.00 P.M. TUESDAY 10 NOVEMBER 1925 (NATIONAL)
Recital: Lionel Tertis (viola), York Bowen (piano)

Sonata	Dohnányi
'Komm, süsser Tod' ('Come, sweet death')	Bach–Tertis
Preludium and Allegro	Pugnani–Kreisler

9.52 P.M. SUNDAY 21 MARCH 1926
Recital: Lionel Tertis (viola), Harold Craxton (piano)

Aria	Porpora–Tertis
Fugue (unacc.)	Tartini–Kreisler
Allegretto	Wolstenholme
La Chasse	Cartier–Kreisler
Andante from Sonata, op. 19	Rachmaninov

9.35–11.04 P.M. MONDAY 9 MAY 1927 (NATIONAL)
'My Programme' by Stacy Aumonier
Tatiana Makushina (soprano), Gertrude Peppercorn (piano), Lionel Tertis
(viola), Eric Gritton (piano), R. Higgins (Monologue), Choir of All Saints'
– Margaret Street, Prof. E. N. da C. Andrade (Talk on 'Energy and Atoms').
The programme included

Sonata in D major	Padre Martini, arr. Endicott
	(Tertis with Gertrude Peppercorn)
Hier au Soir	Tertis
Allegretto	Wolstenholme
Slavonic Dance in G minor	Dvořák–Kreisler
Simplicity	Rebikoff–Tertis
Londonderry Air	arr. Tertis
Le Basque	Marais (Tertis with Eric Gritton)

10.03 P.M. THURSDAY 24 NOVEMBER 1927
(LONDON & DAVENTRY 5XX)

Lionel Tertis: The Future of the Viola with illustrations by himself

Two Songs	Brahms, arr. Tertis
Fugue (unacc.)	Tartini–Kreisler
Kalnins	Polish Folk Song, arr. Tertis
Romance, op. 2	B. J. Dale
Tambourin chinois	Kreisler–Tertis
Hier au Soir	Tertis
Le Basque	Marais

8.40 P.M. THURSDAY 12 JANUARY 1928
(LONDON & DAVENTRY 5XX)
Lionel Tertis Viola Recital

Rondeau	Marais, arr. Tertis
La Chasse	Cartier– Kreisler
Londonderry Air	arr. Tertis
Les Démons s'amusent	Rebikov–Tertis
Berceuse	Saint-Saëns, arr. Tertis
Slavonic Dance in G minor	Dvořák–Kreisler
Allegretto	Wolstenholme
Sunset	Tertis

3.30 P.M. SUNDAY 12 AUGUST 1928
(LONDON & DAVENTRY 5XX)

W.M.B. (Con. Lieut. P.S.G. O'Donnell), Megan Thomas (soprano),
Lionel Tertis (viola), Cecil Dixon (piano)

Sonata in, K305	Mozart, arr. Tertis
(Allegro molto, Thema con variazioni)	
3 Songs	Brahms, arr. Tertis
(Minnelied (Love Song), op. 71 no. 5;	
Wiegenlied (Lullaby), op. 49 no. 4;	
Wir wandelten (We Wandered), op. 96 no. 2)	

9.39 P.M. MONDAY 1 JULY 1929
(LONDON & DAVENTRY 5XX)

Recital: Dorothy Silk (soprano), Lionel Tertis (viola)

Songs: 'The soft complaining flute'	Handel
'Breathe soft ye winds'	Handel–Stark
'My mother bids me bind my hair'	Haydn
Serenade (*Hassan*)	Delius–Tertis

Preludium and Allegro	Pugnani–Kreisler
Andante (Sonata for cello and piano, op. 19)	Rachmaninov–Tertis
Songs: 'Come away, death', 'Polly Willis', 'The plague of love'	Arne
Slavonic Dance in G minor	Dvořák–Kreisler
Fugue (unacc.)	Tartini–Kreisler
Berceuse	Arensky
Le Basque	Marais
Songs: 'Longing in springtime'; 'Margaret's cradle song', 'Good morning', 'A Dream'	Grieg

10.22 P.M. MONDAY 13 JANUARY 1930 (LONDON & DAVENTRY 5XX)
Recital: Lionel Tertis (viola), Eric Gritton (piano)

Sonata no. 2	Delius trans. Tertis
Serenade (*Hassan*)	Delius–Tertis
Sonata in F minor, op. 45	Grieg–Tertis

8.00 P.M. FRIDAY 21 MARCH 1930 (NATIONAL)
Symphony Concert (XVIII) from the Queen's Hall

BBC Symphony Orchestra conducted by Sir Edward Elgar and Sir Thomas Beecham; Lionel Tertis (viola)

Overture 'The Wreckers'	Ethel Smyth
Introduction and Allegro	Bliss
Viola Concerto in E minor, op. 85	Elgar–Tertis
Symphony in C, K425	Mozart
Enigma Variations	Elgar

5.32 P.M. SUNDAY 10 AUGUST 1930 (NATIONAL)
Viola Recital: Lionel Tertis (viola), Cecil Dixon (piano)

Sarabande (Air on the G string)	Sulzer, arr. Tertis
Fugue (unacc.)	Tartini–Kreisler
Breath o' June	McEwen
Allegro vivace (No. 6 from *Six Studies in English Folk Song*)	Vaughan Williams
Londonderry Air	arr. Tertis
Liebeslied	Kreisler–Tertis
Hier au Soir	Tertis
Tambourin chinois	Kreisler–Tertis

10.14 P.M. TUESDAY 25 NOVEMBER 1930 (NATIONAL)
Lionel Tertis: Viola Recital

'Komm, süsser Tod' ('Come, sweet death')	Bach–Tertis
Chaconne from Partita in D minor, BWV1004	Bach, arr. Tertis

9.06 P.M. SUNDAY 11 JANUARY 1931 (LONDON REGIONAL)

Sunday Orchestral Concert (X)

BBC Orchestra conducted by John Barbirolli;

Antonio Brosa (violin), Lionel Tertis (viola), Cyril Scott (piano)

Overture *Rübezahl*	Weber
Early One Morning	Cyril Scott
Sinfonia concertante in E flat, K364	Mozart
Introduction; Ballet; Cortège (*Le Coq d'Or*)	Rimsky Korsakov

8.18 P.M. THURSDAY 26 MARCH 1931 (LONDON REGIONAL)

Royal Philharmonic Society Concert from the Queen's Hall
conducted by Ernest Ansermet; Lionel Tertis (viola)

Concerto Grosso in D minor	Handel
Viola Concerto	Walton
Harold in Italy	Berlioz

8.38 P.M. MONDAY 8 JUNE 1931 (LONDON REGIONAL)

Lionel Tertis: Viola Recital

Aria	Porpora, arr. Corti–Tertis
Fugue (unacc.)	Tartini–Kreisler
A Mosaic in Ten Pieces (acc. by the composer)	Richard H. Walthew

8.00 P.M. THURSDAY 10 SEPTEMBER 1931 (NATIONAL)

Promenade Concert from the Queen's Hall: BBC Symphony Orchestra
conducted by Sir Henry Wood; Lionel Tertis (viola)

Capriol Suite	Peter Warlock
Four Conceits	Eugène Goossens
Chrysilla and The Dance	Ethel Smyth (conducted by the composer)
Ballet Music (*The Perfect Fool*)	Holst
Song of Creation; The Faery Song	
(*The Immortal Hour*)	Rutland Boughton
Viola Concerto	William Walton (conducted by the composer)
The Rio Grande	Constant Lambert (conducted by the composer)

4.16 P.M. SUNDAY 15 NOVEMBER 1931 (NATIONAL)

Chamber Music: Lionel Tertis (viola), Harriet Cohen (piano),
Enid Cruickshank (contralto)

Sonata	Bax
Sonata in D	Martini–Endicott
Sonata no. 2	Delius trans. Tertis

8.15 P.M. WEDNESDAY 25 NOVEMBER 1931 (NATIONAL)

BBC Symphony Concert (VI) from the Queen's Hall conducted by Adrian
Boult; S. Robertson (baritone), Albert Sammons (violin), Lionel Tertis (viola),
& National Chorus

Symphony no. 88 in G	Haydn
Sinfonia concertante in E flat, K364	Mozart
Hammersmith (A Prelude and Scherzo)	Holst
Belshazzar's Feast	Walton (1st London performance)

9.10 P.M. SUNDAY 10 JANUARY 1932 (LONDON REGIONAL)

Sunday Orchestral Concert (XI): BBC Orchestra (Sec.B) conducted
E. Bainton; Lionel Tertis (viola)

Overture, Scherzo and Finale	Schumann
Viola Concerto in E minor, op. 85	Elgar–Tertis
Epithalamion	Bainton
Overture *Les Francs Juges*	Berlioz

7.30 P.M. THURSDAY 21 JANUARY 1932 (MIDLAND REGIONAL)

Symphony Concert from the Town Hall, Birmingham: City of Birmingham
Orchestra conducted by L. Heward; Lionel Tertis (viola)

Overture: *Susanna's Secret*	Wolf-Ferrari
Symphonic Variations on an original theme, op. 78	Dvořák
Viola Concerto	Walton
Romance for viola and orchestra	B. J. Dale

5.30 P.M. EASTER SUNDAY 27 MARCH 1932 (NATIONAL)

Lionel Tertis: Viola Recital

Les Rêves (Dreams) (Naiade)	Rebikov–Tertis
Les Démons s'amusent	Rebikov
Old Irish Air	Traditional–Tertis
Hornpipe	Korngold–Tertis
Plantation Dance	Albert Sammons
Fantasia on Greensleeves:	Vaughan Williams
Allegro Vivace (No.6 from *Six Studies in English Folk Song*)	Vaughan Williams
Elegy and Caprice	Delius–Tertis

8.00 P.M. TUESDAY 23 AUGUST 1932 (LONDON REGIONAL)

Promenade Concert (British Composers) from the Queen's Hall:

BBC Symphony Orchestra conducted by Sir Henry Wood;

Betty Bannerman (contralto), K. Falkner (baritone); Lionel Tertis (viola)

Overture *The Queen of Cornwall*   Rutland Boughton (conducted by the composer)
Viola Concerto in E minor, op. 85   Elgar–Tertis
Three movements from *The Planets*   Holst (conducted by the composer)

9.01 P.M. SATURDAY 29 OCTOBER 1932 (LONDON REGIONAL)

BBC Chamber Concert (III): Lionel Tertis (viola), Solomon (piano)

Sonata   Bax
Sonata in F minor, op. 120 no. 1   Brahms

8.00 P.M. THURSDAY 1 DECEMBER 1932 (SCOTTISH REGIONAL)

from the Usher Hall, Edinburgh: Reid Symphony Orchestra conducted by

Adrian Boult; Lionel Tertis (viola)

Symphony in C minor   Haydn
Springtime on Tweed   W. B. Moonie
Viola Concerto   Walton (played twice)

8.14 P.M. THURSDAY 9 MARCH 1933 (LONDON REGIONAL)

Royal Philharmonic Society concert, from the Queen's Hall

London Philharmonic Orchestra conducted by Sir Thomas Beecham;

Albert Sammons (violin), Lionel Tertis (viola)

Overture *William Tell*   Rossini
Sinfonia concertante in E flat, K364   Mozart
Symphony no.2 in C   Tchaikovsky

9.49 P.M. MONDAY 24 JULY 1933 (NATIONAL)

Chamber Music: Lionel Tertis (viola), Solomon (piano)

Suite   Bloch
Sonata in E flat, op. 120 no. 2   Brahms

9.02 P.M. FRIDAY 3 NOVEMBER 1933 (LONDON REGIONAL)

BBC Chamber Concert (II): Lionel Tertis (viola), Solomon (piano)

Sonata for viola and piano   Bliss (1st performance)
Piano Sonata in B minor, op. 58   Chopin
Sonata no. 3 for viola and piano   Delius–Tertis

9.36 P.M. THURSDAY 28 DECEMBER 1933 (NATIONAL)

Recital: Lionel Tertis (viola), Vitya Vronsky and V. Babin (2 pianos)

'Chant de Roxane'	Szymanowski–Kochanski–Tertis
Les Démons s'amusent	Rebikov–Tertis
Slavonic Dance in G minor	Dvořák–Tertis
Étude no. 4	Scriabin–Kochanski
Mouvements perpetuels	Poulenc–Heifetz–Tertis
Lullaby	Alice Verne-Bredt–Tertis
Le Basque	Marais

7.58 P.M. MONDAY 8 JANUARY 1934 (LONDON REGIONAL)

Fourth concert of British Music from the Queen's Hall

BBC Symphony Orchestra conducted by Adrian Boult;

Parry Jones (tenor), Lionel Tertis (viola), Wireless Chorus

Sinfonietta	Eugène Goossens
Two Songs from *The Immortal Hour*	Rutland Boughton
Flos campi	Vaughan Williams
Symphony no. 4	Bax

WEDNESDAY 10 JANUARY 1934

Gramophone recital programme

included Lionel Tertis (viola); George Reeves (piano)

Minnelied (Love Song), op. 71 no. 5	Brahms–Tertis
Serenade (*Hassan*)	Delius–Tertis

9.10 P.M. SUNDAY 18 MARCH 1934 (LONDON REGIONAL)

Sunday Orchestral Concert (XVIII)

BBC Symphony Orchestra (Sec. B) conducted by Adrian Boult;

Lionel Tertis and Bernard Shore (violas)

Brandenburg Concerto no. 6 in B flat (arr. for 2 solo violas)	Bach–Tertis
Rondino in E flat for wind	Beethoven
Lyric Movement for viola and orchestra	Holst (1st performance)
Symphony no. 3 in A minor	Mendelssohn

8.01 P.M. SATURDAY 4 AUGUST 1934 (LONDON REGIONAL)

Recital: Lionel Tertis (viola), Solomon (piano)

Variations on a Theme of Mozart, op.66	Beethoven–Tertis
Sonata, op. 21	Dohnányi–Tertis
Piano solos	Schumann & Brahms
Andante and Allegro scherzando (Sonata, op. 19)	Rachmaninov–Tertis
Sonata in E flat, op. 120 no. 2	Brahms

8.01 P.M. TUESDAY 14 AUGUST 1934 (LONDON REGIONAL)

Promenade Concert from the Queen's Hall

BBC Symphony Orchestra conducted by Sir Henry Wood; May Blyth
(soprano), P. Heming (baritone), Lionel Tertis (viola)

Symphonic Poem *The Fountains of Rome*	Respighi
Song with orchestra 'To the Forest'	Tchaikovsky
Phantasy for viola and orchestra	Bax
Three Fragments from *Wozzeck*	Berg
La Mer (Three Symphonic Sketches)	Debussy
Theme and Variations from Suite no. 3 in G	Tchaikovsky
Song (with piano) 'Edward'	Loewe
Norwegian Rhapsody	Lalo

8.33 P.M. WEDNESDAY 14 NOVEMBER 1934 (NATIONAL)

BBC Symphony Concert (III) from the Queen's Hall

BBC Symphony Orchestra conducted by Sir Henry Wood;
Lionel Tertis (viola), Pablo Casals (cello)

Brandenburg Concerto no.6 in B flat	Bach
Symphony no. 35 in D, 'Haffner'	Mozart
Cello Concerto in D	Haydn
Symphonic Poem *Don Quixote*	Strauss
Siegfried's Journey to the Rhine	Wagner

9.30 P.M. SUNDAY 2 DECEMBER 1934 (LONDON REGIONAL)

Sunday Orchestral Concert (VII): BBC Symphony Orchestra (Sec.B)
conducted by Aylmer Buesst; Lionel Tertis (viola)

Introduction to Act III, *Lohengrin*	Wagner
Viola Concerto	Walton
Symphonia Domestica	Strauss

9.04 P.M. FRIDAY 25 JANUARY 1935 (REGIONAL)

BBC Chamber Concert (IV)

Lionel Tertis (viola), Artur Rubinstein (piano)

Chaconne from Partita in D minor, BWV1004	Bach, arr. Tertis
Piano solos	Schumann
Variations on a theme of Mozart, op.66	Beethoven–Tertis

(N.B. The concert also included the Bliss Sonata, which was not broadcast)

9.23 P.M. SUNDAY 3 MARCH 1935 (REGIONAL)

Sunday Orchestral Concert (XVI)

BBC Symphony Orchestra (Sec. B) conducted by Adrian Boult;

May Harrison (violin), Lionel Tertis (viola)

Overture *Froissart*	Elgar
Scherzo	Holst
Double Concerto	Delius trans. Tertis
(1st performance of this version)	
Symphony no. 5	Bax

9.21 P.M. SUNDAY 5 MAY 1935 (LONDON REGIONAL)

British Composers Programme

BBC Symphony Orchestra (Sec. B) conducted by Sir Henry Wood;

Dora Labbette (soprano), A. Fear (baritone), Lionel Tertis (viola)

Overture *The Wasps*	Vaughan Williams
Idyll	Delius
Viola Concerto	Walton
Symphonic Poem *Lamia*	Dorothy Howell
Spanish Fantasy	Berners

8.02 P.M. THURSDAY 5 SEPTEMBER 1935 (NATIONAL)

Promenade Concert from the Queen's Hall

BBC Symphony Orchestra conducted by Sir Henry Wood;

J. van der Gucht (tenor), Lionel Tertis (viola)

Overture *Leonora* no. 3	Beethoven
Rondo arlecchinesco	Busoni
Suite for viola and orchestra	Vaughan Williams
Symphony no. 1 in A flat	Elgar

3.15 P.M. WEDNESDAY 18 DECEMBER 1935 (NATIONAL)

Symphony Concert from The Pavilion, Bournemouth

Bournemouth Municipal Orchestra conducted by Richard Austin;

Lionel Tertis (viola)

Overture *Manfred*	Schumann
Suite in D	Bach
Suite for viola and orchestra	Vaughan Williams
Symphonic Suite *Scheherazade*	Rimsky-Korsakoff

9.31 P.M. SUNDAY 22 DECEMBER 1935 (REGIONAL)

Sunday Orchestral Concert (XI)

BBC Symphony Orchestra (Sec. B) conducted by Adrian Boult;

Lionel Tertis (viola)

Overture *Hansel and Gretel*	Humperdinck
Viola Concerto in D (originally for cello)	Haydn–Tertis
Prelude to Act III *Tristan and Isolde*	Wagner
Symphonic Poem *Death and Transfiguration*	R. Strauss

8.31 P.M. WEDNESDAY 26 FEBRUARY 1936 (NATIONAL)

BBC Symphony Concert (IX) from the Queen's Hall

BBC Symphony Orchestra conducted by Sir Henry Wood;

Adolf Busch (violin), Lionel Tertis (viola)

Overture, Elegy and Rondo	Bax
Sinfonia concertante in E flat, K364	Mozart
Symphony no. 1 in E minor	Sibelius

8.15 P.M. TUESDAY 21 APRIL 1936 (NATIONAL)

from the Tonhalle, Bern, Switzerland: BBC Symphony Orchestra

conducted by Adrian Boult; Lionel Tertis (viola)

Prelude *Die Meistersinger*	Wagner
Two Studies from *Doktor Faust*	Busoni
Viola Concerto	Walton

SUNDAY 21 JUNE 1936 (NATIONAL)

Recital: Lionel Tertis (viola), Solomon (piano)

Sonata no. 2	Delius, trans. Tertis
Suite	Bloch

9.31 P.M. TUESDAY 29 SEPTEMBER 1936 (REGIONAL)

BBC Symphony Orchestra (Sec. C) conducted by John Barbirolli;

Lionel Tertis (viola)

Suite for small orchestra	Roger-Ducasse
Suite for viola and orchestra	Vaughan Williams
Norwegian Rhapsody no. 2 in A	Svendsen

9.42 P.M. WEDNESDAY 7 OCTOBER 1936 (NATIONAL)

Sonata Recital: Lionel Tertis (viola), Solomon (piano)

Sonata in F minor, op.120 no.1	Brahms
Variations on a theme of Mozart, op.66	Beethoven–Tertis
Sonata	Bliss

8.31 P.M. FRIDAY 1 JANUARY 1937 (NATIONAL)

Viola Recital: Lionel Tertis

Sarabande (Air on the G string)	Sulzer, arr. Tertis
Two Interlinked French Folk Melodies	Smyth–Tertis
Mouvements perpetuels	Poulenc–Heifetz–Tertis
Slow Waltz (*The Christmas Tree*)	Rebikov
Caprice	Delius–Tertis
Wir Wandelten and Des Liebsten Schwur	Brahms
Fugue (unacc.)	Tartini–Kreisler
Allegretto	Schubert–Tertis

8.14 P.M. WEDNESDAY 24 FEBRUARY 1937 (NATIONAL)

BBC Symphony Concert (XII) from the Queen's Hall: BBC Symphony Orchestra conducted by Ernest Ansermet; Lionel Tertis (viola)

Symphonie *Mathis der Maler*	Hindemith
Viola Concerto	Walton
Harold in Italy	Berlioz

9.30–10 00 P.M. 16 NOVEMBER 1939

Viola Recital: Lionel Tertis

Sonata in D	Martini, arr. Endicott
Allegretto	Schubert–Tertis
Carol and Moto Perpetuo from Suite	Vaughan Williams

9.25–10.00 P.M. SUNDAY 16 FEBRUARY 1941

'The BBC Presents' from Broadcasting House, Bristol

The programme, compèred by Patric Curwen, linked Lionel Tertis with the story of the viola, formerly the 'Cinderella' of string instruments, and told how Mr Tertis had championed the viola and brought it into the limelight. It included 'The Londonderry Air' and a recording of a short discussion between Tertis and the composer B. J. Dale. (Made on the then new glass discs, which broke very easily.)

7.45–8.00 P.M. TUESDAY 15 JULY 1941 (HOME SERVICE)

(Recorded in Studio XX, St John's Parish Hall, Bristol)

Recital: Lionel Tertis (viola), John Wills (piano)

The Holy Boy	John Ireland–Tertis
Hornpipe	Handel–Harty–Tertis
Lullaby	Verne-Bredt–Tertis
Canzona	Wolstenholme–Tertis
Slavonic Dance in G minor	Dvořák–Kreisler

23.30–24.00 GMT/1.30–2.00 A.M. DBST 24–5 July 1941
(BBC North American Service: Evesham)
Lionel Tertis (viola), Frederick Stone (piano)

Serenade (*Hassan*)	Delius–Tertis
'Chant de Roxane'	Szymanowski–Kochanski–Tertis
Sonata in E	Martini–Endicott

01.30–02.00 GMT September 5/6 1941
(BBC Latin-American Service: Evesham)
Lionel Tertis (viola)

Romance, op. 2	B. J. Dale
A Mosaic in Ten Pieces	R. H. Walthew
Lullaby	Verne-Bredt–Tertis

9.15–9.45 P.M. BST 14 November 1941 (BBC African Service)
Tertis gave a recital as part of Empire Music Week.

(A letter from the BBC to Tertis stated that: 'As you probably know it is our custom to pay three-quarter fee for broadcasts given in our Overseas Service between the hours of 9.00 a.m. and 12.00 midnight'. He received £27 11s. 3d. inclusive.)

N.B. Details of all the Overseas Service programmes as broadcast are missing for November 1941

(The *Radio Times* dated 26 December 1941
included an article about Tertis's 65th birthday.)

7.35 P.M. Monday 29 December 1941 (Home Service: Manchester)
BBC Northern Orchestra conducted by Julian Clifford; Lionel Tertis (viola)

Suite	Vaughan Williams
(10.50 p.m.):	
Sonata in F	Handel–Tertis (1st performance in this form)
Romance, op. 2	B. J. Dale
Slavonic Dance in G minor	Dvořák–Kreisler
Sunset	Tertis

(Tertis played as an encore Allegretto by Schubert, arr. Tertis)

02.30–03.00 BST 6/7 March 1942
(BBC Latin-American Transmission)
Live broadcast from Studio 13 Wood Norton, Evesham: Lionel Tertis (viola)

Andante (Sonata, op.19)	Rachmaninov–Tertis
Sonata 3 in C minor, op.45	Grieg–Tertis

5 APRIL 1942

'Everybody's Scrapbook'. Tertis's contributions were:

Minnelied (15th century song)   arr. & words Tertis
with John Morel (baritone) and Alan Paul (piano)
Londonderry Air   arr. Tertis, orch. Henry Reed
with BBC Revue Orchestra conducted by Mansel Thomas

9.45–10.15 P.M. MONDAY 25 MAY 1942 (BBC AFRICAN SERVICE)
broadcast from Studio 13 Wood Norton, Evesham: Lionel Tertis (viola)

Viola Sonata   Bliss

WEDNESDAY 19 AUGUST 1942
BBC Promenade Concert: BBC Symphony Orchestra conducted by
Sir Adrian Boult; Lionel Tertis (viola)

Triptych – 3 Impressions for viola and orchestra   Thomas Dunhill (1st performance)

8.15 A.M. 22 OCTOBER 1942 (BBC PACIFIC SERVICE: LIVE BROADCAST)
Recital: Lionel Tertis (viola), Frederick Stone (piano)

Aria	Porpora–Tertis
Allegro	Martini–Endicott
Rêverie	D'Ambrosio–Tertis
Fugue (unacc.)	Tartini–Kreisler

2.15–2.45 A.M. MONDAY/TUESDAY 30 NOVEMBER/1 DECEMBER 1942
(OVERSEAS LATIN-AMERICAN TRANSMISSION FROM ALDENHAM)
Lionel Tertis (viola), Frederick Stone (piano)

Sonata in F minor, op. 120 no. 1   Brahms
Sonata in D   Martini–Endicott

10.30–10.45 & 11.30–11.45 FRIDAY 11 DECEMBER 1942
(OVERSEAS EUROPEAN TRANSMISSION)
Lionel Tertis (viola), Frederick Stone (piano)

Suite   Vaughan Williams
(N.B. The Suite was broadcast in two parts – Part 1 groups 1 & 2, Part 2 group 3)

10.45–11.10 P.M. MONDAY 14 DECEMBER 1942
(HOME SERVICE: BEDFORD)
Lionel Tertis (viola), John Ireland (piano)

Cello Sonata (arr. for viola)   John Ireland–Tertis
(1st broadcast of the viola version)
Holy Boy   John Ireland–Tertis

2.30–4.30 P.M. SATURDAY 10 JULY 1943 (HOME SERVICE: BEDFORD)

BBC Symphony Orchestra conducted by Clarence Raybould;

Lionel Tertis (viola)

Programme included:

Viola Concerto in B minor   Handel–Casadesus

A Mosaic in Ten Pieces   Richard Walthew

(1st performance with orchestra)

Viola Concerto in B minor   Handel–Casadesus

03.45–04.00 A.M. DBST TUESDAY 3/4 AUGUST 1943

(BBC LATIN AMERICAN SERVICE)

live broadcast from Boreham Wood

Recital: Lionel Tertis (viola), John Wills (piano)

Sonata no. 2   Delius trans. Tertis

9.30–10.00 A.M. MONDAY 15 SEPTEMBER 1943

from London – European Music

Lionel Tertis (viola), John Ireland (piano)

Cello Sonata (arr. for viola)   John Ireland–Tertis

Holy Boy   John Ireland–Tertis

12.45–13.15 18 FEBRUARY 1944 (BBC EASTERN SERVICE)

Purple Network – India, Burma and Indonesia

'Through Western Ears' – Lionel Tertis (viola), John Wills (piano)

Live discussion between Lionel Tertis and Z. A. Bokhari with commercial

discs and live veena playing by Dr. Menon

Tertis's contributions to the programme were:

Slavonic Dance no. 1 in G minor   Dvořák–Kreisler

A short quotation from an Indian raga on the viola

Londonderry Air   arr. Tertis

This was Lionel Tertis's first broadcast to India and the BBC asked him, through his agent Ibbs & Tillett, to do it for a special low fee of 15 guineas.

2.30–3.45 P.M. SUNDAY 5 MARCH 1944 (HOME SERVICE: LONDON)

(Studio VIII Broadcasting House)

Lionel Tertis (viola), Solomon (piano)

Sonata in E flat, op. 120 no. 2   Brahms

Sonata   Bliss

3.30–4.45 P.M. MONDAY 1 MAY 1944 (HOME SERVICE: BEDFORD)
BBC Symphony Orchestra conducted by Sir Adrian Boult;
Lionel Tertis (viola)

Suite for viola and orchestra   Bloch

13 MAY 1944 (BBC: BOREHAM WOOD)
Recital: Lionel Tertis (viola)

Holy Boy	John Ireland–Tertis
Canzona	Wolstenholme–Tertis
Londonderry Air	Tertis
Slavonic Dance in G minor	Dvořák–Kreisler

02.30–02.45 A.M. TUESDAY/WEDNESDAY 13/14 JUNE 1944
(BBC LATIN AMERICAN SERVICE : ALDENHAM)
Recital: Lionel Tertis (viola), Henry Bronkhurst (piano)

7.00 P.M. THURSDAY 10 AUGUST 1944
BBC Promenade Concert from the Royal Albert Hall (broadcast direct)
BBC Symphony Orchestra, with Lionel Tertis (viola)

Viola Concerto   Walton

FRIDAY 11 AUGUST 1944 (HOME SERVICE)
Studio broadcast (from Bedford) of Walton Concerto

5.30–5.45 P.M. DBST 15 SEPTEMBER 1944 (BBC EASTERN SERVICE)
Recital: Lionel Tertis (viola)

'Chant de Roxane'	Szymanowski–Kochanski–Tertis
Fugue (unacc.)	Tartini–Kreisler
Lullaby	Verne-Bredt–Tertis

Tertis was asked by Hubert Clifford, Empire Music Supervisor: 'Ideally it should be quite a serious programme and should be designed to show off various aspects of viola playing'.

3.30–4.30 P.M. 29 OCTOBER 1944 (HOME SERVICE: LONDON)
from Studio IV, Oxford Street
Lionel Tertis (viola), Solomon (piano)

Piano Sonata in C, op.2 no.3	Beethoven
Suite	Bloch

1.30–1.45 A.M. WEDNESDAY/THURSDAY 1/2 NOVEMBER 1944
(BBC LATIN AMERICAN SERVICE: ALDENHAM)
Recital: Lionel Tertis (viola), Henry Bronkhurst (piano)

Sonata in D	Martini–Endicott
Andante (Sonata, op. 19)	Rachmaninov–Tertis

Tertis's inclusive fee was £37 15s. 0d.

11.45 A.M. 14 DECEMBER 1944 (HOME SERVICE)
'Viola and Voice', a programme of gramophone records,
including Lionel Tertis (viola), playing

Preludium and Allegro	Pugnani–Kreisler–Tertis
Chant sans paroles	Tchaikovsky–Tertis
Minnelied (Love Song), op. 71 no. 5	Brahms–Tertis
Old Irish Air	Traditional–Tertis
Sonata no. 2	Delius, trans. Tertis
Serenade (*Hassan*)	Delius–Tertis

The programme also included a number of songs performed by Roy Henderson (baritone)

2.30–3.00 A.M. TUESDAY/WEDNESDAY 15/16 MAY 1945
(BBC LATIN AMERICAN SERVICE)
Recital: Lionel Tertis (viola), John Wills (piano)

Sonata in E flat, op. 120 no. 2	Brahms
Allegro in D	Martini–Endicott
Rondeau	Marais

7.15–7.45 P.M. SUNDAY 9 DECEMBER 1945
(LIGHT PROGRAMME: LONDON)
'Richard Tauber', including Lionel Tertis, who played *Elégie* by Fauré,
with the George Melachrino Orchestra.

2.30–1.00 A.M. TUESDAY/WEDNESDAY 12/13 FEBRUARY 1946
(BBC LATIN AMERICAN SERVICE: ALDENHAM)
Recital: Lionel Tertis (viola), Ernest Lush (piano)

Sonata in E	Martini–Endicott
Variations on a theme of Mozart, op. 66	Beethoven–Tertis
Romance, op. 2	B. J. Dale

WEDNESDAY 27 FEBRUARY 1946
Broadcast from People's Palace: 'Music of our Time'
Lionel Tertis (viola)

Flos campi   Vaughan Williams

1.30–2.00 A.M. TUESDAY/WEDNESDAY 6/7 AUGUST 1946
(BBC LATIN AMERICAN SERVICE: LONDON)
Recital: Lionel Tertis (viola), Ernest Lush (piano)

Allegro in D	Martini–Endicott
A Mosaic in Ten Pieces	Walthew
Lullaby	Verne-Bredt–Tertis
The Answer	Wolstenholme–Tertis
Allegretto	Schubert–Tertis
Rondeau	Marais

27 JUNE 1947 (HOME SERVICE)
This Week's Composer – Mozart (repeat)
Probably included record of *Sinfonia concertante* with Albert Sammons
(violin), Lionel Tertis (viola)

TUESDAY 19 AUGUST 1947 (THIRD PROGRAMME)
BBC Promenade Concert from the Royal Albert Hall
London Philharmonic Orchestra conducted by Basil Cameron;
Lionel Tertis (viola), Moura Lympany (piano) Isobel Baillie (soprano)

Harold in Italy	Berlioz
Piano Concerto no.21 in C, K467	Mozart
Aria: 'A maiden's is an evil plight' (*La finta giardiniera*)	Mozart

12 OCTOBER 1947
Repeated on Home Service (AR) on Sunday Morning Prom

8.00 P.M. MONDAY 13 OCTOBER 1947 (THIRD PROGRAMME)
Vaughan Williams Birthday Concert
Items with Lionel Tertis (viola) included

Flos campi
Four Hymns for tenor, viola and orchestra

10.15 A.M. 1 APRIL 1951
'Sunday Morning Prom' (repeat)

11.30 A.M. 30 DECEMBER 1951 (HOME SERVICE)

'Music Magazine' Tribute to Lionel Tertis on his 75th birthday

Record: Serenade (*Hassan*)   Delius, arr. Tertis

10.15 A.M. 20 JULY 1952 (HOME SERVICE)

Sunday Morning Prom (repeat)

3 AUGUST 1954 (WEST OF ENGLAND HOME SERVICE)

Lionel Tertis presented 'In the Gramophone Library'

His selection of recordings were:

The Musical Box	*(Solomon – piano)*
Hungarian Fantasia for piano and orchestra	Liszt *(Solomon)*
String Quartet in D minor, op.posth. D810, 'Death and the Maiden' (finale)	Schubert
Caprice Viennoise	Kreisler *(Larry Adler – harmonica)*
La Campanella	Paganini *(William Primrose – viola)*
Minnelied (Love Song), op. 71 no. 5	Brahms *(Lionel Tertis – viola)*

Tertis then gave a live performance of *Aria Amorosa* by Galuppi

5.15–6.00 P.M. 12 DECEMBER 1956 (HOME SERVICE)

Included a five minute talk 'Casals and Tertis'

10.00–10.30 P.M. 28 DECEMBER 1956 (HOME SERVICE)

(Supplement to Music Magazine)

Julian Herbage introduced a joint tribute to Casals and Tertis on the eve of their 80th birthdays. Tertis spoke briefly on how the 'Tertis Model' came about, and played a few illustrations on the instrument; a section of Melody on the G String, a few bars on the C string and two songs with viola obbligato with the singer Alvar Lidell – 'Come again, sweet love' and a 15th century folk-song 'The birds are silent in the trees', with piano accompaniment. Finally Bernard Shore paid tribute to his former teacher.

9.30 P.M. 14 JULY 1957 (HOME SERVICE)

Lionel Tertis (viola), Ernest Lush (piano)

Sonata in F minor, op.120 no.1	Brahms
Andante (Sonata, op. 19)	Rachmaninov–Tertis

These performances were recorded on TLO 19013 as a permanent recording for the BBC library.

8.00 P.M. 28 JULY 1957 (BBC TRANSCRIPTION SERVICE: KING'S LYNN)

Lionel Tertis played with the King's Lynn Festival Ensemble

7.00 P.M. 20 NOVEMBER 1957 (HOME SERVICE)

Tertis took part in a programme about the violinist Albert Sammons

1962? (SOUTH-EAST REGION)

Radio 4 PM programme: Sue MacGregor interviewed Tertis on his musical
career and his friendship with Pablo Casals

1.10 P.M. 13 AUGUST 1962

Lionel Tertis was the castaway on the BBC programme 'Desert Island Discs'
in which he spoke to Roy Plomley (the speech inserts were prerecorded on 23
July 1962). His choice of eight gramophone records were:

Overture 'The Bartered Bride'	Smetana *(New York Philharmonic Orchestra conducted by Sir John Barbirolli)*
Piano Concerto no.3 in C minor (part of finale)	Beethoven *(Solomon with the Philharmonia Orchestra conducted by Herbert Menges)*
Oboe Concerto in C major (part of 1st movement)	attrib. Haydn *(Evelyn Rothwell with the Hallé Orchestra conducted by Sir John Barbirolli)*
Waltz Brilliant in A flat, op.34 no.1	Chopin *(Artur Rubinstein – piano)*
String Quartet in A major (1st movement)	Boccherini *(Carmirelli String Quartet)*
Folies Musicales	Betove
Imitations of *Chansonette chinoise*	Betove
Cherry Ripe	Cyril Scott *(Lionel Tertis – viola)*
Tambourin chinois	Kreisler
	(Fritz Kreisler – violin, Franz Rupp – piano)

This programme was repeated in 'Pick of the Week' on 17 August 1962 at 1.10 p.m.

4.15 P.M. 29 SEPTEMBER 1963

'In Praise of Sir John Barbirolli' included a short interview with Lionel Tertis

29 DECEMBER 1963 (HOME SERVICE)

BBC Music Magazine: Pablo Casals and Lionel Tertis –
a birthday greeting by Arthur Jacobs

12.56 P.M. 18 APRIL 1965 (MUSIC PROGRAMME)

There was a short interval discussion with members of the jury
(including Lionel Tertis) for the BBC violin competition

11.00 A.M. 25 DECEMBER 1966

Music Magazine with Julian Herbage:
Ninetieth birthday tribute to Pablo Casals and Lionel Tertis

Tertis gave a short interview (not used) for a programme 'Friends and Contemporaries of Harriet Cohen' introduced by Roy Plomley

3.05–4.10 P.M. 29 DECEMBER 1966

Lionel Tertis 90th birthday, introduced by Lionel Tertis

Sinfonia concertante in E flat, K364	Mozart *(record: London Philharmonic Orchestra conducted by Sir Hamilton Harty; Albert Sammons – violin, Lionel Tertis – viola)*
Variations on a four-bar theme of Handel for viola and cello	Tertis *(Harry Danks – viola, Lillian Tertis – cello)*
Trio, op. 87 for three violas	Beethoven, arr. Tertis *(Harry Danks, Cecil Aronowitz, Margaret Major – violas)*
Preludium and Allegro	Kreisler, after Pugnani, arr. Tertis *(record: Lionel Tertis – viola, Ethel Hobday – piano)*

5.00 P.M. 29 DECEMBER 1970 (RADIO 4)

Lionel Tertis interviewed about his music career on the 'PM' programme

11.00 A.M. 26 DECEMBER 1971

Music Magazine: Double Anniversary: Pablo Casals and Lionel Tertis, who were born on 29 December 1876: Bernard Shore talks about Lionel Tertis

10.25–11.20 A.M. 26 OCTOBER 1972 (RADIO 3)

'For Mrs Elizabeth Sprague Coolidge'.
Tertis spoke for 3 minutes on his recollections of Mrs Coolidge

2.05–2.50 P.M. 28 DECEMBER 1973 (RADIO 3)

'Wrap Him in Gold': A Tribute to Lionel Tertis

The title is the comment of a Concertgebouw Orchestra player after Tertis had rehearsed with them. Bernard Keefe, on the eve of Tertis's 97th birthday, presented a celebration of an artist who raised the Cinderella of instruments out of obscurity, and inspired the admiration and friendship of many other famous musicians. He talked to some of them, and to Tertis himself. There were contributions from Gerald Moore, Sir Arthur Bliss, Lady Dorothy Mayer, Artur Rubinstein, Paul Cropper and Harry Danks. Tertis's recordings played were *Minnelied*, op. 71 no. 5, by Brahms–Tertis, *Song Without Words*, op. 20 in E flat, 'The Fleecy Cloud', by Mendelssohn–Tertis, and part of the 3rd movement of Mozart's *Sinfonia concertante*, with Albert Sammons (violin) and the London Philharmonic Orchestra conducted by Harty.

OTHER BROADCASTS RELATED TO TERTIS

20 FEBRUARY 1959

South African Broadcasting Concert Hall, Cape Town

Lionel Tertis (viola), Arthur Woodland (piano)

Allegretto	Wolstenholme–Tertis
Aria amorosa	Galuppi–Tertis
Allegro	Martini–Endicott
Romance, op. 2	B. J. Dale

11 JUNE 1960

Danish National Radio Station, Copenhagen, Denmark

Lionel Tertis (viola), Lillian Tertis (cello)

Duet for viola and cello 'Eyeglass'   Beethoven

13 SEPTEMBER 1988 (RADIO 3)

'The Tertis Legacy': Harry Danks, viola player, talks to Paul Hindmarsh about his former friend and teacher Lionel Tertis. (Recorded during the 3rd Lionel Tertis International Viola Competition and Workshop at Port Erin, Isle of Man, in August 1988).

AUGUST 1990

Broadcast Prom Talks: Paul Silverthorne talks about Lionel Tertis's arrangement for viola of the Elgar Cello Concerto.

5 DECEMBER 1991 (RADIO 3)

'His Master's Voice': As part of the 200th anniversary of Mozart's death, Robert Philip presents some 'unusual' recordings of his music, including the *Sinfonia concertante* played by Albert Sammons (violin) and Lionel Tertis (viola).

1 AUGUST 1995

BBC Vintage Years: William Walton (1902–1983) presented by John Amis included a Tertis recording

8 AUGUST 1998

David Mellor explores the recorded legacy of great artists of the past. Viola player Lionel Tertis was born in 1876 on the same day as his great friend cellist Pablo Casals. As a boy, Roger Chase had a lesson with Tertis, then in his nineties, and witnessed the energy that had driven him to rescue the viola from its lowly status at the turn of the century. Decades later, that energy still burns in the grooves of Tertis's recordings and in the new life he gave his instrument.

Preludium and Allegro   Kreisler *(Ethel Hobday – piano)*

Chaconne from Partita in D minor, BWV1004   Bach, arr. Tertis

Piano Trio no. 2 in C minor, op.66 (excerpt)   Mendelssohn *(Albert Sammons –*
violin, William Murdoch – piano)

Après un rêve, op.7 no.1   Fauré, arr. Tertis *(unnamed pianist)*

Sinfonia concertante in E flat, K364   Mozart, ed. Tertis *(Albert Sammons –*
violin; London Philharmonic Orchestra
conducted by Hamilton Harty)

Tertis's Honours

1900 Associate of the Royal Academy of Music (ARAM)

1921 Knight of the Order of the Crown
awarded by King Albert of the Belgians for services to the Belgian cause
during the First World War and his efforts to raise the status of the viola

1922 Fellow of the Royal Academy (FRAM)

1946 Cobbett Gold Medal for Services to Chamber Music
endowed by W. W. Cobbett, and presented by the Worshipful Company
of Musicians

1950 Commander of the British Empire (CBE)
awarded by King George VI 'for services to music particularly in relation
to the viola'

1950 Kreisler Award of Merit
awarded by the Musicians' Benevolent Fund

1964 Eugène Ysaÿe Medal

1964 Gold Medal of the Royal Philharmonic Society
presented by Sir John Barbirolli: '... a unique figure in our musical life,
revered as the greatest viola virtuoso of our time'

1966 Honorary Fellow of Trinity College London (Hon. FTCL)

Music with Tertis Connections

Music for solo viola, viola and piano, viola and orchestra, with a selection of other works featuring the viola (or violas) with other instruments or voice plus one original work for solo piano by Tertis.

From the early years of the twentieth century until his sudden retirement in 1937 Lionel Tertis premièred some of the most important viola works of that time and arranged and transcribed numerous short 'salon' type pieces for his own performance, some of which were published, others remaining in ms. During and after the Second World War he continued to promote his beloved viola with further transcriptions and arrangements.

The following list gives an insight into a large and varied repertoire which helped to enhance the development of the viola as a solo instrument.

KEY: [1] Arranger. [2] Commissioner. [3] Dedicatee. [4] Editor.
[5] Première performance. [6] Transcriber.

Ambrosio, Alfredo d', *Aubade* for viola and piano[1]
—— *Canzonetta* for viola and piano[1]
—— *Feuillet d'album* for viola and piano[1]
—— *Petite suite* no. 2 for viola and piano[1]
—— *Rêverie* for viola and piano[1]
Anonymous (1452), *15th-Century Folk Song* for viola, cello and piano[1] (Bosworth 1961)
—— *Minnelied* (15th-century song) for voice, viola and piano[1]
Arensky, Anton, *Berceuse*, op. 30 no. 2, for viola and piano[1]
Bach, J. S., *Adagio* (Organ Toccata and Fugue in C, BWV564) for viola and piano[1] (Boosey & Hawkes, 1935; Comus, 2006)
—— (transcr. A Siloti) *Adagio* (Organ Toccata and Fugue in C, BWV564) for viola[1] and piano (Carl Fischer, 1950)
—— *Adagio* (Easter Offering) for cello and piano or organ[1] (Bosworth)
—— *Air* (Orchestral Suite no. 3 in D, BWV1068) for viola and piano[1]
—— Brandenburg Concerto no. 6 in B flat, BWV1051, for 2 solo violas and ensemble[1] (MS)
—— *Chaconne* (Partita no. 2 in D minor, BWV1004) for solo violin[4] (Augener no. 5568, c.1935)

—— 'Come, sweet death' (Komm', süsser Tod), BWV478, for violin, viola or cello and piano[1] (Schott, 1925)

—— Concerto in D minor for 2 violins, BWV1043, arr. for violin and viola[1] (Hawkes & Son, 1942)

—— Concerto for violin and oboe in C minor, BWV1060, arr. for violin and viola[1]

—— Suite no. 3 in C major for cello, BWV1009, transcribed for solo viola[6]

Bainton, Edgar, Sonata (1922) for viola and piano[5] (MS)

Bate, Stanley, Concerto for viola and orchestra (Schott, 1951)

Bax, Arnold, Concerto (Phantasy) for viola and orchestra[3] (solo part[4])[5] Murdoch (Murdoch & Co., 1922)

—— *Concert Piece* (1904) for viola and piano[5] (Corda Music, 2002)

—— *Elegiac Trio* for flute, viola and harp[5] (Chester, 1916)

—— *Fantasy Sonata* for harp and viola (Murdoch, 1927; Chappell, 1943)

—— *Legend* for viola and piano[5] (Murdoch, 1930; Chappell, 1943)

—— Sonata for viola and piano[3/5] Murdoch (Murdoch & Co., 1923; Chappell, 1943)

—— Trio in E major, op.4, for violin, viola and piano[5] (Avison–Chester, 1906)

Beethoven, Ludwig van, Sonata in G minor for cello, op. 5 no. 2, arr. for viola and piano[1] (Augener, 1947)

—— Duo in E flat (mit zwei obligaten Augenglasern) for viola and cello (Peters, 1952)

—— *Notturno*, op. 42, arr. W. Primrose for viola and piano[3] (Schott, 1952)

—— Trio in C for two oboes and cor anglais, op. 87, arr. for three violas[1/4] (Bosworth, 1952)

—— Variations on a Theme of Mozart, op. 66, for viola and piano[1] (Boosey & Hawkes, 1934)

—— (Burmester), Menuet for viola and piano[5/6] (Schott, 1912, 1925)

Bell, W. H., *An Arab Love Song* (c.1905)[5]

—— *Cantilena* (c.1905)[5]

—— Violin Sonata in E minor, op. 15 (1897), arr. for viola and piano[1/5]

Benjamin, Arthur, *Romantic Phantasy* (1935) for violin, viola and orchestra/piano[4] (Boosey & Hawkes, 1956); solo viola part[4]

Berlioz, Hector, Symphony *Harold in Italy*, op. 16 (Breitkopf & Härtel, 1900; Eulenburg, 1900)

Bizet, Georges, *Adagietto* from *L'Arlésienne* (Suite no. 1), for viola and piano[1]

Bliss, Arthur, Sonata for viola and piano[3/4/5](Oxford University Press, 1934)

—— *Two Wiegenlieder* for voice, clarinet or viola[1] and piano (J. W. Chester 1923): (a) The Ragwort (b) The Dandelion

Bloch, Ernest, Suite (1919) for viola and orchestra/piano (Schirmer, 1920)

Bowen, York, *Allegro de concert* (1906) for cello/viola and piano (Josef Weinberger, 2006)

—— 'At the Midhour of Night', song with piano and viola obbligato

—— *Fantasia* for viola and organ[3/5] (Josef Weinberger, 2006)

—— *Fantasie* for four violas (1907)[3/5] (Rarities for Strings, 1983) (Sometimes referred to as *Fantasia*)

—— *Melody for the G String*, op. 47, for violin/viola and piano[3/5] (Swan & Co., 1923; Josef Weinberger, c. 2000)

—— *Melody for the C String*, op. 51 no.2 [3/5] (Swan & Co., 1923; Josef Weinberger, c. 2000)

—— 'No Tears to Weep', song with piano and viola obbligato

—— *Phantasie-Trio*, op. 24, for violin, cello/viola and piano[3/5] (Ascherberg, Hopwood & Crew) viola part (MS)

—— *Phantasy*, op. 54 (1918), for viola and piano[5] (Josef Weinberger, 1997)

—— *Poem* (Romantic Poem), op. 27 (1911), for solo viola, harp (or piano) and organ[3/5] (Josef Weinberger, 2006)

—— *Romance* (1900; viola version 1904) in D flat for violin/viola and piano[3/5] (Comus, 2004)

—— *Romance* in A (1908) for cello/viola and piano (Josef Weinberger, 2006)

—— Sonata no. 1 in C minor, op. 18, for viola and piano[3/4/5] (Schott, 1907)

—— Sonata no. 2 in F, op. 22, for viola and piano[3/4/5] (Schott, 1911)

—— Viola Concerto, op. 25 (1907)[3/4/5] (Josef Weinberger, 1998)

—— *Londonderry Air* (arrangement of traditional, 1918) for cello/violin/viola and piano[3/5] (MS)

Boyd, Tod, *Samoan Lullaby* for viola and piano[1]

Brahms, Johannes, *Die Ribansten Schwer* for viola and piano[1]

—— *Minnelied*, op. 71 no. 5, for viola and piano[1] (Comus, 2006)

—— *Two Songs*, op. 91, for mezzo soprano, viola obbligato and piano (Simrock, 1920; Peters, 1954). Viola obbligato[4]

—— Sonata in F minor, op. 120 no. 1 for viola and piano[4] (Augener, 1951)

—— Sonata in E flat, op. 120 no. 2 for viola and piano[4] (Augener, 1952)

—— Sonata in E minor, op. 38 for viola and piano[1] (Augener, 1947)

—— Trio, op. 114, for viola, cello and piano (Simrock, 1892)

—— *Wiegenlied* (Lullaby), op. 49 no. 4 for viola and piano[1/4]

—— 'Wir Wandelten' (We Wandered) op. 96 no. 2 for violin/viola and piano[1] (Hawkes & Sons, 1937)

Bridge, Frank, *Allegro Appassionato* (1907) for viola and piano, (Stainer & Bell, 1908, 1981)

—— *Pensiero* (1905 rev. 1908) for viola and piano (Stainer & Bell, 1908, 1981)

—— *Lament* (c.1912) for two violas[5] (Thames, 1981)

—— *Caprice* (*c*.1912) for two violas[5]

Brucken-Fock, Gerard Hendrick, Sonata in B flat, op. 5, for viola and piano (Breitkopf & Härtel, 1906)

Burmester, Willy, *Französisches Lied* (French Song) for viola and piano[1] (Schott, 1912/1925)

Bush, Alan, *Dance Melody and Song Melody*, op. 47[3] (Joseph Williams, 1959)

Carse, Adam, Concerto for viola and orchestra[2]

Clarke, Rebecca, Sonata (1919) for viola and piano (Chester, 1921)

—— Two Pieces for viola and cello (Oxford University Press)

Coates, Eric, *First Meeting* (1941/42) for viola and piano[3/5] (Josef Weinberger, 2006)

Collins, A., Theme and Variations from Divertimento no. 17, K334 for viola and piano[3]

Dale, B. J., 'Come away, Death', op. 9 no. 2 for voice, viola and piano[5] (Novello, 1919)

—— *Introduction and Andante*, op. 5 for six violas[3/5] (Corda, 1996)

—— *Phantasy*, op. 4 for viola and piano[3/4/5] (Schott, 1912)

—— Suite, op. 2 for viola and piano[3/4/5] (Novello, 1913)

—— *Romance and Finale* (Suite no. 2) for viola and orchestra[3/4/5] (MS)

—— (Bowen) *English Dance* for viola and piano[3/4/5] (Comus, 2003)

Debussy, Claude, *Minstrels* for viola and piano[1]

Delius, Frederick, *Caprice and Elegy* for cello arranged for viola[1] and piano (Boosey & Hawkes, 1934)

—— Concerto for violin, cello (arranged for viola)[1] and orchestra/piano (Augener, 1935)

—— Serenade 'Hassan' for viola and piano[1] (Universal/Boosey & Hawkes, 1934; Josef Weinberger, 2006)

—— Violin Sonata no. 2 for viola and piano[1] (Boosey & Hawkes, 1932)

—— Violin Sonata no. 3 for viola and piano[1] (Boosey & Hawkes, 1932)

Dohnányi, Ernő, Violin Sonata in C sharp minor, op. 21 (Simrock, 1913); part for viola (in original key)[1]

Dowland, John, Duet for voice and viola[1] 'Come again sweet love' (1954)

—— Elizabethan Melody for viola and cello[1] (Bosworth, 1961)

Dunhill, Thomas, Phantasy Trio in E flat, op. 36, for violin, viola and piano[5] (Stainer & Bell, 1912)

—— *Triptych*, Three Impressions for viola and orchestra/piano, op.99[3/5] (Oxford University Press, 1945)

Duparc, Henri, 'Extase' and 'Phydilé', Two Songs for soprano, viola[1] and piano

Dvořák, Antonín, *Bagatellen*, op. 47 (2 violins, cello and harmonium) arr. for violin, viola and piano[1]

—— *Slavonic Dance* no. 1 in G minor for viola and orchestra/piano[1/5]

—— (orch. G. Walter/W. Goehr) *Songs my Mother Taught me*, op. 55 no. 4, for viola[1] and orchestra

Eccles, Henry, Sonata in G minor for cello/viola[1] and piano

Elgar, Edward, Concerto for viola[1] and orchestra/piano, op. 85[5] (Novello, 1929)

Farjeon, Harry, *Deux morceaux* (Andante and Scherzo) for viola[4] and piano[3/5] (Schott, 1911/12); (alternative title: *Two Sketches* for viola and piano) (Schott 1917)

—— *Concertstück* for viola and piano

—— Sonata movement for viola and piano

Fauré, Gabriel, *Après un rêve*, op. 7. no. 1, for viola and piano[1]

—— 'Dans les Ruins d'une Abbaye' for mezzo soprano, viola and piano

—— *Élégie*, op. 24, for cello/viola and piano/orchestra (Hamelle), for viola and piano (Comus, 2006)

Forsyth, Cecil, Concerto in G minor for viola and orchestra (piano score by John Ireland) (Schott, 1904)

Franchi, Dorothy, *Rhapsody* for viola and orchestra

Franck, César, (Bowen) Violin Sonata in A arr. for viola and piano[4]

—— (Tertis) Violin Sonata in A arr. for viola and piano[4]

Fry, Bridget, Concerto for solo viola, wind quintet and string orchestra

Fuchs, Robert, Duet for violin and viola from 12 duets, op. 60 (Adolf Robitschek, Vienna, 1903)

Galuppi, Baldassare, *Aria amorosa* for violin, viola or cello and piano[1] (Augener, 1954); arr. Blanche Gerstman for solo viola, string quartet, double bass and harp[5] ; for viola and cello[1] (unaccompanied)

Glazunov, Alexander, *Mélodie* for viola and piano[1]

Godard, Benjamin, *Berceuse de Jocelyn* for viola and piano[1]

—— *Six Duettini*, op. 18 for violin, viola and piano

Grainger, Percy, *Arrival Platform Humlet for middle fiddle* (1912)[4] (Schott, 1916, 1926)

—— *Molly on the Shore* for viola and piano[1]

Grazioli, Giovanni Battista, Sonata in F for viola and piano[1]

Grieg, Edvard, 'I Love Thee', op. 5. no. 3, for viola and piano[1]

—— Violin Sonata no. 3 in C minor, op. 45, arr. in F minor for viola and piano[1]

Guiraud, Ernest, *Mélodrame* for viola and piano[1]

—— Serenade for viola and piano[1] (MS)

Halvorsen, Johan, Passacaglia on a Theme of Handel for violin and viola (Hansen, 1951)

Handel, G. F., *Arietta* for viola and piano[1] (Schott 1912, 1925)

—— Sonata in F, op. 1 no. 12, for viola and piano[1] (Boosey & Hawkes, 1943)

—— Sonata in G minor, op. 2 no. 8, for two violins and continuo; 2nd violin part arr. for viola[1]

—— (Burmester) *Sarabande* for viola and piano[1] (Schott, 1912, 1925)

—— (Casadesus) Concerto in B minor for viola and orchestra/piano (Eschig, 1925); viola part fingered and phrased with original cadenza by Tertis (MS)

Harding, Kenneth, *Concertante* for five violas[3] (Corda Music, 2006)

Haydn, Joseph, Cello Concerto in D arr.[1] for viola and piano with two original cadenzas (Boosey & Hawkes, 1942)

—— (Burmester) *Capriccio* for viola and piano[1] (Schott, 1912; Comus. 2006)

—— (Burmester) *Menuet* for viola and piano[1] (Schott, 1912, 1925)

Holbrooke, Josef, Nocturne 'Fairyland', op. 57 (1911), for viola, oboe d'amore or clarinet/violin/flute and piano[5] (Chester, 1916)

—— *Romance* in D, op. 59, for viola and piano[4/5] (MS)

Holst, Gustav, *Lyric Movement* (1934) for viola and small orchestra (piano reduction)[3/5] (Oxford University Press, 1948, 1971)

Hurlstone, William Yeates, *Four Characteristic Pieces* for viola and piano[4] (Novello)

Inghelbrecht, D. E., *Prelude and Saltarella* for viola and piano (Eschig, 1905)

Ireland, John, Cello Sonata (1923) for viola and piano[1/4] (Augener, 1941)

—— Violin Sonata no. 2 in A minor (1917) arr. for viola and piano[1]

—— *The Holy Boy* (Carol of the Nativity) for unaccompanied viola[1] or viola and piano[1] (Comus, 2006)

Jacob, Gordon, *Nocturne* for viola and cello[3] (Corda Music, 1996)

—— Suite for eight violas 'In memoriam Lionel Tertis' (Anglo-American, 1980)

—— Viola Concerto no. 1 (Oxford University Press, 1926; Simrock, 1980)

Jongen, Joseph, Trio in F sharp minor, op. 30 (1907), for violin, viola and piano (Durand)

Kalniņš, Alfrēds, *Élégie* for viola and piano[1] (MS)

Korngold, Erich, *Vier Stücke*, op. 11, for violin and piano, nos.1 and 4 arr. for viola and piano[1]; no. 4 is Hornpipe from *Much Ado about Nothing* for viola and piano[1] (MS)

Kreisler, Fritz, *Chanson Louis XIII and Pavane* (in the style of Couperin) for viola and piano[1]

—— *Fugue in D* (In the style of Tartini) for unaccompanied viola or viola and piano[1/5] (MS); viola and cello (unaccompanied)[1] (MS)

—— *La Chasse* (In the style of Cartier) for viola and piano[1/5]

—— *La Gitana* for viola and piano[1/5]

—— *Liebeslied* for viola and piano[1]

—— *La Précieuse* (in the style of Couperin) for viola and piano[1/5]

—— *Preludium and Allegro* (in the style of Pugnani) for viola and piano[1] (MS)

—— *Rondino* (after Rondo in C for violin and piano by Beethoven) for viola and piano[1/5]

—— *Rondo* (after Rondo, 'Haffner' Serenade by Mozart) for viola and piano[1/5]

—— *Tambourin chinois* for viola and piano[1/5] (MS); orchestrated by York Bowen for viola and orchestra[5]

—— Theme from *Slavonic Dance* no. 1 in G minor (after Dvořák, op. 46 no. 2, in D minor) for viola and piano[1/5] (MS)

—— *Valse* for viola and piano[1]

Liszt, Franz, *Liebestraum* (Notturno no. 3) for viola and piano[1] (Augener, 1954; Comus, 2006)

—— *Rêverie* for viola and piano

Loeffler, Charles Martin, *Four Poems*, op. 5, for mezzo-soprano, viola obbligato and piano (Schirmer, 1904)

McEwen, J. B., (a) *Breath o' June* (1913) for violin/viola and piano[3/5] (Anglo-French Music Co., 1918); (b) *The Lone Shore* (1913) for violin/viola and piano (Anglo-French Music Co., 1918)

—— Concerto for viola and orchestra (1901)[3/5] (MS, Glasgow University)

—— *Chaleur d'été* for viola and piano[3/5]

—— *Nocturne* in D flat (1917) for viola and piano[3/5]

—— Sonata in E flat for violin and piano, arr. for viola and piano[1]

—— Sonata no. 2 in F minor (1914) for violin and piano, arr. for viola and piano[1]

Marais, Marin, *Rondeau* and *Le Basque* from 5 Old French Dances for viola and piano[1/5] (Chester, 1917)

Martini, Giovanni Battista, (Endicott) Trio Sonata in D arr. for viola and piano[1] (Composers Music Corporation, New York)

—— Trio Sonata in E, arr. for viola and piano[1]

Méhul, Étienne, *Gavotte* for viola and piano[1] (Schott, 1912)

Mendelssohn, Felix, *On Wings of Song*, op. 34 no. 2, for viola and piano[1]

—— Piano Trio no. 2 in C minor, op. 66; cello part arr. for viola[1]

—— *Songs without Words*, op. 19 no. 1 'Sweet Remembrance' for viola and piano[1] (Comus, 2006)

—— *Songs without Words*, op. 20 'Fleecy Clouds' for viola and piano[1] (MS)

—— *Songs without Words*, op. 38 no. 6 'Duetto' for viola and piano[1]

—— *Songs without Words*, op. 53 no. 2 for viola and piano[1]

—— *Songs without Words*, op. 60 no. 6 'Spring Song' for viola and piano[1] (Comus, 2006)

—— (Goehr) *Songs without Words*, op. 38 no. 6 'Duetto' for viola and orchestra[5]

—— *Venetian Gondola Song*, op. 19 no. 6 for viola and orchestra[5]

—— Violin Concerto in E minor, op. 64 arr. for viola in A minor[1] (1st and 2nd movements only)

Meyer-Olbersleben, Max, Sonata in C, op. 14, for viola and piano (Schuberth, 1881)

Mozart, W. A., Aria from *Il re pastore* for soprano, violin/viola[1] and piano

—— Concerto in A, K622, for clarinet and orchestra/piano; clarinet part arr. for viola[1] (Chester, 1947)

—— *Andante* from Duo no. 2 in B flat, K424, for violin and viola, arr. for two violas[1]

—— *Sinfonia concertante*, K364, for violin, viola and orch/piano;[5] + cadenza by Tertis (Augener, 1936, 1947)

—— *Sinfonia concertante*, K364; cadenzas by Ysaÿe (1916)[3] 'A son ami Lionel Tertis' (MS)

—— *Sinfonia concertante*, K364; cadenzas by Kreisler (1924)[3]

—— Violin Sonata in A, K305, for viola and piano (1927)[1] (MS)

—— Trio in E flat, K498, for violin, viola and piano (Barenreiter)

—— Trio in E, K542, for violin, cello and piano; cello part arr. for viola[1]

—— Trio in G, K564, for violin, cello and piano; cello part arr. for viola[1]

Paynter, T. C., *Cradle Song* for viola and piano

Pierné, Gabriel, *Serenade*, op. 7, for viola and piano[1/5] (Joseph Williams, 1908; Stainer & Bell; Josef Weinberger, 2006)

Pitt, Percy, *Solo* (1915) for viola and orchestra[3/5]

Porpora, Nicolò, (Corti), *Aria* for viola and piano[5/6] (Chester, 1924)

Poulenc, Francis, (Heifetz), *Mouvements perpetuels* for viola and piano[1]

Purcell, Henry, 'Golden' Sonata for 2 violins and continuo; 2nd violin part arr. for viola[1]

Rachmaninov, Sergei, *Andante and Scherzo* (Sonata for cello and piano in G minor, op. 19); cello part arr. for viola[1] (MS)

Rebikoff, V. I., *Berceuse, Simplicity, Dance of Satan's daughter, Insouciance, Les Rêves, Les Démons s'amusent, Waltz* (The Christmas Tree) for viola and piano[1]

Reed, W. H., *Rhapsody* for viola and orchestra/piano[3/4/5] (Augener, 1927)

—— Sonata for violin and viola[3/5]

Ropartz, Guy, Sonata in G minor for cello and piano; cello part arr. for viola[1]

Roussel, Albert, Trio in F, op. 40 (1929), for flute, viola and cello (Durand, 1930)

Rubinstein, Anton, Melody in F, op. 3 no. 1, for viola and piano[1]

Saint-Saëns, Camille, *Berceuse* for viola and piano[1]

—— *Melody* for viola and piano[1] (Schirmer, 1959)

Sammartini, G. B., *Allegro* (Sonata in E, op.1 no.2, for 2 violins and continuo) for viola and piano[1]

Sammons, Albert, Duet for violin and viola

—— *Minuet* (1919) for viola and piano (Hawkes & Sons)

—— *Plantation Dance* for viola and piano[1]

—— *Rêve d'enfant* (1915) for viola and piano (Hawkes & Sons)

—— *Theme and Variations in Olden Style* for viola and piano[1]

Schubert, Franz, *Allegretto* for viola or violin and piano/two violins and piano/violin, viola and piano[1] and two violas and piano, op. 161, D887 (Boosey & Hawkes, 1936)

—— *Ave Maria*, op. 52 no. 6, D839 for viola and piano[1]

—— 'Du bist die Ruh', op. 59 no. 3, D776 for viola and piano[1]

—— *Nacht und Traume*, op. 43 no. 2, D827 for viola and piano[1] (MS)

—— Trio in B flat, op. 99, D898; cello part arr. for viola[1] (MS)

—— Sonatina in G minor, op. 137 no. 3, D408 for violin and piano, arr. for viola and piano[1]

Schumann, Robert, *Romance* in F, op. 28 no. 2 for viola and piano[1] (Augener, 1954; Josef Weinberger, 2006)

—— *Abendlied* (Slumber Song) for viola and piano[1]

—— *Albumblätter*, op. 124 for viola and piano[1]

Scott, Cyril, *Fantasie* (1911) for viola and piano[3/5] (Schott, 1930)

Scriabin, Alexander, (Kochanski), *Étude* no. 4 (Violin and piano) for viola and piano[1]

Ševčík, Ottokar, *School of Technique*, op. 1, arr. for viola in 3 parts[1] (parts 1 and 2, Bosworth 1952; part 3, 1953)

—— *School of Bowing Technique*, op. 2, arr. for viola in 3 parts[1] (Bosworth)

—— *Change of Position and Preparatory Scale Studies*, op. 8, arr. for viola[1] (Bosworth, 1952)

Smyth, Ethel, Concerto for violin, horn or viola[1] and orchestra; viola part arr. Tertis

—— Trio for violin, horn (or viola, or cello) and piano (MS)

—— *Two Interlinked French Folk Melodies* for viola and piano[4/5] (Oxford University Press, 1936)

Sowerby, Leo, Trio (1919) for flute, viola and piano (MS)

Stiles, Frank, Viola Concerto no. 2 (1973) for viola and orchestra[3] (MS)

Strauss, Richard, *Don Quixote*, op. 35 for solo cello, solo viola and orchestra (Universal, 1904)

Sulzer *Sarabande* (Air on the G String) for violin or viola and piano[1/4] (Schott; Josef Weinberger, 2006)

Szymanowski, Karol, (Kochanski), *Chant de Roxane* for viola and piano[1]

Tchaikovsky, P. I., *Barcarolle*, op. 37a no. 6 for viola and piano[1]

—— *Chanson triste*, op. 40 no. 2 for viola and piano[1]

—— *Chant sans paroles*, op. 2 no. 3 for viola and piano[1]

—— *Seasons*, op. 37b for viola and piano[1]

—— *Song Without Words*, op. 2 no. 3 for viola and piano[1]

—— *Souvenir de Hapsal*, op. 2 for viola and piano[1]

—— 'None but the Lonely Heart', op. 6 no. 6 for viola and piano[1]

Tertis, Lionel, *Crimond* (Psalm 23) for viola and cello (MS)

—— *Hier au soir: Pensée musicale* for violin or viola and piano (Schott, 1925)

—— *Rêverie* for viola and piano

—— *Romance* for viola or violin and piano (Schott, 1923)

—— *Sunset* (Coucher du Soleil) for violin, viola or cello and piano (Chester, 1923); for cello and string quartet[1] (MS); for viola and piano (Comus, 2006)

—— *Three Sketches* for viola and piano (1) 'Serenade' (MS); (2) 'The Blackbirds' (for viola or violin and piano) (Augener, 1954; Comus, 2006); (3) 'The River' (for soprano or viola and piano) words by Tertis (Comus, 2006)

—— *A Tune* for viola and piano (Augener, 1954; Comus, 2006)

—— *Valse rêve* for piano solo (MS, undated)

—— Variations on a Passacaglia of Handel (from Suite no. 7) for two violas (Comus, 2001)

—— Variations on a Theme of Handel for viola and cello (Francis, Day and Hunter, 1961)

Thomé, François, *Sous la feuillée*, op. 29 for viola and piano[1]

Tovey, Donald, Sonata in B flat for viola and piano

Traditional, *Farewell to Cucullain* for violin, viola or cello and piano[1] (Schott, 1918)

—— *Lament* (An Old Irish Air) for viola and piano[1] (Schott, 1925)

—— *Londonderry Air* for viola and piano (Josef Weinberger, 2006)

—— *Old German Love Song* for viola and orchestra[1]

—— (Cyril Scott) *Cherry Ripe* for viola and piano[1] (Schott, 1925; Joseph Weinberger, 2006)

—— (C. Kennedy Scott) *Provençal Carol* (1672) for voice, viola and piano

Tremain, Ronald, Concertino for viola and orchestra

Trowell, Arnold, Sonata for viola and piano[3]

Turina, Joaquin, *Farruca* for viola and piano[1]

—— *Scène Andalouse* for solo viola, solo piano and string quartet (Mathot, 1913; Salabert, 1940)

Two Lionel Tertis Albums (Comus, 2006)

Two Lionel Tertis Albums (Josef Weinberger, 2006)

Vaughan Williams, Ralph, *Flos campi* for solo viola, mixed chorus and small orchestra.[3/5] (Oxford University Press, 1928)

—— *Six Studies in English Folk Song* for viola and piano (Stainer & Bell, 1927)

—— *Four Hymns* for tenor voice, viola and piano/orchestra (Boosey & Hawkes, 1920)

—— Suite for viola[4] and small orchestra[3/5] (Oxford University Press, 1936)

Verne-Bredt, Alice, *Lullaby* for viola and piano[1]

Vierne, Louis, *Le Soir* for viola and piano[1] (Leduc, Paris)

Vieuxtemps, Henry, *Saltarella* for viola and piano[1]

Walker, Ernest, Sonata in C, op. 29, for viola and piano[4] (Schott, 1912)

Walthew, Richard, *Five Diversions* for string trio[5]

—— *A Mosaic in Ten Pieces* for viola and piano[3/5] (Boosey & Hawkes)

—— *A Mosaic in Ten Pieces* for viola and orchestra[3/5] (MS)

Walton, William, Concerto for viola[4] and orchestra (Oxford University Press, 1930)

Warner, Waldo, Suite in D, op. 58, (a) for solo viola and string orchestra;[3] (b) solo viola and full orchestra; also for viola and piano

Wieniawski, Henryk, Violin Concerto no. 2 in D minor, for viola in G minor[1] (1st and 2nd movements only)

Winkler, Alexander, Sonata in C minor, op. 10, for viola and piano (Belaieff, 1902)

Wolstenholme, William, *Allegretto* for viola and piano (Novello, 1900; Comus, 2006)

—— *Romanza* for viola and piano[1] (Novello, 1900; Comus, 2006)

—— *Canzona* for viola and piano[1/4] (Novello, 1954)

—— *Légende*, op. 45, for viola and orchestra[3] (MS, unknown)

—— *The Answer* for viola and piano[1] (Comus, 2006)

—— *The Question* for viola and piano[1] (Comus, 2006)

Wray, John, Suite for six violas[3] (MS)

Ysaÿe, Eugène, *Rêve d'enfant* for viola and piano

—— Trio for two violins and viola[5] (MS)

Zsolt, Nándor, *Berceuse* for viola and piano[1]

⤜ APPENDIX 7 ⤛
The Lionel Tertis Bequest

After Tertis's death a set of music and manuscripts was donated to Trinity College of Music by his widow, Mrs Lillian Tertis. It includes a few examples of music which he played from and edited. After the death of his first wife in 1951, he gave many manuscripts and recordings to pupils and friends and some of these are now in the possession of the author.

Piano Music

Bowen, *Four Bagatelles*, op. 147. Autographed by the composer, 1956.
Heller, *Tarantella*, op. 85/2. Tertis's first public performance, original copy.
Kabalevsky, Sonata no. 3, op. 46. Autographed by the composer, 1949.
Warner, Waldo, *An Irish Dell*; *Road Breaker*.

Viola Music

Bach, Concerto in D minor for two violins, second violin part arr. for viola (Boosey & Hawkes).
Bax, *Phantasy* for viola and orchestra (Murdoch, 1923).
Beethoven, Variations on a theme of Mozart, op. 66, for cello and piano, arr. for viola and piano by Tertis.
Dale, *Romance*, from Suite for viola and piano, op. 2. Two editions.
Delius, Sonata no. 2 for violin and piano, adapted and edited for viola by Tertis (Boosey & Hawkes).
—— Sonata no. 3 for violin and piano, adapted and edited for viola by Tertis (Boosey & Hawkes).
—— Double Concerto for violin and cello, arr. for violin and viola.
Elgar, Cello Concerto in E minor, op. 85, arr. for viola by Tertis (Novello, 1929).
Galuppi, *Aria amorosa*, for viola and piano, MS and published version by Augener, arr. Tertis.
Grieg, Violin Sonata, op. 45, arr. for viola by Tertis, MS.
Handel, Concerto in B minor for viola, bass realization and orchestration by Henri Casadesus, fingered and phrased with two cadenzas by Tertis, MS.
Ireland, Sonata no. 2 in A minor for violin and piano, arr. for viola by Tertis, MS.
Mozart, Aria from *Il re pastore*, 'L'amero saro constante', for soprano and obbligato violin, arr. for viola by Tertis, MS.

—— Sinfonia concertante in E flat for violin, viola and piano, K364, edited with original cadenza by Tertis (Oxford University Press).

Rachmaninov, Sonata for cello and piano, op. 19, two movements arr. for viola by Tertis, MS.

Savagnore, Giuseppe, Sonata for solo violin, dedicated to Tertis.

Scriabin-Kochanski, *Étude* no. 4, arr. for viola and piano by Tertis, MS.

Sulzer, *Sarabande*, for cello or violin with piano or organ, arr. for viola by Tertis, MS.

Szymanowski-Kochanski, 'Chant de Roxane', for violin and piano, arr. for viola by Tertis, MS.

Tertis, Analysis of Schumann's Sonata, op. 105, 1898.

Vaughan Williams, Suite for viola and orchestra (piano), dedicated to Tertis by the composer, autographed.

Walton, Concerto for viola and orchestra, edited and revised by Tertis.

Wolstenholme, *Canzona* for viola and piano, edited by Tertis. Proof copy (Novello).

The Tertis Legacy

Whenever I listen to Tertis's playing, I am always struck by the volcanic force of his musical personality. That magnificent and heroic tone, that sometimes uncompromising approach to tempo, those daredevil fingerings ... these are qualities which keep me absolutely riveted no matter how many times I listen to his recordings. He must have been a man of tremendous passion and conviction, and I would dearly love to have met him. Fortunately he has left us a great musical legacy, and as with other giants of the past, I can only imagine the communicative power of a live Tertis performance. Alongside his artistry, Tertis's tireless campaign on behalf of his beloved instrument is in itself a great inspiration, generating as it did an enduring energy throughout his own long life, and providing a model of commitment and integrity to the rest of us.

— Martin Outram

◈

The Lionel Tertis International Viola Competition and Workshop
Patron: Mrs Lillian Tertis • Administrator: John Bethell MBE

In 1977 a small group of friends met to discuss how best to honour the memory of Lionel Tertis. It was very quickly agreed that they should form a committee to establish an international viola competition. Initially the Royal Philharmonic Society agreed to administer it, and many distinguished musicians and prominent figures in the arts became patrons.

It was not possible to organize a competition in London at that time but one member of the committee, Ruth, Lady Fermoy, proposed that they should invite to their next meeting John Bethell, who had recently administered the International Double Bass Competition on the Isle of Man. The idea appealed to him, and the first Lionel Tertis International Competition and workshop was held in Port Erin in 1980.

The Competition owes a great debt of gratitude to John Bethell and his splendid team of voluntary helpers in the Arts Centre. In Lillian Tertis's words, 'No thanks can ever be adequate for all they have done for the instrument, for viola players, and for the wonderful tribute to the memory of my husband.'

The original Executive Committee that planned the inaugural competition consisted of John Bethell (Chairman), Myers Foggin, Bernard Shore, Harry

Danks, Ruth, Lady Fermoy, Mrs Lillian Tertis and John White. Members of the present Executive Committee (2006) are John Bethell (Chairman), Sarah-Jane Bradley, Martin Outram, Tully Potter, Mrs Lillian Tertis and John White.

Honorary Presidents

1980   Artur Rubinstein
1981–93 Ruth, Lady Fermoy
1994–   Yuri Bashmet

Jury Members and Prizewinners

1980 *Jury:* Gerald McDonald (UK, Chairman), Harry Danks (UK), Paul Doktor (USA), Csaba Erdély (Hungary), Piero Farulli (Italy), Milan Škampa (Czechoslovakia).
   First Prize: Paul Neubauer (USA)
   Second Prize: Kim Kashkashian (USA)

1984 *Jury:* Lady Evelyn Barbirolli (UK, Chairman), Paul Cropper (UK), Hirofumi Fukai (Japan), Alfred Lipka (DDR), Donald McInnes (USA), Simon Streatfeild (Canada)
   First Prize: Cynthia Phelps (USA)
   Second Prize: Paul Coletti (UK) 'The Artur Rubinstein Memorial Prize'
   Third Prize: Carla Maria Rodrigues (UK) 'The John Bethell Award'

1988 *Jury:* Sir David Lumsden (UK, Chairman), Yuri Bashmet (USSR), Harry Danks (UK), Paul Hindmarsh (UK), Thomas Riebl (Austria), Emanuel Vardi (USA)
   First Prize: Hsin-Yun Huang (Taiwan)
   Second Prize: Jane Atkins (UK) 'The Artur Rubinstein Memorial Prize'
   Third Prize: Jean Eric Soucy (Canada) 'The John Bethell Award'

1991 *Jury:* Sir David Lumsden (UK, Chairman), Yuri Bashmet (USSR), Harry Danks (UK), Jerzy Kosmala (USA), Milan Škampa (Czech Republic)
   First Prize: No award
   Second Prize: (joint) Tomoka Ario (Japan), Andra Darzins (Australia) 'The Artur Rubinstein Memorial Award'
   Third Prize: Esther Geldard (UK) 'The Lillian Tertis Award'

1994 *Jury:* Philip Jones (UK, Chairman), Yuri Bashmet (Russia), Kazuhide Isomura (Japan), Michael Kugel (Russia/Israel), Paul Neubauer (USA), John White (UK)
   First Prize: Gilad Karni (Israel) 'The Ruth Fermoy Memorial Prize'
   Second Prize: Kenta Matsumi (Japan) 'The Artur Rubinstein Memorial Prize'
   Third Prize: Scott Lee (Taiwan) 'The Lillian Tertis Award'

1997 *Jury:* Philip Jones (UK, Chairman), Yuri Bashmet (Russia), Thérèse-Marie Gilissen (Belgium), Lubomir Malý (Czech Republic), Yizhak Schotten (USA), Paul Silverthorne (UK)

First Prize: Roland Glassl (Germany) 'The Ruth Fermoy Memorial Prize'

Second Prize: Steven Larson (Canada) 'The Artur Rubinstein Memorial Prize'

Third Prize: Mikhail Bereznitsky (Russia) 'The Lillian Tertis Award'

2000 *Jury:* Howard Snell (UK, Chairman), Yuri Bashmet (Russia), Sally Beamish (UK), Masao Kawasaki (Japan), Hartmut Lindemann (Germany), Bruno Pasquier (France), Christopher Wellington (UK)

First Prize: No award

Second Prize: Agathe Blondel (France) 'The Artur Rubinstein Memorial Prize'

Third Prize: Arie Schachter (Israel) 'The Lillian Tertis Award'

2003 *Jury:* John Wallace (UK, Chairman), Atar Arad (USA), Yuri Bashmet (Russia), Luigi-Alberto Bianchi (Italy), Martin Outram (UK), Lars Anders Tomter (Norway)

First Prize: Yuval Gotlibovich (Israel) 'The Ruth Fermoy Memorial Prize'

Second Prize: Maxim Rysanov (Ukraine) 'The Artur Rubinstein Memorial Prize'

Third Prize: Maya Rasooly (Israel) 'The Lillian Tertis Award'

2006 *Jury:* John Wallace (UK, Chairman), Vladimir Bukac (Czech Republic) Michael Kugel (Belgium), Kenta Matsumi (Japan), Hariolf Schlichtig (Germany), Roger Tapping (UK/USA)

First Prize: David Kim (Korea) 'The Ruth Fermoy Memorial Prize'

Second Prize: Peijun Xu (People's Republic of China) 'The Artur Rubinstein Memorial Prize'

Third Prize: Ewa Grzywna (Poland) 'The Lillian Tertis Award'

Commissioned Works (compulsory for all competitors)

1980 Viola Concerto no. 2 for viola and string orchestra by Gordon Jacob (Richard Schauer), dedicated to Lillian Tertis. First public performance with orchestra: Queen Elizabeth Hall, London, 11 March 1981. Soloist Paul Neubauer (USA) winner of the 1980 competition, with the English Chamber Orchestra conducted by Sir Charles Mackerras.

1984 Concerto for viola and small orchestra by Wilfred Josephs (Basil Ramsey) 'In Memory of Lionel Tertis'. First public performance with orchestra: Adelaide Town Hall, Adelaide, by Juris Ezergailis with the Adelaide Symphony Orchestra, conducted by David Measham.

1988 *Tides of Mananan*, op. 64, for solo viola by Paul Patterson (Josef Weinberger), dedicated to Sir David Lumsden. First performance at the Erin Arts Centre, Port Erin, Isle of Man, 2 September 1988.

1991 *February Sonatina* for solo viola by John McCabe (Novello). First performance at the Erin Arts Centre, Port Erin, Isle of Man, 31 August 1991.

1994 *Odd Man Out* for solo viola by Michael Berkeley (Oxford University Press), dedicated to John Bethell and Roger Chase. First performance at the Erin Arts Centre, 3 September 1994.

1997 *Rondel* for solo viola by Richard Rodney Bennett (Chester Music). First performance at the Erin Arts Centre, 30 August 1997.

2000 *Pennillion* (1998) for solo viola by Sally Beamish. This work was selected, not commissioned for the 2000 competition (Erin Arts Centre), dedicated to Rebecca Mair Jones. First performance at the Erin Arts Centre, 26 August 2000.

2003 *Through a Limbeck* for solo viola by John Woolrich (Faber Music). First performance at the Erin Arts Centre, 30 August 2003.

2006 *Darkness Draws In* for solo viola by David Matthews (Faber Music).

❖

A Celebration to mark the 125th Anniversary of the Birth of the Distinguished Alumnus and Great Viola Player Lionel Tertis (1876–1975)

Artistic Director: John White FRAM
Guest of Honour: Mrs Lionel Tertis
ROYAL ACADEMY OF MUSIC
31 October, 1 and 2 November 2001

31 OCTOBER

3–6 p.m. Viola Masterclass given by the distinguished Russian-born viola player Michael Kugel. The following students participated: Maya Rasooly, Takashi Kikuchi, Lydia Lowndes-Northcott, Abigail Fenna and Isabel Pereira.

1 NOVEMBER

11 a.m. Tertis lecture by John White

1.05 p.m. Lunchtime concert: a programme of string quartets by Haydn

Haydn, Quartet in D, op. 20 no. 4

Hetherington Quartet: Elizabeth Croad (violin), Charlotte Scott (violin), Sarah Chapman (viola), Kate Hetherington (cello)

Haydn, Quartet in B flat, op. 103, 'The Unfinished'
Haydn, Quartet in D, op. 64 no. 5, 'The Lark'
  Pavao Quartet: Clare Duckworth (violin), Kerenza Peacock (violin), Natália Gomes (viola), Bryony Rump (cello)

2.30 p.m. Concert of works associated with Lionel Tertis
  Yuko Inoue (viola), Kathron Sturrock (piano), Martin Outram (viola)*, Julian Rolton* (piano)

Ralph Vaughan Williams, Suite for viola and piano
Arthur Bliss, Sonata for viola and piano*
John Ireland, arr. Tertis, Sonata for viola and piano

4.30 p.m. Lecture: The Tertis Legacy by Tully Potter

7.30 p.m. Viola ensemble concert
Lionel Tertis, Variations on an 8-bar theme of Handel for two violas
  Martin Outram and Garfield Jackson

Beethoven, arr. Tertis, Trio in C, op. 87, for three violas
  Paul Silverthorne, Isabel Pereira, Alexander Wood

York Bowen, Fantasie Quartet for four violas
  Yuko Inoue, Errika Collins, Natália Gomes, Matthew Cooke

B. J. Dale, Introduction and Andante, op. 5, for six violas
  Paul Silverthorne, Maya Rasooly, Amy Stanford, Anna Smith, Felix Tanner, Sarah Chapman

2 NOVEMBER

11 a.m. Lecture: The Tertis Model Viola by Wilfred Saunders

1.05 p.m. Lunchtime Concert
  Royal Academy of Music Orchestra, conducted by Vernon Handley

B. J. Dale, Romance (Suite op. 2) for viola and orchestra
  Martin Outram (viola)

Edward Elgar arr. Tertis, Concerto in E minor, op. 85 for viola and orchestra   *Paul Silverthorne (viola)*

3.00 p.m. Concert of music written for and arranged by Tertis
  Garfield Jackson (viola), Carole Presland (piano)

Handel, arr. Tertis, Sonata in F (originally for violin)
Schubert, arr. Tertis, Allegretto (String Quartet in G, op. 161)
Beethoven, arr. Tertis, Variations of a theme of Mozart, op. 66 (originally for cello)

Liszt, arr. Tertis, *Liebestraum* (Notturno no. 3) (originally for solo piano)

J. S. Bach, adapted and arr. Tertis, Adagio from Toccata and Fugue in C for organ

Arnold Bax, Sonata for viola and piano 'to Lionel Tertis'

7.30 p.m. Celebrity Recital

Michael Kugel (viola), Mireille Gleizes (piano)

Schumann, Adagio and Allegro, op. 70

Rebecca Clarke, Sonata

Paganini, arr. Kugel, Duo Concertante 'Il Carnevale di Venezia'

Michael Kugel, Prelude Classici

Bizet/Waxman, Carmen – Fantasie

Notes: The programme of Haydn string quartets was given as a tribute to Lionel Tertis who was director of the Academy's ensemble class from 1924 to 1929. During the 1927/8 academic year, four of his students undertook the performance of the complete Haydn string quartets in public concerts in the Duke's Hall.

All the music performed during the festival had close links with Lionel Tertis, except for the final recital, which included only one work he played – the sonata by Rebecca Clarke.

⋐ Discography ⋑

1 – Listed Chronologically by Label

Information is listed in the following order:

Matrix number. Composer. Composition. Assisting artist(s). Availability.

† = Pianist identified in January 1923 Vocalion catalogue, but not on record label

VOCALION

1919

c. AUGUST–DECEMBER

[01310] d'Ambrosio. Petit Suite no. 2. With unknown pianist. Vocalion
R-6099; Biddulph 80219 (4 CDs).

[01477] Wolstenholme. The Answer. With Frank St. Leger (piano).†
Vocalion D-02012; Biddulph 80219 (4 CDs).

[01501] Bach. Air on G String. With Frank St. Leger (piano). Vocalion
D-02067; Pearl GEMM CDS 9148 (2 CDs); Biddulph 80219 (4 CDs).

1920

c. JANUARY

[01611] Kreisler. La Chasse. With unknown pianist. Vocalion R-6007
(alternative take on some copies).

[01613] McEwen. Breath o' June. With Frank St. Leger (piano). Vocalion
D-02006; Biddulph 80219 (4 CDs).

[01617] Dale. Romance from Suite for Viola and Piano (1907). With Frank St.
Leger (piano). Vocalion D-02067; Pearl GEMM CDS 9148 (2 CDs); Biddulph
80219 (4 CDs).

c. FEBRUARY

[01645] Wolstenholme. Allegretto. With Frank St. Leger (piano).† Vocalion
D-02011; Biddulph 80219 (4 CDs).

[01646] Traditional. Londonderry Air. With Frank St. Leger (piano).†
Vocalion D-02011; Wing WCD 24 (CD-Japan); Biddulph 80219 (4 CDs).

[01648] Kreisler. La précieuse. With Frank St. Leger (piano).† Vocalion
R-6019; Biddulph 80219 (4 CDs).

[01649] Fauré. Après un rêve. With Frank St. Leger (piano).† Vocalion
R-6019; Biddulph 80219 (4 CDs).

c. MARCH

[01725] Rubinstein. Melody in F. With Frank St. Leger (piano). Vocalion
R-6007; Biddulph 80219 (4 CDs).

[01726] Godard. Berceuse de Jocelyn. With Frank St. Leger (piano).
Vocalion D-02006; Biddulph 80219 (4 CDs).

[01728] d'Ambrosio. Rêverie. With unknown pianist. Vocalion R-6111;
Biddulph 80219 (4 CDs).

c. APRIL

[01764] Grainger. Molly on the Shore. With Frank St. Leger (piano).†
Vocalion R-6078; Wing WCD 24 (CD-Japan); Biddulph 80219 (4 CDs).

[01767] Kreisler. Tambourin chinois. With Frank St. Leger (piano).†
Vocalion D-02041; Biddulph 80219 (4 CDs).

[01768] Wolstenholme. The Question. With Frank St. Leger (piano).†
Vocalion D-02012.

[01769] Schumann. Abendlied. With Frank St. Leger (piano).† Vocalion
R-6078; Biddulph 80219 (4 CDs).

c. MAY

[01777] Dunhill. Phantasy Trio, part 1. With Albert Sammons (violin) and
Frank St. Leger (piano). Vocalion R-6027; Biddulph 80219 (4 CDs).

[01780] Dunhill. Phantasy Trio, part 2. With Albert Sammons (violin) and
Frank St. Leger (piano). Vocalion R-6027; Biddulph 80219 (4 CDs).

[01782] Mozart. Trio in E flat, K498: Andante. With Albert Sammons
(violin) and Frank St. Leger (piano). Vocalion D-02064; Biddulph 80219
(4 CDs).

[01784/−85] Mozart. Trio in E flat, K498: Menuetto & Rondo. With Albert
Sammons (violin) and Frank St. Leger (piano). Vocalion D-02015; Biddulph
80219 (4 CDs).

c. DECEMBER

[02112] Kreisler. La Chasse. With Frank St. Leger (piano). Vocalion R-6007;
HMV Treasury HLM 7055 (LP); Pearl GEMM CDS 9148 (2 CDs); Biddulph
80219 (4 CDs). (Notes for HMV Treasury HLM 7055 give recording date as
September 1920.)

[02113] Tod Boyd. Samoan Lullaby. With unknown pianist. Vocalion
R-6033; Biddulph 80219 (4 CDs).

[02114] Marais. Le Basque. + St.-Saëns. Berceuse. With unknown pianist.
Vocalion R-6085; Biddulph 80219 (4 CDs).

[02115] Kreisler. Chanson Louis XIII and Pavane. With unknown pianist.
Vocalion R-6111; Biddulph 80219 (4 CDs).

[02118] Kreisler. Prelude and Allegro. With unknown pianist. Vocalion D-02041; Biddulph 80219 (4 CDs).

[02119] Tchaikovsky. Chanson triste. With unknown pianist. Vocalion R-6017; Biddulph 80219 (4 CDs).

[02120] Tchaikovsky. Chant sans paroles. With unknown pianist. American Vocalion 21004; Vocalion R-6017; Biddulph 80219 (4 CDs).

[02121] Kreisler. Rondino. With unknown pianist. Vocalion R-6099; Biddulph 80219 (4 CDs).

[02122] Thomé. Sous la feuillée. With unknown pianist. American Vocalion 21004; Vocalion R-6033; Biddulph 80219 (4 CDs).

1921

c. January

[02176] Handel–Halvorsen. Passacaglia. With Albert Sammons (violin). Vocalion D-02019; Biddulph 80219 (4 CDs).

[02177] Fuchs. Duet for Violin and Viola. With Albert Sammons (violin). Vocalion D-02019; Biddulph 80219 (4 CDs).

c. March

[02285] Handel. Sonata no. 8: movt 1, Andante. With Albert Sammons (violin) and Frederick B. Kiddle (piano). Vocalion D-02023; Biddulph 80219 (4 CDs).

[02287] Handel. Sonata no. 8: movt 4, Allegro. With Albert Sammons (violin) and Frederick B. Kiddle (piano). Vocalion D-02023; Biddulph 80219 (4 CDs).

[02288] Godard. Duettini, op. 18 no. 1, 'Souvenir de Champagne'. With Albert Sammons (violin) and Frederick B. Kiddle (piano). Vocalion R-6063; Biddulph 80219 (4 CDs).

[02289] Godard. Duettini , op. 18 no. 5, 'Minuit'. With Albert Sammons (violin). Vocalion R-6063; Biddulph 80219 (4 CDs).

c. May

[02346] Leroux. Le Nil. With Zoia Rosovsky [Rozovska] (vocalist) and unknown pianist. Vocalion C-01023; Biddulph 80219 (4 CDs).

[02347] Tchaikovsky. None but the Lonely Heart. With Zoia Rosovsky [Rozovska] (vocalist) and unknown pianist. Vocalion L-5012; Biddulph 80219 (4 CDs).

[02349] Duparc. Extase. With Zoia Rosovsky [Rozovska] (vocalist) and unknown pianist. Vocalion L-5015; Biddulph 80219 (4 CDs).

c. OCTOBER

[02538] Schubert. Trio in B flat, op. 99: Andante un poco mosso. With Albert Sammons (violin) and Ethel Hobday (piano). Vocalion D-02050; Biddulph 80219 (4 CDs).

[02539] Mozart. Trio in E, K542: Allegro. With Albert Sammons (violin) and Ethel Hobday (piano). Vocalion D-02064; Biddulph 80219 (4 CDs).

[02540/−41] Mozart. Trio in E, K542: Andante grazioso & Allegro. With Albert Sammons (violin) and Ethel Hobday (piano). Vocalion D-02091; Biddulph 80219 (4 CDs).

c. NOVEMBER

[02583x] Mendelssohn. Spring Song. With unknown pianist. Vocalion R-6085; Biddulph 80219 (4 CDs).

[02584x] Rebikov. Les rêves. With Ethel Hobday (piano). Vocalion X-9696; Biddulph 80219 (4 CDs).

[02585] Schubert. Trio in B flat, op. 99: Allegro moderato. With Albert Sammons (violin) and Ethel Hobday (piano). Vocalion D-02050; Biddulph 80219 (4 CDs).

[02586x] Schubert. Trio in B flat, op. 99: Allegro. With Albert Sammons (violin) and Ethel Hobday (piano). Vocalion D-02060; Biddulph 80219 (4 CDs).

[02587] Schubert. Trio in B flat, op. 99: Allegro vivace. With Albert Sammons (violin) and Ethel Hobday (piano). Vocalion D-02060; Biddulph 80219 (4 CDs).

[02592] Fauré. Élégie. With Ethel Hobday (piano). Vocalion K-05144; Wing WCD 24 (CD-Japan); Biddulph 80219 (4 CDs).

[02593] Tchaikovsky. Barcarolle. With Ethel Hobday (piano). Vocalion K-05174; Wing WCD 24 (CD-Japan); Biddulph 80219 (4 CDs).

[02594] Kalnins. Élégie. With Ethel Hobday (piano). Vocalion D-02082; Biddulph 80219 (4 CDs).

[02595] Schubert. Ave Maria. With Ethel Hobday (piano). Vocalion D-02082; Wing WCD 24 (CD-Japan); Biddulph 80219 (4 CDs).

1922

c. APRIL

[02757] Grieg. I Love Thee. With Ethel Hobday (piano).† Vocalion R-6096; Biddulph 80219 (4 CDs).

[02758] Mendelssohn. On Wings of Song. With Ethel Hobday (piano).† Vocalion R-6096; Biddulph 80219 (4 CDs).

[02759] Dvořák. Bagatelle: Allegretto scherzando. With Albert Sammons (violin) and Ethel Hobday (piano). Vocalion D-02083; Biddulph 80219 (4 CDs).

[02760] Dvořák. Bagatelle: Tempo di minuetto. With Albert Sammons (violin) and Ethel Hobday (piano). Vocalion D-02111; Biddulph 80219 (4 CDs).

[02761] Dvořák. Bagatelle: Allegretto scherzando. With Albert Sammons (violin) and Ethel Hobday (piano). Vocalion D-02111; Biddulph 80219 (4 CDs).

[02762] Dvořák. Bagatelle: Poco allegro. With Albert Sammons (violin) and Ethel Hobday (piano). Vocalion D-02083; Biddulph 80219 (4 CDs).

27 NOVEMBER
exact date from a test pressing

[02999] Tertis. Rêverie. With Ethel Hobday (piano). Vocalion D-02144; Biddulph 80219 (4 CDs).

[03000] Liszt. Liebestraum no. 3 in A flat. With Ethel Hobday (piano). Vocalion D-02144; Wing WCD 24 (CD-Japan); Biddulph 80219 (4 CDs).

[03001X] Tertis. Sunset. With Ethel Hobday (piano). Vocalion X-9696; Biddulph 80219 (4 CDs).

[03002] Schumann. Slumber Song. With Ethel Hobday (piano). Vocalion R-6146; Biddulph 80219 (4 CDs).

[03003] Mendelssohn. Sweet Remembrance. With Ethel Hobday (piano). Vocalion R-6115; Wing WCD 24 (CD-Japan); Biddulph 80219 (4 CDs).

[03004] Mendelssohn. The Fleecy Cloud. With Ethel Hobday (piano). Vocalion R-6115; Biddulph 80219 (4 CDs).

1923
c. JUNE

[03272/−73] Grieg. Sonata in C minor, op. 45: first movement, parts 1 & 2. With Ethel Hobday (piano). Vocalion D-02104.

[03274/−75] Grieg. Sonata in C minor: second movement, parts 1 & 2. With Ethel Hobday (piano). Vocalion D-02106.

[03276/−77] Grieg. Sonata in C minor: third movement, parts 1 & 2. With Ethel Hobday (piano). Vocalion D-02112.

The complete Grieg Sonata no. 3 was released on Wing WCD 24 (CD-Japan) and in Biddulph set 80219 (4 CDs).

c. JULY

[03299] Bizet. Adagietto. With unknown pianist. Vocalion R-6146; Biddulph 80219 (4 CDs).

[03300] Ireland. The Holy Boy. Vocalion K-05144; Biddulph 80219 (4 CDs).

[03301/–02] Mozart. Trio in G, K496 ('no. VII, Op. 16' on label): Allegro & Andante. With Albert Sammons (violin) and Ethel Hobday (piano). Vocalion D-02150; Biddulph 80219 (4 CDs).

[03303] Mozart. Trio in G, K496 ('no. VII, Op. 16' on label): Allegretto. With Albert Sammons (violin) and Ethel Hobday (piano). Vocalion K-05174; Biddulph 80219 (4 CDs).

1924

MAY

[03524/–25] Brahms. Sonata in F minor, op. 120 no. 1: first movement, parts 1 & 2. With Ethel Hobday (piano). Vocalion X-9463.

[03526/–27] Brahms. Sonata in F minor, op. 120 no. 1: second movement, parts 1 & 2. With Ethel Hobday (piano). Vocalion X-9464.

[03528] Brahms. Sonata in F minor, op. 120 no. 1: third movement. With Ethel Hobday (piano). Vocalion K-05117.

[03529] Brahms. Sonata in F minor, op. 120 no. 1: fourth movement. With Ethel Hobday (piano). Vocalion K-05117.

The complete Brahms Sonata no. 1 was released on LP in a limited run of 250 copies by Thomas L. Clear: TLC 2581 – *Historical Anthology of Chamber Music*, vol. 1 (four discs) and in Biddulph set 80219 (4 CDs).

◈

VICTOR

1923

10 DECEMBER
Trial recordings. With Mr Scheid (piano).

Berceuse. Unissued.

Traditional. Londonderry Air (10″). Unissued.

[Bizet?] Adagietto (10″). Unissued.

◈

COLUMBIA

1924

Test recording: unissued on 78 rpm

[T 1709 4a] Korngold. Hornpipe from *Much Ado about Nothing*. With unknown pianist. Biddulph 82016 (4 CDs).

25 NOVEMBER

[AX 755/−58] Bach. Chaconne 'in D minor', BWV 1004. Columbia L 1644/−45; American Columbia 67071-D/−72-D (in Set M 13); Yamano YMCD-1022 (CD-Japan); Pearl GEMM CD 9918 (CD); Biddulph 82016 (4 CDs).

LATE 1924/EARLY 1925

issued February 1925

[A 1468] Bach. Come, Sweet Death. With unknown pianist. Columbia D 1502; Biddulph 82016 (4 CDs).

[A 1471] Porpora. Aria. With unknown pianist. Columbia D 1502; Yamano YMCD-1022 (CD-Japan); Biddulph 82016 (4 CDs).

1925

25 NOVEMBER

[WAX 1160/−63] Dohnányi. Sonata in C sharp minor, op. 21. With William Murdoch (piano). Columbia L 1731/−32; Claremont 78-50 historical series (cassette-produced by Michael Dutton); Biddulph 82016 (4 CDs).

9 DECEMBER

[WAX 1190/−97] Mendelssohn. Trio no. 2 in C minor, op. 66. With Albert Sammons (violin) and William Murdoch (piano). Columbia L 1755/−58; American Columbia 67212-D/−15-D (Set M 43); Biddulph LAB 023 (CD) & 82016 (4 CDs).

[WAX 1198] Traditional. An Old Irish Air. With unknown pianist. Columbia L 1761; Biddulph 82016 (4 CDs).

[WAX 1199] Tertis. Hier au soir. With unknown pianist. Columbia L 1761; Biddulph 82016 (4 CDs).

1926

21 MAY

[WA 3283] Kreisler. La Gitana. With unknown pianist. Columbia D 1554; Wing WCD 24 (CD-Japan); Biddulph 82016 (4 CDs).

[WA 3284] Fauré. Après un rêve. With unknown pianist. Columbia D 1562; Yamano YMCD-1022 (CD-Japan); Biddulph 82016 (4 CDs).

[WA 3285] Schubert. Nacht und Traume. With unknown pianist. Columbia D 1562; Yamano YMCD-1022 (CD-Japan); Biddulph 82016 (4 CDs).

[WA 3286] Sulzer. Air on G String. With unknown pianist. Columbia D 1554; Wing WCD 24 (CD-Japan); Biddulph 82016 (4 CDs).

[WAX 1523] Dvořák. Slavonic Dance Theme no. 1 in G minor. With unknown pianist. Columbia L 2004; Australian Columbia 04064; Yamano YMCD-1022 (CD-Japan); Biddulph 82016 (4 CDs).

[WAX 1524] Kreisler. Fugue in D after Tartini. With unknown pianist. Columbia L 1995; Australian Columbia 04048; Japanese Columbia J 7233; Yamano YMCD-1022 (CD-Japan); Biddulph 82016 (4 CDs).

20 NOVEMBER

[WAX 2189] Schubert. Allegro moderato from Sonatina no. 3 in G minor. With unknown pianist. Columbia L 1981; American Columbia 5084-M; Japanese Columbia J 7054; ARC Inc. T20P-504 (CD-Japan); Biddulph 82016 (4 CDs).

[WAX 2190] Schubert. Andante from Sonatina no. 3 in G minor. With unknown pianist. Columbia L 1981; Japanese Columbia J 7054; Biddulph 82016 (4 CDs).

[WAX 2191] Arensky. Berceuse, op. 30 no. 2. With unknown pianist. Columbia L 1995; Australian Columbia 04048; Japanese Columbia J 7233; American Columbia 5084-M; ARC Inc. T20P-504 (CD-Japan); Biddulph 82016 (4 CDs).

[WAX 2192] Guiraud. Mélodrame. With unknown pianist. Columbia L 2004; Australian Columbia 04064; Biddulph 82016 (4 CDs).

[WA 4489] Wolstenholme. Canzona. With unknown pianist. Columbia D 1569; Biddulph 82016 (4 CDs).

[WA 4490] Scott. Cherry Ripe. With unknown pianist. Columbia D 1569; HMV Treasury HLM 7055 (LP); Biddulph 82016 (4 CDs).

1927

17 June

[WA 5702] Tertis. The Blackbirds (no. 2 of Three Sketches). With unknown pianist. Columbia D 1627; American Columbia 174-M; Biddulph 82016 (4 CDs).

[WA 5703] Schubert. Du bist die Ruh'. With unknown pianist. Columbia D 1647; Australian Columbia 03638; Biddulph 82016 (4 CDs).

[WA 5704] Tertis. Serenade (no. 1 of Three Sketches). With unknown pianist. Columbia D 1627; Biddulph 82016 (4 CDs).

[WA 5705] Tchaikovsky. None but the Lonely Heart (titled 'A Pleading'). With unknown pianist. Columbia D 1628; American Columbia 174-M; Yamano YMCD-1022 (CD-Japan); Biddulph 82016 (4 CDs).

[WA 5706] Bach. Adagio from C major Toccata. With unknown pianist. Columbia D 1647; Australian Columbia 03638; American Columbia 1960-D; HMV Treasury HLM 7055 (LP); Biddulph 82016 (4 CDs).

[WA 5707] Tertis. The River (no. 3 of Three Sketches). With unknown pianist. Columbia D 1628; Biddulph 82016 (4 CDs).

19 November

[WAX 3118/–19] Mozart. Sonata in A major, K305. With unknown pianist. Columbia L 2070; American Columbia 50151-D; Australian Columbia 04156; Japanese Columbia J 7332; Wing WCD 24 (CD-Japan); Biddulph 82016 (4 CDs).

[WAX 3120/–21] Beethoven. Theme and Variations, op. 66. With unknown pianist. Columbia L 2172; Japanese Columbia J 7327; Wing WCD 24 (CD-Japan); Biddulph 82016 (4 CDs).

[WAX 3122/–23] Handel. Sonata in F: Adagio non tanto & Allegro. With unknown pianist. Columbia L 2213; Japanese Columbia J 7521; HMV Treasury HLM 7055 (LP); Wing WCD 24 (CD-Japan); Biddulph 82016 (4 CDs).

1928

19 June

[WA 7513] Rubinstein. Melody in F. With unknown pianist. Columbia 5230; American Columbia 1960-D & 2081-M; Yamano YMCD-1022 (CD-Japan); Biddulph 82016 (4 CDs).

[WA 7514] Tchaikovsky. Chant sans paroles. With unknown pianist. Columbia 5230; American Columbia 2082-D & 2143-M; Yamano YMCD-1022 (CD-Japan); Biddulph 82016 (4 CDs).

[WA 7515] Mendelssohn. On Wings of Song. With unknown pianist.
Columbia D 1637; Japanese Columbia J 5102; HMV Treasury HLM 7055 (LP);
Yamano YMCD-1022 (CD-Japan); Biddulph 82016 (4 CDs).

[WA 7516] Tchaikovsky. Chanson Triste. With unknown pianist. American
Columbia 2082-D & 2143-M; Yamano YMCD-1022 (CD-Japan); Biddulph
82016 (4 CDs).

[WA 7517] Brahms. Minnelied, op. 71 no. 5. With unknown pianist.
Columbia D 1637; American Columbia 2192-D; Japanese Columbia J 5102;
EMI HQM 1055 (LP); Biddulph 82016 (4 CDs).

[WA 7518] Traditional. Londonderry Air. With unknown pianist. American
Columbia 2192-D; Biddulph 82016 (4 CDs).

1929

25 MARCH

[WA 8744/−51] Mozart. Trio in E, K542. With Albert Sammons (violin) and
William Murdoch (piano).

The only extant copy of this recording is, unfortunately, an incomplete set of 10"
test pressings. The first movement is missing the third of three sides, and the third
movement is missing the second of three sides. The incomplete first and complete
second movements are available in Biddulph set 82016 (4 CDs). Unissued on 78 rpm.

27 MAY

[WAX 4947/−48] Handel–Halvorsen. Passacaglia (from Harpsichord Suite
no. 7 in G minor). With Albert Sammons (violin). Columbia L 2364;
American Columbia 67747-D; EMI HQM 1055 (LP); Biddulph LAB 023 (CD);
Yamano YMCD-1022 (CD-Japan); Biddulph 82016 (4 CDs).

[WAX 4949/−54] Bax. Sonata for Viola. With Arnold Bax (piano). Unissued
on 78 rpm. Pearl GEMM 201 (LP); Pearl GEMM CD 9918 (CD); Biddulph
82016 (4 CDs).

4 OCTOBER

[WAX 5190/−92] Delius. Sonata no. 2. With Evlyn Howard-Jones (piano).
Unissued.

7 OCTOBER

[WAX 5193/−95] Delius. Sonata no. 2. With George Reeves (piano).
Columbia L 2342/−43; American Columbia 67761-D/−62-D; Japanese
Columbia J 7609/−10; HMV Treasury HLM 7055 (LP); Pearl GEMM CD 9918
(CD); Biddulph 82016 (4 CDs).

[WAX 5196] Delius. Serenade from *Hassan*. With George Reeves (piano).
Columbia L 2343; American Columbia 67762-D; Japanese Columbia J 7610;
EMI HQM 1055 (LP); ARC Inc. T20P-504 (CD-Japan); Biddulph 82016
(4 CDs).

1930

8 DECEMBER

[WAX 5906] Kreisler. Preludium and Allegro. With Ethel Hobday (piano).
Columbia DX 313; Australian Columbia DOX 267; EMI HQM 1055 (LP);
Yamano YMCD-1022 (CD-Japan); Biddulph 82016 (4 CDs).

[WAX 5907] Liszt. Liebestraum no. 3 in A flat. With Ethel Hobday (piano).
Columbia DX 313; EMI HQM 1055 (LP); Yamano YMCD-1022 (CD-Japan);
Biddulph 82016 (4 CDs).

[WA 10959] Traditional. Lament (Old Irish Air). With Ethel Hobday
(piano). Columbia DB 396; Japanese Columbia J 5204; Biddulph 82016
(4 CDs).

[WA 10960] Mendelssohn. Sweet Remembrance. With Ethel Hobday
(piano). Columbia DB 855; Biddulph 82016 (4 CDs).

[WA 10961] Wolstenholme. Allegretto. With Ethel Hobday (piano).
Columbia DB 1022; Biddulph 82016 (4 CDs).

[WA 10962] Wolstenholme. The Answer. With Ethel Hobday (piano).
Columbia DB 1022; Biddulph 82016 (4 CDs).

[WA 10963] Traditional. Londonderry Air. With Ethel Hobday (piano).
Columbia DB 396; Japanese Columbia J 5204; Yamano YMCD-1022
(CD-Japan); Biddulph 82016 (4 CDs).

[WA 10964] Mendelssohn. The Fleecy Cloud (Song Without Words no. 20
in E flat). With Ethel Hobday (piano). Columbia DB 855; EMI HQM 1055
(LP); Biddulph 82016 (4 CDs).

1933

17 FEBRUARY

[CAX 6704/–09] Brahms. Sonata in F minor, op. 120 no. 1. With Harriet
Cohen (piano). Columbia LX 225/–27; Australian Columbia LOX 175/–77;
American Columbia 68114-D/–16-D (Set M 183); Japanese Columbia
J 8193/–95; HMV Treasury HLM 7055(LP); Pearl GEMM CD 9918 (CD);
Biddulph 82016 (4 CDs).

30 April

[cax 6824/–31] Mozart. Sinfonia concertante in E flat, k364. With Albert Sammons (violin) and the London Philharmonic Orchestra conducted by Sir Hamilton Harty. Columbia dx 478/–81; French Columbia dfx 158/–61; American Columbia 68148-d/–51-d (Set m 188); Odeon 9418/–21; EMI hqm 1055 (LP); BBC cd 757 (CD); Biddulph lab 023 (CD); Naxos 8110957 (CD); Biddulph 82016 (4 CDs).

26 October

[ca 14102] Traditional. Old German Love Song. With orchestra. Columbia db 1390; Biddulph 82016 (4 CDs).

[ca 14103] Mendelssohn. Venetian Gondola Song. With orchestra. Columbia db 1468; Yamano ymcd-1022 (CD-Japan); Biddulph 82016 (4 CDs).

[ca 14104] Dvořák. Songs my Mother Taught me. With orchestra. Columbia db 1390; Yamano ymcd-1022 (CD-Japan); Biddulph 82016 (4 CDs).

[ca 14105] Mendelssohn. Duetto. With orchestra. Columbia db 1468; Yamano ymcd-1022 (CD-Japan); Biddulph 82016 (4 CDs).

◈

HMV

1924

11 September
Special tests. With J. Brath (piano).

[cc5064] no title. Unissued.

[cc5065] Old Irish Air (arr Lionel Tertis). Unissued.

[cc5066] Porpora. Aria (arr. Corti). Unissued.

[cc5067] Porpora. Aria (arr. Corti). Unissued.

1945

17–18 February & 29 May

[2EA.10412/–16] Brahms. Sonata no. 2 in E flat, op. 120 no. 2. With Solomon (piano). Unissued.

18 February

[2EA.10417] Martini. Sonata in D: Allegro. With Solomon (piano). Unissued.

1947

22 August

[2EA.12132] Bach–Tertis. Come, Sweet Death. + Sammartini. Sonata in E: Allegro. With unknown pianist. HMV c.3619; Biddulph 82016 (4 CDs). Abridged version issued on RCA Victor 45-6050 in set E 104 (10").

❖

PEARL

1959

20 February

from South African radio broadcast

Dale. Romance, from Suite for Viola and Piano (1907). With Arthur Woodland (piano). Pearl GEMM 201 (LP).

Galuppi–Tertis. Aria amorosa. With Arthur Woodland (piano). Pearl GEMM 201 (LP).

Martini. Sonata in D: Allegro. With Arthur Woodland (piano). Pearl GEMM 201 (LP).

Wolstenholme–Tertis. Allegretto. With Arthur Woodland (piano). Pearl GEMM 201 (LP).

1960

11 June

from Danish National Radio broadcast

Beethoven. Duet in E flat ('Eyeglasses'). With Lillian Tertis (cello). Pearl GEMM 201 (LP).

❖ ❖ ❖

2 – Listed by Composer

d'Ambrosio, Alfredo. Petit Suite no 2. Vocalion R-6099.

——Reverie. Vocalion R-6111.

Arensky, Anton (arr. Tertis). Berceuse op. 30 no. 2. Columbia L 1995.

Bach, J. S. (arr. Tertis). Adagio from C major Toccata. Columbia D 1647.

——Air on G String. Vocalion D-02067.

——Chaconne 'in D minor', BWV1004. Columbia L 1644/–45.

——(arr. Tertis). Come, Sweet Death. Version 1: Columbia D 1502. Version 2: HMV C.3619.

Bax, Sir Arnold. Sonata for Viola. Columbia [matrix nos. WAX 4949/–54]. Unpublished on 78 rpm.

Beethoven, Ludwig van. Duet in E flat ('Eyeglasses'). Pearl GEMM 201.

——(arr. Tertis). Theme and Variations op 66. Columbia L 2172.

Bizet, Georges. Adagietto. Version 1: Vocalion R-6146. Version 2: Victor [matrix no. unknown]. Unpublished on 78 rpm.

Boyd, Tod. Samoan Lullaby. Vocalion R-6033.

Brahms, Johannes (arr. Tertis). Minnelied op 71 no 5. Columbia D 1637.

——Sonata no. 1 in F minor, op. 120 no. 1. Version 1: Vocalion X-9463/–64 & K-05117. Version 2: Columbia LX 225/–27.

——Sonata no. 2 in E flat, op. 120 no. 2. HMV [matrix nos. 2EA.10412/–16]. Unpublished on 78 rpm.

Dale, Benjamin. Romance from Suite for Viola and Piano (1907). Version 1: Vocalion D-02067. Version 2: Pearl GEMM 201.

Delius, Frederick. Serenade from *Hassan*. Columbia L 2343.

——(arr. Tertis). Violin Sonata no. 2. Version 1: Columbia [matrix nos. WAX 5190/–92]. Unpublished on 78 rpm. Version 2: Columbia L 2342/–43.

Dohnányi, Ernő. Sonata in C sharp minor, op. 21. Columbia L 1731/–32.

Dunhill, Thomas F. Phantasy Trio. Vocalion R-6027.

Duparc, Henri. Extase. Vocalion L-5015.

Dvořák, Antonín (arr. Tertis). Four Bagatelles from op. 47. Vocalion D-02083 & D-02111.

——(arr. Kreisler). Slavonic Dance Theme no. 1 in G minor. Columbia L 2004.

——(arr. Walter). Songs my Mother Taught me. Columbia DB 1390.

Fauré, Gabriel (arr. Tertis). Après un rêve. Version 1: Vocalion R-6019. Version 2: Columbia D 1562.

——Élégie. Vocalion K-05144.

Fuchs, Robert. Duet for Violin and Viola. Vocalion D-02019.

Galuppi, Baldassare (arr. Tertis). Aria Amorosa. Pearl GEMM 201.

Godard, Benjamin. Berceuse de Jocelyn. Vocalion D-02006.

——Duettini, op. 18: Minuit & Souvenir de Champagne. Vocalion R-6063.

Grainger, Percy. Molly on the Shore. Vocalion R-6078.

Grieg, Edvard. I Love Thee. Vocalion R-6096.

——(arr. Tertis). Violin Sonata no. 3 in C minor, op. 45. Vocalion D-02104,
  D-02106 & D-02112.

Guiraud, Ernest (arr. Tertis). Mélodrame. Columbia L 2004.

Handel, G. F. (arr. Johan Halvorsen). Passacaglia. Version 1: Vocalion
  D-02019. Version 2: Columbia L 2364.

——Sonata no. 8: Andante & Allegro. Vocalion D-02023.

——(arr. Tertis). Sonata in F: Adagio non tant & Allegro. Columbia L 2213.

Ireland, John. The Holy Boy. Vocalion K-05144.

Kalniņš, Alfrēds. Élégie. Vocalion D-02082.

Korngold, Erich W. Hornpipe from *Much Ado about Nothing*. Columbia
  [matrix no. T 1709 4a]. Unpublished on 78 rpm.

Kreisler, Fritz. Chanson Louis XIII and Pavane. Vocalion R-6111.

——La Chasse. Vocalion R-6007.

——Fugue in D after Tartini. Columbia L 1995.

——La Gitana. Columbia D 1554.

——La précieuse. Vocalion R-6019.

——Prelude and Allegro. Version 1: Vocalion D-02041. Version 2: Columbia
  DX 313.

——Rondino. Vocalion R-6099.

——Tambourin chinois. Vocalion D-02041.

Leroux, Xavier. Le Nil. Vocalion C-01023.

Liszt, Franz (arr. Tertis). Liebestraum no. 3 in A flat. Version 1: Vocalion
  D-02144. Version 2: Columbia DX 313.

Marais, Marin. Le Basque. Vocalion R-6085.

Martini, Giambattista. Sonata in D: Allegro. Version 1: HMV [matrix
  no. 2EA.10417]. Unpublished on 78 rpm. Version 2: Pearl GEMM 201.

McEwen, John. Breath o' June. Vocalion D-02006.

Mendelssohn, Felix (arr. Walter). Duetto. Columbia DB 1468.

——(arr. Tertis). The Fleecy Cloud. Version 1: Vocalion R-6115. Version 2:
  Columbia DB 855.

——On Wings of Song. Version 1: Vocalion R-6096. Version 2: Columbia
  D 1637.

——Spring Song. Vocalion R-6085.

——Sweet Remembrance. Vocalion R-6115.

——(arr. Tertis). Sweet Remembrance. Columbia DB 855.

——Trio no. 2 in C minor, op. 66. Columbia L 1755/–58.

——(arr. Walter) Venetian Gondola Song no. 1. Columbia DB 1468.

Mozart, W. A. Sinfonia concertante in E flat, K364. Columbia DX 478/–81.

——(arr. Tertis). Sonata in A major, K305. Columbia L 2070.

——(arr. Tertis). Trio in E, K542. Version 1: Vocalion D-02064 & D-02091. Version 2: Columbia [matrix nos. WA 8747/–48]. Unpublished on 78 rpm.

——Trio in E flat, K498. Vocalion D-02064 & D-02015.

——(arr. Tertis). Trio in G, K496 ('No. VII, op. 16'). Vocalion D-02150 & K-05174.

Porpora, Niccolò. Aria (arr. Corti). Versions 1 and 2: HMV [matrix nos. CC5066/–67]. Unpublished on 78 rpm. Version 3: Columbia D 1502.

Rebikov, V. I. Les rêves. Vocalion X-9696.

Rubinstein, Anton (arr. Tertis). Melody in F. Version 1: Vocalion R-6007. Version 2: Columbia 5230.

Saint-Saëns, Camille. Berceuse. Vocalion R-6085.

Sammartini, G. B. Sonata in E: All°. HMV C.3619.

Schubert, Franz. Ave Maria. Vocalion D-02082.

——(arr. Tertis). Du bist die Ruh'. Columbia D 1647.

——(arr. Tertis). Nacht und Traume. Columbia D 1562.

——Sonatina no. 3 in G minor: Andante & Allegro moderato. Columbia L 1981.

——(arr. Tertis). Trio in B flat, op. 99. Vocalion D-02050 & D-02060.

Schumann, Robert. Abendlied. Vocalion R-6078.

——Slumber Song. Vocalion R-6146.

Scott, Cyril. Cherry Ripe. Columbia D 1569.

Sulzer, Johann. Air on G String. Columbia D 1554.

Tchaikovsky, P. I. Barcarolle. Vocalion K-05174.

——(arr. Tertis). Chanson Triste. Version 1: Vocalion R-6017. Version 2: American Columbia 2082-D.

——(arr. Tertis). Chant sans Paroles. Version 1: Vocalion R-6017. Version 2: Columbia 5230.

——None but the Lonely Heart. Version 1: Vocalion L-5012. Version 2: Columbia D 1628 (titled 'A Pleading').

Tertis, Lionel. The Blackbirds (no. 2 of 'Three Sketches'). Columbia D 1627.

——Hier au soir. Columbia L 1761.

——Rêverie. Vocalion D-02144.

——The River (no. 3 of 'Three Sketches'). Columbia D 1628.

——Serenade (no. 1 of 'Three Sketches'). Columbia D 1627.

——Sunset. Vocalion X-9696.

Thomé, François. Sous la feuillée. Vocalion R-6033.

Traditional (arr. Tertis). Lament (Old Irish Air). Columbia DB 396.

——Londonderry Air. Version 1: Vocalion D-02011. Version 2: Victor [matrix no. unknown]. Unpublished on 78 rpm. Version 3: American Columbia 2192-D. Version 4: Columbia DB 396.

——Old German Love Song. Columbia DB 1390.

——(arr. Tertis). Old Irish Air. Columbia L 1761.

Wolstenholme, William. Allegretto. Version 1: Vocalion D-02011. Version 2: Columbia DB 1022. Version 3: Pearl GEMM 201.

——The Answer. Version 1: Vocalion D-02012. Version 2: Columbia DB 1022.

——Canzona. Columbia D 1569.

——The Question. Vocalion D-02012.

◈ ◈ ◈

I wish to thank the following people for generously sharing their research in order to make this discography as complete as possible. Ross Laird for his extensive knowledge of the Aeolian-Vocalion label and, in the absence of original documentation, his expertise in estimating recording dates. Roger Beardsley for his information on Tertis's recordings for His Master's Voice and Columbia. Jon M. Samuels for information on Tertis's unpublished Victor sides as well as general confirmation of Columbia and Vocalion recording dates and matrix numbers. Christopher Nozawa for sharing information from his extensive collection of rare recordings, and to Shuichiro Kawai for making copies of several of Mr Nozawa's recordings available to me in digital format and for providing information on Japanese CD reissues of Tertis 78s. John White for sharing recordings from his collection, especially Tertis's own copies of rare and unpublished Columbia sides. Donald Hodgman and Raymond Glaspole for making it possible to obtain many rare original Tertis recordings for review.

Bibliography

Anonymous. 'Lionel Tertis'. *Musical Standard*, 31 July 1915.

—— 'Lionel Tertis'. *Musical Times*, March 1922.

—— 'Tertis and his Viola'. *Picture Post*, 36/10 (6 September 1947).

—— 'An Artist among the Musicians' [featuring drawing of Tertis seated playing his viola], *Penguin Music Magazine*, no. 5 (February 1948).

Applebaum, Samuel and Sada. 'Lionel Tertis'. *Violins and Violinists Magazine*, 18/2, no. 146 (March–April 1957).

—— *The Way They Play*, vol. 1 (Neptune, NJ: Paganiniana Publications, 1972.

Atkins, E. Wulstan. *The Elgar–Atkins Friendship*. Newton Abbott: David & Charles, 1984.

Baker, Theodore. *Baker's Biographical Dictionary of Musicians*, 7th edn, rev. Nicolas Slonimsky. Oxford: Oxford University Press, 1984.

Bainton, Helen. *Remembered on Waking: Edgar L. Bainton*. Sydney: Currawong Publishing, 1960.

Barr, Cyrilla. *Elizabeth Sprague Coolidge: American Patron of Music*. New York: Schirmer Books, 1998.

Bax, Arnold. 'Lionel Tertis: An Appreciation'. *Musical News and Herald*, 27 May 1922, p. 656.

—— *Farewell, my Youth*. London: Longmans, Green, 1943.

Beecham, Sir Thomas. *A Mingled Chime: Leaves from an Autobiography*. London: White Lion, 1973.

Bliss, Arthur. *As I Remember*. London: Faber & Faber, 1970.

Calvocoressi, M. D. *Musician' Gallery: Music and Ballet in Paris and London, Recollections*. London: Faber & Faber, 1933.

Carley, Lionel. *Delius: A Life in Letters*, vol. 2: *1909–1934*. London: Scolar Press, 1988.

Coates, Eric. *Suite in Four Movements: An Autobiography*. London: Thames, 1986.

Cobbett, W. W. *Cobbett's Cyclopedic Survey of Chamber Music*, 2nd edn, ed. Colin Mason. Oxford: Oxford University Press, 1963.

Cohen, Harriet. *A Bundle of Time: The Memoirs of Harriet Cohen*. London: Faber & Faber, 1969.

Craggs, Stewart. *William Walton: A Source Book*. Aldershot: Scolar Press, 1993.

Crimp, Bryan. *Solo: The Biography of Solomon*. Hexham: Appian Publications, 1994.

Dalton, David. *Playing the Viola: Conversations with William Primrose.* Oxford: Oxford University Press, 1988.

Douglas-Home, Jessica. *Violet: The Life and Loves of Violet Gordon Woodhouse.* London: Harvill Press, 1997.

Draper, Muriel. *Music at Midnight.* London: William Heinemann, 1929.

Dunhill, David. *Thomas Dunhill: Maker of Music.* London: Thames, 1997.

Dunhill, Thomas F. *Chamber Music: A Treatise for Students.* London: Macmillan, 1913; repr. 1925, 1938.

Elkin, Robert. *Queen's Hall, 1893–1941.* London: Rider, 1944.

—— *Royal Philharmonic: The Annals of the Royal Philharmonic Society.* London: Rider, 1946.

Fenby, Eric. *Delius: As I Knew Him.* London: Bell & Sons, 1936.

—— *Fenby on Delius: Collected Writings on Delius to mark Eric Fenby's 90th Birthday*, ed. Stephen Lloyd. London: Thames, 1996.

Foreman, Lewis. *Bax: A Composer and his Times*, 2nd edn. Aldershot: Scolar Press, 1988.

Gibson, John Carrington. *A Musician's Life: Alfred Gibson, by his Son.* London: Frederick Books, 1956.

Ginsburg, Lev. *Ysaÿe.* New Jersey: Paganiniana, 1980.

Goossens, Eugène. *Overture and Beginners: A Musical Autobiography.* London: Methuen, 1951.

Hawkins, Frank V. *A Hundred Years of Chamber Music.* London: South Place Ethical Society, 1987.

Heath, Edward. *Music: A Joy for Life.* London: Sidgwick & Jackson, 1976.

Hinrichsen's Year Book 1944: Music of Our Time, ed. Ralph Hill and Max Hinrichsen. London: Hinrichsen Editions, 1944.

Holst, Imogen. *The Music of Gustav Holst*, 3rd rev. edn, *and Holst's Music Reconsidered.* Oxford: Oxford University Press, 1986.

Hull, Robert. 'Some Music of Ernest Walker'. *Musical Opinion*, July 1931.

Jaffa, Max. *A Life on the Fiddle.* London: Hodder & Stoughton, 1991.

Kennedy, Michael. *The Hallé Tradition: A Century of Music.* Manchester: Manchester University Press, 1960.

—— *Portrait of Elgar*, 2nd edn. London: Oxford University Press, 1982.

—— *Adrian Boult.* London: Macmillan, 1989.

King-Smith, Beresford. *Crescendo!: 75 Years of the City of Birmingham Symphony Orchestra.* London: Methuen, 1995.

Kirk, H. L. *Pablo Casals: A Biography.* London: Hutchinson, 1974.

Lahee, Henry C. *Famous Violinists of Today and Yesterday.* London: Putnam, 1902.

Langrish, Vivian. 'The Last Years in Tenterden Street'. *Royal Academy of Music Magazine*, no. 224 (Autumn 1980).

Lloyd, Stephen. *Sir Dan Godfrey: Champion of British Composers: A Chronology of Forty Years' Music-Making with the Bournemouth Municipal Orchestra.* London: Thames, 1995.

Maine, Basil. *Elgar: His Life and Works*, 2 vols. London: Bell & Sons, 1933.

Marney, Fiona. 'The Tertis Influence'. diss., University of Leicester, 1989.

MacRae, Julia. *Wigmore Hall, 1901–2001: A Celebration.* London: Wigmore Hall Trust, 2001.

Meadmore, W. S. *South Place Sunday Popular Concerts: The Story of a Thousand Concerts (1887–1927).* London: South Place Ethical Society, 1927.

Menuhin, Yehudi, and William Primrose. *Violin and Viola*, Yehudi Menuhin Music Guides. London: Macdonald & Jane's, 1976.

Moore, Gerald. *Am I Too Loud? Memoirs of an Accompanist.* Harmondsworth: Penguin, 1979.

—— *Farewell Recital: Further Memoirs.* Harmondsworth: Penguin, 1979.

—— *Furthermoore: Interludes in an Accompanist's Life.* London: Hamish Hamilton, 1983.

Northrop Moore, Jerrold. *Edward Elgar: A Creative Life.* Oxford: Oxford University Press, 1984; Clarendon paperbacks, 1987.

Ottaway, Hugh. *Walton.* Sevenoaks: Novello, 1972.

Palmer, Russell. *British Music: An Encyclopaedia of British Musicians.* London: Skelton Robinson, 1948.

Primrose, William. *Walk on the North Side: Memoirs of a Violist.* Provo, Utah: Brigham Young University Press, 1978.

Procter-Gregg, Humphrey, ed. *Beecham Remembered.* London: Duckworth, 1976.

Railton, Ruth. *Daring to Excel: Story of the National Youth Orchestra of Great Britain.* London: Secker & Warburg, 1992.

Reed, William H. *Elgar as I Knew Him*, 2nd edn. Oxford: Oxford University Press, 1989.

Reid, Charles. *Malcolm Sargent: A Biography.* London: Hodder & Stoughton, 1973.

Riley, Maurice. *The History of the Viola*, 2 vols. Ann Arbor, Mich.: Braun-Brumfield, 1980; 1991.

Rubinstein, Artur. *My Young Years.* London: Jonathan Cape, 1973.

—— *My Many Years.* London: Jonathan Cape, 1980.

Russell, Thomas. 'Lionel Tertis: A Study'. *Musical Times*, June 1937.

—— *Philharmonic.* London: Hutchinson, 1942.

—— *Philharmonic Decade.* London: Hutchinson, 1944.

Sachs, Harvey. *Arthur Rubinstein: A Life.* London: Phoenix, 1997.

Saint John, Christopher. *Ethel Smyth: A Biography.* London: Longmans, Green, 1959.

Savage, Richard Temple. *A Voice from the Pit: Reminiscences of an Orchestral Musician.* Newton Abbot: David & Charles, 1988.

Scholes, Percy A., ed. *The Mirror of Music, 1844–1944: A Century of Musical Life in Britain as Reflected in the Musical Times,* 2 vols. London: Novello/ Oxford University Press, 1947.

Self, Geoffrey. *In Town Tonight: A Centenary Study of the Life and Music of Eric Coates.* London: Thames, 1986.

Shore, Bernard. *The Orchestra Speaks.* London: Readers Union, Longmans, Green, 1939.

—— *Sixteen Symphonies.* London: Readers Union, Longmans, Green, 1950.

—— 'Obituary: Lionel Tertis'. *Royal Academy of Music Magazine,* 208 (Summer 1975).

Tatton, Thomas. 'English Viola Music, 1890–1937'. DMA diss., University of Illinois at Urbana, 1976.

Tertis, Lionel. 'Introduction to an English Viola'. *Music & Letters,* vol. 28 (1947), pp.214–22.

—— *Cinderella No More.* London: Peter Nevill, 1953.

—— *My Viola and I: A Complete Autobiography.* London: Paul Elek, 1974.

Walton, Susana. *William Walton: Behind the Façade.* Oxford: Oxford University Press, 1989.

Watkins, Hadley, ed. *The Bournemouth Municipal Orchestra: Twenty-One Years of Municipal Music, 1893–1914.* Bournemouth, May 1914.

Watson, Monica. *York Bowen: A Centenary Tribute.* London: Thames, 1984.

Wetherell, Eric. *Albert Sammons: Violinist.* London: Thames, 1998.

White, John, ed. *An Anthology of British Viola Players.* Colne: Comus Edition, 1997.

Willeby, Charles. *Masters of English Music.* London: James R. Osgood, McIlvaine & Co., 1896.

Wood, F. H. (Wolstenholme). 'Lionel Tertis'. *Musical Times,* 1931.

Wood, Sir Henry. *My Life of Music.* London: Gollancz, 1938.

Young, Percy. *Elgar O.M.: A Study of a Musician.* London: Collins, 1955.

Ysaÿe, Antoine, and Bertram Ratcliffe. *Ysaÿe: His Life, Work and Influence.* London: William Heinemann, 1947.

Zeyringer, Franz. *Literatur für Viola.* Hartberg: Julius Schönwetter, 1976.

Index